HOMELAND WANTED: INTERDISCIPLINARY PERSPECTIVES ON REFUGEE RESETTLEMENT IN THE WEST

HOMELAND WANTED: INTERDISCIPLINARY PERSPECTIVES ON REFUGEE RESETTLEMENT IN THE WEST

PETER WAXMAN
VAL COLIC-PEISKER
EDITORS

Nova Science Publishers, Inc.
New York

Production Coordinator: Donna Dennis
Editorial Production Manager: Donna Dennis
Senior Production Editor: Susan Boriotti
Office Manager: Annette Hellinger
Graphics: Andrea Charles, Magdalena Nuñez and Annemarie VanDeWater
Editorial Production: Marius Andronie, Maya Columbus, Keti Datunashvili, Andrew Kallio, Vladimir Klestov, Lorna Loperfido, Marlene Nuñez, Joann Overton and Rusudan Razmadze
Circulation: Ave Maria Gonzalez, Vera Popovic, Luis Aviles, Alexandra Columbus, Raymond Davis, Cathy DeGregory, Melissa Diaz, Jeannie Pappas, Lauren Perl and Katie Sutherland

Library of Congress Cataloging-in-Publication Data
Homeland wanted : interdisciplinary perspectives on refugee resettlement in the West / Peter Waxman and Val Colic-Peisker, editors.
p. cm.
Includes index.
ISBN 1-59454-266-X (hardcover)
1. Refugees--Services for--Cross-cultural studies. 2. Refugees--Legal status, laws, etc.--Cross-cultural studies. I. Waxman, Peter. II. Colic-Peisker, Val.
HV640.H582 2005
305.9'06914--dc22 2005000175

400 Oser Ave, Suite 1600
Hauppauge, New York 11788-3619
Tele. 631-231-7269 Fax 631-231-8175
e-mail: Novascience@earthlink.net
Web Site: http://www.novapublishers.com

Printed in the United States of America

CONTENTS

ACKNOWLEDGEMENTS

This volume is a result of one year of concerted efforts of sixteen authors and two editors to present a refereed selection of recent research in refugee studies under the title *Homeland Wanted: Interdisciplinary Perspective on Refugee Resettlement in the West.* We thank our contributors for their consistent cooperation and effort in meeting editors' requests for revisions and amendments, as well as deadlines. We are much indebted to our external reviewers who provided insightful critiques of the chapters: Prof. Emeritus Reginald Appleyard of the University of Western Australia, Linda Bartolomei of the University of New South Wales (Sydney, Australia) Barry Edmonston of Portland State University, Dr. Elzbieta Gozdziak of Georgetown University, Assoc. Professor Robyn Iredale of the University of Wollongong (Australia), Assoc. Professor Konia Kollehlon of Trinity University (Washington D.C.), Assoc. Prof. Salim Lakha of University of Melbourne, Assoc. Professor Larry Lam of York University (Canada), Dr. Cheryl Lange of the University of Western Australia, Dr. Eileen Pittaway of the University of New South Wales, Assoc. Professor Jan Rath of the University of Amsterdam, and Dr. Farida Tilbury of Murdoch University (Western Australia). We extend our warm thanks to Prof. Stephen Castles of Oxford University for writing a preface to our volume and Mr. Hariz Halilovich of RMIT University (Melbourne) for joining us late in the process to contribute his personal story of refugeedom. We are also grateful to Nova Science Publishers, New York, for having the foresight and an interest in an under-researched topic afflicting many millions. Finally, we thank the many refugees who contributed their time, energy and trust in assisting the researchers. We hope this volume will help readers deepen their understanding of the theory, policy and practice of refugee resettlement in the West.

Peter Waxman and Val Colic-Peisker
5 September 2004

FOREWORD

This book is about the small minority of the world's refugees who are allowed to 're-settle' in highly-developed countries. We call this 'the West' for convenience — and rarely even stop to think that the West includes a country as far to the east as Australia. The term is really a label for the prosperity, security and human rights seen as typical of the rich countries. Those who manage to cross our well-guarded borders are regarded as 'the lucky ones'. Are they really lucky? The overwhelming majority of the world's displaced people would prefer to return to their homes in safety and dignity. It is only those who have no hope of return who get resettled in the West.

There are millions of forced migrants in the world – people displaced by violence, persecution, human rights abuse, disasters, large dams and other development projects. Only about ten million are counted as refugees, according to the official definitions — and these are the only ones who enjoy the protection of the United Nations High Commission for Refugees (UNHCR). Very few of them are offered resettlement — over seven million have become what the US Committee for Refugees calls 'warehoused refugees': people forced to vegetate in camps on meagre rations for ten years or more. Other groups are often forgotten completely, such as the four and a half million Palestinians, 25 million internally displaced persons (IDPS), and ten million development displaces a year (according to the World Bank).

The other reason to ask if 'resettled refugees' are lucky lies in the way our societies treat them on arrival. In the past, refugees were welcomed as heroic fighters against oppression. Today, we see them with suspicion and fear — they are accused of bringing in poverty, disease and crime, of being terrorists, of taking our jobs, or sponging off welfare. Never has the public stereotype been so negative. Never have populist politicians and sensationalist media been so eager to encourage and exploit such views. The anti-refugee climate is used to justify stereotyping asylum seekers as bogus, locking them up, providing only 'temporary protection', denying them the right to work, and providing reduced and humiliating forms of welfare.

Such views forget the shared responsibility of the West for some of the world's violent conflicts. Many struggles in Africa and Asia are a legacy of divisions deliberately created by European colonialism. Underdevelopment and impoverishment are partly the results of unequal trade rules and neo-liberal structural adjustment policies. Poor governance and unrepresentative regimes often derive from the interventions of western secret services to undermine democratic governments which refused to accept the dominance of the multinationals — think of Iran, DR Congo, Nicaragua and so on. Europe and North America remain the world's largest weapons exporters, providing the cheap, light weapons that make internal conflicts so brutal.

This book explores the meaning of such contradictions for those refugees who do reach the rich countries. The authors examine the situation in the main receiving countries, providing cross-national and interdisciplinary perspectives. Personal accounts make it clear that there is no 'typical refugee': people vary enormously in their experience, resources, skills and aspirations. Government policies and the attitudes of receiving populations matter a great deal too. The treatment of vulnerable groups like refugees says a great deal about the openness and confidence of a society. In many places, unfortunately, the current climate of fear and mistrust has meant growing social exclusion. The important thing is to find ways of helping refugees to participate in society and — in the long run — to cease to be perceived as refugees, but rather as full and active citizens. Hopefully, this work will raise understanding and provide support to the many organisations and individuals working to combat prejudice and exclusion.

Stephen Castles
August 2004

In: Homeland Wanted
Editors: P. Waxman and V. Colic-Peisker, pp. xi-xxii
ISBN 1-59454-266-X

INTRODUCTION: HUMANITARIANISM VS. REALPOLITIK IN THE WEST[1]

Val Colic-Peisker

'It takes an enormous effort of the imagination, as well as a great deal of knowledge, to break out of our comfortable, protected and self-absorbed enclaves and enter an uncomfortable and unprotected larger world inhabited by the majority of humans' (Eric Hobsbawm, The new century, London: Little, Brown and Company, 1999, pp. 166-167)

At the beginning of the 21st century, the global population of forced migrants would suffice for a reasonably-sized state: UNHCR (2004) identifies 17 million people 'of concern' to the organisation. These are people who have been involuntarily displaced from their homes and everyday lives, and often traumatised not only by violence in their homelands but also by inadequate circumstances in refugee camps and other situations of 'temporary protection'. Their need for a stable and permanent residence and a possibility to resume whatever signifies a 'normal life' to them, represents the humanitarian aspect of the global 'refugee crisis'. As I write these lines, the 'worst humanitarian disaster on record', as media like to call it, unfolds in the Darfur region of Sudan. But there is another, 'Realpolitik' aspect of the refugee problem — the need of the luckier countries of the world, usually abbreviated as 'the West', to keep the refugee flows, emanating from 'failed and troubled states', under control.

Only ten countries of the West have annual quotas to resettle refugees on a permanent basis: Australia, Canada, Denmark, Finland, the Netherlands, New Zealand, Norway, Sweden, Switzerland and the United States. Other countries accept refugees on an ad hoc basis, and in most cases only provide temporary protection.[2] Thus researching refugees[3] who

1 The meaning of the 'West' has been shifting throughout history. Here it is used as a shorthand to denote the 'developed and pacified Western world' (Hobsbawm, 1999, p. 127), or the main target countries for immigrants and asylum seekers: the so-called 'First World' in Europe ('Western Europe', now expanding into the EU) and the developed part of the 'New World' claimed by Europeans through colonial expansion in the early modern times (North America and Australia).

2 Top five refugee hosting countries are: Pakistan (UNHCR estimate: 1.1 million), Iran (UNHCR estimate: 985,000), Germany (960,000), Tanzania (650,000) and the United States (UNHCR estimate: 452,500). See UNHCR, 2004 at www.unhcr.org

3 This word is used to cover all categories of forced migrants.

resettle in the West means focusing on a minority — between 5 and 10 per cent — of the current global population of forced migrants, but the minority who, for obvious reasons, have been researched the most. The editors of this book wish this would be different, and the large refugee populations who resettle in the African and Asian 'countries of first asylum' received more attention from Western researchers and media, and with it more assistance from international refugee and other aid organisations. We also wish a larger number of the world's displaced would receive a warmer welcome in the West. As it stands, however, a majority of Westerners seem to be less and less inclined to discomfort themselves thinking about troubles outside their own countries: the *Losing perspective* Report (Stone, 2000) revealed a dramatic decline in the amount of coverage of the developing world and its problems in British TV programs over the 1990s.

While we are producing this volume, millions of refugees and displaced people from African and Asian countries as well as some countries in Latin America and Europe continue their temporary existence in refugee camps and other environments that do not allow for structured and fulfilling lives. For the majority of these people, the return to their countries and homes is too risky or simply impossible, and the resettlement in the 'third country' delayed for years. According to many refugee officials, the 'third country' resettlement — and this usually means resettling in the West — is the 'least preferred solution', to be used only when efforts to either help refugees return home or settle permanently in the country of the first asylum have failed (Refugee Reports 2002).

The Changing Context of the Refugee Reception in the West and the 'Refugee Debate'

This book is concerned with refugees who are, paradoxically, often considered 'lucky' to be able to experience the 'least preferred solution' of resettling in the West. Those who have been granted permanent asylum try to rebuild their lives in what is for many of them a considerably alien environment. These people, however, are not only small in number but also a shrinking minority. Many asylum seekers are only found 'deserving' of temporary protection: this is the case with the 'boat people' in Australia since 1999 (HREOC, 2003), as well with many asylum seekers in Britain who are granted an 'exceptional leave to remain'. Chapter 9 of this volume is devoted to the troubled and anxiety-filled settlement based on a temporary protection visa (TPV). Temporary protection was introduced in Europe in response to the Bosnian refugee crisis; it was adopted in the US in response to Salvadorians in 1990; Australia first introduced temporary protection in 1990 for Chinese students, survivors of the Tiananmen massacre, then abolished it in 1992 and reintroduced it in 1999 at the peak of the influx of 'boat people' arriving on its northern shores. The most notorious of the recent refugee policies, however, is the mandatory detention of asylum seekers, introduced in Australia in 1992 (York, 2003) and in recent years fiercely debated, but still enjoying the support of both Australia's major parties.

Refugee settlers seem to attract more suspicion nowadays than half a century ago (Harding, 2000; York, 2003). During the Cold War, those who fled communist countries were welcomed in the West as heroes who mastered their way across the heavily guarded Iron Curtain in order to find refuge in the 'free world'. In this context they had a considerable propaganda value in the West. Their popularity was also supported by the fact that they were usually the communist countries' elites — typically academics, scientists, artists and sporting heroes — and thus seen as people able to make a contribution to the host societies. Because of the closed borders of communist countries, only those who could mobilise considerable financial and social resources and connections could make their way to the West in spite of formidable obstacles. This meant that there was only a refugee trickle rather than a torrent. And at last, but not least, they were 'people like us': white 'Eastern' Europeans.

A large majority of today's refugees differ considerably from this cold-war image. The 1970s, 80s and 90s saw refugees coming from new source countries outside Europe, (apart from ex-Yugoslavia and ex-USSR in the last decade). During the 1990s, ex-Yugoslavia, the Middle East and Africa were the largest sources of refugees. In 2000s it is the Middle East and Africa. The humanitarian intake is usually the topic of the most heated debate within a broader debate between immigration 'expansionists' and 'restrictionists'.[4] The fears that the conservative opponents of humanitarian immigration create or reinforce in the Western voters originate from the sheer number of people in the refugee-like situation around the globe: therefore, many Westerners fear that if they are 'too generous' they will be 'swamped'. On top of the impressive number of refugees comes the 'fact' that these days they are not 'people like us': they are visibly different, they wear different clothes and speak different languages. There is another fear, far removed from rational political and economic considerations, a fear that belongs to the depth of the psyche of a comfortable Westerner: that refugees who come from countries torn by war and violence must somehow be partly responsible for what's going on in their countries, and in who knows what arcane ways they may bring the germ of 'evil' and disturbance to our stable, peaceful and prosperous societies. This irrational fear is exacerbated by the current global upsurge of terrorism.

Another issue that affects refugee admission in the West is a perception of porous borders created through the influx of asylum seekers and illegal immigrants to the US and Europe, and in much smaller numbers also in Australia (IOM, 2003; BBC, 2000). This perception, engineered by the conservative opponents of immigration and asylum seeking, creates waves of immigration panic in the target countries (see Moore, 2002; U.S. Border Control, 2003). Over the past decade, it led the governments of refugee-receiving countries, and particularly the US, EU and Australia, to introduce new restrictive laws, policies and measures (Helton, 2002; Jupp, 2002). The September 11 terrorist attacks caused a new type of anxiety in the citizens of the West. A fortress mentality triggered in the aftermath of the event severely limited the refuge intake. In 2002 for example, the approved US ceiling for refugees was 70,000, but because of the stricter security checks only 26,508 refugees actually entered the country (The Refugee Council USA, 2003). This was the lowest refugee admission in the US in 25 years (Refugee Reports, 2002), and a rather dramatic reduction compared to 1993, when 154,300 humanitarian immigrants were approved to enter the country (Isbister, 1996, p.75). The sudden realisation of their own vulnerability did not result in more empathy by the Westerners for the most vulnerable people — refugees — who were now instead associated with international organised crime and terrorism (Humphrey, 2002).[5] In recent years, the Western governments shifted their view on refugees from the issue of humanitarian

---

4 For some extreme views on both sides see for example Brittan, 2003 and Hanson, 2003.

5 See for example 'U.S. Border Control' website at www.usbc.org subtitled 'America's last best chance to reform our border and immigration policies...before it's too late', with its 'ring of websites' created in 1997, see http://h.webring.com

responsibility towards the issue of national interest, and especially national security. In effect, the intake of refugees to the West has been reduced in the last couple of years (UNHCR, 2003).

Australia, one of the less than dozen countries which receive refugees on a regular basis, had its own, appropriately smaller crisis that triggered tightening of its asylum regime: the 'Tampa crisis'. On 26 August 2001, the Norwegian freighter 'Tampa' rescued 433 asylum seekers from a leaking boat off the northwestern Australian coast. The Australian government did not allow the Tampa to berth in Australia and the unwanted people were instead transported to several Pacific islands. Those among them who were found to be genuine refugees were only entitled to a three-year temporary protection visa (TPV). Not allowing refugees to reach the Australian mainland and diverting them to neighboring Pacific island nations to claim asylum from there, a strategy devised during the Tampa affair, became an official policy called the 'Pacific solution'. In the aftermath of the Tampa incident, small islands off the northern Australia coast were legally excised from the Australia immigration zone to prevent boat people from claiming Australian asylum when they arrived there (DIMIA, 2003). Australia conservative government, in power since 1996, today claims great success in stemming the tide of boat people arriving on Australia's northern shores (DIMIA, 2003a).

Humanitarianism vs. Pragmatism

The international refugee regime (IRR) has always been embedded in *Realpolitik* and interests of the powerful states rather than on humanitarian feelings (Keely, 1996). Ethical postulates are conventionally respected as a basis of culture, values and legal systems of liberal democracies, but they rarely, if ever, determine political action on their own. Refugee flows are a result of serious cracks in the global system of sovereign states, and large refugee waves have the potential to destabilise it further, hence there is a pragmatic need to keep them contained. In the ongoing refugee debate, the ethical considerations and justifications for refugee admissions are voiced by humanitarian and human rights organisations and refugee supporters through the 'discourse of humanitarianism', while pragmatic political considerations are articulated by governments and usually framed within the 'discourse of national interest'. The discourse of humanitarianism is based on Western ethical thought, theological as well as secular philosophical,[6] which starts from the premise of intrinsic and equal moral worth of every person regardless of their legal status as 'citizens' or 'aliens'. The ethical stance therefore calls for a broader sense of solidarity than the one prevalent in a world divided into nation-states (Wilbanks, 1993).

The discourse of national interest is embedded in 'political realism': a legitimate government is seen as a guardian of sovereignty which is 'increasingly defined as control over population movements' (Dauvergne, 2003, p.6). Within this discourse, the government's duty is to promote the interests of citizens, if necessary at the expense of aliens: in this case, refugees. This way, two political principles that underpin liberal states, sovereignty and human rights, have come to contradict each other, and as stricter border control has strong

6 As, for example, in the well-known Christian postulate 'Do unto others as you would have them do unto you' or Kant's (1785/1964, p. 88) categorical imperative: 'Act only on that maxim through which you can at the same time will that it should become a universal law'.

popular support, democracy has come to deny human rights when asylum seekers are concerned (Joppke, 1999). In the pragmatic discourse, these contradictions are reconciled by the principle of citizenship: from a perspective of the nation-state, citizens and aliens not only have unequal rights and prerogatives, but their interests are often seen as opposed.

Legal bases of the International Refugee Regime (IRR), the 1951 Refugee Conventions, and the 1967 Refugee Protocol, as well as its institutional bases, primarily UNHCR within the UN system, did not change in a more than half a century, but the world has changed enormously during that time. IRR, first created after the First World War and later further developed through the UN after the Second World War, is still based on the long-gone Cold War realities. However, after the fall of communism new global antagonisms replaced the old ones, and global inequalities have deepened (Speth, 1999; Thomas, 2000; Gilpin, 2000). In the 21st century, refugees no longer symbolize the conflict between the West and the East, the 'democracy' and 'totalitarianism' but they are rather one of the consequences of the gap, or indeed chasm, between the world's 'North' and the 'South', the rich and the poor. Reshaping the IRR is the process in which governments of the refugee-receiving Western countries will be key actors.

As recent developments have shown, security is no longer guaranteed to anyone in the increasingly indivisible but nevertheless antagonistic world. Thus, the mandate of IRR needs to be broadened beyond the semblance of apolitical humanitarianism to include pressing political, economic and environmental issues. In order to seriously address the current refugee crisis, IRR must become an integral part of international relations (Loescher and Monahan, 1989). Globalisation, the most pervasive buzzword of the last couple of decades, can hardly be omitted in this context. The benefits of globalisation are not evenly distributed and the neoliberal claim that the economic growth based on free market forces will eventually benefit everyone rings hollow in the developing world (Gilpin, 2000). The Third World's pervasive poverty and deepening global inequality are politically and socially explosive. As Thomas (2000, p.3) argued, development, security and refugee issues are intimately linked. As poverty is no basis for refugee status, more people are likely to become illegal immigrants (Harding, 2000).

With intensification of the global circulation and exchange of goods, capital and ideas, nation-states are less and less imaginable as territorially bounded and self-reproducing units. The movement of people, however, is still strictly controlled and, in spite of globalisation, nation states are still fundamental political, economic, cultural units in which and through which our lives are organised in all their aspects: health, education, welfare, security, legal protection. In the future, exercising sovereignty of the territorially bounded units by defending their borders from the incursion of aliens may become exceedingly expensive. For the populations of developing countries, the access to information about life opportunities in the West has increased, and their global mobility has expanded (IOM, 2002; OECD, 2003). As the established international migration and refugee channels have been restricted and overloaded, people-smuggling rackets have stepped in to meet part of the migration demand (Cornelius, 2001; FH, 2002a; FH, 2002b). The costs of border control sharply rose in the US, EU and Australia during the 1990s (IOM, 2003). In the long run, containment of refugee flows is not likely to be effective and will also involve political and social costs (Helton, 2002). In addition, it may not be possible to sustain restrictive policies of asylum and naturalisation in the West without jeopardising the constitutional ideals of liberty, equality and justice, as well as ideals on which the UN system is based. It is difficult to sustain these ideals in a closed society solely committed to its citizens, while disregarding the basic rights and needs of aliens (Scaperlandra, 1999; Joppke, 1999). Can we, citizens of the West, have a good life in a prosperous household protected by barbed wire from our poor relatives banging at the door?

Some authors argue that the West is currently undergoing the 'historic transition between two epochs' of the magnitude of the industrial revolution that radically changed the world two centuries ago (Halal and Taylor, 1999). There is no doubt that the West is in a stage of dynamic social change as well as imminent crises. We are expected to live our high-tech lives longer than ever before, we are better off, better informed and more mobile than ever, but new problems are lurking behind the spectacular successes of the West: environmental issues, the increasing danger of terrorism, aging population and 'obesity epidemics' are some of them. As is always the case in social affairs, the refugee issue is inextricable connected with other social, and increasingly, also environmental issues (Castles, 2002).

The Economics of Refugee Resettlement in the West

Economic arguments are always heard on the pragmatic side of the refugee debate in the West (Harris, 1995; Roche, 2003). Refugees are often seen as a burden to taxpayers, as people who need assistance rather than offering contribution to the host society. Those who want to minimise the humanitarian intake, especially in Europe where the pressure of asylum seekers is the highest, have expressed concerns about whether the welfare, health and education infrastructure of the most affected countries such as Britain and Germany, can absorb the intake without jeopardising interests of the locals (Sargeant and Forna, 2001). Higher unemployment rates among refugee groups are often quoted as evidence supporting the argument about refugees being a burden to host societies (ibid, p. 8; Jupp, 2002).

However, the demographic situation — for example, the net reproduction rate is well below the replacement level — in the countries traditionally closed for permanent immigration, such as Japan, Germany and most other continental European countries, has recently started to influence the economic argument against refugees and immigration in general. Japanese and German populations are the oldest in the world, and immigration represents a possible partial remedy for the demographic decline. However, many citizens of these countries are deeply suspicious towards increased levels of immigration. The imminent population crisis in the developed Western countries — ageing population and imminent labour shortages as millions of the so-called 'baby-boomers'[7] approach retirement age — requires global management and is increasingly seen as connected with the refugee crisis, as refugees can provide a large pool of labour (NCPA, 2001; NCPA, 2002; Sassen, 1999).

The small minority of world refugees who eventually resettle in the West are in most cases young and have good 'resettlement potential' (Jupp, 1994). The economic inclusion of refugees typically happens at the bottom of the host country's labour market (Harris, 1995). In other words, refugees often become, at least at the early stages of their resettlement, marginal members of host societies who take the '3D jobs',[8] unwanted by local population (Hanson, 2003; Canberra Times, 2003; The Economist, 2003). Labor market segmentation

[7] This expression that usually refers to the generation born between 1946 and 1964 when the birth rates in the developed West were at their highest.

[8] dirty, dangerous, difficult

and job discrimination largely 'protects' the host population from the effects of refugee employment (Cohen and Joly, 1989). This argument, which may be seen as 'cynical humanitarianism', seems at least as plausible as the one which demands 'zero immigration' in order to protect domestic labor.

Recent Australian developments can illustrate imminent changes in the debate about the economic contribution of refugees or a lack of it. Several country towns, mainly in the inland Australia, started 'fighting to keep their [temporary protected] refugees' a couple of years ago (Canberra Times, 2003). Refugees on TPVs, most of them from Afghanistan, took jobs in local abattoirs, poultry plants and farms, providing keen and reliable workforce where none could be found previously. The local population was initially suspicious of the influx of a visible minority, but the refugees were later found to have 'contributed significantly to the local economy' and rural towns started lobbying the government to grant them permanent visas (Walker, 2003). In response to the recognition that many refugees on TPVs have made important contributions to the Australian community, particularly in rural and regional areas, the Australian government announced that TPV holders who arrived in Australia before 27 August 2004 may apply for permanent visas. Apparently, where moral reasons calling for humanitarianism and compassion could not penetrate, arguments expressed in dollars and cents were instantly convincing. A policy that is currently developing in Australia is to 'direct more unlinked humanitarian entrants to settle in regional Australia' (DIMIA, 2003b); this would address the perenial Australian problem of dwindling populations outside major cities. In a media release from the Minister for Citizenship and Multicultural Affairs that followed the release of the report titled 'Refugees to Help Build Sustainable Regional Communities', it is stated that 'refugees arriving in Australia should be encouraged to settle in regional Australia in order to address the demand for less skilled labour in regional economies and to help humanitarian entrants achieve early employment' (Minister for Citizenship and Multicultural Affairs, 2003). Thus, there is a chance that refugees will be increasingly seen as a potential benefit rather than as a drain to the public purse, and that not only those temporary or permanently protected in Australia, or still in immigration detention, but also more refugees and asylum seekers worldwide, will be given a chance to continue their interrupted lives. Humanitarianism on firm pragmatic foundations? Yes, it seems that such foundations are the only viable long-term options in our 'economically rational' societies where the most convincing arguments are those which rely on number crunching, and ultimately show that the returns are higher than investment.

WHAT CAN YOU FIND IN THIS BOOK?

Just how lucky the refugees are to find themselves in the West is the topic of eleven chapters collected in this book. Ten academic papers and one personal story look at how successfully refugees resettle in the West and to what degree they are 'socially included', thus sharing in the prosperity of their host countries. The encounter of refugees with the 'host society' happens in a variety of circumstances, depending on resettlement policies of any given country as well as many other, less regulated factors, such as public opinion and current levels of xenophobia.

This volume presents to the reader a cross-disciplinary selection of recent empirical research on refugee resettlement in the West by established scholars in a range of social sciences. We see students and scholars in social sciences, as well as policymakers as our primary audiences, and are confident that the interdisciplinary nature of this volume is its great strength. There are more aspects to the issue than what our volume can cover, and they are all heavily intersected. Due to the nature of the contemporary academic life, however, no individual scholar is able to develop a truly integrated perspective. The lack of such a perspective, in spite of the proliferation of academic writing, can be blamed on the necessity to fit into the world of research specialisation and disciplinary segmentation. In order to attract research funding and to produce what is considered 'serious scholarship', we have to keep within our ever smaller disciplinary precincts and produce discipline-specific knowledge in a discipline-approved way. However, the fragmented perspective can seriously limit our understanding of complex social issues and their contexts (cf. Martinelli 2003). Refugee resettlement is one such complex issue that requires a cross-disciplinary perspective if it is to be understood: in this volume we attempt juxtaposing economic, political, sociological, anthropological and cultural perspectives and arguments.

This volume is a contribution to the interdisciplinary field of refugee studies. Various perspectives presented in the assembled chapters, and different methodologies used, can give the reader an insight into the variety of aspects and angles that make refugee studies. Over the past decade or two, forced migration became a larger issue than ever before and refugee studies, a new specialized area of research and scholarship, reflect this reality. Our volume follows the tradition of strong policy links of refugee studies (Black 2001). Each chapter includes a reference to the refugee policy (and other relevant policies) of the respective country of resettlement, and in some chapters the policy is a major element in the analysis (e.g. chapters by Korac and Hannah).

This rigorously peer-reviewed selection of chapters features contributions from established authors in the area of refugee studies who provide authoritative analyses of diverse aspects of resettlement of a number of refugee groups. Our contributors come from traditional refugee receiving countries: Australia, the US, the UK, Canada and Sweden, and write about various refugee groups resettling in the US, Great Britain, Australia, Sweden, Canada, Netherlands and Italy. Chapters 1 and 4 are devoted to the broad analysis of the refugee resettlement in Canada and the UK: in Chapter 1 Devoretz, Beiser and Spivenko provide an economic analysis of adaptation of refugees in Canada. and in Chapter 4, Hannah looks at resettlement and integration of refugees in the UK. In chapter 2, Bloch takes a gender perspective on refugees' labour market integration in Britain. Other chapters focus on particular aspects of resettlement and on a particular refugee group. The resettlement of Bosnians, the refugee group with the greatest access to the Western humanitarian visas during the 1990s, features in five chapters. Analysis of their resettlement in four different countries (the US, Italy, Netherlands and Australia), can be found in Chapters 3, 5, 6 and 7 (by Colic-Peisker and Waxman; Korac; Matsuo; and Owens and Coughlan). In other chapters, you can find the analyses of resettlement of several other refugee groups in the West: Ugandan Asians in Sweden (Westin and Cyberg's in Chapter 8), temporary protected Afghanistan's Hazara in Australia (Glazebrook in Chapter 9) and Ethiopia's Oromo in Australia (Gow in Chapter 10).

In order to make this book more useful to students and researchers each chapter contains a section on methodology. The reader will notice that some contributors come from the tradition of qualitative research, and some others apply quantitative methods. One of the two approaches tends to be prevalent in particular disciplines and also in particular countries or even 'schools': economics and psychology, for example, mostly subscribe to the quantitative approach and tend to rely heavily on numbers, while cultural studies and anthropology rely on narratives and in-depth interpretative analysis within the qualitative tradition. Sociology is a mixed bag: American sociology tends to be more quantitative than European and Australian. In addition, there are 'schools' based at different research centres and universities which develop specific theoretical perspectives and methodologies. Just as we argue in favour of inter-disciplinarity, we also argue in favour of both qualitative ad quantitative approaches which we see as complementary rather than mutually exclusive or even opposed.

The order of chapters of this book follows the logic of 'gradually softening perspectives' Chapters 1 (by DeVoretz, Beiser and Pivnenko), 2 (by Bloch) and 3 (by Colic-Peisker and Waxman) are rather hard-nosed analyses by economists and sociologists who used quantitative methods and their chapters contain quantitative data presented in tables and graphs. Chapter 3 authored by the editors of this volume consciously combines quantitative and qualitative approaches. Chapters 4 (by Hannah), 5 (by Korac) and 6 (by Matsuo) present qualitative sociological perspectives. Chapter 7 by Coughlan and Owens-Manly combines a sociological and social work perspective, while chapter 8 by Westin and Nyberg represents a collaboration of a political scientist and a sociologist. Chapter 9 by Glazebrook is an anthropological take on the issue of refugee resettlement, and Chapter 10 by Gow introduces cultural studies perspective into the domain of refugee studies. Several chapters employ the concepts of 'human capital' and 'social capital' in the analysis of refugee resettlement (chapters by DeVoretz et al; Colic-Peisker and Waxman; Hannah; Korac; Matsuo; Coughlan and Owens-Manley), thus reflecting the fact that these concepts captured the imagination of social scientists during the past decade. Another two concepts that enjoy considerable popularity in the recent years — transnationalism and diaspora — feature prominently in chapters by Westin and Nyberg, and Gow.

It is not usual for editors to say that they have their favourite chapter in an edited volume, but we do: it is Chapter 11, the highly illuminating personal story of a Bosnian refugee and the reader can indeed take it as a dessert. In the last chapter Hariz Halilovich, now a university researcher in Melbourne, Australia, describes his amazing seven-year journey through cultures and languages.

We hope that scholars and students in social sciences, and especially those in refugee studies, will find the diversity of perspectives presented in this volume interesting and illuminating.

References

Black, R. (2001). 'Fifty years of refugee studies: From theory to policy', *The International Migration Review*, *35*(1), 57-79.

British Broadcasting Corporation (BBC) (2000, July 26). Real-life tale of Moroccan migration. BBC News Online. Retrieved from *http://news.bbc.co.uk/1/hi/world/africa/851936.stm* .

Brittan, S. (2003). Bring me your huddled masses, Social Market Foundation Talk, 18 November 2003,. Retrieved from *http://www.smf.co.uk/sbmigration.pdf*

Canberra Times. (2003, February 27). NSW town fights to keep its refugees. *Canberra Times*.

Castles, S. (2002, October). Environmental change and forced migration: making sense of the debate, UNHCR, New Issues in Refugee Research, Working Paper No. 70. Retrieved from *http://www.unhcr.ch/cgi-bin/texis/vtx/publ*

Cohen, R. & Joly, D., (Eds.). (1989). *Reluctant Hosts: Europe and Its Refugees*. Aldershot: Avebury.

Cornelius, W. A. (2001). Death at the Border: Efficacy and Unintended Consequences of US Immigration Control. *Population and Development Review*, *27*(4), 661–685.

Dauvergne, C. (2003). Challenges to sovereignty: migration laws for the 21st century. New Issues in Refugee Research. UNHCR, Evaluation and Policy Analysis, Working Paper No. 92. Retrieved from *www.unhcr.org*

Department of Immigration and Multicultural and Indigenous Affairs (Australia). (DIMIA). (2003a). Australia's Excised Offshore Places. Fact Sheet No. 81 Retrieved from *http://www.immi.gov.au/facts/pdf/81excised.pdf*

____(2003b). Review of Settlement Services for Migrants and Humanitarian Entrants. Released on 27 May 2003. Retrieved from *http://www.immi.gov.au/ settle/settle_review/05.htm#*

_____(2004). New Measures to Strengthen Border Control, Fact Sheet No. 71. Retrieved from *http://www.immi.gov.au/facts/71border.htm*

Films for Humanities (FH) (2002a). *Dying to Get In: Illegal Immigration to the E.U.* Princeton, NJ: Films for the Humanities and Sciences (A video-tape documentary, 60 minutes).

_____(2002b). *Escape to the EU? Human Rights and Immigration Policy in Conflict*. Princeton, NJ: Films for the Humanities and Sciences (A video-tape documentary, 60 minutes).

Gilpin, R. (2000). *The Challenge of Global Capitalism: The world economy in the 21st century*. Princeton: Princeton University Press.

Halal, W. E. & Taylor, K.B. (Eds.). (1999). *21st Century Economics: Perspectives of Socioeconomics for a Changing World*. London: Macmillan.

Hanson, V. D. (2003, August). California, Here they come (and come): E Pluribus Unum is losing to La Raza. *National Review*, *55*(15).

Harding, J. (2000). *The Uninvited: Refugees at the rich man's gate*. London: Profile Books London Review of Books.

Harris, N. (1995). *The New Untouchables: Immigration and the New World Worker*. London, New York: I.B.Tauris Publishers.

Helton, A. (2002). *The Price of Indifference: Refugees and Humanitarian Action in the New Century*. Oxford: Oxford University Press.

Hobsbawm, E., & A. Polito (1999). *The New Century*. London: Little, Brown and Company.

Human Rights and Equal Opportunity Commissioner (HREOC). (2003). Face the Facts: Refugees and Asylum Seekers. Canberra: Australian Government Publishing Service. Retrieved from *www.humanrights.gov.au/ racial_discrimination/ face_facts/ ref_htmhtm#10*

Humphrey, M. (2002). Humanitarianism, terrorism and the transnational border. *Social Analysis*, 46(1), 118–126.

International Organisation for Migration (IOM), (2002). Comprehensive and Solution-Oriented Approaches to Addressing Irregular Migration, at *http:// www.iom.int/ en/PDF_Files/mprp/workshop%20summary/Irregular_E.pdf*

______(2003). Prepared by Phillip Martin (2003). *Bordering on Control: Combating Irregular Migration in North America and Europe*.

IOM Isbister, J. (1996). *The Immigration Debate: Remaking America.* West Hartford, Connecticut: Kumarian Press.

Joppke, C. (1999). *Immigration and the Nation-State.* Oxford: Oxford University Press

Jupp, J. (1994). *Exile or Refugee? The Settlement of Refugees, Humanitarian and Displaced Immigrants.* Bureau of Immigration and Population Research, Canberra: AGPS.

_____(2002). *From White Australia to Woomera, The Story of Australian Immigration.* Cambridge: Cambridge University Press.

Kant, I. (1785/1964). *Groundworks for the Metaphysics of Morals* (translated and analyzed by H. J. Paton). New York: Harper and Row Publishers.

Keely, C. B. (1996). How nation-states create and respond to refugee flows. *International Migration Review*, 30(4), 1046-1067.

Loescher, G. & Monahan, L. (Eds.). (1989). *Refugees and International Relations.*Oxford, New York: Oxford University Press.

Martinelli, A. (2003). Markets, Governments, Communities and Global Governance. *International Sociology*, *18*(2), 291-323.

Minister for Citizenship and Multicultural Affairs (2003, May 27). Media release. Refugees to help build sustainable communities. Retrieved from *http:// www.minister.immi.gov .au/cam/media/media03/h03073.htm.*

Moore, A. (2002, January 4). Is Mexico reconquering the U.S. southwest? *WorldNetDaily.* Retrieved from *http://www.worldnetdaily.com/news/article.asp* ARTICLE_ID=25920

National Center for Policy Analysis (NCPA). (2001). U.S. Depends on Immigrant Workers. Daily Policy Digest July 23, 2001. Retrieved from *www.ncpa.org/pd/immigrat/ pd072301e.html*

_____(2002). Immigrant Welfare Receipt Versus Taxes Paid. *Daily Policy Digest* June 14, 2002. Retrieved from *www.ncpa.org/iss/imm/2002/pd062402a.html*

Organisation for Economic Cooperation and Development (OECD). (2003). International Migration: Flow of Immigrants into OECD Countries Continues to Rise. Retrieved from *http://www.oecd.org/document/20/0,2340,en_2649_37415_2495572_1_1_1_37415,00.html*

Refugee Reports (2002, May). 2002: Lowest Refugee Admissions in Two Decades? *Refugee Reports*, *23*(4), at *http://www.refugees.org/world/articles/RR_May_2002_lead.cfm*

Roche, B. (2003). *Rethinking Migration for the 21st Century* (Speech to the Social Market Foundation 18 Nov 2003). Retrieved from *www.smf.co.uk/roche_migration.pdf*

Sargeant, G. & Forna, A. (2001). *Poor Reception. Refugees and Asylum Seekers: welfare or work?* (Policy paper). London: Industrial Society.

Sassen, S. 1999. *Guests and Aliens.* New York: The New Press.

Scaperlandra, M. A. (1999, December). Immigration Justice: Beyond Liberal Egalitarianism and Communitarian Perspectives. *Review of Social Economy*, *57*(4), 523-542.

Speth, J. G. (1999, May). The Plight of the Poor. *Foreign Affairs*, *78*(13), 13-17.

Stone, J., for 3WE (Third World and Environmental Broadcasting Project, 2000). *Losing Perspective: Global Affairs on British Terrestrial Television 1989-1999.* Retrieved from *http://www.ibt.org.uk/4TV%20Research/Losing%20Perpective/Losing%20Perspective. pdf*.

The Economist (US). (2003, July 26). An answer or a problem? Day-labor centers: Helping hired-by- the-day workers. *The Economist* (US), p.32.

The Refugee Council USA (2003, May). *US Refugee Admissions Program for Fiscal Year 2004, Recommendations of the Refugee Council US.* Retrieved *from http://www. refugeecouncilusa.org/rcusa2004doc.pdf*

Thomas, C. (2000). *Global Governance, Development and Human Security: The Challenge of Poverty and Inequality*. London, Sterling, VA: Pluto Press.

United Nations High Commissioner for Refugees (UNHCR). (2003). *Asylum levels and trends in industrialized countries, January to June 2003.* Retrieved from *http://www.unhcr.ch/cgibin/texis/vtx/home/opendoc.pdf?tbl=STATISTICS&id=3f3cd9df4 &page=statisticsU.*

_____(2004). *Refugees by Numbers* 2004 Edition. *Retrieved from http://ww.unhcr.org/.*

U.S. Border Control (2003). Troops on the Border by Edward I. Nelson, Chairman. Retrieved from *http://capwiz.com/usbc/issues/alert/?alertid=1283741&type=CO* .

Walker, J. (2003, October 25-26). Home, where the work is. *The Weekend Australian*, 22–23.

Wilbanks, D. (1993). The moral debate between humanitarianism and national interest about U.S. refugee policy: a theological perspective. *Migration World Magazine*, *21*(5), 15-20.

York, B. (2003). Australia and Refugees, 1901-2002, Annotated Chronology Based on Official Sources. Canberra: Parliament of Australia, Department of the Parliamentary Library. Retrieved from *http://www.aph.gov.au/library/pubs/chron/2002-03/03chr02.htm*

In: Homeland Wanted
Editors: P. Waxman and V. Colic-Peisker, pp. 1-21
ISBN 1-59454-266-X

Chapter 1

THE ECONOMIC EXPERIENCES OF REFUGEES IN CANADA

Don DeVoretz, Morton Beiser and Sergiy Pivnenko

ABSTRACT

Admission of refugees into Canada is claimed by its government to be based on compassionate grounds rather than economic criteria. It is, however, important to document the economic successes or failures among Canada's refugee population in order to understand how post arrival integration policies affect refugee economic performance. This chapter examines a set of economic indicators from Canada's IMDB database to assess the post 1981 Canadian refugee economic experience. With the aid of a standard human capital model, we address a series of economic questions including the length of time required for refugee economic integration, the use by refugees of Canada's social safety net, refugee poverty levels and refugee economic performance vis-à-vis Canada's family-class immigrant. Our main findings are that employed Canadian refugees earn an amount equal to that earned by their family-class reference group circa 1980-2001. However, the incidence of social assistance dependency for refugees is substantial and, for those refugees who receive any assistance, their total income is at the near destitute level.

Key words: Refugees, immigrant earnings, human capital.

INTRODUCTION

Canada's immigration and refugee legislation admits permanent residents through a variety of gateways which all require prior assessment to qualify for admission: the independent or economic class which includes business migrants and skilled workers, a family reunification class and humanitarian (refugee) class. The independent class is further subdivided into entry gates for principal applicants and dependents, where only the principal applicants are assessed for their potential economic contribution through Canada's points system. The accompanying dependants (spouse and children) are not assessed but can not enter Canada unless the principal applicant passes the points test. Importantly, from an economic viewpoint, the government's designation of the assessment gateway influences the economic outcomes of the foreign-born. In fact, most foreign arrivals to Canada, including refugees, are not economically screened: only 25 per cent of all non-refugee arrivals must pass economic criteria to earn 67-plus points on human capital attributes and thus qualify for admission.

Canada clearly attempts to insure a bone fide approach to asylum seekers but there is no explicit selection technique employed by Canada in regards to their human capital.[1] The latter also holds for the family class of immigrants. Those who self-select to leave home, but experience no further economic screening upon arrival to Canada will be referred to in this chapter as 'singly selected'. 'Double selection' in the immigrant literature means that the immigrant first self-selects by leaving, and then the destination country selects them again if they apply for an economic (skilled-based) visa.

The selection based upon human capital attributes of the Canada-bound economic immigrants presumably leads to their speedier integration into the Canadian economy. In turn, the condition of the Canadian economy at the refugee's or immigrant's time of arrival is often an important influence on their ultimate economic success. If the economy is weak upon arrival, then many immigrants may never realize the economic "catch-up" that immigrants who arrive in economically robust times have experienced.

This chapter concentrates on the economic performance of refugees. As one of more than 150 signatories to the UN Convention on refugees, Canada is committed to protecting the persecuted and stateless. Canada also belongs to a much smaller section of Convention signatories who offer not just temporary protection, but the option of permanent resettlement. Humanitarian concerns presumably motivate the decision to offer refugees the opportunity for permanent resettlement, and such concerns probably provide sufficient justification to perpetuate this policy. Critics, however, suggest that the policy is misguided, because it brings grave economic consequences in its wake. This chapter addresses these concerns by investigating the question: what are the labour market outcomes for refugees in Canada?

To qualify for Canadian admission, refugees who arrive in Canada must meet several criteria. There are the 'convention refugees' who leave their country because of a well-founded fear that they will be persecuted due to their religious beliefs, race, nationality, political opinion or membership in a persecuted group. Asylum seekers, on the other hand, are defined as those persons "seriously and personally affected by civil war, armed conflict, or massive violations of human rights." Inhabitants of the designated countries meet the definition of convention refugees, and can include people who suffer because their country denies them the rights of freedom of expression, dissent, or the right to engage in trade union activity. In addition to convention refugees, Canada has been admitting Protected Persons, that is, inhabitants of designated refugee-producing countries. However, unlike asylum seekers, protected persons must apply for resettlement from outside Canada These refugee applicants are admitted under special rules and are considered either a convention refugee or a member of a 'humanitarian designated class'. The humanitarian designated class was introduced by the federal government in 1997 to provide for the possibility of resettlement to individuals seriously affected by situations such as civil war and armed conflict. Refugees may be selected abroad for resettlement in Canada or may apply for and receive Convention

---

1 The new *Immigration and Refugee Protection Act* (IRPA) of 2002 made some substantial changes in both economic criteria for entry of the economic class and the adjudication of refugees (Shi, 2003). However, all the refugee arrivals covered in this chapter were admitted under the 1978 Immigration Act.

refugee status from the Federal Immigration and Refugee Board within Canada. As mentioned, Canada's refugee assessment contains no explicit economic criteria for entry although a suitability criterion based on the refugee's presumed ability to integrate is used in the selection procedure. Under the Canada-Quebec Accord, Quebec has the responsibility for selecting refugees abroad who are destined for Quebec. The federal government is responsible for ensuring that people selected by Quebec are eligible for refugee status.

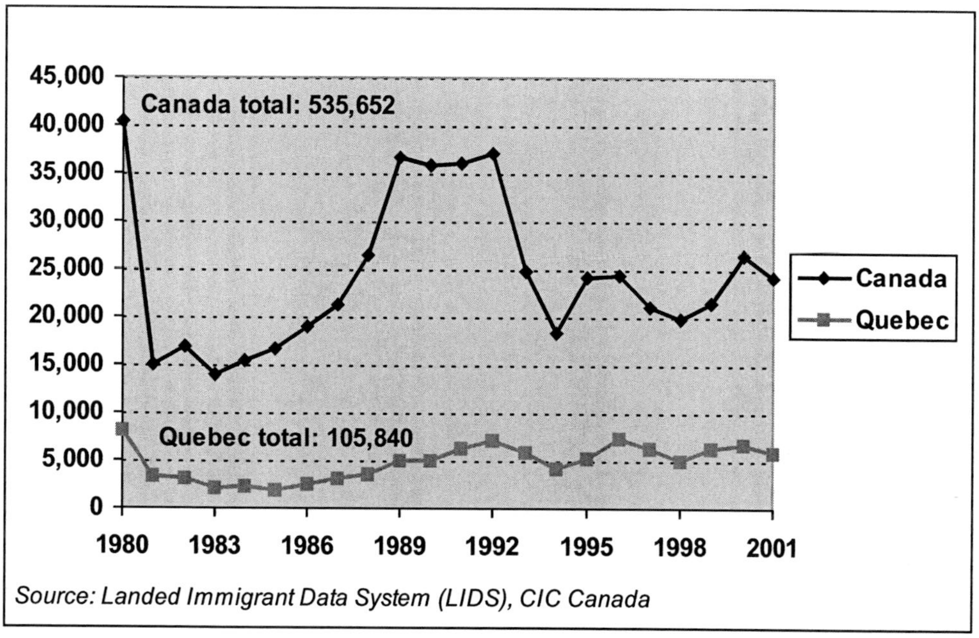

Figure 1: Refugee Arrivals to Canada: 1980-2001

Between 1980 and 2001 Canada received a total of 535,131 refugees from a wide variety of source countries. Figure 1 documents dramatic fluctuations in refugee arrivals between 1980 and 2001, with numbers ranging from a high of 40,000 in 1980 (corresponding to the "Boat People" crisis in Southeast Asia which stimulated the largest admission of refugees in Canada's history) to a low of 15,000 in 1983. While Canada does not have an explicit or implicit refugee quota, the total number of yearly refugee arrivals is a product of both external events and Canada's overall yearly immigrant target levels. Since the early 1990s Canada's goal has been to admit 50 per cent of its immigrants in the economic (doubly-selected) class. The rest of the admissions including refugees is a residual of any year's total target. Thus, any change in total immigrant intake affects the absolute number of refugees admitted. For instance, the fall in refugee levels in the 1980s and the rise in the early 1990s largely reflects the movement of total announced immigration targets. During the last seven years, the number of refugee arrivals has become stabilized at fewer than 25,000 per year, roughly 10 percent of the immigrant total.

Figures 2 and 3 provide insights into political hot spots of a given era, demonstrating the manner in which changing world conditions influence refugee flows to Canada. During the period 1980-1995, Southeast Asia, Poland and El Salvador accounted for more than half of all refugee admissions. By contrast, between 1995 and 2000, refugees from Bosnia Herzegovina, Sri Lanka, Somalia and the Middle East made up 54 percent of all such admissions.

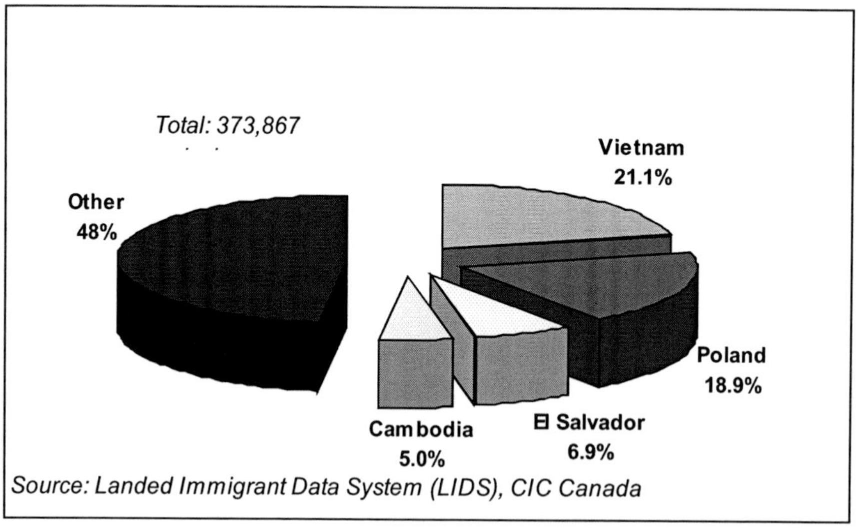

Figure 2: Refugee Arrivals to Canada in 1980-1994 by Source Country

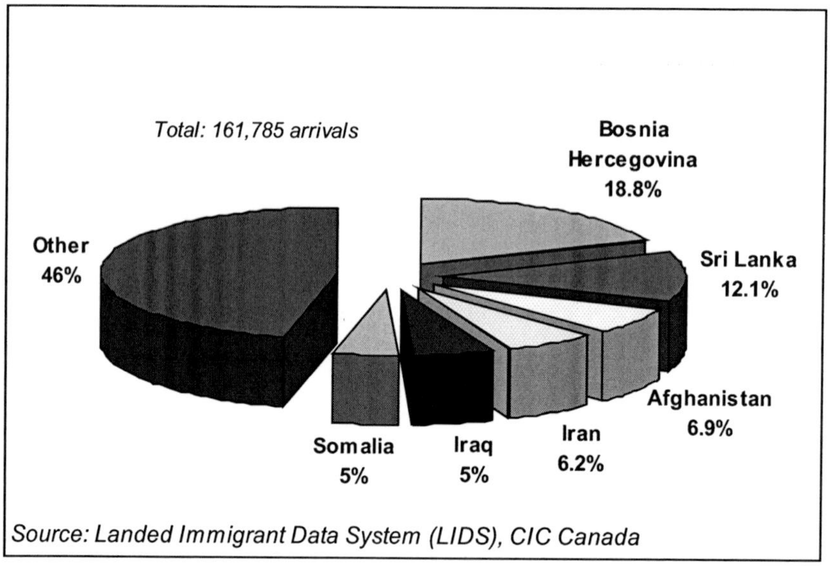

Figure 3: Refugee Arrivals to Canada in 1995-2000 by Source Country

Given the fluctuating number of refugee claimants and their heterogeneity across source countries, it is appropriate to ask how these various refugee groups fared in the Canadian economy. The central goal of this chapter is to answer this question. It proposes to analyze the economic performance of Canadian refugees in terms of the standard human capital model. This model basically states that individuals, before or after arrival in Canada, differentially invest in themselves to increase their endowment of human capital (education and language) depending on their age and ability. In turn, differential rates of investment by individuals lead to different outcomes in the labor market.

To date, very few economists have analyzed the economic performance of refugees in Canada. What we seek to measure is the refugee economic integration over time in Canada. For example, how long does this process of economic integration take, how does it compare to the family reunification class and does it vary by the date of the refugee arrival or across particular refugee gateways? Moreover, what is the refugee experience with poverty and the use of social assistance or unemployment insurance in Canada? Finally, does refugee economic performance depend on how refugees are sponsored?

We provide a brief literature review and present some stylized facts about the human capital characteristics of refugees. On this background, we then report refugee earnings and their relative rates of economic integration into the Canadian economy after arrival and their use of Canada's social safety net. Finally, we assess Canadian refugee economic integration in general.

LITERATURE REVIEW

The academic literature has primarily focused on legal, political, social and health issues of refugees in Canada, and the economic aspect of refugee resettlement has received little attention. Research on the "boat people," Southeast Asian refugees from Vietnam, Laos and Cambodia who were admitted to the U.S. and Canada suggests that, after an initial decade of economic struggle, refugee employment rates approximate, and perhaps better those of the receiving society and that refugee service demands are lower (see Beiser 1999; Caplan, Whitmore & Choy 1989; Haines 1987; Strand & Jones, 1985; Fass 1986). Because these studies have focused on a particular refugee group that arrived in North America during a particular historical era, the conclusions are necessarily limited.

The lack of comprehensive research on the economic status of refugees is partially due to inadequate census data. Census data in the U.S. or Canada only discloses foreign birth status and does not reveal entry status (e.g. refugee, family class immigrant, etc.) of an immigrant, thus precluding any detailed economic analysis of the refugee sub-group. Nonetheless, some imaginative census-based work has been reported. For example, in the U.S., Cortes (2001) used the 1980 and 1990 U.S. Censuses to generate a synthetic panel of refugee and economic immigrants. Even with these limitations, Cortes found that refugees had higher rates of human capital accumulation and thus even though their earnings start below other U.S. immigrants, their annual earnings grow faster than the earnings of other immigrants.

A more reliable data source is available to refugee scholars in Canada. The Longitudinal Immigration Data Base (IMDB) combines information from landing records compiled by Citizenship and Immigration Canada (CIC) with information from refugee or immigrant personal income tax returns. If we combine these two data sets we can track income performance of different immigrant admission categories including refugees after 1980. However, education, occupation and language ability in Canada's official languages are recorded as "tombstone" information.[2] The IMDB data set allows an economic analysis

[2] Tombstone is a set of data collected upon arrival which does not alter over time. An example in this case would be language ability.

across immigrant entry categories over a sufficiently long time period to identify cohort, period and aging effects on differential refugee economic outcomes.

A study by Citizenship and Immigration Canada (1998) utilizing the IMDB database revealed important differences (and some similarities) in the labour market behavior of Canada's major immigrant admission categories that included the family class, economic principal applicants, the spouses and dependents of these economic principal applicants and refugees. An important example of both differential and then converging behavior is the finding that although Canadian refugees reported substantially lower employment earnings than economic principal applicants, their earnings patterns relative to three other immigrant entry categories (including family class and the spouses and dependents of economic principal applicants) were very similar. Moreover, refugees who had been in Canada for twelve or more years reported average earnings at or near the Canadian-born average. Nonetheless, this study reported that refugees admitted prior to 1990 typically reported the highest rates of unemployment benefit usage when compared with any other immigrant category or the Canadian-born population. Also, after two years in Canada, refugees again report the highest rates of social assistance usage.

DeSilva (1997) employed a IMDB sub-sample of male immigrants who landed during the period 1981-1984 to test the commonly held belief that Canadian refugees perform poorly when compared with other immigrant categories. His analysis was restricted to four immigrant entry classes: independents, assisted relatives, convention refugees, and the designated class, the last two being combined into one group for the purposes of regression analysis. DeSilva found that although independently selected immigrants were the highest foreign-born income earners, they experienced the smallest earnings growth after arrival. In contrast, the designated refugee class reported the most rapid increase in earnings.

Overall, DeSilva's (1997) study demonstrated a rapid convergence in earnings among immigrants and refugees over time. Although the refugee and assisted relative classes initially showed a significant earnings disadvantage compared with the independent entrants, the gap narrowed over time. Given that refugees had the weakest language ability upon landing, their economic progress was deemed strong.

DeSilva's (1997) research also reveal that differences between refugee and immigrant human capital endowments at the time of landing account for only a small portion of their subsequent earnings across these groups. This implies that one has to look at factors other than educational and demographic characteristics at arrival to explain the observed earnings differentials. Finally, DeSilva argues that the economic success of refugees was highly conditioned on their region of origin. The most successful among them were those from Europe whereas many refugees from Africa and Southeast Asia performed poorly. In another study, based on the data from the Refugee Resettlement Project (RRP), Beiser and Hou (2000) examined gender differences in English-language acquisition and employment consequences of language proficiency. The results of the study confirmed that English proficiency was a significant determinant of the unemployment rate and labour force participation of refugees in the long term.

In sum, the literature on the economic performance of refugees in Canada points to the use of the IMDB as the primary data source. In addition, these studies argue that earnings convergence occurs between refugees and any reference group over time (12 years), with educational attainment and language acquisition conditioning the speed of convergence. We will explore this presumed earnings convergence in more detail in the following section.

STYLIZED FACTS

Canadian researchers, as noted, are fortunate in having at their disposal two administrative databases which, when combined, yield the researcher a portrait of the immigrant upon arrival (LIDS: Landed Immigrant Data System) and records of their economic performance while residing in Canada (IMDB: Immigration Data Base). The LIDS or landings records are exhaustive and cover every permanent legal immigrant to Canada who arrived after 1980. It is a snapshot that records various socio-economic and demographic features on arrival. The 2002 version of LIDS which we use covers 4.1 million entrants between 1980 and 2001. The IMDB or immigration database combines both the LIDS database to the immigrant's yearly tax records. This administrative database only covers immigrants who file an income tax and hence the coverage is limited to 40-50 percent of all past arrivals. It should be noted that although the major weakness of the IMDB is the disappearance of immigrants over time through death, emigration or retirement, it, nevertheless, does provide a time series picture of refugee and immigrants. We will employ this data set to generate some stylized facts below and in our more extensive analysis in the next section.

The human capital attributes of refugees varied considerably and were, to some extent, a reflection of educational opportunities available in refugees' countries of origin.

Figure 4 illustrates the influence of source area on educational heterogeneity. For example, approximately 50 percent of refugees from Europe who arrived between 1980 and 2001 had some post-secondary education compared to only 20 percent who came from other regions. In particular, the reported percentages for post-secondary educational levels for Africa (28 per cent), Asia (23 per cent) and South and Central America (25 per cent) were all about half the European rate. If we compare the educational levels for European immigrants across entry gates, we can see that refugees from Europe were as well educated as skilled Canadian immigrants in general. Refugees from non-European sources were the least educated of all immigrant classes: 80 per cent had no more than a secondary level of education. It should be noted that the non-European refugee groups contain a wide variety of source countries at different levels of development which masks the true diversity of the entrants' backgrounds.

As shown in Figure 5, knowledge of Canada's official languages followed a different pattern. English or French language ability is one of a number of ways in which applicants for skilled (independent) immigrant status earn points in order to qualify for admission. As a consequence, it is not surprising that almost 70 per cent of all immigrants in this category spoke at least one of Canada's official languages regardless of their source region. The proportion of family-class immigrants who spoke either English or French was substantially lower – about 50 percent – a proportion which, once again, did not vary by source region. Refugees were less likely to have a command of English or French than other immigrant classes: however, the group least likely to possess this advantage was refugees from Europe. Further analysis demonstrated the uneven distribution of official language ability across refugee groups: circa 75 percent of refugees from Europe spoke neither of Canada's official languages, in comparison with 57 per cent of refugees from other regions who spoke neither language.

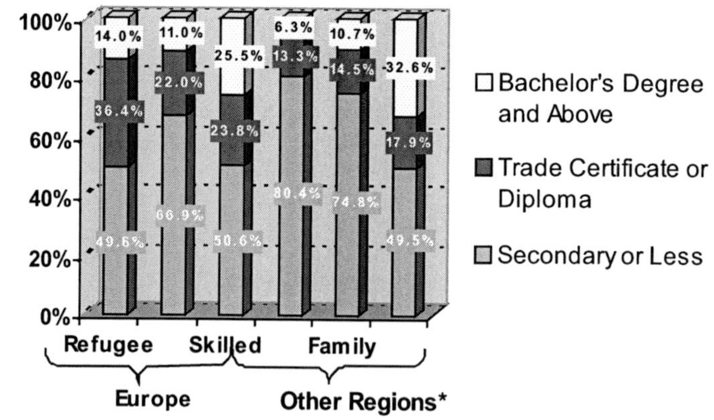

Source: Landed Immigrant Data System (LIDS), CIC Canada

Figure 4: Educational Qualifications of Foreign-born by Entry Class and Source Region: 1980-2001 arrivals

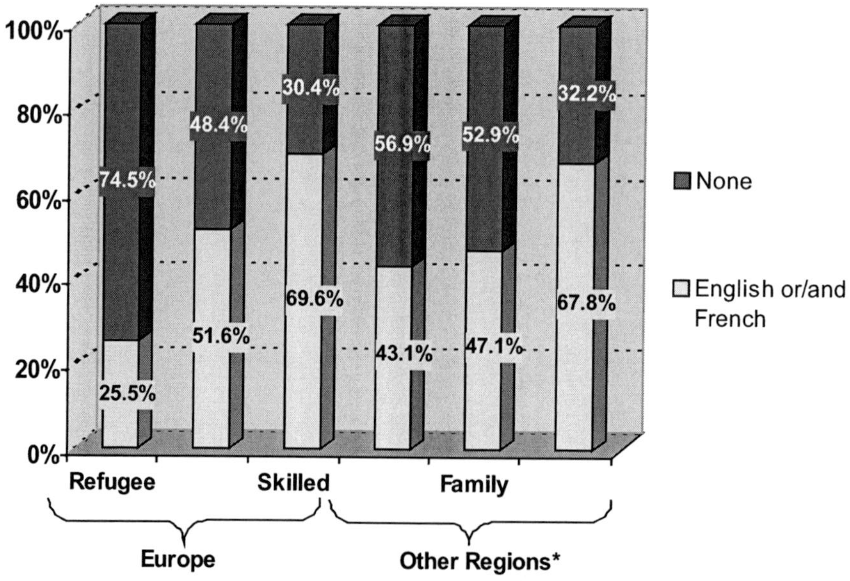

Source: Landed Immigrant Data System (LIDS), CIC Canada

Figure 5: Canadian Language Ability of Foreign-born by Entry Class and Source Region: 1980-2001 arrivals

A consideration of Figures 4 and 5 together allows a comparison of educational and linguistic skills for Canada's family and refugee classes circa 1980-2001. The comparisons are striking. European refugees were more highly educated than either skilled or family class immigrants from other regions, but were more severely linguistically disadvantaged (25.5 per cent of refugees had Canadian language ability compared to 51.6 per cent and 69.6 per cent for family and skilled migrant cohorts respectively). The relatively low level of language proficiency for European refugees is no doubt due to the fact that they came from non-English/French-speaking areas (former Yugoslavia and Poland), whereas over 25 per cent of family class and skilled workers emigrated from British Islands and France.

The educational attainments and linguistic skills of non-European family class immigrants are very similar to those of non-European refugees, while levels of educational attainment and linguistic skills for skilled immigrants were more akin to their European counterparts. In sum, European refugees are a unique group in terms of higher educational levels and less linguistic skills. These differential human capital endowments of education and language affect refugees' economic performance, which we document below.

Refugees' Economic Outcomes

Economic Outcomes: Entry Cohorts and Immigrant Admission Categories

The IMDB data set allows us to analyze the economic outcome of refugees from several dimensions. Essentially, the methodology employed here is to identify a class or type of earnings (e.g. employment income, social assistance) and ask how the refugee group who reported this type of earnings fared vis-à-vis other entry categories. We also expand this analysis by computing refugee total income, that is, we combine the refugee's target income (e.g. employment earnings) with all other sources of earnings (self-employed, social assistance, etc.) reported for the refugee.

Figure 6 presents an overview of total earned income (in 1992 dollars) by all employed refugees seven years after arrival for three different cohorts based on date of arrival: 1980, 1985 and 1990. A further distinction is made to isolate regional differences by specifying the earnings of refugees in Canada and for the province of Quebec since Quebec selects its own refugees. This figure allows us to detect if there is an entry or period effects. In other words, have the earned income prospects of refugees changed between those refugees who entered in the 1980s or 1990s? The answer is no, since seven years after their respective arrival dates, the 1980 and 1990 refugee cohorts reported near identical earned incomes. A period effect nevertheless appears in 1992 when refugees for the 1985 cohort earned about $2,000 more after seven years in Canada than either the 1980 or 1990 cohorts. Thus, although no long-term decline in refugee earnings appears after 1980, it was better to have arrived before Canada's recession of the early 1990s. In addition, figure 6 clearly portrays the 'economic penalty' for refugee settlement in Quebec. The provincial difference could arise because of the Quebec economy's weakness or the weak endowment of human capital found in Quebec refugees or both. We return to the cause of this 15 per cent provincial penalty in a later section.

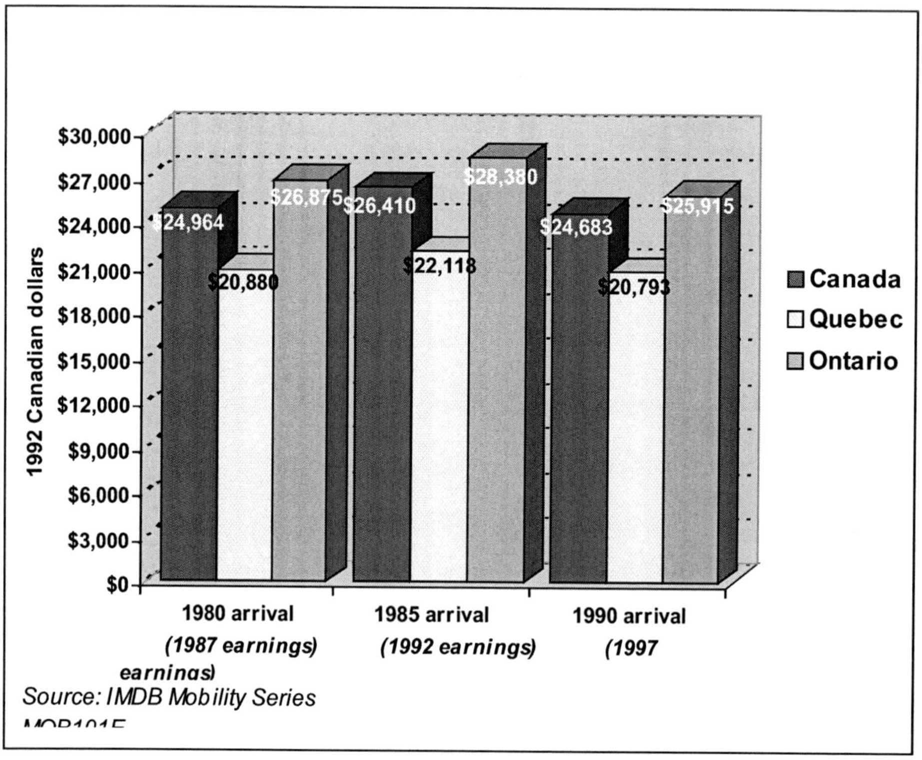

Figure 6: Total Income of 3 Employed Refugee Cohorts: 7 years since arrival (1992 dollars)

Figures 7-A, 7-B and 7-C (below) report the earnings for employed refugees across three subdivisions of the refugee entry gate for three cohorts. Each refugee gate reflects a presumed different degree of sponsorship or support mechanism after arrival in Canada. In short, those refugees who fall in the category "In Canada" are self sponsored asylum seekers. The remaining two categories: Private and Government reflect respectively the presence of a Canadian sponsor in the private or public sector. Given our above arguments, we would expect that after seven years sponsored refugees would do better economically than asylum seekers who lack some of these support mechanisms. A clear pattern emerges in favor of the privately sponsored refugees since between 1987 and 1997 the income prospects of Canadian refugees changed dramatically by refugee entry gates. The "In Canada" category (asylum-seekers) experienced a 20 percent decline in constant 1992 dollars even after allowing for 7-year integration period. Government sponsored refugees experienced a more modest decline over this period (12 per cent) while the earnings of privately sponsored refugees showed a modest 5 per cent rise.

Moreover, there exist little absolute earnings differences across entry gates except for the privately sponsored 1985 and 1990 cohorts of refugees who did earn significantly more than the other two entry groups after seven years in Canada.

These refugee earnings performances greatly exceed the Low Income Cutoff (LICO) level, if we assume that both partners in a refugee household found employment. In 1997, the low income cutoff for a two-person household in a city with a population of 500,000 or more was $20,233 (in 1992 dollars), while Figure 7-D demonstrates that combined male and female refugee employment earnings for the 1990 entry cohort ranged from $33,663 to $41,163 (1992 dollars) at that time.

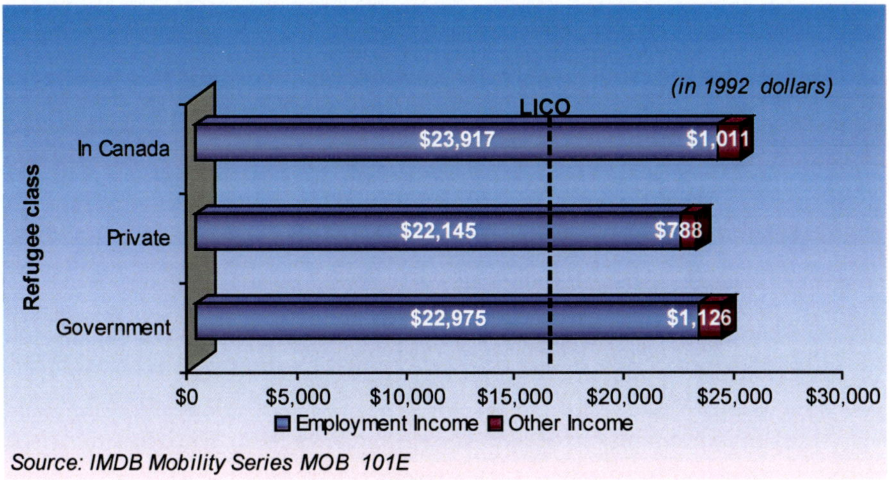

Figure 7-A: Total income of employed principal applicant by refugee entry class: 1980 arrivals, 1987 income

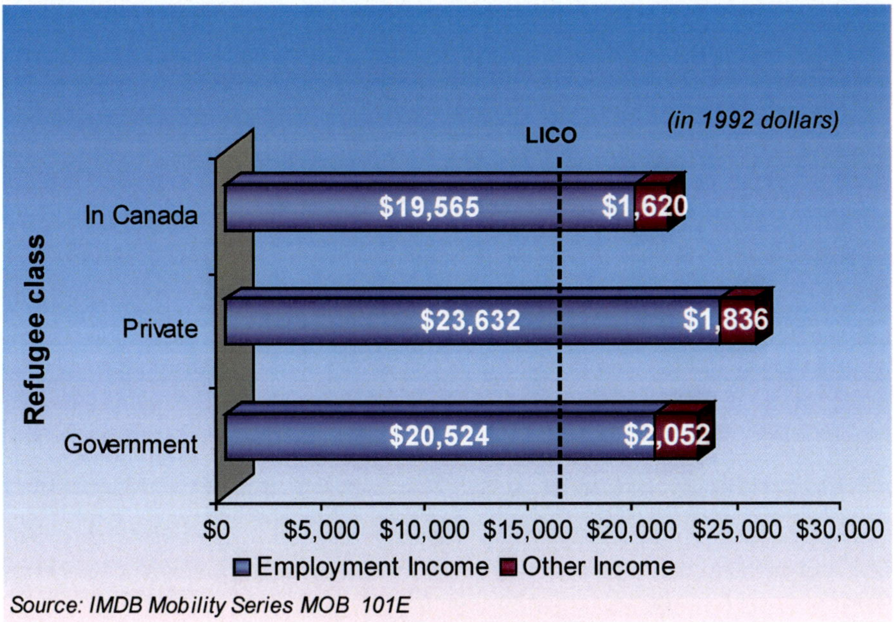

Figure 7-B: Total income of employed principal applicant by refugee entry class: 1985 arrivals, 1992 income

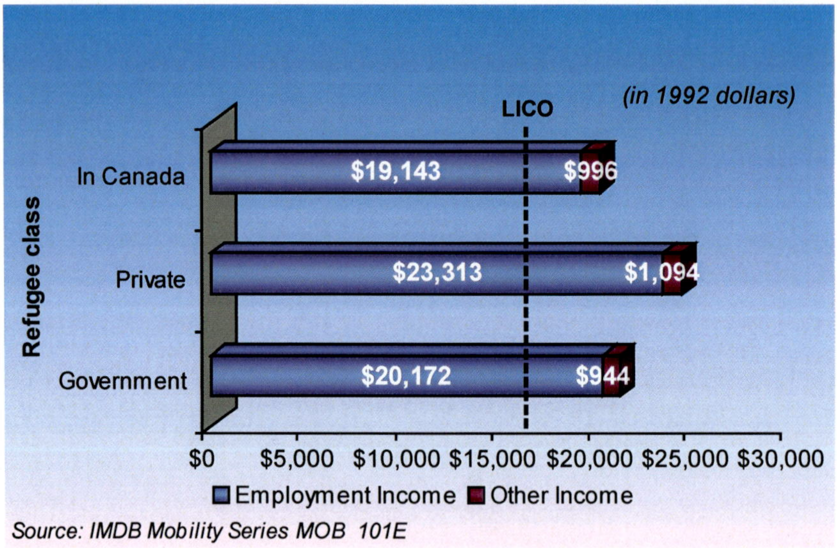

Figure 7-C:Total income of employed principal applicant by refugee entry class: 1990 arrivals, 1997 income

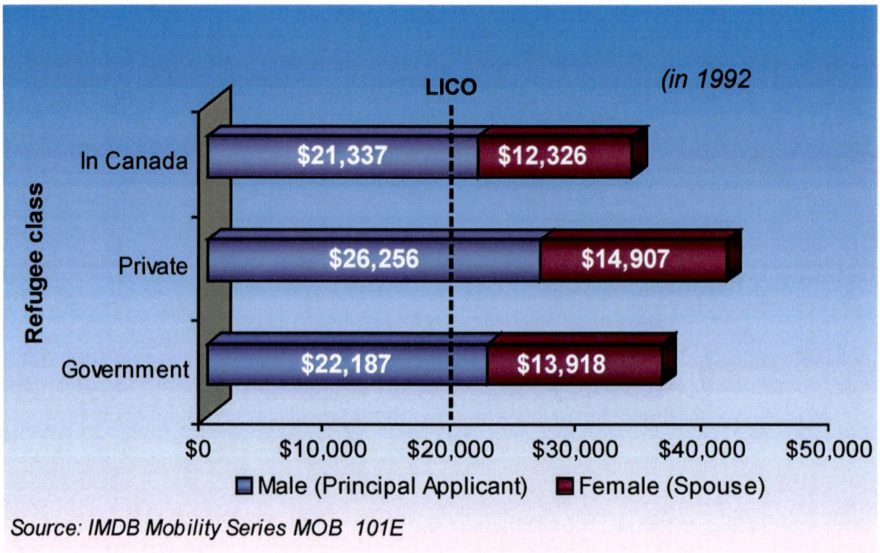

Figure 7-D: Total income of the two-person (both employed) refugee family by entry class: 1990 arrivals, 1997 income

Nonetheless, the absolute level of earnings for any of these entry groups is not high. Thus, we must ask two further questions. How did other non-refugee entry groups to Canada fare after arrival in Canada? Furthermore, what effect did this weak and declining income-earning performance in general have on refugee poverty levels and use of Canada's social assistance programs? We answer these questions below.

Refugee Economic Integration

Previous research (DeVoretz, 1995) has demonstrated the important effect of length of resettlement on economic performance. On average, it takes immigrants 12 years or more to achieve their full economic potential. Analyses in this section describe the effects of time on economic performance for different immigrant classes.

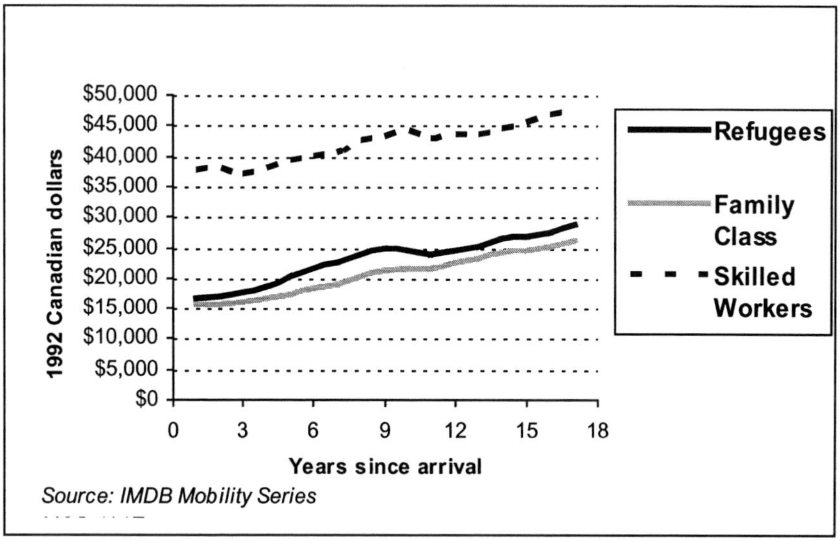

Figure 8-A: Assimilation Profiles for 1980 Family Class, Skilled and Refugee Cohorts: Employment Earnings

In particular, in this section we attempt to answer the earlier posed questions of degree of refugee economic integration by comparing refugee economic performance to family class immigrants over time. Figures 8-A and 8-B report the degree of refugee earnings integration in terms of years since arrival in Canada for both the 1980 and 1985 cohorts respectively. For the 1980 cohort refugee employment earnings slightly exceed the earnings of family class members for the entire reporting period. Note, however, that these earnings were controlled only for year of entry and entry class. Moreover, real (1992 dollars) earnings for the 1980 cohort of refugees doubled from $15,000 to $30,000 after 17 years in Canada. In both these dimensions, earnings relative to the family class and the growth in refugee earnings over time, it can be argued that the 1980 refugee cohort successfully assimilated into the Canadian labour market. However, if we used the doubly-selected skilled worker group as the reference group than the degree of refugee integration would be nil. In fact, the effect of double selection is made clear from the earnings of skilled workers who uniformly earn approximately $20,000 more than the singly-selected family and refugee classes for the 1980 cohort.

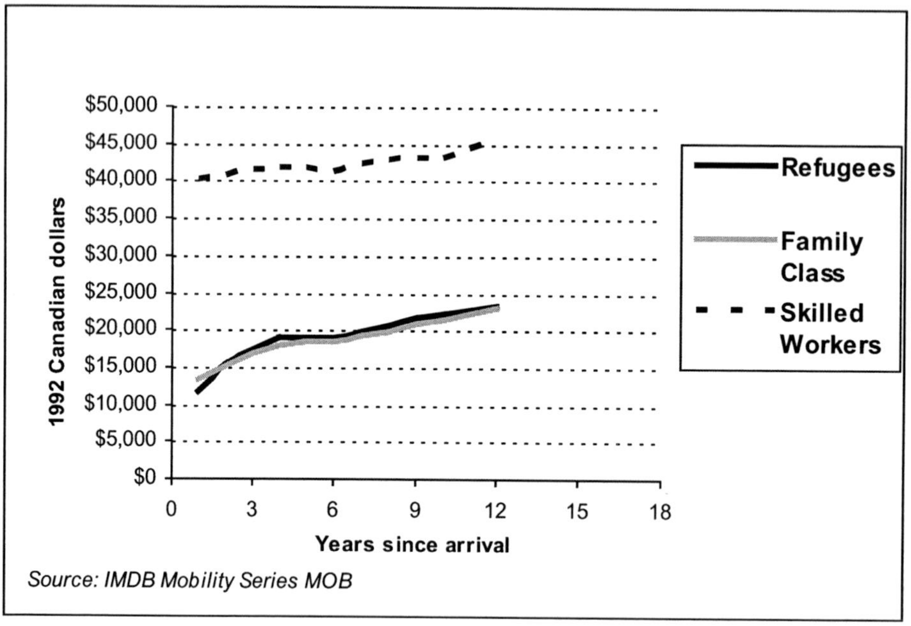

Figure 8-B Assimilation Profiles for 1985 Family Class, Skilled and Refugee Cohorts: Employment Earnings

Figure 8-B reinforces this pattern of divergent earnings between the singly-selected (refugee and family class) entrants and the doubly-selected (economic) group. However, over the twelve year period reported in Figure 8-B refugees doubled their employment earnings from $12,000 to $25,000 while skilled workers only experienced a $5,000 gain during the same period.

Age-Earnings Profiles

An alternative method of measuring economic integration is to construct age earnings profiles for a given entry year (1980) cohort of the family class and refugee arrivals to test the human capital model of earnings. The human capital model would predict that these earnings profiles would be quadratic in form (i.e. concave) with a greater intercept for that group who acquired more human capital.

The human capital model is supported by Figure 9. Both groups' earnings initially rise as investment in language increases their productivity in Canada's labour market: A peak in earnings occurs at age interval 35-49 and then earnings decline to reflect the 'depreciation' of human capital. Figure 9 also amplifies Figure 8-A findings that refugees and family class members have near similar earnings performance. In particular, before approximately age 40, family class earners outperform refugees but afterwards the trend is reversed.

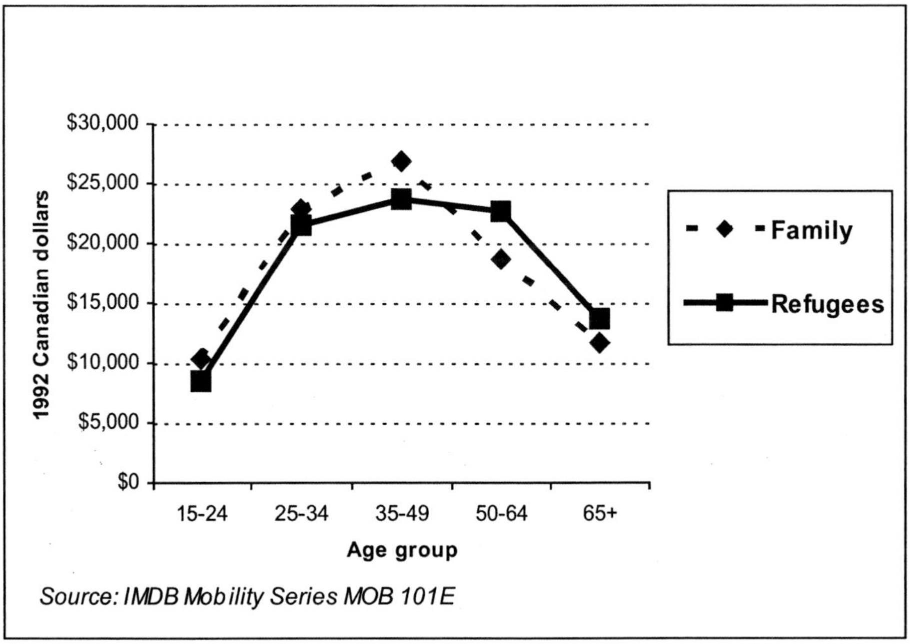

Figure 9: Family Class and Refugee Employment Earnings in 1992 by Age Group (1980 arrivals)

Regional Variations

In addition to entrance category and time in Canada, the place of settlement may exert an independent effect on economic performance (DeVoretz and Pivnenko, 2004). The underlying proposition in this section is that due either to differential selection criteria or a weak economy (or both), Quebec-bound refugees would have a weaker performance. Also, it should be noted that to the extent that Quebec-bound refugees are francophone, they will have limited out-migration possibilities after arrival (DeVoretz, Pivnenko and Coulombe, 2003). All of these forces should contribute to differential regional refugee earnings. Table 1 presents two measures of earnings (employment earnings and total income) across the three provinces for employed refugees and family class entrants over time.

Ontario clearly offers superior income prospects for either refugees or family class entrants. The 1980 refugee cohort which lived in Ontario in 1987 earned $21,720, which is $5,809 and $4,261 more than the 1980 refugee cohort resident in Quebec and British Columbia respectively at that time. By 1997, the relative advantage of refugees living in Ontario versus Quebec and British Columbia slightly declined. Family class immigrants, our reference group, experienced a similar disparity in earning outcomes across provinces. However, contrary to the refugee experience, the inter-provincial earnings differential among the family-class cohorts of British Columbia and Ontario narrowed markedly (as the former's earnings rose from 80.7 per cent of the latter's in 1987 to 94.2 per cent a decade later), while those in Quebec continued to languish as earnings only approached 73 per cent of Ontario's in 1997. In sum, after seven years in Canada, earnings differentials persisted by province of residence for both refugees and the family class immigrants, with Quebec's outcome particularly weak.

Table 1. Total Income of Employed Family Class Immigrants and Refugees 7 Years after Arrival by Entry Class (in 1992 dollars)

Immigrant cohorts	All Canada		Quebec		Ontario		British Columbia	
	Employment Earnings ($)	Total Income ($)	Employment Earnings ($)	Total Income ($)	Employment Earnings ($)	Total Income ($)	Employment Earnings ($)	Total Income ($)
1980 (1987)								
Family	18,888	20,401	16,888	18,736	20,434	21,506	16,488	19,071
Refugees	19,341	20,346	15,218	17,017	21,720	21,903	17,459	19,530
1985 (1992)								
Family	19,176	21,072	16,405	18,406	20,944	22,558	17,224	20,088
Refugees	19,749	21,524	15,911	18,026	21,457	23,130	16,846	19,216
1990 (1997)								
Family	18,546	19,532	14,252	15,239	19,557	20,430	18,416	19,975
Refugees	19,200	20,117	15,723	16,946	20,301	21,121	17,907	18,989

Source: IMDB Mobility Series MOB 101E.

Refugee Use of Canada's Social Safety Net

Earnings constitute an important measure of economic integration. To balance this measure, however, it is important to know the extent to which refugees use Canada's social safety net. How do the successive refugee cohorts of 1980, 1985 and 1990 fare with respect to poverty levels? Canada has a relative poverty index or Low Income Cutoff criterion which, according to Statistics Canada (Statistics Canada, 1998), "is used to delineate family units into "low income" and "other" groups. A family unit with income below the cut-off for its family size in an urbanization classification is considered a "low income" family. Any family with income equal to or above the cut-off is considered in the "other" category." For our purposes, we chose a LICO level at $16,186 (in 1992 dollars) based on a household in a city with a population of 500,000 or more with one employed refugee.[3] It is apparent from Figure 7-A that after seven years in Canada, the 1980-refugee cohort, regardless of selection gate, earned an average total income in excess to LICO. Subsequent cohorts in 1992 and 1997 also exceeded the poverty levels if they had reported earned income. What these diagrams indicate is that on average, refugees were not members of the working poor. However, this does not mean that those refugees who did not report employment earnings or belonged to a multiple member household were not poor. We return to this important issue below. For purposes of completeness, Figure 10 reports that the family class or the reference group had a similar experience as the employed refugee group. In other words, if you arrived in Canada in the family class and reported earned income, on average, your income did not fall below the poverty line.

The concept of total income used in this analysis includes both earned income and government transfers for those refugees who reported at least some earned income. This masks the true extent of refugee poverty in Canada since it excludes those who do not report or earn any income. The analytical concept must be reversed for a more accurate picture. We must analyze the refugee group which reported receiving social assistance as a primary source of income, and then compute that dependent group's total income. Figures 11-A and 11-B

3 We chose this configuration because the IMDB, our principal data source, does not provide data on household income for multiple earning households.

report the total income of refugees (principal applicants) for the 1985 and 1990 arrival cohorts who also first reported receipt of some social assistance.

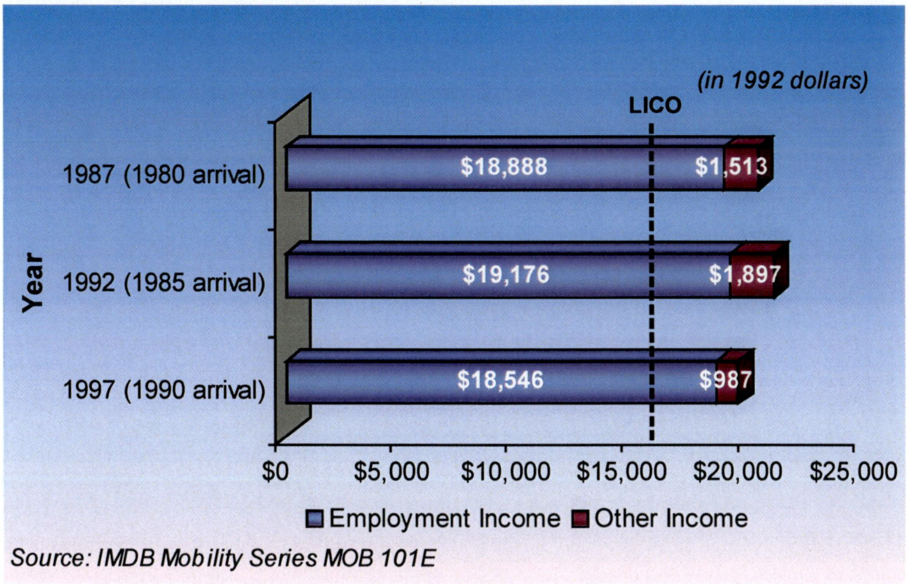

Figure 10: Total income of employed family class immigrants: 7 years after arrival

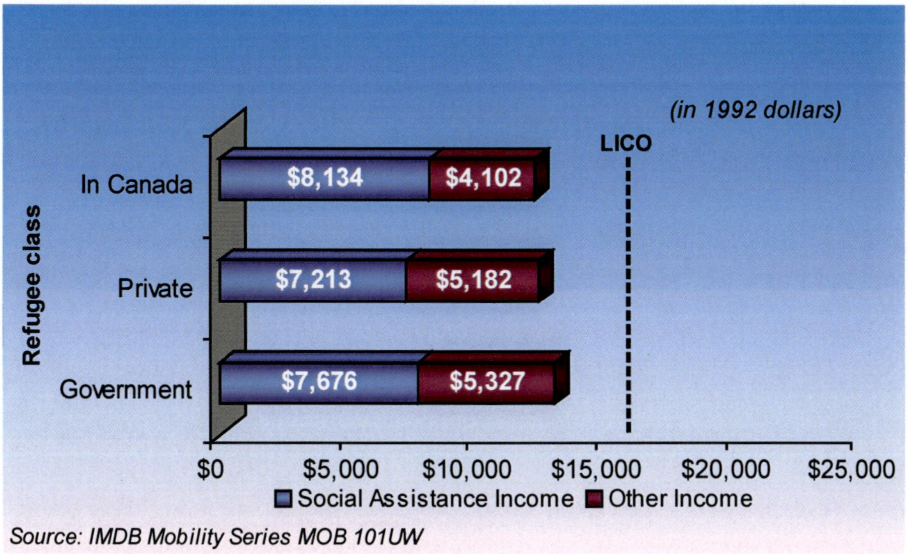

Figure 11-A: Total income of principal refugee applicants by entry class who received social assistance: 1985 arrivals, 1992 income

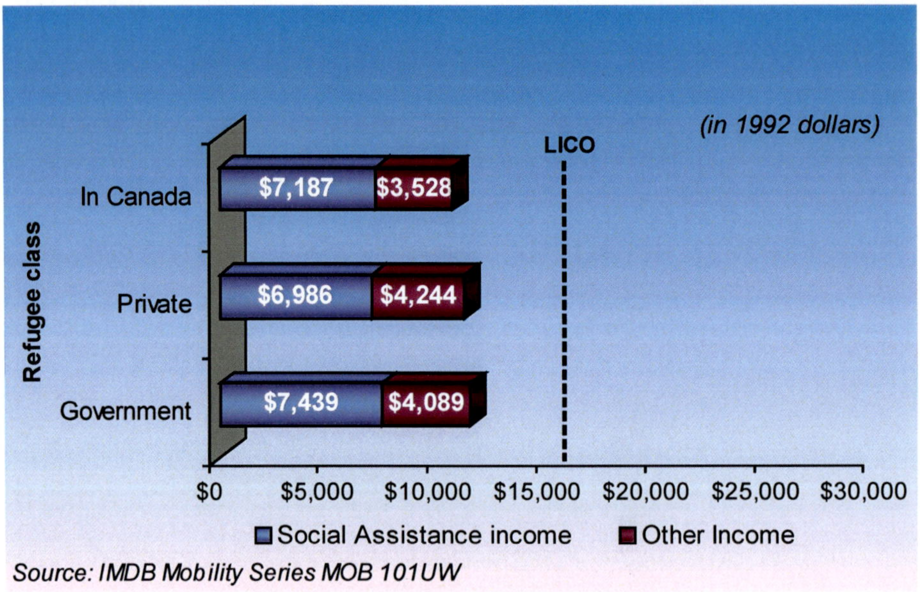

Figure 11-B: Total income of principal refugee applicants by entry class who received social assistance: 1990 arrivals, 1997 income

The experience of refugee social assistance recipients is vastly different from the experience of refugees who secured employment (Figures 7-A to 7-C). For example, government sponsored refugees who entered in 1990 and were employed in 1997 earned $21,116 (1992 dollars, see Figure 7-C) while those government sponsored refugees who arrived in 1990 and received social assistance in 1997 received a total income of only $11,528. In short, in 1997, government sponsored refugees who received some social assistance had a total income level which was only 71 per cent of the LICO level. An additional disturbing finding shown in Figures 11-A and 11-B is that both earned income and social assistance declined in real terms across the cohorts between 1992 and 1997. Thus, long-term refugee poverty (after seven years in Canada) worsened in the 1990s. Given these outcomes we now analyze the incidence of social assistance use by refugee, family and skilled cohorts. The reader should be aware that different eligibility rules apply to the family and refugee classes for the collection of social assistance. By law, in most cases, family class members are denied access to social assistance and should they receive benefits, their sponsors may be required to repay the government for these benefits. This rule does not apply to refugees.

Figure 12 indicates that over their lifetime refugee entrants are more likely to use social assistance benefits than any other foreign-born entry category. In particular, during the peak earning years of 35-64, refugees have almost twice the incidence of social assistance use as the similarly aged family class members. Beyond age 65, the incidence of use of social assistance by refugee claimants who arrived in 1980 rose to about 44 per cent of that age group still resident in Canada in 1992.

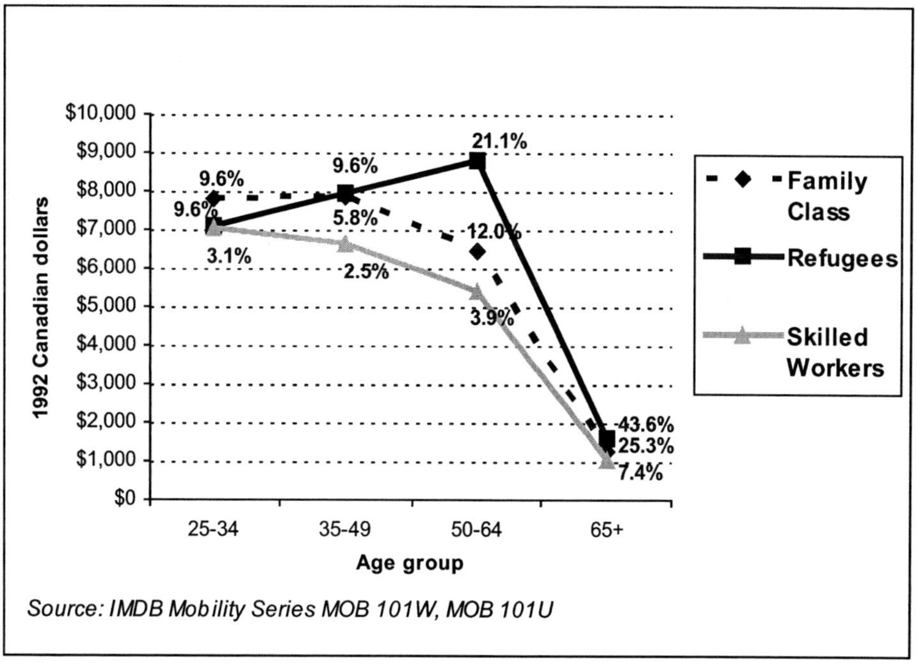

Figure 12: Utlization Rates and Amounts Received by Immigrant and Refugee Recipients of Social Assistance in 1992 by Age Group, 1980 arrivals

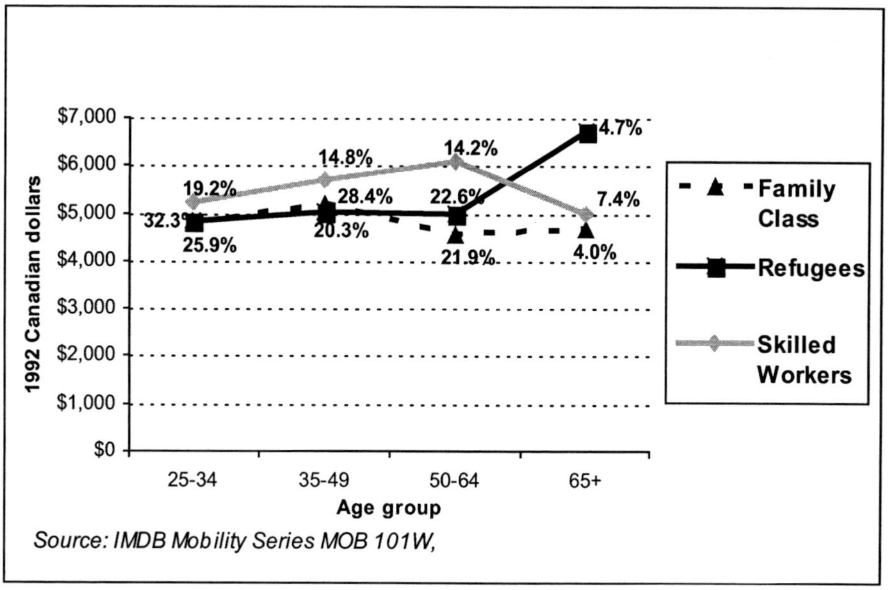

Figure 13: Utilization Rates and Amounts Received by Immigrant and Refugee (Un)Employment Insurance Recipients in 1992 by Age Group, 1980 arrivals

Did refugees use social assistance benefits once their unemployment insurance benefits expired? In Canada, the normal procedure is to first use any insurance benefits that the worker paid for during periods of employment before social assistance or social assistance can be claimed. Figure 13 lends some support to the view that refugees substitute insurance claims by social assistance. As refugees age, their use of (un)employment insurance declines from 32 per cent in the 25-34 aged group to 22.6 per cent in the 50-64 year old group. Nonetheless, refugees use employment insurance more than any other group and this reflects the weak employment prospects of refugees relative to either family or independent class immigrants who arrived in 1980.

SUMMARY AND CONCLUSION

This summary will review our findings against a number of key questions asked at the beginning of this chapter. We first asked if refugees experienced economic integration after a significant period of residence (seven years) in Canada. We offered two metrics to answer this question. We initially measured refugee earnings relative to independent and family class immigrants over time in Canada and, subsequently, as the refugee group aged. In both their ability to catch-up to others earnings and the absolute growth in earnings, employed refugees have integrated into the Canadian economy. With respect to their reference group (family class), employed refugees earned an equal amount of income, both at their time of arrival and in each successive year of residence.

We next asked if this performance varied by refugee date of arrival or across particular refugee entry gates. Evidence appears that refugees have been affected, sometimes positively, by their date of arrival during the 1980-1997 study period: the 1985 arrival group earned the highest income after seven years in Canada. There is some evidence that privately sponsored refugee earnings exceed other refugee groups over the study period. This may be because private sponsors have more time or motivation than the regular social system to help refugees find first jobs or help then certify their qualifications. Our major proposition that Canadian refugees follow a human capital model of earnings performance is supported by the available evidence.

Finally, even given this relatively strong economic performance of the average employed refugee, economic poverty was an endemic and growing problem for refugees. For those refugees who arrived as the principal applicants in 1990 and who received social assistance in 1997, the total income level was extremely low (less than $12,000 in 1992 dollars per principal refugee). Thus, whether a refugee fared well in Canada's labour market ultimately depended upon employment prospects. Evidence from Canada's IMDB records for the 1980-1997 study period indicates that only 52 percent of those refugees aged 20 to 64 found employment. Thus, the refugee population's economic performance is truly bi-modal.

It should be noted that all of the above conclusions must be tempered by the weakness of the primary data source (IMDB). The IMDB covers only 40 percent of all refugees and many refugees who have disappeared from the data set have retired, died, returned home, moved on or left the Canadian labour force. In sum, our analysis is limited to those Canadian resident refugees who reported income. In addition, it is difficult with our data set to distinguish between the effects of pure aging and years of residence in Canada. Thus, we can make no definitive judgment whether the improvement in refugee earnings reported in this paper was due to either aging or integration into Canada's labour market (years in Canada) or both. In the future, a more ambitious study of refugees could use the confidential individual files and thus avoid these ambiguities.

ACKNOWLEDGEMENTS

We would like to acknowledge the financial support of RIIM (Research on Immigration and Integration in the Metropolis), Vancouver's Centre of Excellence and IMER (International Migration and Ethnic Relations), Malmö University while writing this paper, and excellent referee comments which greatly improved the paper. The research assistance of D. Coulombe is noted with appreciation.

REFERENCES

Beiser, M. & Hou, F. (2000). Gender Differences in Language Acquisition and Employment Consequences among Southeast Asian Refugees in Canada. *Canadian Public Policy, 26*(3), 311–30.

Beiser, M. (1999). *Strangers at the Gate: The 'Boat People's' First Ten Years in Canada.* Toronto: University of Toronto Press.

Caplan, N., Whitmore, J., & Choy, M. (1989). *The 'Boat People' and Achievement in America.* Ann Arbor: The University of Michigan Press.

Citizenship and Immigration Canada. (1998). The Economic Performance of Immigrants: Immigration Category Perspective'. *IMDB Profile Series.*

Cortes, K. E. (2001). *Are Refugees Different from Economic Immigrants? Some Empirical Evidence on the Heterogeneity of Immigrant Groups in the United States.* Center for Labor Economics, University of California at Berkeley. Working Paper No. 41.

DeSilva A. (1997). Earnings of Immigrant Classes in the Early 1980s in Canada: A Re-examination. *Canadian Public Policy, 23*(2), 179–202.

DeVoretz, D. J. (Ed.). (1995). *Diminishing Returns: The Economics of Canada's Recent Immigration Policy.* Toronto: C.D. Howe Institute; and Vancouver: The Laurier Institution.

DeVoretz, D. & Pivnenko, S. (2004). Immigrant Public Finance Transfers: A Comparative Analysis by City. *Canadian Journal of Urban Research 13*(1):155–69.

DeVoretz, D., Pivnenko, S. & Coulombe, D.S. (2003). *The Immigration Triangle: Quebec, Canada and the Rest of the World.* RIIM, Simon Fraser University, Working Paper 03-11.

Fass, S. (1986). Innovations in the Struggle for Self-Sufficiency: The Hmong Experience in the United States. *International Migration Review, 20*, 351–80.

Haines D.W. (1987). Patterns in Southeast Asian Refugee Employment: A Reappraisal of the Existing Research. *Ethnic Groups, 7*, 39–63.

Shi, Y. (2003). The Impact of Canada's Immigration Act on Chinese Independent Immigration. *Canadian Journal of Urban Research* 13(1):140-54.

Statistics Canada, Household Surveys Division. (1998). Low Income Cut-Offs. *Catalogue no. 13-551-XIB.* Ottawa.

Strand, P. J. & Jones, Jr., W. (1985). *Indochinese Refugees in America: Problems of Adaptation and Assimilation.* Durham: Duke University Press.

In: Homeland Wanted
Editors: P. Waxman and V. Colic-Peisker, pp. 23-41
ISBN 1-59454-266-X

Chapter 2

REFUGEE[1] WOMEN IN THE LABOUR MARKET: THE UK CASE

Alice Bloch

ABSTRACT

This chapter examines the labour market participation of refugee women by drawing on data from a survey of refugees from Somalia, Sri Lanka (Tamils), Kosovo, Iraq and Turkey living in Britain. It explores the main factors that affect the labour market participation of refugee women and places these within a broader policy context such as dispersal to areas around the country away from social and community networks that can provide valuable support and advice. The chapter shows the low level of economic activity among refugee women and the extremely disadvantaged position that refugees as a whole, and refugee women in particular, occupy in the UK labour market. Economic activity is determined by a number of personal and structural factors including language and literacy skills, educational background, employment experience, household composition and social and community networks. This survey found that fluency in English and participation in training and obtaining educational qualifications in the UK had the greatest positive effect on economic activity. However, it is not possible to generalise the experiences of refugee women, as there is much diversity within and between communities.

Key words: refugee women, employment, UK asylum policy.

INTRODUCTION

The role of employment in the successful settlement of refugees is widely recognised as it increases social and economic integration, and offers the opportunity to gain self-esteem, to learn or improve in the language of the country of asylum and to facilitate new social contacts (Valtonen, 1999; Valtonen, 2004). Research carried out by Colic-Peisker in Australia, notes

---

[1] The term refugee will be used to describe forced migrants at all stages of the determination process – that is refugees, people with Exceptional Leave to Remain, Humanitarian Protection, asylum seekers, those with Indefinite Leave to Remain and refugees who have become naturalised citizens of an EU member state.

that employment 'seems to be the single most important aspect of successful resettlement and social inclusion in general' (2003, p. 17) while Valtonen (2004) notes the social exclusion that results from unemployment not just in terms of economic activities but also in terms of social participation in community life. The importance of facilitating access to the labour market for refugees in Europe has been recognised by policy makers (European Commission, 2003), though many of the asylum policies that have emerged in Europe in the last decade are in direct conflict with this goal (Flynn, 2003; Bloch, 2004a; Schuster, 2004).

In the United Kingdom (UK), with the exception of a small minority who arrive as part of the resettlement programme or on Temporary Protection, the majority of forced migrants arrive as spontaneous asylum seekers and wait for the Home Office to make a decision on their case. The Home Office can grant refugee status or Humanitarian Protection or it can reject an asylum seekers' claim. In spite of the recognition of the importance of economic participation in the settlement of forced migrants, asylum seekers waiting for a decision on their asylum case are not given permission to work and are not allowed to access statutory job search provision and training. One of the concerns about the initial exclusion of asylum seekers is that those with professional skills, such as doctors, will become rapidly deskilled and will be unable to work in their professions again (Stewart, 2003).

Access to the labour market is of course complex as refugees are a diverse selection of people and arrive in the country of asylum with different pre-migration experiences. This chapter will focus on the economic participation of refugee women in Britain and will explore the main factors that affect economic activity. This includes structural barriers that have emerged through restrictive policy initiatives, as well as individual factors such as English language competency, the level of education and qualifications, participation in training and methods of job seeking that can be culturally specific.

This chapter presents findings from a survey of refugees in Britain.[2] It shows the low levels of economic participation among refugee women. The minority who are working are, for the most part, in secondary sector jobs, with low pay and poor terms and conditions of employment regardless of the skills and experiences they had on arrival. However, due to differences in the causes of flight, social class, education, employment status, household composition, cultural norms and religious beliefs there are variations within and between refugee groups that all contribute towards varying circumstances in exile. Refugee women are, on the whole, more likely to experience barriers to the labour market that are based on cultural, social and religious factors than there male counterparts.

Although this research was carried out in Britain, similar examples of high unemployment rates among refugees and the under employment of refugees with professional qualifications has been found in research elsewhere (see for example, Coughlan, 1998; Valtonen, 1999; Liebaut & Blichfeldt, 2000; Colic-Peisker, 2003).

---

2 The research on which this chapter is based was commissioned by the Department for Work and Pensions in the UK and is available as a research report Bloch. A. (2002) *Refugees' Opportunities and Barriers to Employment and Training*, Research Report 179, Leeds: Department for Work and Pensions. See http://www.dwp.gov.uk/asd/asd5/rrep179.asp

METHODS

The data used in this chapter is derived from a sub-sample of 200 refugee women from a survey population of 400 refugees, all of whom had permission to work in the United Kingdom. The respondents were from five communities living in five localities in England. The five refugee communities were originally from Somalia, Iraq, Kosovo, Sri Lanka (Tamils) and Turkey. The countries chosen were selected to reflect the diversity of the refugee experience by including a mix of pre-migration characteristics such as education, migration trajectories, social and community networks and different historic links with the UK in the form of imperial/colonial relations. There also had to be sufficient numbers in each group to enable their inclusion in the study. The five groups included in the study had been arriving in the UK in relatively large numbers for the few years that preceded the survey (see Heath et al., 2003).

The five areas in Britain where the fieldwork was carried out were London, Manchester, Leeds/Sheffield, Newcastle and Birmingham. In the absence of a sampling frame of refugees from which to draw a representative sample (Robinson, 1998), quotas were set for country of origin, length of residence, age, gender and geographical region. Representatives from organisations that work with refugees, or that refugees are involved in, were used to identify respondents for the study in order to maximise the extent to which the survey represented the diversity of the refugee experience. The fieldwork took place between February and May 2002.

The exact quotas were not met for each community. For example, it was not possible to locate Kosovars who had been in Britain for more than five years due to their relatively recent migration (since 1999). However, trying to achieve the quotas meant that there were sufficient numbers of respondents in each category to enable analysis by key variables. Table 1 shows the sample characteristics by the main quota variables.

The survey was administered using face-to-face interviews conducted in the relevant community language. The questionnaire mostly contained structured questions with pre-coded response categories. This limits the extent to which the data allows for the in-depth exploration of the individual experience although the economic participation of refugees can be quantified applying such an approach. Bilingual interviewers were recruited to work on the translations of the questionnaires into the relevant community languages and to carry out the interviews. The questionnaires were translated using the dual strategies of back translation and the translation decentralising procedure (Brislin et al., 1973). Using the translating decentralising procedure leaves the source and target language open to modification in order to achieve comparability. Back translation is a process whereby a bilingual person, in this case one of the survey interviewers, translates the source language into the target language while another bilingual, the other interviewer from the same community, translates from the target language back to the source language without seeing the original. Every question is subsequently examined and where necessary changes were made to the translations and/or the English language version.

Representatives from statutory, community, voluntary, religious and social organisations working with refugees as well as further education colleges and training providers with refugee students helped to identify respondents for inclusion in the study. This helped to ensure diversity of respondents rather than the homogeneity that is associated with using a limited number of access points with snowball sampling techniques.[3]

Table 1. Sample Characteristics: Length of Residence, Age and Region

	Frequency	Percentage
Length of residence		
Less than 5 years	113	56.5
5 years or more	87	43.5
Total	*200*	*100*
Age		
18-24	26	13.0
25-29	38	19
30-34	41	20.5
35-39	35	17.5
40-49	47	23.5
50 or over	13	6.5
Total	*200*	*100*
Geographical location (City/region)		
Manchester (North West)	15	7.5
Leeds/Sheffield (Yorkshire and Humberside)	27	13.5
Birmingham (West Midlands)	29	14.5
Newcastle (North East)	3	1.5
London	126	63
Total	*200*	*100*

Access to the Labour Market: The Policy Context

Refugees are more likely to be affected by unemployment than the general population; this also holds if they are compared with minority ethnic groups. The factors which impact on the level of economic participation include the refugee's proficiency in the language of the receiving country, levels of education, the length of residence in the country of asylum, the economic climate on arrival, and the age and gender of the refugee (Bloch, 2004c). However, there are also structural barriers that affect refugees' access to the labour market and these cut across any individual or group characteristics. Thus, any analysis of refugee employment needs to be located within the context of asylum and immigration policies. This section examines the development of policy that progressively excludes asylum seekers from social and economic participation. The rights afforded to different categories of forced migrant: asylum seekers, those on temporary protection, those with humanitarian protection (HP)[4] and refugees have become increasingly differentiated. Asylum seekers have the fewest rights, for example no legal access to the labour market and, for those who need financial assistance, no

[3] See Bloch (2004b) for more information about the methods of data collection used in the survey.
[4] Before 2003, this category was known as exceptional leave to remain (ELR).

control over where they live under the policy of dispersal. Such policies are not unique to the UK but have been used throughout Europe during and since the 1990s (Schuster, 2004).

In the UK, since 1993, there have been five pieces of legislation, dealing with this issue, the most recent, the Asylum and Immigration (Treatment of Claimants etc) Act, 2004 received Royal Assent in July 2004. One of the aims of the asylum and immigration legislation has been to reduce the social and economic rights of asylum seekers as they await decisions on their respective cases (Flynn, 2003).

In 1996, the Asylum and Immigration Act was introduced and it included a clause relating to employment. Under the legislation, a system of penalty fines for employers hiring staff without the appropriate documentation was introduced. The result is that some employers have been reluctant to take on refugees as employees because of the burden of checking this information or because they are concerned that they might be in breach of the legislation (Brophy et al., 1998; Refugee Council, 1999).

From the employer side, there is also the issue of discrimination which is more difficult to measure empirically, especially as it is illegal under the UK Race Relations legislation. However, perceptions of employer discrimination have been strongly identified in research carried out by the Policy Studies Institute which reported that that a fifth of ethnic minority respondents said that they had been refused a job on the grounds of their race or religion (Modood et al., 1997). In terms of religion, Brown (2000) notes the differences between South Asian religious groups: for example Muslims are less likely to be employed than other religious minorities. Moreover, those Muslims who are employed tend to earn less than people from other religious minorities (Lindley, 2002).

Another structural barrier with longer-term implications was introduced in July 2002 when the government withdrew the right for asylum seekers to apply for permission to work. Prior to this, asylum seekers could apply for permission to work after six months in the UK. While this was usually granted, it was not an automatic entitlement, delays of over a year were not uncommon and permission was usually given to the principal applicant who in most cases is male. The longer-term affect on the economic activity of refugees, after an initial period of unemployment, has been identified both in general (Valtonen, 1999) and more specifically among professionals (Stewart, 2003). Removing the rights of asylum seekers to work jeopardises the longer-term integration of those who are given HP or refugee status.

The introduction of dispersal in 2000, under the 1999 Immigration and Asylum Act, has created another barrier to the labour market integration of refugees. Prior to the introduction of the Act, asylum seekers tended to cluster in areas where they had pre-existing community or kinship networks. These networks were important in helping to negotiate a new system and by providing important information and advice in a number of areas including employment and training (Bloch, 2002). However dispersal, which is the geographical placement or distribution of asylum seekers to areas round a country, takes away the choice for asylum seekers to decide where they want to live without forfeiting subsistence support.

Nevertheless, since the introduction of dispersal, some refugees have opted to forfeit governmental support in favour of living with family or friends rather than be dispersed to areas where they have no networks. Others end up in localities where community structures do not exist and hence lose the possibility of community support. Table 2 shows the regions of residence and the large number of asylum seekers who lived in London (28,555) with subsistence-only support.

Table 2. Asylum Seekers Supported by National Asylum Support Service (NASS) in Regions as at the End of December 2002 (Including Dependants)

Government Office Region	Subsistence only	NASS accommodation
North East	210	6010
North West	925	10325
Yorkshire and Humberside	800	10225
East Midlands	1170	4540
West Midlands	1185	10305
East of England	1405	535
Greater London	28555	2605
South East	2445	1180
South West	590	925
Wales	180	1585
Scotland	335	5665
Northern Ireland	20	170
Total	*37820*	*54070*

Source: Home Office http://www.homeoffice.gov.uk/rds/pdfs2/asylumq402.pdf

Sales (2002) notes that women, especially those with children, are more likely to be forced to stay wholly within the system as they can not afford to lose any benefits. This may have the affect of leaving them more isolated from community networks than their male counterparts. Refugees rely heavily on informal social contacts for obtaining work and the greater isolation of women than men from community networks whether or not they have been dispersed can disadvantage women job seekers. Al-Rasheed (1993) notes, in her study of Iraqis, that there is a gender dimension to community organisations because they provide support for men but can leave women marginalised.

Regional variations in terms of information, advice, training, language learning and local labour markets may all impact on the labour market participation of refugees as some were dispersed to areas with mono-ethnic populations with high levels of unemployment and little provision for groups with diverse needs. Thus, policy developments in the area of asylum are in direct conflict with longer term strategies for refugee settlement.

The Position of Women in the Labour Market

Research on the situation of refugees in the labour market consistently reveals the relatively low levels of participation among all refugees, and particularly so among refugee women (Carey-Wood et al, 1995; Bloch, 2002). Even women with professional qualifications who are in demand, such as doctors and teachers, are unable to find commensurate work. A study in London of refugee women from the teaching and medical professions found that while about three-quarters (74 per cent) had been working in their country of origin, only 20 per cent were in paid employment in the UK, but not in their chosen profession. The main reasons why women were not practicing their chosen profession were childcare responsibilities, and the need to both improve English language competency and to re-qualify because qualifications were not transferable at the equivalent level (Dumper, 2002).

In this study, 15.5 per cent of women (31 out of 200) were in paid employment which is considerably fewer than the 27.5 per cent (55 out of 200) who had been in paid work in their country of origin. Furthermore, in their country of origin the women were more likely to be engaged as professionals or skilled workers; for example, among those who had been employed, 12 were teachers, seven were health care professionals and 10 were in clerical and administrative jobs. This contrasts with the positions that refugee women occupied in Britain, as Table 3 shows.

Table 3. Current job in Britain

Job title/type of work	Frequencies
Administration/clerical	7
Interpreter/translator	5
Advisor	4
Factory work	3
Shop assistant/cashier	3
Catering: waiter/kitchen porter/chef/delivery	2
Nurse	1
Community/social work	1
Shop owner	1
Engineer	1
Cleaner	1
Receptionist	1
Total number	30
Missing=1	

Only five of those who were working in Britain and had worked in their country of origin were doing comparable jobs. A majority of refugee women experienced downward occupational downgrading. For example, a shop owner was working as a shop assistant, teachers as administrative/clerical workers or interpreters and an administrative/clerical worker was employed as a cleaner in Britain. The clustering of refugees in just a few sectors of employment and downward occupational downgrading has been found in other research with refugees (Girbash, 1991; Bloch, 2002) and with minority ethnic groups more generally (Owen et al., 2000). More than half (18 out of 31) of those who were working at the time of the survey were employed in the private sector, around one quarter (eight) was in the voluntary sector, three were in the public sector and two were not sure of their sector of employment. More refugees work in the voluntary sector than others because of the need for people with relevant community language skills to work as interpreters, translators and advisors.

The terms and conditions of employment were generally poor. Around one-third (10 out of 31) of those working were in temporary posts and for half of those the reason why they were in temporary work was because their job was casual and because they could not find a permanent job (7 out of 10). While over half (17 out of 31) were in full-time work, half of those who were working part-time were doing so because they were not able to find a full-time job.

A large proportion (42 per cent) of those employed were working unsocial hours (before 8.30 am and after 6.30 pm) and regularly on weekends (at least two weekends every month) (42 per cent). Moreover, average levels of pay were lower among refugees than among ethnic minority women in general (£7.39 and £8.79 an hour respectively). Kosovar women, on average, earned less than other refugee women (£5.43 an hour). Although for the whole population in Britain, there are regional variations in earnings with average earnings in London around 30 per cent higher than elsewhere (Owen et al., 2000), among refugees there was little variation and refugee women were in fact earning slightly more outside London.

Table 4. Labour Market Participation, by Country of Origin, Age, English Proficiency, Length of Residence and Qualifications

	% in paid Employment	Total number
Country of origin: Cramers V=.256		
Somalia	17.5	40
Turkey	22.5	40
Iraq	2.5	40
Sri Lanka	27.5	40
Kosovo	7.5	40
Region; Cramers V=.083		
London	17	126
Manchester	20	15
Birmingham	13	29
Leeds/Sheffield	11	27
Newcastle	0	3
Age on arrival: Cramers V=.237		
< 35	19	155
35 or more	2	45
Age at time of survey: Cramers V=.278		
< 35	24	105
35 or more	6	95
Spoken English: Cramers V=.326		
Fluently	36	44
Fairly well	15	67
Slightly	6	71
Not at all	6	18
Length of residence in Britain: Cramers V=.126		
< 5 years	11.5	113
5 years or more	21	87
Whether obtained qualification in Britain: Cramers V=.399		
Yes	44	41
No	8	159
Whether qualification from country of origin: Cramers V=.206		
Yes	22	104
No	7	95
		Missing: 1

It is clear that refugee women are not working to their capacity (both in terms of hours and qualifications) and the minority who are working are, for the most part, employed in the secondary labour market, with accompanying poor terms and conditions of employment. Table 4 shows some of the key variables that interact with employment. Refugee women who are fluent in English are more likely to be working than others. Age, length of residence in Britain and obtaining a UK qualification also interact with employment.

An examination of Cramers V[5] in Table 4 reveals that there are no strong associations between labour market activity and the control variables. Whether or not the respondent had obtained a qualification in Britain was more strongly associated with employment than any other variables, although gaining qualifications in Britain was a function, in part, of English language proficiency. The next strongest association was between spoken English and employment. The lowest level of association was between the region of current residence and employment, with the small numbers in regions outside London affecting the outcome.

Pre-Migration Characteristics

The skills and experiences that refugees bring to Britain can affect economic activity. Pre-migration characteristics include language and literacy skills in the first language as well as the language of the country of asylum, education, qualifications and employment experience. The sample provided a great deal of diversity among refugee women in terms of language and literacy, education and activity before coming to Britain.

Levels of first language literacy vary by country of origin. The lowest levels of first language literacy were found among Kurdish women from Turkey who spoke Kurmanji as their first language but were not literate in the language. Kurmanji was illegal in Turkey between 1935 and 1991 and though most Kurds speak the language, their education was carried out in Turkish so for the most part Kurds are illiterate in their first language but literate in Turkish (Carr-Hill et al., 1996). Of the 29 Kurmanji speakers in this study, 26 could read and write Turkish fluently. When Kurmanji speakers' fluency in Turkish is accounted for, Table 5 shows that Somali women had the lowest levels of first language literacy.

As shown in Table 6, 15.5 per cent of women spoke English fluently or fairly well on arrival in Britain. This was fewer than the 31 per cent of men who spoke English fluently or fairly well on arrival to Britain (not in the Table). Levels of spoken English, on arrival, varied between communities and in some cases reflected former links with Britain. Sri Lanka, Northern Somalia and Iraq all had colonial links with Britain and in some cases English was taught in schools. Women from countries where there were previous links, most notably women from Iraq and Sri Lanka, were most proficient in English on arrival while Kosovar and Turkish women were most disadvantaged in terms of proficiency in English.

Levels of English language on arrival did affect labour market participation though not to a great extent. While 19 per cent of those who spoke English fluently or fairly well on arrival to Britain were working, 15 per cent of those who spoke slightly or not at all were also employed. What were most important were English language skills at the time of the survey.

---

5 Cramers V measures the association between two variables where 0 is no association and 1 is a perfect association.

However, arriving with some English language did make it easier to improve language skills and this was more influential in terms of employment prospects.

Table 5. First Language Literacy by County of Origin

Frequencies	Somali	Arabic	Tamil	Turkish	Kurdish Sorani	Kurdish Kurmanji	Albanian	Malay alam	%
Read/Write									
Fluently	22	30	39	9	5	0	33	1	69.5
Fairly Well	3	1	0	0	3	1	4	0	6
Slightly	3	0	0	1	1	3	3	0	5.5
Not at all	12	0	0	1	0	25	0	0	19
Total	40	31	39	11	9	29*	40	1	200

* Kurmanji was the only first language where there was variation between reading and writing. Four respondents were able to write slightly and 24 not at all.

Table 6. Spoken English on Arrival to Britain by Country of Origin

Frequencies	Somalia	Turkey	Iraq	Sri Lanka	Kosovo	Total %
Fluently	3	0	2	6	0	5.5
Fairly well	1	0	13	5	1	10
Slightly	15	4	18	20	2	29.5
Not at all	21	36	7	9	37	55
Total	40	40	40	40	40	200

Levels of education on arrival can have an effect on labour market participation. One difficultly faced by refugees with qualifications obtained overseas is that they are often not recognised by employers and this can lead to jobs that are not commensurate with pre-migration skills, experience and qualifications. In some cases qualifications are recognised, but not at the same level, so retraining or additional training is required to enter professions, which can be expensive and time-consuming (Dumper, 2002; Stewart, 2003).

There are differences between and within refugee communities in terms of education and qualifications obtained in the country of origin, with gender being an important differentiating variable (Bloch, 2002). Some refugee women arrived in Britain with high levels of education while others had no formal education. Somali women were more likely than others to have received no formal education.

Linked to this were levels of qualifications obtained. More than half of the refugee women (52 per cent) had a qualification on arrival to Britain (See Table 7). Women from Iraq arrived with the highest qualifications with half having professional, graduate or post-graduate level qualifications, while those from Kosovo and Somalia were the two groups least likely to have any formal qualifications.

Of those women with qualifications on arrival to Britain, only 13.5 per cent had tried to get them recognised in Britain although most of those who tried had been successful. The reasons mentioned most frequently for not attempting to have qualifications recognised revolved around the lack of English language skills, lack of knowledge about the system for transferring qualifications or not having copies of the necessary certification.

Table 7. Highest Level of Qualification on Arrival to Britain by Country of Origin

Frequencies	Somalia	Sri Lanka	Iraq	Turkey	Kosovo	Total %
Post grad/Degree	1	5	13	5	1	12.5
Professional	1	0	7	2	0	5
Technical/ skills	1	0	2	2	0	2.5
A' level or equivalent	7	9	9	10	6	20.5
O'level or equivalent	0	5	0	15	1	10.5
Other	0	2	0	0	0	1
None	29*	19	9	6	32	48
Total	39	40	40	40	40	199

* 3 Somali respondents had been pre-school children on arrival to Britain.
Missing: 1.

Table 8. Main Activity before Coming to Britain by Country of Origin

	Somalia	Turkey	Iraq	Sri Lanka	Kosovo	Total %
Employed	7	14	13	12	3	24.5
Self-employed	1	2	0	0	3	3
Unemployed	0	0	1	0	2	1.5
Student	10	8	7	10	4	19.5
Home/family	18	16	18	18	28	49
Other	4	0	1	0	0	2.5
Total	40	40	40	40	40	200

Before coming to Britain, 27.5 per cent of refugee women had been working either as employees or self-employed, one-fifth had been students and 49 per cent had been looking after the home and family. Table 8 shows the main activity of the surveyed refugee women in their country of origin. The profile of Turkish, Iraqi and Sri Lankan women was very similar. Kosovar women differed most from the others as a much higher proportion (nearly three-quarters) had been looking after the home and family before coming to Britain.

The main activity prior to migration affected employment in Britain. Of those who were working in the Britain, 88 per cent had been working or had been students in their country of origin, although fewer were students or working in Britain. The examination of refugee women's pre-migration characteristics showed diversity in terms of language and literacy skills, educational qualifications and employment experiences and these influence the labour market outcome. The following sections focus on refugee women's activities in Britain and their association with employment.

English Language and Language Learning

Proficiency in English affects economic incorporation, with rates of employment rising dramatically where there is fluency in English (Sargeant and Forna, 2001). Research in Australia, however, found that even when the effects of an initial period of unemployment and cultural factors were controlled for, the lower levels of employment among refugees compared with others was due to a combination of employer discrimination and differences in English language skills (Wooden, 1991).

This section explores the English language skills of respondents at the time of the survey and the links between competency in the host language and employment. It will then explore participation in English as a Second Overseas Language classes (ESOL) and views about improving the effectiveness of ESOL. Obtaining the language skills of the country of asylum is crucial to the settlement outcome because those without language skills can be marginalised from the wider community.

A comparison of spoken English language skills at the time of arrival and at the time of the survey shows an overall improvement. While 5.5 per cent spoke English fluently on arrival to Britain, the proportion had increased to 22 per cent by the time of the survey. Likewise, the proportion speaking English slightly or not at all had decreased from 84.5 per cent on arrival to 44.5 per cent at the time of the survey. There was still a core group of respondents – 9 per cent – who spoke no English on arrival to Britain and still spoke no English at the time of the survey. Women from Kosovo then Turkey were less likely to speak English than others.

Table 4 showed the link between language skills and employment and the massive difference that fluency in English made to the propensity to be employed. English language skills also affected aspirations for entry into the labour market. Among those who weren't working in Britain, nearly a quarter said that they were looking for paid work (23 per cent). However, of those who were not looking for work, around one third (32 per cent), gave reasons related to learning or needing to learn English. The largest proportion, more than half (52 per cent), said they were not looking for work because of family and childcare commitments.

One of the ways in which people learn or improve their English competency is through attendance at English classes, either English for Speakers of Other Languages (ESOL) or English as a Foreign Language (EFL). Two-thirds of refugee women had either attended English language classes in the past or were attending at the time of the survey. However, as Table 9 shows, 29 per cent of those who spoke English slightly or not at all on arrival to Britain had not attended an English class. Kosovar and Turkish women with language needs were less likely to have attended English language classes than others.

Previous research has found that lone parents found it more difficult to access services (Bloch, 2002). The same trend was not replicated in this study. Of those who arrived in Britain speaking English either slightly or not at all, fewer women with children and a spouse (67 per cent) had attended English classes than those who were lone parents (82 per cent). Seventy-three per cent of those who either lived on their own or in households without children had attended an English language class. Thus more lone parents had accessed ESOL than others. Part of the reason for this might be the availability of childcare for those studying English language. Not everyone knew whether or not childcare was available for students on their course but among those that did, 70 per cent said that there was childcare provision for those who needed it.

Table 9. Whether Attended ESOL or EFL among those who Spoke English Slightly or not at a ll on Arrival to Britain by Country of Origin

	Whether attended ESOL/EFL		Frequencies
	Yes	No	Total number
Somalia	28	8	36
Turkey	26	14	40
Iraq	19	6	25
Sri Lanka	25	4	29
Kosovo	22	17	39
Total	120 (71%)	49 (29%)	169

Nevertheless, lone parents had lower rates of course completion. In total, 32 per cent of those who had attended an English course, in the past, had started a course and not completed it. Half the lone parents had started a course but not finished compared with 34 per cent of those who were living with their spouse as well as children and 20 per cent of those who lived on their own or in households without children. More than half (14 out of 26) of those who had not completed an English course said that childcare or family commitments were the reasons for non-completion. Not everyone who needed childcare was accessing it or choosing to access it. Research with refugee women has found that, in some cases, women prefer to look after their own children because leaving them with strangers can undermine the role of the mother and might affect the maintenance of cultural traditions (Ryan, 1997). Therefore, even when childcare is available, it might not be appropriate and/or might not be wanted as cultural norms can dictate women's status relative to their childcare role.

Education

This section explores participation in education in Britain. Table 4 shows there is an association between obtaining a qualification in Britain and being employed. Obtaining a qualification in Britain had more influence on economic participation than arriving with a qualification and it was also important in terms of salary remuneration. As shown earlier, the average hourly rate of earnings for refugee women in work was £7.39 an hour. However, the average rate for those with a qualification from the UK was £8.04 per hour compared with £6.48 among those without UK qualifications. This was less than that earned, on average, by women from ethnic minority groups as a whole, regardless of whether or not they had any qualifications from the UK or elsewhere, whose average hourly rate was £8.79 (Bloch, 2004c).

At the time of the survey, 15.5 per cent of women were studying for a qualification and 20.5 per cent had obtained a qualification in Britain in the past. Of the 31 women studying at the time of the survey, six were studying for a degree or higher though the majority were studying at a lower level and taking vocational qualifications. Nearly a quarter (24 per cent; 17 respondents) was studying both at the time of the survey and had obtained a qualification in Britain in the past. For some women there was an element of progression in their study. For instance some had studied an access to higher education course or a diploma in higher education in the past and were doing a degree course at the time of the survey though progression was not always evident with some doing more of the same level study.

Those who were studying at the time of the survey were, on the whole, less than 35 years old, spoke English fluently or fairly well and could read and write fluently or fairly well. A higher proportion of those with a qualification on arrival to Britain were studying than those without (21 per cent and 10 per cent respectively) and women without children were more likely to be studying than those with children (20 per cent and 8 per cent respectively). The profile of those who were studying at the time of the survey was similar to that of those who had studied and obtained a qualification in the past. Therefore, it is likely that some of those who complete their courses will progress into work. However, as with the ESOL courses, there was a proportion that had started courses but did not complete them (13 per cent) with more than half citing childcare and/or family commitments as their major reason for not finishing their course.

Training

One of the ways in which the unemployed gain the skills and experience necessary to enter the labour market is through participation in training. Take up of training among refugees as a whole is known to be low and fewer refugee women than men participate (Bloch, 2002). Reasons for the low rate of training include a lack of knowledge and awareness of the available schemes and an emphasis, among training providers, on job outcomes that can result in the 'creaming' off of those who are most likely to achieve them and so disadvantage ethnic minority people (Rolfe et al., 1996). In addition, people from ethnic minorities who complete their training are less likely to progress into the labour market than their white British counterparts (Moody, 2000).

In this study, 10 per cent of refugee women were either training at the time of the survey (5.5 per cent) or had trained in the past (4.5 per cent). Of the 20 respondents who were training or had trained in the past, eight were from Sri Lanka, six from Iraq, five from Somalia, one was from Turkey and none were from Kosovo. Only a minority had attended statutory schemes, with such schemes the key government strategy for getting long-term unemployed into work.

The profile of those who had participated in training was similar to those who had studied in Britain. A greater proportion of those who were fluent in English had participated in training than others, they were likely to have been living in England longer and have a secure immigration status (i.e. refugee status, indefinite leave to remain or a naturalised citizen of an EU country).

Though the numbers are small, they still illustrate that a much greater proportion of those who had taken some kind of training or were training at the time of the survey were in paid employment than others (50 per cent and 12 per cent). However, there is little evidence to suggest that those who had done training had found jobs relating to the subject of their training.

There was a demand for training with 60 per cent of respondents indicating that they were interested. The areas where training was wanted most often were information technology, dress making, office and typing skills and English. However, many of those who said they wanted training did not participate, often because they lacked information about the availability and entitlements to training (31 per cent), had child-care and/or family commitments that prevented attending a training course (31 per cent) or felt that their language skills were not sufficient to enable them to participate (19 per cent).

Methods of Job Seeking

Methods of job seeking can be culturally specific (Marshall, 1989). Women from Turkey who had worked before coming to Britain were more likely to have found their jobs through informal social networks than others while those from Sri Lanka were the most likely to have found their job through a newspaper advertisement. A comparison of successful job seeking methods in the UK and in the country of origin, shown in Figure 1, demonstrates this variation.

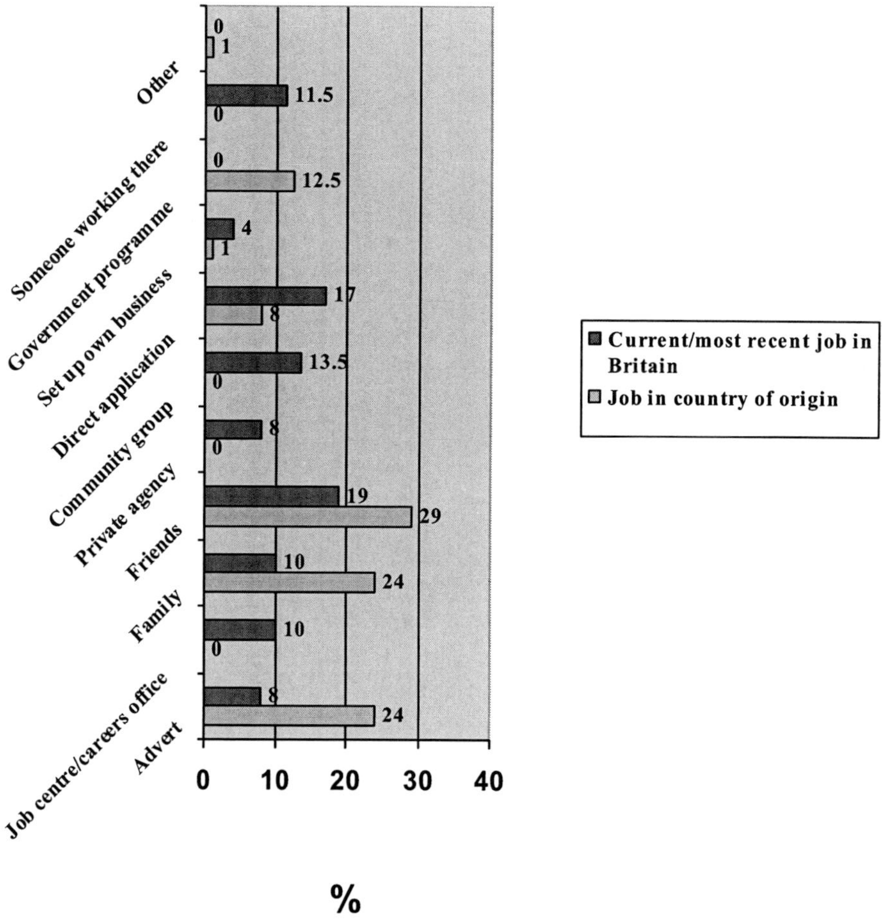

Figure 1. Successful methods of job seeking in Britain and in the country of origin (Percentages rounded to nearest whole number).

Base number in Britain: 52.

Base number in country of origin: 72.

Before coming to Britain, the informal networks of family and friends were much more important routes to employment than in the UK. In the UK, people used private employment agencies and community groups more often due, in part, to having fewer social networks in countries of asylum than in the country of origin. Even where networks existed, the very high rates of unemployment meant that networks were not necessarily a useful route to employment.

Though the numbers are small, there was also evidence of regional variations in terms of successful methods of job seeking. Those living outside of London were less likely to have found their jobs through informal networks and personal contacts than those in London (43 per cent and 58 per cent respectively). However, similar proportions were working within and outside London so those outside were accessing jobs through other, more formal routes and were no more excluded from the labour market.

When the areas outside London were disaggregated, there were regional variations in terms of rates of employment as Table 4 shows. Dispersal makes it difficult to move to areas with more jobs, even after a positive determination of an asylum case. Moving would mean the additional upheaval imposed on refugee households, which is especially problematic to those with children. As a consequence, the dispersal policy has long term negative implications for the labour market integration of refugees.

CONCLUSION

This chapter has presented findings from a survey of refugee women in Britain and has found that they have low levels of participation in education, training and the labour market. There are a number of reasons for the low rate of economic activity, some are related to personal characteristics and pre-migration skills and experiences and some are structural. Though structural barriers affect all refugees, to differing degrees, and indeed some other migrants, many of the barriers can have a disproportionate impact on refugee women. This is because refugee women are more likely to arrive with fewer qualifications and less employment experience than their male counterparts. Moreover, they experience greater difficulty accessing courses and completing them when they have childcare commitments. Dispersal also increases the probability of women finding themselves in areas where they have no social or kinship networks that can help them to negotiate a new system, access basic services as well as help with childcare. The absence of a social support structure based on friends and family can have a big impact on the lives of refugees, and even more so on refugee women, and can leave them marginalised, socially and economically, in the longer term.

The main factors that affect refugee women's participation in the labour market have been explored in this chapter and the data shows that some pre-migration experiences directly affect employment, though of greater relevance was the fluency in English at the time of the survey. Linked to fluency in English was participation in training and obtaining UK qualifications which also affected employment. However, the skills base that people 'bring' with them to the country of asylum affected their capacity to develop English language skills and obtain UK qualifications.

The heterogeneity of the sample of refugee women, both between and within communities, emerges clearly from the data. Refugee women arrive in exile with different language and literacy skills, educational backgrounds, work experience and family commitments all of which can affect access to the labour market. In spite of this diversity, there was an element of uniformity in terms of the characteristics of the minority of refugee women who were working: they were likely to have English language skills and UK qualifications. However, many of those who were well qualified and had been in professional jobs before coming to the UK had been unable to work in their chosen professions. The minority who were working in Britain were in secondary sector jobs with low pay, poor terms and conditions of employment and few opportunities for promotion.

The findings from this and other research on refugee employment show the extremely disadvantaged position of refugees as a whole, and more specifically that refugee women occupy economically. Given the importance of employment in achieving economic independence, increasing self-esteem, providing opportunities to practice and develop skills in the language of the country of asylum and opportunities to make social contacts and create new social networks, poor refugee employment outcomes are a concern of policymakers (Department for Work and Pensions, 2003; European Commission, 2003). However, state run integration strategies, that also include an employment dimension, are only accessible to those who have received a positive decision on their asylum case. For many refugees with professional qualifications, rapid deskilling can occur which has longer-term implications for economic activity. This is not a situation that is unique to Britain but one that is apparent across Europe where asylum seekers are excluded from economic activity in the short term, and increasingly subjected to compulsory dispersal, which can result in their longer-term exclusion. Immediate access to language tuition and labour market and the removal of other structural barriers such as refugee dispersal could help longer-term resettlement. In addition, the cultural diversity of refugee women means that a number of initiatives and options need to be in place if they are to have a range of choices which would facilitate their successful economic integration.

REFERENCES

Al-Rasheed, M. (1993). The meaning of marriage and status in exile: The experience of Iraqi women. *Journal of Refugee Studies, 6* (2), 89-104.

Bloch, A. (2002). *The Migration and Settlement of Refugees in Britain.* Basingstoke: Palgrave-Macmillan.

____ (2004a) *Making it Work: Refugee employment in the UK*, London: Institute for Public Policy Research. *http://www.ippr.org/research/index.php?current=19&project=183*

____ (2004b). Survey Research with Refugees: A methodological perspective. *Policy Studies, 25*(2), 139-151.

____ (2004c). Labour Market Participation and Conditions of Employment: a Comparison of Minority Ethnic Groups and Refugees in Britain. *Sociological Research Online, 9*(2), *http://www.socresonline.org.uk/9/2/bloch.html*

Brislin, R., Lonner, W. & Thorndike, R. (1973). *Cross-Cultural Research Methods*, New York: Wiley-Interscience.

Brophy, M., Maxey, K., Abraham, T., Aybek, T., Bird, P. & Stanikzai, F. (1998). *Refugee Education, Training and Employment in Inner London.* London: FOCUS TEC.

Brown, M.S. (2000). Religion and economic activity in the South Asian population. *Ethnic and Racial Studies, 23*(6), 1035-1061.

Carey-Wood, J., Duke, K., Karn, V. & Marshall, T. (1995). *The settlement of refugees in Britain*, London: HMSO.

Carr-Hill, R., Passingham, S., Wolf, A. & Kent, N. (1996). *Lost Opportunities: The language skills of linguistic minorities in England and Wales.* London: The Basic Skills Agency.

Colic-Peisker V (2003). Bosnian refugees in Australia: Identity, community and labour market integration. *New Issues in Refugee Research.* Working Paper 97. Geneva: UNHCR.

Coughlan, J. (1998). Occupational Mobility of Australia's Vietnamese Community: its Direction and Human Capital Determinants. *International Migration Review, 32*(1), 175-201.

Department for Work and Pensions. (2003). *Working to Rebuild Lives: A preliminary report towards a refugee employment strategy,* Sheffield: DWP, *http://www.dwp.gov.uk/publications/dwp/2003/wrl/main_rep.pdf*

Dumper, H. (2002). *Missing Opportunities: A skills audit of refugee women in London from the teaching and medical professions*, London: Greater London Authority.

European Commission (2003). Communication on 'immigration, integration and employment'.COM 336, Brussels: Commission of the European Communities. *http://europa.eu.int/eur-lex/en/com/cnc/2003/com2003_0336en01.pdf*

Flynn, D. (2003). *Tough as Old Boots: Asylum, immigration and the paradox of New Labour policy.* London: Joint Council for the Welfare of Immigrants.

Girbash, C. (1991). *Manchester Vietnamese Employment and Training Survey.* Manchester: Manchester Polytechnic.

Heath, T., Jefferies, R. & Lloyd, A. (2003). *Asylum Statistics 2001.* London: Home Office.

Liebaut, F. & Blichfeldt, T. (2000). *Legal and Social Conditions for Asylum Seekers and Refugees in Western European Countries* (4th ed.). Copenhagen, Danish Refugee Council.

Lindley, J. (2002). Race or religion? The impact of religion on the employment and earnings of Britain's ethnic communities. *Ethnic and Racial Studies, 28*(3), 427-442.

Marshall, T. (1989). *Cultural Aspects of Job Hunting.* London: Refugee Council.

Modood, T., Berthoud, R., Lakey, J., Nazroo, J., Smith, P., Virdee, S. & Beishon, S. (1997). *Ethnic Minorities in Britain – diversity and disadvantage.* London: Policy Studies Institute.

Moody, A. (2000). New deal and ethnic minority participants. *Labour Market Trends,* February 2000.

Owen, D., Reza, B., Green, A., Maguire, M. & Pitcher, J. (2000, November). Patterns of labour market participation in ethnic minority groups. *Labour Market Trends*, 505-510.

Refugee Council (1999). Catch 22. *iNexile, 6*, 18-19.

Robinson, V. (1998). The importance of information in the resettlement of refugees in the UK. *Journal of Refugee Studies, 11*(2), 140-160.

Rolfe, H., Bryson, A. & Metcalf, H. (1996). *The Effectiveness of TECs in Achieving Job Outcomes for Disadvantaged Groups.* London: Policy Studies Institute.

Ryan, L. (1997). *Refugee Women: Issues facing Bosnian women in Ireland.* Discussion paper drafted for the Bosnian Community Development Project, Dublin.

Sales, R. (2002). The deserving and the undeserving? Refugees, asylum seekers and welfare in Britain. *Critical Social Policy*, *22*(3), 456-476.

Sargeant, G. & Forna, A. (2001) *A Poor Reception: Refugees and asylum seekers: welfare or work*. London: The Industrial Society.

Schuster, L. (2004). Inclusion and Exclusion of Refugees in Europe. Paper presented at *The Refugee Problem and the Problems of Refugees in the Twentieth and Twenty-first Centuries Conference*, sponsored by the British Academy, Birkbeck, CRASSH and the Weiner Library, London 22-23 March 2004.

Stewart, E. (2003). A bitter pill to swallow: Obstacles facing refugee and overseas doctors in the UK. *New Issues in Refugee Research,* Working Paper 96. Geneva: UNHCR.

Valtonen, K. (1998). Resettlement of Middle Eastern Refugees in Finland: The elusiveness of integration. *Journal of Refugee Studies, 11*(1), 38-60.

____ (1999). The societal participation of Vietnamese refugees: Case studies in Finland and Canada. *Journal of Ethnic and Migration Studies,25* (3), 469-491.

____ (2004). From the margin to the mainstream: Conceptualising refugee settlement processes. *Journal of Refugee Studies, 17*(1), 70-96.

Wooden, M. (1991). The experience of refugees in the Australia labour market. *International Migration Review, 25*(30), 514-534.

In: Homeland Wanted
Editors: P. Waxman and V. Colic-Peisker, pp. 43-68
ISBN 1-59454-266-X

Chapter 3

HUMAN AND SOCIAL CAPITAL IN THE PROCESS OF ECONOMIC ADJUSTMENT OF REFUGEES: BOSNIANS IN AUSTRALIA

Val Colic-Peisker and Peter Waxman

ABSTRACT

This chapter is a joint endeavour of a sociologist and an economist and its theoretical background mainly draws from the economic sociology of migration. Both authors undertook empirical research among Bosnian refugees in Australia, in the metropolitan cities of Sydney and Perth. The earlier fieldwork in Sydney took place in the mid-1990s, when Bosnians were arriving in Australia in large numbers and their resettlement was at the early stages; the later fieldwork took place in both cities, from late 2001 to 2003, when Bosnians refugees who arrived in the 1990s reached a degree of stability and adjustment to their new environment. We start from the premise that the economic adjustment is a crucial, and a relatively measurable aspect of refugee resettlement and that the main element of economic adjustment is labour market integration. We analyse two crucial factors that influence labour market integration: the 'human capital', that is, skills, English language proficiency, age, gender and all the other elements of a person's 'marketability', and social capital, that is, networks that facilitate successful re-investment of people's human capital into the labour market. In the case of Bosnians, we identified a number of difficulties that devalue their human and social capital and therefore slow down and hamper their labour market integration. Some of these are language barrier, non-recognition of skills, age, a loss of social networks as a result of forced migration, and cultural differences in the way they tend to approach job-search. We also address the issue of housing as an important element of refugee resettlement and economic adjustment, as well as an issue of specific cultural relevance for this refugee group.

Key words: refugees, Australia, economic adjustment, housing, human capital, social capital.

INTRODUCTION

This chapter is a joint endeavour of a sociologist and an economist and its theoretical background draws mainly from the economic sociology of migration. We seek to explore the economic adjustment of Bosnian refugees in Australia and our main conceptual tools are two concepts that are increasingly used by economic sociologists of migration as well as other social scientists: 'human capital' and 'social capital'.

Refugee movements are often conceptualised as a variant of labour migration models, in spite of the obvious differences (Portes, 1987). Richmond (1988; 1993) claimed that the distinction between voluntary and involuntary migration is misleading and should be more appropriately replaced by a continuum between proactive and reactive migration, where reactive migration points to far more constraints than the proactive. Whichever model one chooses in one's analysis, applying the models of economic adjustment on refugee resettlement requires caution. There are, clearly, refugee-specific issues that require a refugee-specific conceptualisation. This pertains primarily to the different motivational structure of refugee settlers and their traumatic experiences.

As a response to these refugee-specific factors, a mental health perspective on refugee experience has been developed, not only in clinical psychology and psychiatry but also in social science disciplines that constitute refugee studies (Colic-Peisker and Tilbury, 2003). This perspective often focuses on traumatic experiences of violence, war, civil disorder and expulsion and tends to see post-arrival stressors, such as language barrier, unemployment and a lack of supportive networks as secondary. Rumbaut (1991) argued that resettling refugees are confronted with dual crises: 'a crisis of loss' — coming to terms with the past — and a 'crisis of load'— coming to terms with the present and the immediate future. Losses involved in forced migration — social status, material possessions and 'meaningful sources of identity and self-validation' — can in extreme cases threaten mental heath (ibid, p. 57). However, the clinical perspective on the refugee resettlement process, although relevant, is beyond the scope of our research.

In this chapter we analyse the economic adjustment of the largest recently arrived (during the 1990s) refugee group in Australia through two major factors: labour market integration and housing tenure. We define successful economic adjustment as a state where a refugee settler achieved satisfactory labour market integration and stable housing. 'Satisfactory' refers to subjective appraisal of the employment outcome rather than to the mere state of being employed; the minimal prerequisite of such satisfaction is in most cases, although not always, a success in reaching the pre-migration occupational status and a satisfactory level of income. Therefore, it does not necessarily follow that once refugees find employment their successful economic adjustment has been achieved, as they may be underemployed or may have experienced a significant down-adjustment. We define stable housing as living in an owner-occupancy situation (i.e., owning or paying off a home) or, alternatively, living in public housing, which does not expose the occupant to the vicissitudes of the private rental market including frequent moving. For Bosnians in particular, one's own home is a highly valued goal and a great source of peace and satisfaction (Colic-Peisker, 2002).

THE CONCEPTS OF HUMAN AND SOCIAL CAPITAL

These two concepts, central to our analysis, straddle both economic and sociological perspectives on migration. In sociology, they are sometimes seen as a penetration of economic thinking, perhaps as part of a larger social trend of 'economic fundamentalism'. For economists, the introduction of concepts such as human and social capital may be met, as Gittins (2003) put it, with 'raised eyebrows', as an introduction of 'warm and fuzzy' concepts in the hard-nosed science based on number-crunching. On the other hand, it may be greeted as a 'partial retreat from the economic fundamentalism of earlier times' (ibid.).

The concept of human capital seems to have first appeared as part of corporate management vocabulary, expressing a corporate desire for effective 'tracking, procurement and management' of human resources. This is achieved through the 'scientific measurement' of the economic value of an employee in the economy where 'skill and competences' of the high-performance workforce become the 'key variables' of productivity and competitiveness of the organization (Saba, 2003). In essence, this is an approach committed to the maximization of profit through "making leaders more impactful, employees more satisfied, and organizations more productive", thus "optimizing the return on their human capital" (Human Capital Resource Center (HCRC), 2003).

The idea of human capital in migration studies conceptualises the mobility of skilled people, who are presumably motivated by an expectation of attracting higher returns to their skills in another country. In the context of international migration, however, there is more to human capital than skills: other aspects include language (predominantly English), globally valid cultural knowledge (i.e. urban Western culture) and local knowledge, especially the knowledge of the local labour market and the local formal and informal work and corporate subcultures. People with high human capital, and especially 'Westerners' among them, move across international borders with relative ease and are usually welcomed to the places of popular desire. This is radically different from the experiences of refugees, even for those with high skills, as they come from cultures which do not automatically qualify as 'insiders' in the globally dominant Western-urban-cyberspaced-English-speaking culture.

In a recent research paper by Australian Productivity Commission (APC), social capital has been defined 'a resource that facilitates cooperation within or between groups of people', and whose key elements are social norms, social networks and trust (APC, 2003, p. x). In theoretical sociology, social capital was first defined by Bourdieu in the early 1980s. He argued that social capital consisted of two elements: the social relationship that allows individuals to claim access to resources possessed by their friends and associates, and the amount and quality of such resources (Portes, 1998). Theorists of social capital emphasise its intangible character relative to other forms of capital (see Coleman, 1988; Portes, 1998).[1] As Portes (1998, p. 4) summarized, "whereas economic capital is in people's bank accounts and human capital is inside their heads, social capital inheres in the structure of their relationships." In his writing on social capital, Coleman (1988) sought to "introduce social

[1] Still, the Australian Bureau of Statistics will attempt to measure social capital in a research project announced to start next year (see D. Macken, 'Real wealth is a measure of 'regrettables', The *Australian Financial Review*, 14-15 February 2004, p. 26)

structure into the rational action paradigm." He explored three forms of social capital: obligations and expectations, information channels and social norms.[2]

Although these two concepts have an economic sound to them, they are essentially sociological terms: they denote certain non-quantifiable qualities of individuals and communities, as detailed below (cf. Portes, 1995). Similarly, migration and resettlement are complex phenomena and cannot be reduced to a cost-benefit analysis; although we focus on economic adjustment, there is much more to it than what numbers (as in "household income", for example) can express. Nevertheless, quantitative information is presented in this qualitative-analysis based chapter.

In the following sections we outline our methodology and then briefly elaborate on the Australian refugee policy. In the bulk of the chapter we present findings of our research. We show some findings in tabular form, along with an analysis of several key adjustment variables (e.g. job satisfaction and owner-occupancy). Quotations from interviews as well as written comments from the survey are offered to confirm and/or illustrate major concerns. We also analyse the role of bureaucratic structures of support in refugees' job search as well as the role of informal networks (at the early stage of resettlement predominantly 'ethnic community' networks). A separate section is devoted to housing tenure and residential location choice as important aspects of economic adjustment.

METHODOLOGY

This chapter is based on two separate empirical research projects on Bosnian refugees in Australia, conducted in the metropolitan cities of Sydney and Perth. The earlier project was conducted in Sydney between 1996 and 1998, immediately following the peak of Bosnian refugee intake and at the early stages of their resettlement. The project involved three refugee groups, Afghanis, Iraqis and Bosnians, and the data were collected through questionnaire-based interviews with refugees (167) and key informants (44). The latter were people working for government and non-government service providers catering to the needs of refugees in Sydney: officers of the departments of immigration, health, housing and social security, as well as employees at various non-governmental services providers. A comprehensive questionnaire formed the basis for semi-structured interviews with key informants, where respondents could expand and discuss points beyond specific questions. Subsequently, seven bilingual interviewers conducted 50 structured questionnaire-based interviews with Bosnian refugees who arrived in Sydney between 1994 and 1996. Although the questionnaire consisted of nine sections, data used in this chapter relate to the economic adjustment, i.e. English language competency, residential location, overseas qualifications and their recognition in Australia, current employment status and those factors stifling employment and/or labour mobility.

The fieldwork for the recent project was conducted in Perth and Sydney from late 2001 to early 2003 and targeted Bosnians who had been in Australia for at least two years. After two

[2] Current sociological writing on the subject presents a thesis that social capital is decreasing in developed societies. The argument about the need for rebuilding of social capital in modern society states that despite the highly rationalised, productive, regulated and institutionalized society, primary face-to-face relationships as well as the intangible qualities as trust and the sense of community, still count not only in the intimate sphere of family and close friendships, but also in the broader social domains, as well as in the public arena.

years, most of them reached a degree of stability and adjustment to their new environment. The fieldwork which included interviews, focus groups and a survey, was conducted by the chief investigator. Semi structured interviews were conducted with refugees (35) and refugee service providers (25) that lasted about 1.5 hours on average. The survey was conducted in Perth in 2002, and 46 out of 100 distributed questionnaire packages were returned. Each pack contained two parts: a 3-page household questionnaire asking about household size, composition, income, home ownership, and demographic data about members of the household, and a 6-page individual questionnaire (two identical copies for two adults in the household in the each pack). The individual questionnaire consisted of 3 sections: 1) demographic data 2) assessment of resettlement services received and 3) general questions on resettlement in Australia, inquiring about resettlement outcomes and personal satisfaction with these outcomes. Demographic information was collected on 46 households (a total of 182 people) and 87 individuals who completed the individual questionnaires with the data from this survey presented below together with quotations and comments relating to key issues.

Research data were analysed using descriptive and inferential statistics through the application of Statistical Package for Social Sciences (SPSS). The descriptive statistics identify major data characteristics in our sample and include the production of frequency distributions, percentages and cross tabulations, which allowed for a more thorough data analysis and interpretation. In order to determine if a significant relationship exists between two or more categorical variables, we applied Pearson's chi square hypothesis test. In addition, qualitative data are presented in the form of first-hand quotations.

Australia's Refugee Immigration: Resettling Human Capital?

Since 1945, over six million people have migrated to Australia through a planned immigration program, and approximately 600,000 of these settlers have been refugees (Department of Immigration & Multicultural & Indigenous Affairs (DIMIA), 2003b). Stilwell (1987) argued that economic factors increasingly shaped Australian immigration policy in the 1980s. Similarly, Iredale, Fox and Sherlaimoff (1994) argued that over recent decades Australia's immigration policy is increasingly seen as part of its economic policy. This economic emphasis is known as the human capital approach in immigration, where skilled migrants, who can arguably contribute to the receiving country's economic prosperity, are more likely to be admitted (Iredale, 2001; Jupp, 2002). Although this cannot be directly applied to refugees, who are by definition forced migrants, the human capital approach affects refugee selection. Many authors, including the Refugee Resettlement Working Group (RRWG, 1994), argue that Australian immigration authorities base their selection of refugees not only on people's need for safety but also on their 'resettlement potential' (Jupp, 1994, Iredale et al., 1996) as determined by age, education, type of skills/employability, as well as socio-economic background, gender and health, which are also elements of human capital. Once the chosen refugees arrive in Australia, they make their own decisions on how to put their human capital to use. The decision depends on their own assessment of its value in the new environment and the feedback they receive from the environment, primarily from the labour market once they venture out to seek employment.

Australian government assists and influences refugee resettlement through resettlement programs. The current program called 'Integrated Humanitarian Settlement Strategy' (IHSS) was introduced in 1997-98. The aim of IHSS is to provide a national framework for improving settlement assistance for humanitarian entrants and to build partnerships with community organizations involved in its provision. IHSS consists of a variety of time-limited services that are available to refugees free-of-charge (while 'voluntary' migrants have to pay for some of the services), such as English tuition, short-term subsidized on-arrival-accommodation (OAA), help in accessing public housing and the private rental market for a longer-term accommodation, assistance in the skill-recognition process and securing employment, special provisions in health and dental care, torture and trauma as well as 'general' counseling, and advocacy and community development (DIMIA, 2003a). In Perth and Sydney, where our research was conducted, there are a number of Migrant Resource Centres (MRCs), where advice, assistance and referrals to other specialised service providers are offered to refugees and other migrants. Unlike voluntary migrants in Australia, permanently protected refugees are entitled to welfare assistance immediately upon arrival. Since 2001, most refugee services within Australian IHSS have been tendered out by DIMIA and effectively privatized. As Beer and Morphett (2002, p.7) aptly suggested, "...the Australian 'liberal' welfare regime is so structured that it is assumed that most new arrivals will meet their needs through the labour market. In Australia, successful settlement is independence in settlement. Those who cannot meet their needs, and the needs of their household, through privately earned income or other resources, present a significant policy dilemma [...]".

BUREAUCRATIC STRUCTURES OF SUPPORT IN THE PROCESS OF ECONOMIC ADJUSTMENT: EMPLOYMENT ASSISTANCE

Migrants and refugees from non-English speaking backgrounds (NESB), and Bosnians among them, come from considerably different cultures and labour markets and many find it difficult to cope in Australia, especially if their English language skills are limited. Specific and migrant-focused employment services should therefore assist them in order to avoid unwanted outcomes: welfare dependence, on the one hand, and considerable occupational down-adjustment on the other, which are, reportedly, common outcomes for NESB migrants, and especially refugees (VandenHeuvel and Wooden, 1999; Puls, 2000; 2001; Jupp, 2002; Colic-Peisker, 2003).

Shortly after taking office in 1996, the current Liberal government announced, and in 1998 introduced, major changes in active labour market assistance (APC, 2002). In the new model based on a so-called 'Job Network',[3] government contracted out employment assistance to a number of private providers through competitive tendering. Competition among service providers and a degree of choice for clients (job seekers) was expected to make services more efficient and cost-effective. However, according to APC's Independent Review of the Job Network (2002) report, the benefits of the new model of job assistance on

3 Previously called 'Case Management' within the Commonwealth Employment Service (CES).

net employment outcomes remain small, similar to past programs (ibid, p. xxvii). In addition, the Job Network has no policies in place to cater for specific populations such as NESB migrants and refugees. As a consequence, refugees are likely to be provided with intensive assistance (for example regular meetings with a case manager) as especially 'problematic' cases at a time when it may not be appropriate and without taking specific refugee issues into account. Job seekers have to accept the offered intensive assistance even if they feel they do not need it. Some of the clients are 'parked' (…and made "invisible within the apparatus of the government" Beer and Morphett, 2002, p. 6), earning sign-on fees for the service provider, regardless of the outcome of the refugees' involvement with the Job Network.

In our recent (2002) Perth survey, we asked respondents to assess services provided by Centrelink — the single Australian welfare benefit payment agency and the gatekeeper to the employment services — and the employment assistance embodied in the Job Network. The answers to one of the questions ("If you work, or have worked in Australia, how did you find employment") are presented in Table 1. People were encouraged to complement multiple choice questions by written comments. Some of these comments are listed later in this section.

Table 1. If You Work, or have Worked in Australia, How did you Find Employment? (N = 87 Respondents)

Through own ('ethnic') networks	61.5 %
Through Job Network	3.1 %
Independently through job ads	20.0 %
Other (self-employed, or with help of other agencies such as TAFE and MRCs	15.4 %

The following account from an interview conducted with a bilingual settlement worker in Perth, herself a refugee, illustrates the issues that many Bosnian respondents reported through interviews or written comments in the questionnaire. Mrs. M. commented on the experience of her family as well as her Bosnian clients with the Centrelink and Job Network:

> The [Australian] system offers a lot of possibilities but you need to know about them and our people don't and there's no-one to tell them... and also things change all the time... at Centrelink there are new people all the time...you can never talk to the same person twice, so you do not feel supported [...]
> Our people find very little support in Job Network ... They find jobs by themselves, or through friends and acquaintances... they start with cleaning [jobs]... I had a client who got a full time job as soon as he arrived in Australia... he's a carpenter, and his relative employed him... he didn't speak any English, but he was a good tradesmen. After a year his boss told him he could not keep him anymore because he could not work independently because of the language [barrier] […] So he started learning English [...] but Centrelink was always after him. They assigned him to the intensive job assistance, but this did not make any sense [...]. He needed to learn English and when he acquired a level of functional English he could find job in no time... They [Centrelink] called him all the time, threaten to cut his payment off... while he was only 100 hours into his 510 hours [of the migrant English course] […]
> My husband was given the intensive [job] assistance in the first year in Australia, while he didn't even know what that meant... appointments with case managers... They would fill the form with his personal data, write down his level of English and good-bye [...] My husband's English teacher recommended him to a private plumbing firm and that's how he found a job, a full-time job... not through the Job Network... his intensive assistance was completely useless,

it was at the wrong time, and later when it would have been useful he could not get it, what an irony [...] Our people are very disenchanted with the system and they look for their own ways to get jobs.

Below are short comments from our respondents about the Centrelink services and the employment assistance received through the Job Network. Overall, comments gleaned through the recent survey and interviews were seldom positive and often negative. 41 out of 87 surveyed people had been registered in the Job Network for some time, but only two of them said they found jobs through this avenue. Comments on Centrelink were somewhat less negative, but very often critical. We chose comments that are representative of the overall sample.

Comments about Job Network:

A 42 year old part-time cleaner and a 'casual chemist', found work through her own networks:
They [Job Network officers] always listened to what I'd done and asked what I was going to do next. They encouraged me but never gave any suggestion what to do: no initiative [came] from them.

Draftsman, 48, an electrical engineer in Bosnia:
Me and people like me were of more use for them [Centrelink and Job Network employees], so they can have jobs, rather than them being able to help us.

A doctor, 37, now a registrar in a Perth hospital, who previously did pamphlet delivering, cleaning and worked as a sleep technologist:
[I received] no help at all from them in the job search: I had to do it all myself.

A chemical technician who found work independently but assessed Job Network services as 'acceptable':
They increase pressure to look for work...

Bilingual settlement worker, 47, a lawyer in Bosnia, who found a job through her teacher's recommendation:
I have never met anybody whom they [Job Network] found a job.

The following comments indicate that older job seekers may receive less attention from the Job Network and may be 'parked' as a 'headcount'.

A man, 55, with a postgraduate degree from Bosnia:
Their services are sheer formality.

A 54 year old woman, with 12 years of schooling and limited English, in casual employment which she found through her Bosnian networks:
Their services are absolute zero... in four years that I was registered with them no-one ever asked about me as if I didn't exist.

A cleaner, 55, with university education from Bosnia:
[They are] insufficiently engaged in looking for ways to find a job on the level of one's qualifications.

The following are the comments about the Centrelink services:

A self-employed painter and decorator, 46, a journalist in Bosnia:
Their ignorance is catastrophic. They send you from one counter to another for trivial assistance because they are absolutely unprepared for the job they do.

A quality control officer, 49:
Centrelink should be there to help clients, not to torture them... [they are] non-functional and [it is] not easy to access rights that we actually have. They should be there to help not to keep threatening people.

Mrs. B., 39, a social worker, studying at university to get her qualifications recognised:
We started learning English from zero...we kept getting letters from Centrelink, but we couldn't read them. I didn't understand how to report my income, as I was receiving Austudy... after tax, before tax... but if you want to clarify something [at Centrelink], four people will give you four different answers...

About one third of respondents gave neutral comments about Centrelink, but positive comments were rare and critical comments predominated. Puls (2000) who conducted her research in Perth also reported dissatisfaction of Bosnian refugees with the Centrelink and Job Network. According to Puls (2000, p. 7), "not a positive comment was made" and Centrelink and Job Network were described as systems that are "difficult to understand". Puls (2001, p. 15) reported that respondents from other refugee groups also found the job assistance hard to understand and "almost none (definitely one and possibly three) of the 41 participants reported that they had found a job through the Job Network system". The quotes presented above also point to another widespread problem: Bosnians working in jobs considerably below the level of their formal qualifications.

In analysing job-search methods, it is important to note that a typical Bosnian, even a highly educated urban dweller, is not a 'self-sufficient' Western individual supported by the rule of law and well established social institutions and professional services. Rather, an individual coming from a country where many services taken for granted in Australia are non-existent, rudimentary or inefficient, is accustomed to providing assistance to those within their private support network while expecting it reciprocated when the need arises. For people with such cultural background, coming from a communist system with the weak civil society and little private initiative, the decline of the social capital of their communities in suburban Australia and their replacement by formal organizations may be experienced as a cultural shock. In Bosnia, much more than in Australia, social connections are instrumental to accessing employment, while official channels are often a mere façade. When assessing the formal employment assistance they received in Australia, a considerable number of our respondents mentioned that genuine help with job search came from institutions they dealt with but whose primary role was not to provide employment assistance. For example, Adult Migrant English Program (AMEP) and Technical and Further Education (TAFE) teachers were often mentioned as helpful, as were the MRC staff in several instances. Employment services were perceived by most people to be doing a headcount rather than genuinely helping their clients. This perception is partly attributable to the deficiencies of the system, and partly it is 'in the eye of the job seeker': apart from the cultural differences, the importance of finding employment to overall resettlement success probably made respondents more inclined to judge employment assistance more harshly than other resettlement services. However, recently released internal documents from the Department of Employment and Workplace Relations, which is responsible for Job Network, state that "...bureaucrats were trying to find a new 'stock' of job seekers for the agencies to stay afloat" (Tingle, 2004, p. 6). Some of our refugee respondents expressed a similar view.

It should be mentioned that, as Puls (2001, p.12) reported, service providers saw their NESB clients as very focused on finding work and generally more motivated than the 'mainstream clients'. The refugees' culturally conditioned lack of appreciation for the highly bureaucratic system based on "much form-filling", as many respondents remarked, seems to be another reason for their dissatisfaction (cf. Puls, 2001). However, it is up to particular service providers to take into account cultural differences and find ways to deal with them, as well as to make the system more transparent to people from different cultures, often with limited English language competency.

Social Capital of the Refugee Community in the Process of Economic Adjustment

In all societies, regardless of the level of urbanisation and modernisation, social capital is instrumental in the job search process and affects labour market outcomes (Stone *et al.*, 2003). However, the established understanding of determinants of job search show that the relative weight of informal networks, compared with the strictly formalised process of human resource allocation, vary enormously from one society to another. Bosnia is, in this respect, a much more social capital-oriented society while Australia can be regarded as more 'meritocratic'. As our respondents reported, human capital was unlikely to be realized or 'invested' in the Bosnian labour market unless the person could also mobilize considerable social networks in the process of job search. This, and the fact that social capital was highly instrumental in furthering individual mobility, was indeed considered one of the main weaknesses of communism, where social connections overshadowed the relevance of selection based on more objective criteria of merit. This in effect meant that human capital was often wasted, which eroded work motivation, productivity and work ethic. The weakness of institutional arrangements, which either operated on rudimentary levels or were corrupt, made people rely almost exclusively on informal networks. In Coleman's (1988) words, the density of outstanding obligations (what he calls 'informal credit slips') was high, and therefore the social capital in the local community on which individuals could draw, was high. This was, however, only the case on the level of dense face-to-face networks and communities: extended family, friendship, collegial networks and neighbourhoods, whereas social capital on a societal level, represented in generalised civic trust in strangers, and trust in institutions and formal arrangements, was notoriously low in communist societies (Rose 1994).

In such an environment, the 'strength of weak ties' (Granovetter, 1974) — those outside the family and face-to-face community which may connect an individual with other groups in society and serve as informal employment referral system — can be instrumental to a very limited degree. In the early stages of their resettlement in Australia, Bosnians of course would not have many 'weak ties' in the wider community, and would have to rely on 'strong ties' in the family and immediate ethnic community, which could only assist in accessing low-skilled jobs. As a result, at the current stage of their resettlement, the employment of Bosnians is still concentrated in ethnic enclaves (spatially) and ethnic niches (in specific businesses such as cleaning and building industries).

Social values and customs of their society of origin continue to operate after Bosnians migrated to Australia, especially in the early stages of resettlement.[4] The tension between the old face-to-face and the new 'impersonal' and highly institutionalised environments is expressed in the following quote from a 40-year old professional woman:

> The old system [in Bosnia] with all the family support, you could sort of sleep peacefully [...]. [Here in Australia] when you have a problem, you ring a service and they make an appointment in 20 days... that's not what I see as help, I need help *now*... You feel like a number... 'Please report to the reception' 'Do you have an appointment?' [...] Our people just do not accept this cold bureaucratic interaction... [they] need to know that there's a place where they can come and seeks help any time, now, today...or at least first thing tomorrow morning.

The appreciation of the Australian system and awareness that not everything's rosy about the community support are expressed in a following quote coming from a 41-year old GP turned taxi driver:

> Things are well organised here in Australia, and one can cope without friends... You do not need to help me, just do not abuse me, I'm happy to be left alone... left in peace... given a break. Back home people are really nosy, they want to know everything. The best welcome [to Australia] for me is to be left alone [...]. I can say that I feel Australians are largely indifferent... and that's a fantastic approach as far as I'm concerned. Our people receive you with open arms, but one day those same arms might strangle you, if you know what I mean...

Consistent with much research on ethnic communities in the US and Australia, Bosnian community networks have a vital role to play in helping to find work. This enables individuals to access employment while avoiding unfamiliar requirements of the formal job search, and ethnic businesses, on the other hand, gain a pliant, disciplined and highly motivated labour force. However, as Portes (1998, p. 9) observed, "social capital in the form of social (community) control may clash with social capital in the form of network-mediated benefits". In other words, an individual who feels able to look for employment outside ethnic networks may experience downwards-leveling pressure from their ethnic community (Portes 1998; Bloch 2002).

---

4 For example, borrowing money from friends and relatives rather than from a bank (apart from large sums required for a home loan) is entirely acceptable among Bosnians and works as a system of mutual support, based exclusively on trust. This is in clear dissonance with a prevalent attitude of Australia expressed in a bank's advertising slogan 'Keep your friends and borrow from us'. Among Bosnians, borrowing from an institution with interest is considered wasteful and only used as a last resort.

SATISFACTORY LABOUR MARKET INTEGRATION: THE KEY ELEMENT OF ECONOMIC ADJUSTMENT

In the context of economic adjustment, access to employment is a major determinant of the financial health and social well-being of the migrant household. This was confirmed in our research where we found a statistically significant relationship between the financial situation and whether the person was happy with his/her life (p=0.010). People entirely happy with their financial situation were more likely to be satisfied with their life (see Appendix 1). Furthermore, there was a strong association between the financial situation and whether the respondent felt his/her life was back to normal (p=0.009) as 40 per cent of those who were entirely happy with their financial situation felt their life was entirely back to normal compared with none of those not at all happy with their financial status (see Appendix 2). Following these findings, the role of labour market integration in influencing the success (or lack thereof) of resettlement was investigated further.

The household and individual demographic data relevant for economic adjustment, or elements of economic adjustment, which were collected in our recent (2002) survey of 182 Bosnian respondents in Perth is presented below.

Most of our respondents lived in 4-member households. Average household income (after tax) per fortnight in the group of Bosnian respondents was $1,595, or $399 per person per fortnight (which is roughly the amount of the individual welfare benefit). Converted to an annual basis, income for each member of the Bosnian household is equivalent to 29.1 per cent of Australia's per capita income which was $35,693 in 2001-02 (ABS, 2003). However, in our surveyed group, there were 18 households with above average fortnightly incomes ($1600 - $5000) and 14 of these had at least one person with a university degree in the family. These families had an average income per member per fortnight of $587 (41.8 per cent of the per capita income in Australia). However, eight households with members who held tertiary qualifications had below average household income ($740-1460), which translated to $319 per person per fortnight. Thus, considerable human capital could not be re-invested on the Australian labour market.

In the tables below, we present some demographic data relevant for labour market integration:

Table 2. Year of Arrival

1992	2.3%
1993	3.5%
1994	14.5%
1995	15.0%
1996	20.8%
1997	6.4%
1998	16.7%
1999	4.6%
2000	13.3%
2001	2.9%

N= 173, excluding Australia-born children.

Table 3. Age relevant to Employment (N= 182)

Adults of working age (19-64)	119
Children under 18 (includes 9 Australian-born children)	54
People over the age of 65	9

Not surprisingly, language proficiency was higher overall in the most recent survey as respondents' length of residence was higher on average. Furthermore, 76 per cent of Bosnians in Sydney interviewed in the earlier survey found the migrant English tuition inadequate for employment purposes, results aligned with findings of previous Australian studies, such as Pittaway (1991) and Jupp (1994). On the other hand, AMEP's Client Satisfaction Survey (2001) showed that migrants (from different ethnic groups) considered the provided English course satisfactory. This discrepancy in assessment may be explained by the higher expectations of Bosnians compared to other migrant groups (an observation that we heard from service providers, see below).

According to Table 4, 80 per cent of the later sample and 56 per cent of the earlier sample declared their English to be either excellent or satisfactory and this should presumably be a sufficient language basis for labour market integration in Australia. More than half of the respondents in 2002 declared they are "proficient enough to do their previous Bosnian job". However, only 16.5 per cent of working-age respondents worked full-time, and another 33 per cent worked more than 10 hours a week (see Table 5).

Table 4. Self-assessed English Language Proficiency for Adults of Working Age

2002 survey		1997 survey	
Excellent	18%	Excellent	9%
Satisfactory	62%	Satisfactory	47%
Poor	18%	Poor	36%
None	2%	None	8%

Note: Approximately 76 per cent of respondents answered this question in the later survey and 98 per cent in the earlier survey.

Table 5. Employment Status for People of Working Age (N=115, Excluding 4 Full-time University Students)

2002 survey	
Unemployed (looking for work)	13.9 %
On pension / household duties	31.3 %
Employed part time - less than 10 hours a week	5.2 %
Employed part time – more than 10 hours a week	33.1 %
Employed full time	16.5%

Note: 12 people under 50 years of age described themselves as 'retired'.

This distribution may not be the accurate representation of the Bosnian refugee community, as people with higher education were more likely to supply the answer to this question as well as more likely to return the questionnaire. The difference in language proficiency between the earlier and more recent survey may reflect the difference between Perth (2002) and Sydney (1997) communities, where the Sydney settlers appear somewhat better educated although it may also be the reflection of our relatively small samples. The results of both surveys indicate that, contrary to popular belief, Bosnian refugees have higher levels of education than Australian born with, for example, 20.4 per cent of Australians between the ages of 25 and 64 completed a Bachelors Degree or above (compared with 46 per cent and 34 per cent in the 1997 and 2002 surveys respectively), while 34.9 per cent did not completing year 12 (ABS, 2003, p.86). This may confirm the earlier argument that the selection criteria for humanitarian entrants are based not only on humanitarian grounds but also on educational qualifications of applicants. Despite the higher level of educational attainment reached by the Bosnians, their economic adjustment process in Australia is upset as many Bosnian qualifications are either not recognised or partly recognised. Compounding this problem is the fact that some refugees lack documentation of their qualifications due to the urgency of their escape, while others, who lack English proficiency, find it incongruous to try to get qualifications recognized if they cannot communicate with prospective employers. Furthermore, formal recognition of overseas qualifications and finding a satisfactory job are two separate issues, with the latter stifled by the lack of local experience and failure of individual employers to de facto recognise or accept overseas qualifications and skills.

Table 6. Highest Qualifications of People of Working Age

	1997 survey	2002 survey
Primary school (8 years) or less	2%	10%
High school (12 years) / skilled trade	52%	55%
Tertiary degree	40%	30%
Postgraduate degree	6%	5%

The 1996 Australian Census showed high unemployment of 30.5 per cent among the Bosnia-born, compared to 9.2 per cent unemployment in the general population (Jupp, 2002, p.156). More recent data based on the 2001 Census indicate a drop in Bosnian unemployment rate as they settle in Australia: 16.8 per cent compared to 7.4 per cent for the general population (DIMIA, 2004)

Many authors argue that employment is the single most important resettlement issue (Puls 2000; 2001; Beer and Morphett 2002; Colic-Peisker 2003). Yet for refugees, acquiring satisfactory employment, or indeed any employment, and resuming a 'normal life' may be in some cases significantly delayed by psychological trauma. Other obstacles to successful economic adjustment can be conceptualised as a lack of human capital relevant in the Australian environment, and primarily pertain to age, English language proficiency, formal skills and relevant work experience (in one's occupation/profession).[5] Once refugees arrive in Australia, these characteristics are crucial for their economic adjustment. As a counselor at

[5] These four elements of human capital at the same time represent those characteristics of applicants for a permanent Australian visa that are evaluated by the immigration authorities through a 'points test'.

AMEP commented, the issue may be compounded by relatively high expectations among Bosnians:

> Age, health, personal resources...education...problems get compounded... it's all connected. Um...their expectations are very high... my impression is that their overall standard of living in the former Yugoslavia was quite high...

High expectations were quoted as one of the problems by Mr. B., a surgeon who passed the Australian Medical Association exam and now practices his profession in Australia:

> [Our] people's [Bosnians] memory is short... they solve all their problems [in Australia] but they still complain. They cannot socialise [acculturate], they have a feeling that they are not at the level they were at before...our people want Italian shoes, Ray Ban sunglasses and German cars...

The loss of occupational status because of unrecognized formal qualifications or failure to secure an adequate job, seems pervasive among Bosnians. Some people adjust to this situation well as long as they can satisfactorily provide for their families, but for a majority the loss of occupational status represents an ongoing source of dissatisfaction. The following quotes cover a range of reactions to the situation of down-adjustment.

> Mr. B., a GP in Bosnia, now driving a taxi:
> Someone had to work...and also, I came here to live, not to study all over again... I would have accepted to volunteer in a hospital for three years if needed, but not to sit at home and learn…with such a uncertain outcome… My best friend who lives in Sydney, also a doctor from Sarajevo, studied for five years and still didn't pass the [AMA] exam, which is terribly, terribly hard. [...] I went to do this [driving a cab]. I am not unhappy... it's a no-stress job...when I come home I can forget about it.
> Mrs. S, a specialist dentist turned dental hygienist:
> It was a horrible realisation that I cannot do my job [here in Australia]. I thought, what else can I do? [...] I chose this job [a dental hygienist] as something close enough to what I was doing before. I am immensely grateful that I could study, and I was treated the same as anyone else [...]. I feel appreciated at work, I have built my reputation... and that's fantastic. I am happy at the moment... I'm not saying I'll be happy forever, [because] this job does get monotonous. I work part time, and perhaps I should work full time while still young, but I am really tired, and I wanted to have some time for the family.
> Mrs. M., a social worker in Bosnia:
> After 6-7 months some friends of ours offered us [my husband and I] a cleaning job; we were in debt as we borrowed $3,500 from the Conference of Churches of Western Australia to pay for the air-fare for the three of us; we spent 2.5 years as refugees in Serbia and we came here with no money at all... so we had to work, we didn't have anything... no furniture...and doing anything is better that sitting at home and despairing.
> Mrs. B., who works as a bank-teller, holds a 4-year degree in economics from Croatia and has completed an additional year in banking and finance at an Australian university:
> I found a job shortly after I completed my studies, but I'm not happy with the job, not at all! Not only it is below my qualifications, but I also feel I am exploited... How shall I put it... the job is demanding and stressful but very poorly paid... [...] people born here do this job with 12 years of schooling and with no particular qualification... and then there's the work vs. family issue as well [...]. Back in Bosnia we had great family support so kids were no obstacle to full-time work...

Job satisfaction is an important element of general well being. In the case of migrants the satisfaction with their economic adjustment may influence not only their general satisfaction with life and their well-being, but also their attitude towards the host society. The following two tables represent the answers to two questions in the recent survey: 'Are you satisfied with your current job?' and 'Do you get a "fair go" in Australia?' Tables 7 and 8 reveal that some people who were not satisfied with their jobs, or only somewhat satisfied, were still ready to consider Australia a fair country. This may mean that they were ready to see the failure to find satisfactory job as a consequence of their limited English and their lack of local knowledge rather than to prejudice or discrimination. Similarly, levels of satisfaction with life in Australia were high among 52,000 immigrants who participated in the three waves of the Longitudinal Survey on Immigrants to Australia (LSIA) despite their lack of English competency and often a marginal position in the labour market (Beer and Morphett, 2002).[6]

Table 7. Job Satisfaction

Entirely satisfied	23.6%
Satisfied to a degree	62.4%
Not at all satisfied'	14%

N=85 people of working age, as not everyone provided the answer.

Table 8. Australia is a Country where Everyone has an Opportunity to Succeed

Yes	40%
To a degree / not sure	49.4%
No	10.6%

N=85, as not everyone provided the answer.

We found no statistically significant relationship between job satisfaction and the personal assessment that 'Australia is a country where everyone has an opportunity to succeed'. Nevertheless, 53.9 per cent of those entirely happy with their job believed Australia was a country where one could experience a degree of a 'fair go' while not a single person "not at all happy with his/her job" felt Australia was a country offering a fair go to everyone.

Integration in the labour force unfolds unevenly over time, especially for refugees (Waxman, 2001) and, as a consequence, they are disproportionately reliant on government services. Khoo (1994) examined the correlates of welfare dependency among immigrants in Australia from 1971 to 1990 and found that refugee status was positively correlated with welfare dependency although the coefficient was not significant. Birrell and Jupp (2000) found English proficiency the critical factor in determining reliance on welfare benefits. Whiteford (1991) claimed that the period of residence, along with English competency, were the dominant factors explaining the level of welfare dependency, a sentiment shared by Beer and Morphett (2002). These factors, along with those cited earlier, including pre-arrival experiences, qualification recognition in Australia and health issues, may explain why the levels of unemployment for refugees continue to remain considerably higher than for the

6 The LSIA surveyed migrants who came to Australia between September 1993 and August 1995 and their settlement experiences were recorded after six months, 18 months and 3.5 years post arrival.

general population or other immigration categories (Jupp, 2002, p.156; Richardson *et al.*, 2002, DIMIA, 2001).

HOUSING AND RESIDENTIAL LOCATION

Many authors have noted the significance of housing and residential location in the resettlement process (Junankar *et al.* 1993; Tonkin 1993; Hugo 1994; Richardson et al., 2002). The National Population Council (NPC 1990) found housing to be a major determinant of successful settlement. Furthermore, housing outcomes reflect the individual's capacity not only to enter the labour market but also his/her position within that market (Beer and Morphett 2002). Sianni (1992), RRWG (1994), Iredale *et al.* (1996) and Beer and Morphett (2002) stressed stable, affordable and suitable accommodation as essential to the effective adjustment and successful resettlement of refugees. Their analysis of housing and other service needs of recently arrived immigrants shows that kinship and community networks are vital for successful resettlement for many immigrants, with housing the centre of family life and 'the focus for receiving community support' (ibid., 2002, p.31). Thus stable housing contributes to strengthening and activating the social capital within the ethnic community.

However, refugees are under considerable housing stress.[7] Hassel and Hugo (1996, p.64) argued about the existence of an 'accommodation gap' for newly arrived immigrants, particularly refugees. Once the short respite in OAA expires, most refugees are not able to meet the financial rigours of the private rental sector, while adequate public housing is usually only available after extended waiting periods. These problems are more pronounced in Sydney, where housing prices and, therefore also private accommodation rentals, are considerably higher than elsewhere in Australia.

Almost without exception, Bosnian respondents from the recent survey placed home ownership on the top of the list of their resettlement goals. We found a statistically significant relationship between housing tenure and whether the respondent felt his/her "life was back to normal" (p=0.024): 28.1 per cent of owner-occupiers felt their life was entirely back to normal compared with 12.5 per cent of people in public housing and no renters (see Appendix 3). Yet, while there was a statistically significant relationship between housing tenure and satisfaction with financial situation (p=.020), most people in rented accommodation and public housing felt somewhat satisfied with their financial situation (81 per and 100 per cent respectively). In addition, 50 per cent of owner-occupiers were somewhat satisfied with their life at the moment, 28 per cent were very satisfied and 22 per cent were not at all satisfied (This data is not found in the Appendices). The burden of carrying a mortgage in an often precarious and insecure employment circumstances may have contributed to the relatively high proportion of home owners who were not at all satisfied.

Despite the housing stress, at the time of the interviews two-thirds of our respondents have made the crucial move towards the goal of stable housing which they considered a necessary condition of stable family life. Although the average length of residence in Australia at the time of the survey was only 5.1 years, Bosnians already had achieved high

---

[7] Housing stress is defined as those in the lower 40 per cent of income-earners spending at least 30 per cent of their disposable income on housing.

rates of home ownership: 65.9 per cent of survey respondents were owner-occupiers (only marginally below the Australia-wide rate of 66.2 per cent) while 25 per cent rented privately (compared to 21.5 per cent Australia-wide), and 8.9 per cent lived in public housing (versus 4.5 per cent Australia-wide) (ABS, 2002a). The rest lived in alternative arrangements. In the earlier survey, when the average length of residence was only one year, the situation was expectedly different: no respondents were owner-occupiers, 77.6 per cent were renting privately, 8.2 per cent lived with relatives and friends, four per cent lived in public housing with the remainder in alternative arrangements.

According to the 2001 Australian Census, 23.4 per cent (5,528) of the Bosnia-born population fully owned their homes, 27.7 per cent (6,555) were purchasing them and 43.8 per cent (10,358) lived in rental accommodation, with 5.1 per cent (1,200) of people declaring 'other tenure types' and not stated (ABS, 2002b). The difference between our figures and census figures can be explained by at least two factors. First, in our recent survey we targeted respondents who have been in Australia for at last two years, while the Census covers everyone, including the most recent arrivals. Second, housing in Perth, where the recent survey was conducted, is far more affordable than in Sydney and Melbourne where the largest number of Bosnians settled during their large influx over the past decade. During our fieldwork in Perth, many respondents proudly showed us their impressively furnished houses (see also Matsuo, this volume). Bosnian women take pride in their homes as their family nests and do not spare any effort in keeping them neat, tidy and pleasant. The homemaker's role and care for the family seem to provide women with a sense of purpose which is an important psychological stabiliser in the stressful period of resettlement: this may be the secret of refugee women coping better than men, which is an often repeated observation by other researchers as well as our respondents (cf. Franz, 2003; Colic-Peisker, 2000). The following quote from a migrant English coordinator illustrates Bosnian passion for their own roof above their head:

> One couple [...] they bought a house in Quinn's Rock [a far northern coastal suburb of Perth], and travelled to the city twice a day rather than renting. [...] They do cleaning and their teenage son does too. [...] Lot of our students do cleaning and paper delivery, that's' the usual thing among Yugoslavs [refugees]... some are very motivated, they work in the morning and in the evening, and come to school in the middle of the day, and some of them are buying houses.

It is important to note that this quote describes very early arrivals, as a great majority of refugees attend migrant English during their first year in Australia. The following observation comes from a Homeswest (public housing in Perth) manager:

> Many Bosnians obtained their Perth homes through Homeswest's Good Start Shared Equity Scheme, which enables tenants to buy a share of their property for a start. Our clients from ex-Yugoslavia maintain their properties very well and are excellent payers. Their homes seem to be their first priority: professional people — we had doctors and engineers among them — were ready to take cleaning jobs while they go back to study or sit for exams in order to have their qualifications recognised. [...] They are hard-working people, everyone in the family goes out and works, including teenage children, in order to pay off the home loan and secure a decent life.

Private rental tenure is rare in Bosnia and it conveys a pariah status, resulting in a cultural reflex to rent only if it is absolutely unavoidable. Some respondents indicated, however, that the high value placed on home ownership may have a downside in regard to gaining satisfactory employment. A bilingual settlement worker in Perth explained:

> Our people [refugees from ex-Yugoslavia] would do anything to buy a house as soon as possible, and then they need to furnish it 'properly', which cannot be done without a job, and job requires time, so they do not allocate time for learning the language. They do manual low-paid jobs, everyone in the family does cleaning and newspaper delivery...

The pattern apparently held in Sydney as well. The following quotes come from several bilingual settlement workers who work in the areas of highest concentration of Bosnians, such as Auburn and Liverpool:

> (1) Community competition is one factor and the other thing is to feel settled, to be in one's own house, rather than paying rent for years.
> (2) There is a push from the community: get a job, go to the building [industry], do Gyprock [plastering], money's good there, so you can buy a house... you do not wait for a long time to buy a house. But they work a lot, from the daybreak to nightfall; people even go into buying expensive houses, have high mortgages, and have to keep working hard no matter what.
> (3) They [Bosnians] do not want to rent and they do not want to live in weatherboard houses...

A considerable number of people accepted low-skilled but readily available jobs in order to get a home loan and establish a secure family base as soon as possible. Community pressure seems to play a role in this. This way, however, many people postponed or gave up updating their skills/education, and thus their chances of gaining employment commensurate to their formal skill were reduced.

Distinctive residential concentration patterns can be discerned among Bosnians settlers in Perth as well as in Sydney. As established in earlier research on immigrants, these patterns are strongest at the time of initial settlement but become less pronounced over time (Lieberson and Waters, 1987; Viviani et al., 1993). Immigrants gaining entry under the family reunion or humanitarian program are likely to reside in close proximity to their sponsors or the first place of abode (e.g. OAA). Following this pattern, the largest concentration of Bosnians in Perth can be found in the areas around the OAA (northern suburbs of Balga, Mirrabooka, Girawheen and Beechboro). In Sydney, our earlier research showed that 79 per cent of Bosnians first lived in the south-western suburbs of Auburn, Fairfield and Liverpool, where OAA were also located. OAA is usually provided in affordable areas and this fact encourages refugees, usually under considerable financial stress, to stay in these areas, where public housing is also located. Their early employment and financial stress reinforce residential concentration by minimising residential choices (cf. Burnley, 1989, p.131). The pattern of residential stability thus combines the voluntary residential concentration, the purpose of which is to keep the access to established support networks and social capital, with the involuntary residential segregation caused by the low socio-economic status. For Bosnians, these residential patterns may change in the later stages of resettlement.

Our earlier research showed that a key factor found to influence the selection of the second residential location (after OAA) was the location of employment opportunities. In many cases this location coincided with the suburbs where co-nationals resided. The area of the highest concentration of Bosnian refugees in Sydney metropolitan area is Liverpool, which is also the area where earlier arrivals from the former Yugoslavia established their businesses. Virtually all our respondents in both surveys reported that the majority of their contacts and friends are from their former country of origin.

Conclusion

Ideally, resettlement ultimately results in the refugee feeling her/his life is back to normal. This was confirmed in our recent Perth study, where a statistically significant relationship between 'life being back to normal' and overall 'satisfaction with life' was found.[8] Our findings indicate that acquiring satisfactory employment — which implies a successful 'human capital re-investment' — is a crucial element of not only economic adjustment of Bosnian refugees in Australia, but also of the overall success of their resettlement. This makes employment assistance a critical service within the refugee resettlement program. Currently, employment assistance is a 'mainstream service' and not a part of the refugee resettlement scheme, and this may be a problem in itself. As already suggested by other researchers (see Jupp, 2002, p. 156), more specific programs for refugees may be needed in order to improve their chances to update their skills in the new environment and subsequently secure jobs appropriate for their skill level. Our research also suggests that the existing migrant English tuition classes may be not focused enough on the practical and especially employment needs of refugees. Housing seems to be a issue that Bosnians handle well. This is due to their high motivation to acquire their own home, their resourcefulness and readiness for hard and low-skilled work, and the assistance from their informal community networks, rather than any specific program aimed at helping them towards home ownership. Therefore, the lack of adequate English language provision and specialised labour market programs seem to be the problems that require more attention within the refugee resettlement program.

Our Bosnian respondents found many institutional arrangements designed to help them in their resettlement to be inadequate; this is not necessarily due to a low quality of services, as cultural differences and culturally-specific expectations play a considerable role in this assessment. However, service providers need to take cultural factors into account more than is currently the case with many 'mainstreamed' services. This is crucially important in the case of employment assistance. The result of the current situation is that Bosnians predominately rely on their social capital embodied in their informal networks for support in finding jobs, which leads many people to accept jobs below their skills. In addition, notwithstanding the fact that Australia's institutional support to migrants is well developed, many recent arrivals cannot use it because of the language barrier. As a consequence of the Australian policy of 'mainstreaming' the migrant services during the last decade, NESB migrants have much to learn before they are able to make good use of the provided institutional support. This idea is

8 82.4 per cent per cent of those who believed their life was entirely back to normal were satisfied with their life while none of those who did not feel their life was back to normal expressed satisfaction with life.

echoed by Beer and Morphett (2002, p.29) who recommend that assistance to humanitarian entrants be given through programs that integrate them into mainstream social and economic life, including English-language training, employment and financial counseling. However, a consolidated approach to the provision of such services is currently lacking (Beer and Morphett, 2002, p.vi).

High social capital in the Bosnian families and communities seems to have already started translating into high human capital in their children's generation, as many of them strive for high educational achievement (cf. Coleman, 1988). Spatial and social arrangements in Australian cities will inevitably decrease the social capital of Bosnian refugee communities past the first migrant generation, but the second generation is likely to experience social mobility and cease to be primarily reliant on the 'ethnic' network — as indeed is the case in many other migrant groups.

Many of our respondents, because their language skills were poor and qualifications not recognised, initially took low-skilled jobs, often in 'ethnic' businesses, and although some had full-time jobs, many were not happy with their situation. The Australian labour market may secure employment for immigrants through lowering their occupational status, without regard for the appropriate use of their skills and their job satisfaction. This, in turn, exerts negative influence on the overall well-being of individuals and families and their attitude towards the host society. Unemployment, with its pervasive negative influence on physical and mental heath, housing and general well-being of individuals, as well as its destructive effect on families, is not the only problem that needs to be addressed. Professional people are, as a rule, frustrated when they are reduced to low-skill jobs, not just because of the job satisfaction and status, but also because of diminished financial security and inability to live according to their previously established spending and lifestyle patterns. A comprehensive resettlement program should help people realize their full potential rather than merely integrating them into the labour market in the way that wastes their human capital. As a consistent human capital approach is not only in the interest of refugees but also in the interest of the host country, refugees' loss of occupational status and devaluation of their skills is deserving of far more attention from policymakers.

Appendix 1

financial situation * happy with your life? Crosstabulation

			happy with your life?				
			yes	mostly	not really	not at all	Total
financial situation	entirely happy	Count	7	8	3		18
		% within financial situation	38.9%	44.4%	16.7%		100.0%
		% within happy with your life?	28.0%	22.9%	13.6%		20.7%
	somewhat	Count	16	22	15	1	54
		% within financial situation	29.6%	40.7%	27.8%	1.9%	100.0%
		% within happy with your life?	64.0%	62.9%	68.2%	20.0%	62.1%
	not at all	Count	2	5	4	4	15
		% within financial situation	13.3%	33.3%	26.7%	26.7%	100.0%
		% within happy with your life?	8.0%	14.3%	18.2%	80.0%	17.2%
Total		Count	25	35	22	5	87
		% within financial situation	28.7%	40.2%	25.3%	5.7%	100.0%
		% within happy with your life?	100.0%	100.0%	100.0%	100.0%	100.0%

Appendix 2

financial situation * life back to normal? Crosstabulation

			life back to normal?			
			yes,entirely	partly	no	Total
financial situation	entirely happy	Count	7	10	1	18
		% within financial situation	38.9%	55.6%	5.6%	100.0%
		% within life back to normal?	41.2%	16.4%	12.5%	20.9%
	somewhat	Count	10	41	3	54
		% within financial situation	18.5%	75.9%	5.6%	100.0%
		% within life back to normal?	58.8%	67.2%	37.5%	62.8%
	not at all	Count		10	4	14
		% within financial situation		71.4%	28.6%	100.0%
		% within life back to normal?		16.4%	50.0%	16.3%
Total		Count	17	61	8	86
		% within financial situation	19.8%	70.9%	9.3%	100.0%
		% within life back to normal?	100.0%	100.0%	100.0%	100.0%

Chi-Square Tests

	Value	df	Asymp. Sig. (2-sided)
Pearson Chi-Square	13.604[a]	4	.009
Likelihood Ratio	13.856	4	.008
Linear-by-Linear Association	10.195	1	.001
N of Valid Cases	86		

a. 4 cells (44.4%) have expected count less than 5. The minimum expected count is 1.30.

APPENDIX 3

housing * life back to normal? Crosstabulation

			life back to normal?			
			yes,entirely	partly	no	Total
housing	renting	Count		20	1	21
		% within housing		95.2%	4.8%	100.0%
		% within life back to normal?		32.8%	12.5%	24.4%
	public housing	Count	1	5	2	8
		% within housing	12.5%	62.5%	25.0%	100.0%
		% within life back to normal?	5.9%	8.2%	25.0%	9.3%
	owner-occupancy	Count	16	36	5	57
		% within housing	28.1%	63.2%	8.8%	100.0%
		% within life back to normal?	94.1%	59.0%	62.5%	66.3%
Total		Count	17	61	8	86
		% within housing	19.8%	70.9%	9.3%	100.0%
		% within life back to normal?	100.0%	100.0%	100.0%	100.0%

ACKNOWLEDGEMENTS

We thank Dr. Narelle Smith of the University of Technology Sydney for her assistance in the application of SPSS in this chapter.

REFERENCES

Australian Bureau of Statistics (ABS). (2002a). *2001 Census of population and housing*, Cat.No. 2015.0. Canberra: AGPS.

_____ . (2002b).2001 Census of Population and Housing, *Birthplace of Individual by Tenure Type and Sex for Persons, Australia*, Cat. No. 2016.0. Canberra: AGPS.

ABS (2003). *Social Trends 2003.* Cat. No. 4102.0, Canberra: AGPS.

Adult Migrant English Program (AMEP). (2001). National Client Satisfaction Survey, prepared by Urbis Keys-Young (DIMA), July 2001. Retrieved from *http://www.immi.gov.au/amep/reports/client_survey.pdf*

Australian Productivity Commission (APC). (2002). *Independent Review of the Job Network*, Report No. 21. Canberra: AusInfo.

_____ . (2003). *Social capital: Reviewing the Concept and its Policy Implications*, Research Paper. Canberra: AusInfo.

Beer, A. & Morphett, S. (2002). *Housing and Other Service Needs of Recently Arrived Immigrants.* Melbourne: Australian Housing and Urban Research Institute.

Birrell, B. & Jupp, J. (2000). *Welfare Recipient Patterns among Migrants.* Canberra: Department of Immigration and Multicultural and Indigenous Affairs.

Bloch, A. (2002). *The Migration and Settlement of Refugees in Britain*, Hamphire, UK and New York, NY: Palgrave.

Burnley, I. (1989, October). Settlement dimensions of the Vietnam-born population in Metropolitan Sydney. *Australian Geography Studies*, (*27),* 120-54.

Coleman, J. S. (1988). Social capital in the creation of human capital. *American Journal of Sociology, 94*, S95-121.

Colic-Peisker, V. (2000). Croatian and Bosnian Migration to Australia in the 1990s. In C. Lange (Ed.), *Being Australian Women: Belonging, Citizenship and Identity* in *Studies in Western Australian History*, No. 21, 2000, Nedlands, WA: UWA, Centre for Western Australian History.

Colic-Peisker, V. (2002). The process of community and identity building among Bosnian Muslims in Western Australia. *Mots Pluriels.* Retrieved from http://www.arts.uwa.edu.au/MotsPluriels.

Colic-Peisker, V. (2003). Bosnian refugees in Australia: Identity, Community and Labour Market Integration. *New Issues in Refugee Research.* Retrieved from http://www.unhcr.org.

Colic-Peisker, V. & Tilbury, F. (2003). Active and Passive Resettlement: the Influence of Support Services and Refugees' own Resources on Resettlement Style. *International Migration, 41*(5), 61-91.

Department of Immigration & Multicultural & Indigenous Affairs (DIMIA) (2001). *Migrant Labour Market Outcomes,* Immigration Fact Sheet No. 14. Retrieved from http://www.dimia.gov.au/facts/14labour.html.

_____ . (2003a). *Integrated Humanitarian Settlement Strategy*, Immigration Fact Sheet No.66. Retrieved from http://www.dimia.gov.au/facts/66ihss.html.

_____ . (2003b). *More than Fifty Years of Post-war Migration* Fact Sheet No.4. Retrieved from http://www.dimia.gov.au/facts/4ihss.html.

_____ . (2004). *Australian Immigration Statistics*, Community Information Summaries: The Bosnia-Herzegovina-born community. Retrieved from http://www.immi.gov.au/statistics/infosummary/bosniaherzegovina.pdf.

Franz, B. (2003). Bosnian refugee women in (re)settlement: gender relations and social Mobility. *Feminist Review, 73*, 86-103.

Gittins, R. (2003, July 26-27). Diehards start to get that warm, fuzzy feeling. *The Sydney Morning Herald*, p. 46.

Granovetter, M. S. (1974). *Getting a job: A Study of Contacts and Careers*. Cambridge, MA: Harvard University Press.

Hassel Consultants & Hugo, G. (1996). *Immigration and Public Housing.* Canberra: AGPS.

Hugo, G. (1994). Demographic and spatial aspects of immigration. In M. Wooden, R. Bolton, G. Hugo & J. Sloan (Eds.), *Australian Immigration: A Survey of the Issues (pp.30-110).* Canberra: AGPS.

Human Capital Resource Center (HCRC) (2003). Retrieved from http://www.humancapitalresources.com.

Iredale, R., Fox, C. & Sherlaimoff, T. (1994). *Immigration, Education and Training in New South Wales*. Canberra: AGPS.

Iredale, R., Mitchell, C., Pe-Pua, R., & Pittaway, E. (1996). *Ambivalent Welcome: thesettlement experiences of humanitarian entrant families in Australia.* Canberra: AGPS.

Iredale, R. (2001). The Migration of Professionals: Theories and Typologies. *International Migration, 39,* 7-21.

Junankar, P., Pope, D., Kapuscinaki, C., Ma, G. & Mudd, W. (1993). *Recent Immigrants and Housing*. Canberra: AGPS.

Jupp, J. (1994). *Exile or Refugee?* Canberra: AGPS.

_____ . (2002). *From White Australia to Woomera: The Story of Australian Immigration.* Cambridge: Cambridge University Press.

Khoo, S. (1994). Correlates of Welfare Dependency Among Immigrants in Australia. *International Migration Review*, *26*, 68-92.

Lieberson, S. & Waters, M. (1987). The location of ethnic and racial groups in the United States. *Sociological Forum*, *2*(4), 780-810.

National Population Council (NPC) (1990). *Immigration and Housing in the Major Cities.* Canberra: AGPS.

Pittaway, E. (1991). *Refugee Women–Still at Risk in Australia.* Canberra: AGPS.

Portes, A (1987). One Field, Many Views: Competing Theories of International Migration. In J. Fawcett & B. Carino (Eds.), *Pacific Bridges, The New Immigrants from, Asia and the Pacific Islands (pp. 53-70)*. New York: Center for Migration Studies.

_____ . (1995). Economic Sociology and the Sociology of Immigration: A Conceptual Overview. In A. Portes (Ed.), *Essays on Networks, Ethnicity and Entrepreneurship*. New York: Russell Sage Foundation.

_____ . (1998). Social capital: its origins and applications in modern sociology, *Annual Review of Sociology*, *24(*1), 1-24.

Puls, J. (2000). *The settlement experience of the Bosnian community in Perth*, (Report). Fremantle, WA: South Metropolitan Migrant Resource Centre.

_____ . (2001). *Migrants and refugees and the Job Network: A report on the Job Network experiences of three Western Australian ethnic communities* (Report). Fremantle, WA: South Metropolitan Migrant Resource Centre.

Richardson, S., Miller-Lewis, L., Ngo, P. & Ilsley, D. (2002, August). *The Settlement experiences of New Migrants: A Comparison of Wave One of LSIA 1 and LSIA2.* Adelaide: National Institute of Labour Studies, Flinders University, Adelaide, for DIMIA.

Richmond, A. (1988). *Immigration and Ethnic Conflict.* New York: St. Martin Press.

_____ . (1993). *Global apartheid: refugees, racism, and the new world order.* Toronto: Oxford University Press.

Rose, R. (1994). Postcommunism and the problem of trust. *Journal of Democracy, 5(3)*, 18-30.

RRWG (Refugee Resettlement Working Group). (1994). *Let's Get it Right in Australia.* Sydney: Refugee Resettlement Working Group.

Rumbaut, R. (1991). The Agony of Exile: A Study of the Migration and the Adaptation of Indochinese Refugee Adults and Children. In F. Ahearn & J. Athey (Eds.), *Refugee Children (pp. 53-91).* Washington, D.C.: John Hopkins Series in Contemporary Medicine and Public Health.

Saba (Saba Software Inc.) (2003). Saba human capital development and management solutions. Retrieved from *http://www.humancapitalresources.com*

Sianni, A. (1992). *Shelter for refugees: a new perspective.* Sydney: National Council of Churches.

Stilwell, F. (1987). Immigration Policy: Sound Economic Foundations? *Journal of Australian Political Economy, 21*, 49-65.

Stone W., Gray, M. & Hughes, J. (2003, April). *Social capital at work: How family, friends and civic ties relate to labour market outcomes.* Australian Institute of Family Studies, Research Paper No. 31.

Tingle, L. (2004, February 18). Job Network fiasco exposed. *The Australian Financial Review*, pp.1, 6.

Tonkin, S. (1993). *Initial Location Decisions of Immigrants: Results from the Longitudinal Survey of Immigrants to Australia Pilot.* Bureau of Immigration Research, Canberra: AGPS.

VandenHeuvel A. & Wooden, M. (1999). *New Settlers Have Their Say: How immigrants fare over the early years of resettlement*, The National Institute for Labour Studies, Flinders University of South Australia (for DIMIA).

Viviani, N. Coughlan, J. & Rowland, T. (1993). *Indochinese in Australia: The Issues of Unemployment and Residential Concentration.* Canberra: AGPS.

Waxman, P. (2001). The Economic Adjustment of Recently Arrived Bosnian, Afghan and Iraqi Refugees in Sydney, Australia. *International Migration Review, 35*(2), 472-505.

Whiteford, P. (1991). *Immigrants and the Social Security System.* Canberra: AGPS.

In: Homeland Wanted
Editors: P. Waxman and V. Colic-Peisker, pp. 69-86
ISBN 1-59454-266-X

Chapter 4

REFUGEE RESETTLEMENT AND INTEGRATION IN THE UK

Janet Hannah

ABSTRACT

This chapter presents an overview of current policy and practice of the resettlement and integration of refugees in the UK, and relevant co-ordinated European Union (EU) developments. It is recognised that whilst economic and social integration is the key policy goal of both UK and European policy, it remains a controversial and problematic concept to define and to measure. Empirical evidence of the impact of recent resettlement and integration initiatives, drawing upon a range of sources, is presented, focusing in particular upon refugees' access to, and experience of, education, training and the labour market, as various studies have highlighted its importance in successful resettlement and integration. The implementation of the recently launched *Gateway Protection Programme*, in co-operation with the UNHCR, provides encouraging evidence of the UK's capacity to operate a comprehensive and effective resettlement programme. However, beneficiaries of this programme are very few in number, in comparison with those granted refugee status after arrival in the UK and, for the foreseeable future, this is likely to remain the case.

Key words: migration, asylum, refugees, resettlement, integration

INTRODUCTION

In recent years, migration and asylum issues have assumed a high political profile in the UK and in the European Union, with governments increasingly concerned about how to respond to the growing numbers of people seeking entry to Europe in pursuit of asylum or work. A framework for developing a more coherent approach to managing the provision of support to asylum-seekers and the transition to full refugee status, was launched in November 2000 in a document entitled *"Full and Equal Citizens: a strategy for the integration of refugees into the United Kingdom"*. In February 2002, the UK Home Office produced a White Paper *"Secure Borders, Safe Haven: Integration and Diversity in Modern Britain"*, outlining the government's principles underlying policies on nationality, immigration and asylum. This document represents an attempt, for the first time in the UK, to produce a coherent strategy on these issues, and develop a formal refugee resettlement programme, called *the Gateway Protection Programme*, in co-operation with the United Nations High Commissioner for Refugees (UNHCR). Planned resettlement will, however, affect small numbers of people –up to 500 during the 2003/2004 financial year. This compares with 103,100 applications for asylum lodged in 2002, with 28,405 asylum seekers being granted refugee status or leave to remain (Home Office, 2003). It can reasonably be expected that a significant majority of those eventually granted refugee status in the UK will, for the foreseeable future, have arrived spontaneously as asylum-seekers, and that numbers will not fall dramatically. As Zetter et al. (2003, p. 2) observe: "the growth in asylum seeking is the outcome of a complex set of factors but driven mainly by increased global mobility linked to the increasing incidence of complex humanitarian emergencies".

Both global mobility and complex humanitarian emergencies show little evidence of abating. Instead, both the "push" and "pull" factors are becoming stronger with high levels of social, political and economic instability in the poorest parts of the world, whilst richer countries experience ageing populations and labour shortages in some areas of the labour market. In the UK, the government has launched a series of policy initiatives designed to promote a more coherent and co-ordinated approach to economic migration and asylum. It is now accepted that the economy requires inward migration to meet occupational and regional labour market shortages, and legitimate avenues for migrant workers to fill these are being extended. An implicit assumption is that an expansion in legal routes of entry to the labour market will reduce asylum applications, as those who previously used the asylum system to gain access to the labour market will have less incentive to do so.

Until relatively recently, migration and asylum did not attract much media and political attention. In the 1970s, refugees fleeing the war in Vietnam, and fascist dictatorships in Chile and elsewhere, were generally welcomed, and actively supported by solidarity campaigns. In the mid-1990s, media images of the war-torn former Yugoslavia, and reports of the atrocities committed in that region, facilitated a relatively high level of public sympathy towards those fleeing eastern Europe to seek asylum in the UK, and those resettled here under UNHCR schemes. In contrast, the recent significant growth in the number of asylum-seekers in the UK has attracted considerable negative media attention, with a number of newspapers running sustained campaigns against UK asylum policy, portraying asylum-seekers as economic migrants abusing our national reputation for hospitality and generosity[1]. This hostile campaign reached a crescendo in the period leading up to the closure of the Sangatte refugee reception centre in Calais in December 2002. British people watched nightly television pictures of large groups, of mainly young men, attempting to gain entry to the channel tunnel under cover of darkness, as commentators questioned why asylum-seekers were unwilling to stay in France and prepared to risk so much to enter Britain. The apparent unwillingness of asylum-seekers and the French authorities to adhere to the principle that asylum should be sought in the first "safe" country travelled through further undermined confidence in existing European policy on this issue, which was clearly in disarray.

---

[1] Sensationalist, factually inaccurate newspaper headlines are monitored by the Refugee Council (2004a). These include "Asylum-seekers: 9 out of 10 are conmen" (Daily Star 22 May 2002) and "Britain the No. 1 refugee magnet" (*The Sun* 14 September 2002)

This chapter presents an overview of current policy and practice in relation to the resettlement and integration of refugees in the UK, and relevant recent developments at European Union level. Since the vast majority of refugees in the United Kingdom arrive as asylum seekers, their experience whilst their claims are being processed will have a significant influence upon the integration process and policy in relation to asylum-seekers is therefore also considered. Whilst integration is the key policy goal of both UK and European policy, it is nevertheless a controversial and problematic concept to define and to measure. Measurement requires the adoption of indicators, which are also contentious, and of limited value in the UK as they are not underpinned by comprehensive and systematic data collection. Various studies have highlighted the role of refugees' access to, and experience of, language support, education, training and the labour market in successful resettlement (Audit Commission, 2003; Rudiger and Spencer, 2003). These issues are therefore considered in relation to evolving government policy, particularly in relation to the National Asylum Support Service (NASS) and the policy of regional dispersal.

Evidence is drawn from a range of sources, including official documents and existing research studies, and from a small scale study exploring the provision and experience of technical and vocational education and training for asylum seekers and refugees in Scotland, undertaken by the author in 2002. This preliminary qualitative study explored how the further education sector in Glasgow and Edinburgh was responding to the challenges presented by the arrival of significant numbers of asylum seekers under the national dispersal scheme. Interviews were conducted with key members of college staff responsible for formulating and implementing college policy. English as a Second or Other Language (ESOL) classes for asylum seekers were observed, and interviews with individual asylum seekers and refugees were conducted. As this chapter is concerned with both asylum seekers and refugees, it is important to begin by clarifying how these terms are applied in the UK, and the various categories of protection applied.

Asylum in the UK: Status and Procedures

Refugees being resettled under the *Gateway Protection Programme* have already been accepted by the UNHCR as meeting the criteria for refugee status within the terms of the 1951 Convention on the Status of Refugees. In-country applications for asylum in the UK are dealt with by the Immigration and Nationality Directorate (IND) of the Home Office. After lodging a claim, the applicant is screened, and fingerprints and a photograph are taken, along with personal details. These are then recorded on an Application Registration Card (ARC), issued to the applicant and required to access services. Since January 2003, fingerprints are entered on a European database known as Eurodec. The transfer of documentation between EU member states is facilitated through Dublinet, introduced as part of a package of measures to co-ordinate and manage asylum, discussed further below. In the process of determination of refugee status, a decision is made as to whether another safe country is responsible for considering the application, and if so, the applicant is returned there. If not, the applicant attends a full asylum interview to make his or her case, supported if possible by documentary evidence. The current target is that an initial decision should be reached within two months (Home Office 2004). The decision can take three forms:

1. The applicant is recognised as a refugee under the terms of the 1951 United Nations Convention and granted asylum.
2. The applicant is refused asylum, but it is recognised that there are humanitarian or other reasons for allowing the applicant to stay in this country, and humanitarian protection or discretionary leave for a limited period is granted.
3. The applicant is refused both asylum and humanitarian protection or discretionary leave and must voluntarily leave the country or face deportation.

The first wave of refugees arriving under the *Gateway Protection Programme* arrived in the UK in late 1993. As acknowledged by the Refugee Council, this is a well-planned and co-ordinated initiative involving a number of agencies, including the British Red Cross and the International Rescue Committee, that collectively constitute the *Resettlement Interagency Partnership.* Prior to arrival in the UK, the refugees have been through a "drawn out but well worked out" pre-resettlement process (Refugee Council, 2004b, p.8). In the case of 70, mostly Liberian refugees arriving from camps in Guinea, this began with a mission by Home Office officials to interview applicants, and in some cases also dependents, who had registered applications for resettlement with the UNHCR. Interview results were then used to establish eligibility for the programme, and to check security status. Once eligibility was confirmed, the International Organization of Migration arranged health checks and transportation to the UK, and the group undertook a four-day orientation programme that provided information about life in the UK (ibid.). Since arrival, locally-based support has been provided by the Refugee Council, which has already been sent background information including the refugees' family circumstances, education and work experience, eliminating the need to repeat information already given during extensive pre-arrival questioning. Housing is provided, and support workers are allocated to each household to offer advice and guidance in how to access education, training and employment, health and other services.

Having spent many years living in camps, these refugees might have been expected to experience significant difficulty in adjusting to life in the UK, but this has not commonly been the case. A strong sense of shared identity and group cohesion, and the fact that their homes are located within walking distance of each other, has facilitated resettlement. Most already have a high level of proficiency in English. Refugee Council staff applaud their "positive frame of mind and 'can-do' attitude" (Refugee Council 2004b, p. 8), but recognise that this is facilitated by a complex range of factors not always shared, or made available to, other arrivals to the UK. The compassionate treatment and level of support provided through the *Gateway Protection Programme* is not extended to asylum-seekers. International evidence points to a significant relationship between early experience and the subsequent integration of refugees (Ndofor-Tah et al., 2003), and alienating experiences during the asylum-seeking period, which in the worst cases can last for years, are therefore likely to impede the process of settlement and integration. In a country such as the UK where the vast majority of refugees arrive as asylum-seekers, their experiences during this period are therefore of crucial importance, and the arrangements for the treatment of asylum seekers is considered next.

The National Asylum Support Service (NASS) and the National Dispersal Scheme

Historically, London has been a major destination for successive generations of refugees, and the Audit Commission (2003) estimates that at least 85 per cent of all asylum seekers and refugees who arrive in the UK live in London. As the estimated total UK refugee population is 350,000 (Department of Work and Pensions, 2003), this represents a significant figure. With large, established ethnic minority communities and a buoyant labour market, it is unsurprising that London and the South East is so attractive to migrants. However, increasingly severe housing shortages and an overstretched public sector fuelled the belief that London could no longer cope with such a disproportionate share of the asylum-seeking population, and the government decided to introduce a programme to disperse asylum-seekers throughout the UK whilst their claims are being considered. Responsibility for the co-ordination and implementation of this strategy was given to the National Asylum Support Service (NASS) in the Immigration and Asylum Act of 1999. The establishment of NASS was a significant and decisive step in the development of a coherent and co-ordinated approach to managing support for asylum-seekers in the UK, but the dispersal policy was not universally welcomed and continues to face many challenges to successful implementation.

The operation of NASS must also be understood within the context of the government's drive to minimise the incentives for economic migration, and so too should the development of reception and accommodation centres. Although common across Europe, these centres are a relatively recent development in the UK, and attempts to increase their number are proving controversial and encountering considerable local opposition. Housing inhabitants from application through to initial decision and any subsequent appeal, the centres will offer limited access to educational and recreational facilities, and are presented very positively by the government:

The centres will provide a range of educational and other purposeful activities for all age groups, including ESOL skills and training, volunteering opportunities, sport and creative activities. The aim is that asylum seekers spend their time in the UK productively and are able to develop skills that will be useful either in the UK or if they are expected to return to their home country" (Department of Work and Pensions, 2003, p. 10).

Asylum-seekers had their entitlement to cash benefits under the UK social security system withdrawn in 2000. Instead, they must apply to NASS for accommodation and subsistence support, and eligibility will be determined by taking into account the amount of money or assets at the claimant's disposal. Those with no other means of financial support are provided with an income set at 7 per cent of income support rates that vary according to a person's age or family size. In December 2003, a total of 80,120 asylum seekers were in receipt of NASS support, but 30,360 of these were not in NASS supported accommodation and received subsistence only. It is salient to note that 22,025, (73 per cent) of those in receipt of subsistence-only support were located in London (National Statistics, 2004a). Although there are other contributory factors, this highlights the extent to which significant numbers of asylum seekers are very reluctant to leave London and will refuse accommodation support rather than be relocated.

Before the establishment of the NASS dispersal scheme in 2000, a voluntary initiative was launched in the previous year by the Local Government Association to relieve pressure on London and the South East. Multi-agency consortia, led by local authorities, were established in eight English regions (outside London), Wales and Scotland to co-ordinate arrangements for new arrivals and to identify appropriate accommodation in their area. This scheme struggled on a number of fronts: in the absence of hard information about the numbers and needs of asylum-seekers to be dispersed, local authorities could not predict how much accommodation to bring on stream, what level of support was required or the scale of the long-term financial implications. Some asylum-seekers were sent to areas that could not meet their needs for specialist services such as mental health support (Audit Commission, 2003). However, the experience underlined the crucial importance of a co-ordinated, multi-agency approach and the need to develop more effective partnerships, sharing expertise, information and resources. Multi-agency consortia currently exist in Scotland, Wales, and eight English regions: the North West, Yorkshire and Humberside, the West Midlands, the East Midlands, the North East, the South West, South Central and Eastern England. Typically, these consortia include health authorities, training and employment services, housing providers and voluntary and community groups. Each is expected to: a) develop a strategy for commissioning accommodation and monitoring its quality, b) facilitate liaison and joint working between local agencies providing support, c) promote positive media and public relations and d) co-ordinate services for resettlement and tackle any gaps in services (ibid., p. 21).

Whilst asylum claims are being processed, claimants are not entitled to mainstream UK social security benefits, nor are they entitled to undertake paid work. For asylum seekers accommodated outside the reception and accommodation centres, denied access to the labour market and with limited opportunities to engage in education, daily life can be one of "enforced leisure". Aimlessness and feelings of isolation are compounded for dispersed asylum-seekers, as the following description of the daily life of a Rwandan asylum seeker demonstrates:

> "During the day he is bored; he has to leave his hotel in the morning and spends his days wandering up and down the streets. Although some of the staff at the hotel are friendly, he feels very visible and exposed in the town; people stare at him as if he is from another planet. He is very anxious for news about his missing wife and children, but without any community groups it is hard for him to get news from his country. When, after six months in the UK, he gets the right to work he intends to move back to London to be nearer to other Rwandans" (Audit Commission 2003:8).

As emphasised in this chapter, there is a significant relationship between the early experience of asylum seekers and their subsequent integration as refugees. This is a point made frequently by refugee organisations, and confirmed in an interview conducted by the author in January 2004 with a civil servant involved in the implementation of the employment strategy for refugees:

> The process around what happens initially, and the experience of asylum seekers at the beginning, on entering the country, affects their own perceptions and expectations, and also promotes the public negativity surrounding asylum seekers. The local population can become hostile when they see them hanging around street corners begging, but are usually not aware that asylum seekers are not allowed to work.

Denied the opportunity to be economically active or access education and training beyond some entitlement to language training, asylum seekers have very limited opportunities to practice or develop their skills during this period. Viewed from an economic or human capital perspective, policy and practice in relation to the treatment of asylum seekers therefore appears irrational, and a period of forced inactivity undermines their ease of transition back into the labour market if granted refugee status. If not granted refugee status, it is nevertheless a waste of opportunity to maintain or develop skills that may be useful on return to the country of origin. This benefit is acknowledged by the government in the statement, quoted earlier, on accommodation centres which provide ESOL and training facilities. Whilst physical capital and human capital operate together to secure economic activity and economic growth, it is argued that the presence of a third element – social capital – is also crucial to create the environment in which these can be successfully bound together. Its popularity as a conceptual tool re-emerged in the 1980s, primarily through the work of Coleman (1988) and Putnam (1993; 1995). Whilst it is not difficult to define physical or human capital, social capital poses a challenge as it exists in the relations between people: in the norms, levels of trust and networks that enable people to act collectively. Rooted in "second generation" theories of collective action, social capital theory recognises that "individuals do not live in an atomised world. Many collective-action problems are embedded in pre-existing networks, organisations, or other ongoing relationships among individuals (Ostrom and Ahn, 2003, p. xv). The concept of social capital, with its focus on trust and social and family networks, is therefore relevant to debates about settlement and integration.

Kinship and community networks have been found to be important in the lives of asylum seekers and refugees (Hannah, 1999; Bloch, 2002). In Bloch's study, seventy per cent of respondents attended groups or meetings for refugees. Nearly one-third (31 per cent) of refugees gave their main reason for living in a particular locality as family, 16 per cent because of friends and 10 per cent the existence of a community (Bloch, 2002). Acknowledging the importance of established communities is a welcome feature of the national asylum seekers dispersal scheme, which has learned the lesson that settlement and integration is immensely less stressful if a pre-established community exists. In the words of one Iraqi asylum seeker in Glasgow interviewed by the author in 2002:

> When I was told that I was coming to Glasgow, I was frightened and very upset. I didn't know where Glasgow was, and whether anyone from my country lived here. However, since I arrived, I have made friends with other Iraqi families and we meet regularly to discuss the situation in Iraq. Although the community is much smaller here than in London, we support one another.

He went on to say that it was through fellow Iraqis living in the area that he had become aware of the language classes at the local college. Iraqi friends whose status allowed them to work had also secured part-time jobs in a factory through an Iraqi refugee who was already working there. However, the reliance on friends in finding employment may perpetuate the situation whereby refugees become locked in a cycle of relatively low status, low paid employment (Bloch, 2002). Similarly, the selection of education and training opportunities on the basis of personal recommendation by friends may be narrowing options (Hannah, 1999). In this respect, the use of kinship networks can have potentially negative or limiting consequences. The policy challenge here must be the development of easily accessible sources of comprehensive and impartial advice and guidance. As part of the refugee employment strategy, those granted refugee status receive a fact sheet, translated into 17 languages, detailing the support available from Jobcentre Plus. Staff from this government agency work nationally and locally with other government agencies, voluntary and private sectors to help individuals move from welfare into work, recognising the benefits of working in partnership with refugee and community support groups. Staff are also being trained in cultural awareness, discrimination and valuing diversity (Department of Work and Pensions, 2003).

From a social capital perspective, asylum seekers' relationship with the state is conducted within a framework of low trust. The state's assumption is that a significant number of applicants are "bogus", and the asylum seekers' perception is that the government is seeking to minimise the number of successful claims. If asylum seekers are experiencing resentment or hostility within the communities in which they are located, low trust relations will be compounded. These conditions are ultimately counter-productive to the achievement of the policy goal of integration of refugees. Negative experiences during this period may leave a lasting impression upon individuals' levels of trust, and willingness to engage in, British society. In view of the government's promotion of "citizenship", it would be a cause for concern if, by the time asylum seekers are granted citizenship, their experiences have depleted their levels of trust and reduced their propensity to actively participate in the mainstream community life. However, disillusion with formal political structures and processes need not necessarily result in hopelessness, alienation and withdrawal. Individuals may instead channel their efforts through pressure group politics. Some evidence of this is found in studies showing that, relative to the general population, a high percentage of asylum seekers and refugees engage in voluntary activity (Department of Work and Pensions, 2003). Engagement in voluntary work is actively encouraged by the government, although it is very precisely defined to protect people from being exploited though unpaid work. Each summer, a Purposeful Activities Scheme is funded to encourage asylum seekers to undertake voluntary activity in the communities within which they live (ibid.). A high level of willingness to engage in voluntary activity was found amongst the asylum seekers and refugees who were interviewed by the author in 2002, but was found to be contingent upon the degree of self-confidence, nurtured by high trust relations, in this case with college staff, as well as English language proficiency. In the words of one interviewee:

> It was eighteen months before I was given Exceptional Leave to Remain. During that time, I was so afraid and nervous, and humiliated by my helplessness and dependency. I couldn't have got through that time without the support of people who trusted that I was telling the truth, and did everything they could to help me. Of course, some of these were people from my own community, but they were also the staff at the college where I studied English. They were kind and didn't ask questions – they just wanted to help me, and that made me want to repay their trust. I already spoke some English, but I worked hard, and made progress very quickly. Since then, I've been helping recent arrivals when they need someone they can trust to translate documents, or go with them to the college, the doctor, the lawyer, or wherever… .

The emphasis on trust in this quote underlines its importance in creating the conditions for settlement and integration for this particular refugee, which he then repays and perpetuates through engagement in voluntary activity by helping newcomers who need support from someone they can trust. It would seem reasonable to assume that volunteering may have both human and social capital benefits. It helps to overcome isolation, contributes to the development of networks and may also be looked upon favourably by employers. The most common voluntary activities amongst asylum seekers and refugees are supporting other asylum seekers and minority groups by providing interpretation and translation services, or advice and advocacy (Bloch, 2002). These activities require high levels of English language proficiency and are further discussed below.

Managing migration and asylum in tandem is a key feature of the current government's strategy and policy, and represents a significant recent development in an island with a long history of emigration and immigration. As a member state of the European Union, and one of its key asylum destinations, the UK is part of a wider and increasingly managed European response to asylum and migration issues. Recent developments in the UK must be understood within this context.

The European Context

In November 2000, the European Commission announced the way "towards a common asylum procedure and a uniform status, valid throughout the Union, for persons granted asylum" (European Commission, 2000; Europa, 2004). In April 2001, the Dublin Convention came into force, seeking to put an end to "refugees in orbit" and "asylum shopping". The former refers to the successive transfer of applicants between states without any single stake taking responsibility to determine the claim, whilst the latter refers to multiple, parallel or successive claims in different states (Home Office, 2004). On 1st September 2003, the Dublin II Regulation came into force, providing an agreed framework to determine which member state is responsible for the consideration of asylum claims made in the EU where applicants have travelled between states. However, successive restrictive measures, including the expansion of visa requirements and the fining of airlines carrying passengers without proper documentation, have significantly reduced the opportunities for asylum seekers to arrive spontaneously. Ruud Lubbers, the United Nations High Commissioner for Refugees, raises frequent concerns that European policy is in danger of breaching the 1951 Convention. (*Guardian*, 30 January 2004). Choking off the opportunities to enter legally has fuelled a growth in illegal entry, with criminal gangs organising people smuggling operations in boats and lorries, often with tragic consequences (ibid.).

The need to re-open legal channels for bona fide asylum seekers to apply for refugee status offshore was one of the principles underpinning the Communication "Towards more accessible, equitable and managed asylum systems", adopted by the European Commission on 3 June 2003. This document presents three separate but inter-linked policy objectives for a common EU approach. The first of these is the "protected entry procedure" whereby a claim for international protection can be made at EU embassies overseas, and is being pioneered by Austria, France, the Netherlands, Spain and the UK. Burden and responsibility sharing within the EU as well as other host countries in the regions of origin is the second policy objective. This is intended to reduce the burden on the neighbouring, often impoverished, countries to which asylum-seekers initially flee, but also needs to be understood within the context of the unequal distribution of the resident asylum-seeking population across the EU. In 2002, the total number of asylum seekers resident in the EU, including dependants, was estimated to be 386,100 (Home Office, 2003). The UK received the highest total number of applications: 103,100, whilst Germany received 71,100 and France 58,100. Expressed in terms of applications per 1,000 of the population, however, the UK, at 1.7, lies in sixth place, significantly lower than Austria at the top at 4.9 and Sweden at 3.7. At the opposite end of the scale, Portugal received only 200 asylum applications in 2002. Thus, the desire to share responsibility more evenly is understandable, but to be effective, would require a more harmonised approach to reception and integration. An infrastructure to support refugees would need to be developed in those countries that are currently not significant destinations.

The third and final policy objective of the June 2003 Communication is the development of an integrated approach to efficient and enforceable asylum decision-making and procedures for the deportation of failed applicants. Whilst this has been generally well-received by refugee and human rights groups, an important exception is the proposal for "closed processing centres", in which asylum-seekers would be held whilst their claims were processed and which are being challenged on humanitarian and legal grounds (European Council on Refugees and Exiles, 2004). At both the UK and European level, the intended policy outcome of a more managed and integrated approach to asylum and migration is the successful economic and social integration of migrants and refugees. However, this begs the fundamental question of how integration is to be defined and opens up wider debates about the nature of society, cultural diversity and identity.

Integration, Inclusion or Participation?

Whilst the term integration is commonly used in the literature on migration, there are relatively few attempts to provide a clear definition. As Castles et al. (2002, p.112) observe: "There is no single agreed understanding of the term 'integration'. Meanings vary from country to country, change over time, and depend on the interests, values and perspectives of the people concerned. It is considered by some to be a value-laden and normative concept, implying the existence of a monocultural society with a common set of norms and values, where the incomers are expected to adapt to the existing or mainstream culture and society, without any reciprocal adaptation (Rudiger and Spencer, 2003). However, this raises the question of what kind of society it is that migrants are being integrated into – is it a monocultural or a multicultural society? Are the incomers expected to subordinate or abandon their cultural identity in order to be assimilated into the mainstream, or is the society one in which a variety of communities and identities co-exist and are accorded equal rights? Viewed through this lens, criticisms of the term integration appear valid when applied to monocultural societies with low experience or tolerance of diversity and which operate discriminatory access to political and legal rights. However, it seems less applicable to a multicultural country such as the UK with a non-European population of 4.6 million people from a wide range of diverse ethnic and religious communities. Some evidence that British citizens are comfortable with the expression of dual identity can be found in the results of the 2001 census, in which the majority of Britain's ethnic minority citizens voluntarily describe themselves as "British". (National Statistics, 2004b). The UK is a multicultural society where refugees and asylum seekers come from a wide variety of ethnic, cultural, religious and linguistic backgrounds. It would therefore appear axiomatic to conclude that integration should not be measured against a single, monolithic standard, but needs to recognise the existence within society of various distinct and overlapping social groups which shape individuals' identities, values and priorities. (Woodcock, 1998, p.155).

There is also some, albeit limited, evidence that a significant number of refugees (65 per cent) see “Britain as home” (Bloch, 2002). Whilst this varied by country of origin, those who cited “the different way of life” as a reason for not seeing Britain as home were disproportionately female and unable to speak English. Nearly three-quarters (74 per cent) of those who spoke English fluently saw Britain as home, compared to 57 per cent who did not speak any English (ibid.). This would appear to support the contention that language proficiency is a major determinant of effective settlement, as discussed below.

Perhaps a more salient criticism of the term integration is its implication of passivity, with the incomer cast as lacking agency. As integration has fallen out of favour for its alleged negative connotations, alternative terms, particularly inclusion and participation are commonly used in preference (Rudiger and Spencer, 2003; Castles et al., 2002), and have the advantage of being consistent with social inclusion as a policy goal throughout the EU:

> Inclusion refers to how immigrants and refugees have access to, use, participate in, benefit from and feel a sense of belonging to a given area of society. Inclusion is a useful concept for policy formation, because it helps indicate what specific authorities or agencies can do in their own areas of responsibility (Castles et al., 2002, p. 115)

However, the term inclusion, like integration, may be alleged to imply a passive role for the incomer. The term participation has more active connotations and is therefore increasingly employed by NGOs and community groups. Integration is nevertheless the term still used by policy-makers at a UK and European level and is therefore adopted in the remainder of this chapter when discussing UK and EU policy and practice. Evaluation of the extent to which integration is taking place and the impact of policy interventions, cannot proceed without addressing the questions of: integration into what, and how should it be measured? However, just as there are conceptual problems in defining integration, so too are there problems in identifying indicators of integration.

Indicators of Integration

The UK is a relative newcomer to attempts to define and implement an integration strategy, and, as such, is looking to the experience of countries like Australia and Canada for direction (Ndofor-Tah et al., 2003). Fundamental to the efforts of both of these countries is the existence of longitudinal databases that systematically gather the information to which the indicators can be applied. The establishment and maintenance of such databases is a large and costly undertaking, but provide rich sources of quantitative and qualitative data. Recognising the desirability of such data in the UK, the government is currently considering the establishment of a longitudinal survey. The Longitudinal Survey of Immigrants to Australia (LSIA) is a sample survey of a recent time selection of immigrants to Australia. Information is gathered through personal interviews undertaken in approximately sixty languages, with three hundred questions asked. Canada draws data from two databases. The first is the Immigration Database (IMDB), which provides information about the characteristics of individuals at arrival: for example, levels of education, French or English language proficiency, age, martial status and occupation or intended occupation. The second is the longitudinal tax filer database that provides comprehensive information about the financial situation of individuals and has three waves: at six, twenty-four and forty-eight months after arrival in Canada (ibid.).

The settlement indicators have been developed out of the Australian LSIA and can be broadly characterised in relation to two types of participation: social and economic, and two types of well-being: economic and physical. Social participation is measured by English language proficiency, participation in education by young adults and Australian citizenship. Economic participation is measured by labour force activity, employment status and job satisfaction, whilst physical well-being is measured by instances of long term health problems, stress levels and general health. Whilst these generic measures would appear reasonable, there is always a danger in applying a monolithic standard or norm which takes no account of cultural and other differences between different groups of immigrants. For example, levels of female labour force activity will vary amongst groups and low levels cannot automatically be assumed to represent a "failure" to integrate. The most commonly used indicators, such as those adopted in the Canadian and Australian longitudinal studies, seek to measure socio-economic status. Cultural indicators can also be developed and include the extent to which different religious needs are accommodated and rates of inter-marriage, as it is assumed that these are indicative of the breaking down of barriers between communities. However, it is important to recognise the lack of linearity between various indicators, as the case of inter-marriage and socio-economic status illustrates. The inter-marriage rate for men in Britain is highest for black Caribbeans (38 per cent) and lowest for Indians (7 per cent). However, the economic position of these two groups and their experience of equal treatment is completely the reverse (Rudiger and Spencer, 2003, p.14). As Castles et al. argue (2002, p. 130):

> Undue emphasis on a limited number of indicators (such as employment, residential concentration or rates of criminality) may lead to misleading results. It is essential to use an integration framework based on a wide range of indicators. Moreover, such indicators should not be set in a top-down way by government agencies, but should rather be the result of consultations including a range of community groups, and spokespersons for immigrant and refugee communities.

Whilst recognising this cautionary note, various studies have highlighted the importance of language proficiency and access to education, training and the labour market in refugee resettlement (Audit Commission, 2002; Rudiger and Spencer, 2002), and this is considered in the following section.

Language Proficiency, Education, Training and the Labour Market

Various UK studies have concluded that command of the host nation's language is the single most significant factor affecting settlement and integration generally, and access to education, training and the labour market in particular (Africa Educational Trust 1998; Schellekens, 2001; Audit Commission, 2003). This is consistent with a number of international studies (Department for Immigration and Multicultural Affairs 1999, Iredale et al., 1996; European Council on Refugees and Exiles, 2000; Department for Work and Pensions, 2003). A 2001 study of 400 refugees and asylum seekers found that, overall, twenty-nine per cent had been involved in voluntary work in Britain, but this ranged from more than fifty per cent of fluent English speakers who had done so compared with eleven per cent who spoke no English (Bloch, 2002). Language proficiency would therefore appear to be a key factor in the promotion of both social and human capital, as discussed above. Other studies have highlighted the difficulties and frustration that migrants, refugees and asylum seekers experience when they are unable to communicate (Hannah, 2001).

In *"Secure Borders, Safe Haven: Integration with Diversity in Modern Britain"*, English language acquisition, and the promotion of citizenship encompassing the exercise of political rights and social engagement, is given particular significance:

> It is a fundamental objective of the Government that those living permanently in the UK should be able, through adequate command of the language and an appreciation of our democratic processes, to take their place fully in society (2001, p. 32).

Possession of an "adequate" command of English, demonstrated by passing a test, will be required of applicants who apply for naturalisation (Home Office, 2002). However, not all refugees and asylum-seekers plan to resettle permanently in the UK or another English-speaking country but hope to return to their home country when circumstances allow. In this case, the degree of proficiency sought is likely to be different to that of someone who expects to live a long time in the UK or to resettle permanently. The English language and numeracy skills which migrants, refugees and asylum seekers will perceive themselves to have will be also be influenced by other factors including social class, level of literacy in the mother tongue, previous education and occupational background and economic and social aspirations whilst in the UK.

Entitlement to, and the ability to access, English language tuition for asylum seekers and refugees currently remains highly variable and problematic in the UK, as highlighted in a Home Office-commissioned scoping study into the provision of ESOL in London and the asylum seeker dispersal regions (Griffiths 2003. Provision is concentrated mainly in the further education sector, although independent providers are also significant. Courses are generally free or low cost and many are offered on an outreach basis. However, there is a general shortage of classes in London and the dispersal regions, and long waiting lists are common. In some regions, there is a severe shortage of qualified ESOL teachers (ibid.). In another study, the Audit Commission found several authorities with waiting lists of over 200 people, and concluded that: "consortia need to consider how local provision can be developed to meet growing demand" (2003, p.74). Levels of co-ordination between the various providers and between providers and refugee community organisations also vary across the regions. There is some evidence that not only the quantity, but also the quality of ESOL provision, is variable. A study of 236 skilled refugees in London found that over one-third of those who received language training were dissatisfied with the support that they received, primarily because courses were too short, particularly in the early stages when English language proficiency was non-existent or poor (Peabody Trust/LRC 1999). Of course, individual needs vary enormously. This highlights the need for appropriate initial diagnostic assessment of literacy and language (and numeracy) needs, and the flexibility for provision to adapt to individual circumstances. Recognition of the importance of identifying and responding to individual learner needs was high in the Further Education colleges visited by the author in autumn 2002. Teaching methods and appropriate learning support was also identified as key, but somewhat problematic, by an ESOL lecturer:

(Bloch, 2002; NIACE, 2001; Greater London Authority, 2002). These suggest that the most significant barriers are: language competence, recognition of existing qualifications and lack of information and advice. The problem with recognition of qualifications is being addressed on a number of fronts: providing more information about the comparability of qualifications for employers, negotiating recognition with professional bodies, and providing bridging and specialist courses for professionals. Specific projects to provide training opportunities to enable the qualifications for refugee doctors, nurses and teachers to be recognised have been launched in recent years in the UK, at least partly inspired by the need to address skill shortages in these occupations. The Race Relations Amendment Act of 2000 also places an obligation upon public authorities to promote equality and cohesion in employment and promotion policy as well as service delivery. The employment of refugees and other migrants clearly has a contribution to make in achieving these employment objectives, and also promoting more inclusive service delivery by utilising their language skills and cultural understanding.

Raising employer awareness in the private sector would appear to be more challenging, and whilst a lack of awareness of qualifications is an important issue, so too is a fear of breaking the law if an employee turns out to be "illegal". Whilst few employers would be willing to state it publicly, hostile media attention would appear to be an additional factor. In an interview with the author, a civil servant involved in the refugee employment strategy reported that feedback from refugee organisations highlighted the fact that, often, "Employers don't want to shout about the fact that they are employing refugees. It isn't seen as good for their image". In recent years, refugee support organisations have increased their efforts to make employers more aware of the positive benefits of employing refugees, stressing their quite exceptional combination of qualities and experience. There may, however, be some drawbacks to this emphasis. As a refugee has cautioned, "It can seem like there is a pressure on refugees to justify their existence by out-performing the indigenous population. But refugees have a right to be here and they have a right to be ordinary" (Refugee Council, 2001).

Conclusion

There are few who would dispute that the aim to provide a safe, welcoming and enabling environment in which refugees can resettle successfully and achieve their potential, is not only in the interest of refugees but also of the host country. This chapter has explored current policy and practice in relation to the resettlement of refugees and the treatment of asylum seekers in the UK, taking account of recent developments in the European Union. These must be understood within the context of the intended policy outcome of a more managed and integrated approach to asylum and migration, and the successful economic and social integration of migrants and refugees. The implementation of the recently launched *Gateway Protection Programme*, in co-operation with the UNHCR, provides encouraging evidence of the UK's capacity to operate a comprehensive and effective resettlement programme. However, beneficiaries of this programme are very few in number in comparison with those granted refugee status after arrival in the UK and, for the foreseeable future, this is likely to remain the case. Thus, the experience of asylum-seekers remains of critical importance in creating the conditions for the successful resettlement of the majority of the UK's refugees.

_____ . 2000. Education, training and adult refugees in the UK and Australia in Field, J and Leicester, M (eds.) *Lifelong Learning: Education across the Lifespan* London: Routledge 174-190

Home Office 2000. *Full and Equal Citizens: A strategy for the integration of refugees into the United Kingdom.* London: Home Office.

_____ . 2002 .*Secure Borders: Safe Haven: Integration and Diversity in Modern Britain* London: HMSO CM 5387.

_____ . 2003. *Control of Immigration: Statistics United Kingdom, 2003.* Retrieved 4 January 2004 at homeoffice.gov.uk/rds/pdfs2/hosb1003.pdf

_____ . 2004. *Immigration and Nationality Directorate Fact Sheet – Asylum Policy,* retrieved 5 January 2004 at http://www.ind.homeoffice.gov.uk/default.asp?PageId=3659

Iredale R, Mitchell C, Pe-Pua R and Pittaway E. 1996. *Ambivalent Welcome: the settlement experiences of humanitarian entrant families in Australia.* Canberra: Bureau of Immigration, Multicultural and Population Research.

National Institute for Adult and Continuing Education (NIACE) 2001. *Asylum Seekers' Skills and Qualifications Audit Pilot Project* Leicester: NIACE

National Statistics (2004a) UK Asylum Statistics 2003. 4th Quarter London: Home Office National Statistics (2004b) *Focus on Ethnicity and Identity.* Retrieved on 21 January 2004 at http://www.statistics.gov.uk/focuson/ethnicity

Ndofor-Tah, C., Clery, L. & Makarewich-Hall, J. 2003. *UK National Integration Conference: an evidence-based approach to integration.* Retrieved 5 January 2004 at http://www.homeoffice.gov.uk/rds.index.html

Ostrom, E. & Ahn, T.K. (eds.) 2003. *Foundations of Social Capital.* Cheltenham: Elgar Peabody Trust/London Research Centre 1999.

Refugee Skills-Net. *The Employment and Training of Skilled and Qualified Refugees,* Peabody Trust/LRC, June 1999.

Putnam, R. 1993. The Prosperous Community: Social Capital and Public Life, *American Prospect*, 13, Spring, 35-42

_____ . 1995. Tuning In, Tuning Out: The Strange Disappearance of Social Capital in America, *PS: Political Science and Politics*, XXVIII (4) December, 664-83

Refugee Action and the International Organisation for Migration 2002. *Supporting the Somali Community in West London.* London: Refugee Action

Refugee Council 2001. Life and Livelihood: reclaiming a future in*exile* August 2001 London: Refugee Council

_____ . 2004a. *News: Press Myths.* Retrieved 8 January 2004 at http://www. refugeecouncil.org.uk/news/myths/myth001.htm

_____ . 2004b. Gateway to a Future *inexile* May 2004 London: Refugee Council

Rudiger, A. & Spencer, S. 2003. *Social Integration of Migrants and Ethnic Minorities: Policies to Combat Discrimination.* Paper presented to The Economic and Social Aspects of Migration conference organised by the European Commission and the OECD

Schellekens, P. 2001. *English as a Barrier to Employment, Education and Training.* London: DFEE Research Brief RBS3/01

Woodcock, M. 1998. Social capital and economic development: Toward a theoretical synthesis and policy framework *Theory and Society* 27: 151-208

Zetter, R., Griffiths, D., Ferretti, S & Pearl, M. 2003. *An assessment of the impact of asylum policies in Europe 1990-2000.* Home Office Research Study 259. London: Home Office Research, Development and Statistics Directorate.

In: Homeland Wanted
Editors: P. Waxman and V. Colic-Peisker, pp. 87-107 ISBN 1-59454-266-X

Chapter 5

THE ROLE OF BRIDGING SOCIAL NETWORKS IN REFUGEE SETTLEMENT: THE CASE OF EXILE COMMUNITIES FROM THE FORMER YUGOSLAVIA IN ITALY AND THE NETHERLANDS[1]

Maja Korac

ABSTRACT

The chapter examines how different refugee settlement policies in Italy and the Netherlands affect the process of formation of social networks within and outside a group of compatriots. I explore the social condition of exile communities from the former Yugoslavia and examine how different policy interventions, intentionally and unintentionally, affect micro-level social interactions in these specific settlement contexts. Data for this study were collected during several months of ethnographic fieldwork in Rome (1999-2000) and Amsterdam (2000-2001). The discussion aims to emphasise the connection between specific policy contexts, structural constraints they embody, and the type of human agency they engender. Special emphasis is placed on the examination of the role of 'bridging social networks' established outside the refugee group, which seem to facilitate considerably the successful integration of refugees. I suggest that although governments cannot directly affect the formation of bridging social capital, it is possible to develop policies that facilitate it. Without such policies, integration remains plagued by relative social isolation, even when there are employment opportunities and relaxed naturalisation policies.

Keywords: settlement, social networks, integration policies, refugee experiences, social capital.

---

[1] This chapter is based upon some findings of my research entitled 'Dilemmas of Integration: Two policy contexts and refugee strategies for integration', carried out at the Refugee Studies Centre, University of Oxford, between 1999 and 2001. The research was funded by the Lisa Gilad Initiative, the European Commission through the European Council for Refugees and Exiles, as well as The British Council, The Heyter Travel Fund, and The Oppenheimer Fund. The Lisa Gilad Initiative is a charitable trust, set up in 1998, to commemorate the life and work of the late Lisa Gilad, an anthropologist and a founding member of Canada Immigration and Refugee Board.

INTRODUCTION

Refugee settlement has become a much-debated issue in the past decades. Problems of integration are both conceptual and practical, as the term has been defined differently and policies aiming at facilitating settlement developed in a variety of ways (Castles *et al.*, 2003; Robinson, 1998). Although the reception and integration policies of European states vary widely, from the highly centralised state-sponsored programmes, to the provision of minimal and decentralised assistance, a prevailing concern within the EU has been how to facilitate the decision-making process on asylum claims and how to meet the immediate and pressing needs of refugees. Moreover, there is a growing tendency to establish specialised reception centres for the newly arrived (European Commission, 2001). The effects of policy approaches for the settlement of those who are granted asylum are seldom posed, despite a growing realisation among the researchers and practitioners working with refugees that such policies may effectively facilitate their social isolation and stigmatisation.

While it is understandable and important that the policy focuses on the initial phase of refugee settlement, this approach fails to address some other, equally important aspects of long-term integration. It neither acknowledges the fact that the initial and later phases of settlement are interrelated and that the needs of refugees are complex and long-term (Duke *et al.*, 1999), nor the need to build initial conditions for the establishment of bridging social networks in receiving societies (Korac, 2003a). If any policy concerns have been centred on creating conditions for the development of social ties and connections of refugees in receiving societies, such policy initiatives put emphasis on the development of 'ethnic' ties within communities.

The emphasis on the establishment of refugee community organisations (RCOs), and therefore on the development of connections and social networks among compatriots, is linked to two main developments within the European context. First, a lack of sufficient service provision for asylum seekers and refugees in many EU states is increasingly transforming community organisations into alternative service providers (Joly, 1996; Bloch, 2002). Second, in many European states, refugee and migrants' associations are regarded as important for maintaining links with the native culture as well as for 'voicing' the needs and interests of specific groups within the multicultural milieu of receiving societies (Eastmond, 1998). The former process and the establishment of 'ethnic networks' in receiving societies are considered as essential at the early stages of settlement, They provide refugees with emotional support, and a sense of roots and continuity (Gold, 1992; Joly, 1996; Eastmond, 1998; Bloch 2002).

While it is believed that refugee associations are also important for establishing links with the mainstream society and for overcoming social isolation, the establishment of formal (refugee associations), and informal ('ethnic' networks) connections among compatriots does not necessarily increase co-operation within the receiving society. Volunteering at their local community organisation or spending time at their house of worship or any other type of involvement with their ethnic community may be beneficial for refugees and their community, but spending time with 'people like ourselves', as Dekker and Uslaner (2001, p. 7) remark, cannot spread social trust. They emphasise that the development of trust 'come when we put our faith in people who are different from ourselves' (ibid.).

Social capital theory and its emphasis on the value of social networks is a useful framework for addressing problems of refugee integration. Social capital, as Dekker and Uslaner (2001, p. 3) noted, is about the value of social networks through which we bond with similar people and build bridges between diverse groups and individuals. Putnam (2000) introduced the concept of 'bridging social capital' to emphasise its potential to generate broader identities and reciprocity as opposed to 'bonding social capital' which 'bolsters our narrower selves' (pp. 22-23). He pointed out that 'bonding and bridging are not "either-or" categories' (ibid., p. 23). Rather, 'many groups simultaneously bond along some social dimensions and bridge across others' (Putnam 2000, p. 23). Consequently, an approach to integration that puts emphasis on the formation of bridging social capital does not imply abandonment of 'ethnic' roots and native cultures.

Bridging social networks facilitate the access of refugees to the types and quality of societal resources that are otherwise not readily available to them. These networks should be regarded as complex formations that 'channel, filter, and interpret information, articulate meanings, allocate resources, and control behaviour' (Fernárdez Kelly, 1995, p.219). Opportunities to integrate thus depend 'not only on the availability of material and intangible assets in the society at large but also on the way in which interpersonal contacts shape information and relate to structures of opportunity' (ibid.).

Building connections between the refugees and the established community is an essential pre-requisite for the formation of social capital in multicultural societies, as these connections increase trust and reduce racism and xenophobia.[2] In addressing the problems of trust and the related boundary formation in receiving societies, it is important to explore how micro-level social interactions between people in specific settlement settings and policy contexts occur, and to examine their character. It is also vital to investigate how such interactions affect the process of change and adaptation of refugees.

BRIDGING SOCIAL NETWORKS IN THE PROCESS OF REFUGEE SETTLEMENT

The recognition that settlement of refugees is shaped and constrained by governmental policies and cultural norms of the receiving societies informed this comparative study (cf. McSpadden, 1999, p. 244). The Netherlands and Italy have been chosen for comparison because they represent two contrasting policy models of admission, reception and integration of refugees. The Dutch system is state controlled and embedded in a 'welfare model' of assisting refugees, while the Italian model is chaotic, lacking an overarching strategy and is embedded in an *ad hoc* approach to refugee assistance. The refugee populations I studied in the two countries come from the former Yugoslavia and are of a similar background; their social upbringing is embedded in the shared socio-economic system of their country of origin, educational system, system of values, and some elements of shared traditions and culture. It was envisaged that the policy and country contexts of the receiving societies affect how this 'accumulated set of conditions of life' (Bourdieu, 1984) position the refugee towards others.

2 The term 'host' community is not used in the text, as 'it suggests welcome that is not always present' (for more on this issue of terminology see Van Hear, 1998, p. 55).

Refugees usually bring with them considerable human capital, such as education and skills, and most of them are also of working age. However, they lack social capital, or networks, not only within their own ethnic group but more importantly in the wider society, which limits their ability to make use of their human capital. It is through these ties and networks, 'ethnic' as well as 'mainstream', that refugees experience their new social environment; understand it and adjust their attitudes and behaviour.

It is often argued that the establishment of 'bridging social networks' outside the group of compatriots emerges at later stages of refugee settlement, in the work-place and area of residence or in associations and clubs frequented by members of the established community. The establishment of these 'mainstream' social networks, it is emphasised, depends on the aim and objectives of migration (Robinson, 1986; Bloch, 2002). If refugees consider their stay as temporary, they may be less prone to engage in creating bridging social networks, and hence unwilling to undergo the process of adjustment necessary for their full participation in the receiving society. Consequently, they will be less willing to reshape their identity (Weiner, 1996, p. 52-53).

Willingness of immigrants to integrate, as Weiner (1996) points out, is indeed an important determinant of integration, as are the willingness and ability of the receiving society to absorb them, through the labour market participation and naturalisation. The question remains, however, what is the connection between this structural and institutional integration and the character of micro-level social interactions between people in specific settlement settings and policy contexts? If refugees are employed, naturalised and willing to engage in the process of adjustment, can they be considered integrated? More importantly, do they consider themselves socially included and no longer isolated? What makes them feel that they are full participants and that they belong?

The central question concerning the willingness of newcomers to integrate, according to Weiner (1996), is what are the incentives for them 'to adopt behavioural patterns that make them more *acceptable to the host population*?' (p. 54; emphasis added). There is no doubt that integration involves reshaping of identities and sometimes also a change in patterns of an individual's behaviour to make such behaviour more congruent with the culture of the receiving society. However, the discussion in this chapter calls for a shift in attention away from the notion of integration as a 'top-down' process, based on the assumption that refugees have to change in order to 'fit in' and become 'acceptable' to the receiving society. This approach implies hierarchy and opposition of cultures and considers refugees as having 'immature social identities' who therefore have to be re-educated in order to be integrated (Knudsen, 1991). Knudsen (1991, p. 34) argues that this kind of approach tends to remain within the structural framework of a minority situation. Is there a way to overcome this minority situation framework?

Establishing bridging social networks at the micro-level may be part of the answer to this question. I argue that bridging social networks can emerge at a relatively early stage of integration in a policy context that provides refugees with an opportunity and need for fast mobilisation of resources as these networks facilitate functional integration of refugees, ranging from fostering acquisition of language skills, re-training and employment. Furthermore, I suggest that when the process of building bridging social networks emerges early in settlement, these ties provide the basis for the development of mutual trust. Experience of refugees embedded in such social contacts and ties becomes central to their openness toward the receiving society, its culture and customs. When such interpersonal, informal communication exists, refugees are less likely to feel threatened and in need for 'entrenching a symbolic boundary' (Bauböck, 1996) between themselves and the established community — and vice versa.

In addition, the existence of bridging social ties and networks can, in specific circumstances, compensate for the dissatisfaction of refugees with some aspects of their settlement, such as underemployment and consequently the lack of a desired social status. I argue that although governments cannot directly affect the formation of bridging social capital, it is possible to develop policy approaches that create initial conditions for the establishment of micro-level networks between the refugees and the established community. Without such policies integration remains plagued by relative social isolation. Without bridging social networks, social isolation persists even when there are employment opportunities and relaxed naturalisation policies.

The main aim of this chapter is to contribute to a debate about the integration of refugees in receiving societies by examining the role of social networks in the process of settlement. While the economic adjustment of refugees is a critical determinant of settlement, and citizenship is the ultimate symbol of full participation in the receiving society, there are many more, subtle components and mechanisms affecting successful integration of individuals and groups. In this chapter, I focus on some of these less readily visible mechanisms that facilitate the ability of refugees to make sense of the 'rules' underpinning social structures and societal relations in the new society, and thus enable their successful adjustment. The analysis also includes the interpretation or meanings that refugees themselves attach to the networks they belong to or aspire to create. The remainder of this chapter is divided into three parts. First, I outline the methodology. Then I provide an account of the social conditions of refugees from the former Yugoslavia in Amsterdam and Rome, and discuss development of social networks and their effect on their settlement outcomes. The concluding section summarises findings and implications of this research.

METHODOLOGY

This chapter is based on qualitative data collected during several months of ethnographic fieldwork in Rome (1999-2000) and Amsterdam (2000-2001), where there was a considerable concentration of refugees from the former Yugoslavia. Integration is a process that can take a lifetime, so it is important to specify the time span to be examined. This study examined the situation of refugees from the post-Yugoslav states who arrived in Italy and the Netherlands between 1991 and 1995. It was considered that after six to ten years in exile these people were able to come to terms with some of their losses, to refine the perception of their situation in Italian/Dutch society, and to formulate their goals. My research focused on individuals rather than groups, because refugees are considered to be agents who are actively involved in reconstructing their lives in exile. It was envisaged that the analysis of individual cases and experience of exile would point to the factors that facilitate or hinder interaction within and outside the group of compatriots and the role of such interaction(s) in the process of settlement as defined by refugees themselves.

Qualitative methods were used in this study for several reasons. Their use is linked to a critical view of a 'top-down' approach to integration adopted in this study and its aim to give refugees a 'voice'. Qualitative interviewing is considered as an important way of learning from refugees, and crucial in addressing the problem of 'asymmetry of power and voice' between the state and the refugees (Indra, 1993). Robinson (1998, p. 122) argued that 'since integration is individualised, contested and contextual it requires qualitative methodologies which allow the voices of respondents to be heard in an unadulterated form.' Qualitative methods help to avoid treating refugee subjects as 'data-gathering' objects.

This study does not aim to produce ambitious generalisations. Rather, it seeks to offer insights into the complexity of the settlement process based on an in-depth knowledge of a small 'slice' of reality. The empirical relevance of this research is enhanced by its comparative nature and its focus on the refugees from a single country of origin in two different cultural and policy contexts.

Contacts with the NGO sector, statutory agencies and community organisations in Italy and the Netherlands assisted in identifying refugees for interviewing. Informal contacts I was able to make with the refugees in Rome and Amsterdam were important in establishing a relationship of trust. The fact that I am originally from the former Yugoslavia and can speak their language and to some extent share their cultural background as well as their experience of life 'outside homeland' facilitated this.

During the fieldwork in Rome and Amsterdam, I established around 180 informal contacts with refugees from the former Yugoslavia (around 120 and 60 informal contacts respectively). These contacts were useful for collecting general information about their situation in Italy and the Netherlands. As these interactions were usually not on one-to-one basis and, therefore, not suitable for collecting more personal data, I chose 40 refugees in Rome and 20 in Amsterdam for formal, in-depth interviewing. In addition, I tried, as much as possible, to share day-to-day lives with refugees in both study-sites and made every effort to participate in their social life. When the circumstances permitted, I visited them at work, at home, and took part at many social gatherings involving my respondents and their friends, who were either also refugees or people they met in exile. This enabled me to gain a more in-depth understanding of their social situation.

The principal concern in selecting interviewees for this study was to ensure they come from different networks in order to cover a variety of refugee situations. I sought to interview refugees of different age, gender, ethnicity, marital status, parental status, education, region and place of residence before flight. The profile of my sample reflects the characteristics of the refugee population from the former Yugoslavia in the two cities. Tables 1 and 2 show the social characteristics and legal status of the refugees interviewed.

As shown in the tables, refugees in Amsterdam were older and of moderately lower educational level than those in Rome. Most importantly, however, practically all refugees in Rome were employed except for a few young adults still living with their parents. Furthermore, refugees in Rome were overwhelmingly single or cohabiting, without children, and without family networks in Italy. In Amsterdam, parents or siblings of the overwhelming majority of those who were single were also refugees in the Netherlands. While intermarriage or cohabitation with native population was present in the group in Rome it did not exist among my interviewees in Amsterdam. Finally, the overwhelming majority of interviewees in Amsterdam had Dutch citizenship, while the majority of those interviewed in Rome still had temporary, humanitarian refugee status.

Table 1. Social Characteristics and Legal Status of the Interviewees in Amsterdam

Characteristics	Number	Percentage
Age		
20 to 30	6	30
31 to 40	6	30
41 to 50	4	20
over 50	4	20
Total	*20*	*100*
Gender		
Female	9	45
Male	11	55
Total	*20*	*100*
Marital status		
Single	6	30
Married	11	55
To Dutch		0
To their compatriots	11	
Cohabiting		0
Divorced	3	15
From Dutch	0	
From their compatriots	3	
Total	*20*	*100*
Parental status		
Single with children	0	0
Married with children	11	55.0
Cohabiting with children	0	0
Divorced with children	3	15.0
Total	*14 out of 20*	*or 70 out of 100*
Educational level acquired in the home country		
Elementary level	0	0
High or Secondary level	7	35
University degree	7	35
Interrupted by war	6	30
Education continued or vocational training taken	6	
Did not continue	0	
Total	*20*	*100*
Time of arrival		
1991	1	5
1992	3	15
1993	7	35
1994	3	15
1995	3	15
1996	0	0
1997	3	15
Total	*20*	*100*

Table 1. Social Characteristics and Legal Status of the Interviewees in Amsterdam (Continued)

Characteristics	Number	Percentage
Legal status		
Convention ('A') status	0	0
Humanitarian ('C') status	2	10
Provisional permit to stay ('F' status)	1	5
Dutch citizenship	17	85
Total	*20*	*100*
Current labour market status		
Employed	8	40
Casual contracts	2	10
Study	5	25
Unemployed	5	25
Total	*20*	*100*

Table 2. Social Characteristics and Legal Status of the Interviewees in Rome

Characteristics	Number	Percentage
Age		
20 to 30	15	37.5
31 to 40	17	42.5
41 to 50	7	17.5
over 50	1	2.5
Total	*40*	*100*
Gender		
Female	21	52.5
Male	19	47.5
Total	*40*	*100*
Marital status		
Single	19	47.5
Married	10	25.0
To Italians	4	
To their compatriots	6	
Cohabiting	10	25.0
With Italians	2	
With their compatriots	8	
Divorced	1	2.5
From Italians	0	
From their compatriots	1	
Total	*40*	*100*

Table 2. Social Characteristics and Legal Status of the Interviewees in Rome (Continued)

Characteristics	Number	Percentage
Parental status		
Single with children	0	0
Married with children	6	15.0
Cohabiting with children	0	0
Divorced with children	1	2.5
Total	*7 out of 40 or*	*17.5 out of 100*
Educational level acquired in the home country		
Elementary level	0	0
High or Secondary level	7	17.5
University degree	16	40.0
Interrupted by war	17	42.5
Education continued or vocational training taken	13	
Did not continue	4	
Total	*40*	*100*
Time of arrival		
1991	9	22.5
1992	17	42.5
1993	12	30.0
1994	0	0
1995	2	5.0
Total	40	100
Legal status		
Humanitarian status	22	55.0
Work permit	13	32.5
Italian citizenship or permit to stay for family reasons	5	12.5
Total	*40*	*100*
Current labour market status		
Employed	28	70
Work and study	7	17.5
Only study	5	12.5
Unemployed	0	0
Total	*40*	*100*

Refugee Accounts on Reconstructing Lives in the Netherlands and Italy

Following the 'Integration' Rules in the Netherlands

The Dutch model of refugee integration is based on a number of measures and interventions by the state intended to meet the immediate needs of refugees and to facilitate their gradual structural and institutional integration in Dutch society. The main goal of the Dutch integration policy is to 'activate citizenship' by enhancing the opportunity of individual migrants to exercise responsibility involved in membership/citizenship in Dutch society (Lechner, 2000). The emphasis on responsibility leads to a contractual relationship between refugee/immigrant and the government/municipality, as the basis of the policy. The rights and obligations of both parties are guaranteed. The government/municipality is obliged to provide an integration programme, including language and re-training courses; the newcomer is obliged to complete the programme successfully within a specified period. If the newcomer fails to meet requirements stipulated in the contract/policy, the government might reduce his/her social security benefits or penalise those who receive income from other sources.

The Dutch integration policy is embedded in the country's well-developed welfare system and provides a considerable level of social services for refugees. The system is therefore favourable for those fleeing with children and the elderly. However, to protect the welfare system from abuse, the government introduced restrictive admission and reception policies, which have affected the process of integration of refugees. At the time of my research (2000-2001), those seeking asylum in the country usually experienced a two-stage admission and reception procedure involving a stay of up to 48 hours in an investigation centre (OC), and a several months long stay in an asylum centre (AZC). For some, in cases when a provisional permit to stay ('F' status) was granted, the reception procedure involved a third stage. This stage usually lasted up to three years and involved provision of housing and a modest allowance, but no provision directed at integration into Dutch society, such as compulsory language training, the right to re-train and work. This phased, state-led settlement process may therefore last for years. A relatively relaxed naturalisation policy at the time, meant, however, that most of those who were allowed to stay in the country could obtain Dutch citizenship relatively shortly after this period.

Although the national government devises integration policy, the local municipalities and the NGO sector implement it 'on the ground'. The Dutch NGO sector, whose work with refugees goes back to the 1970s, is well-developed and funded, although traditionally it relies heavily on volunteers. The 1990s, however, were characterised by a tendency to increase the involvement of professionals in work with refugees.[3] Due to the organisational and financial capacity of these organisations, as well as the responsibilities that individual immigrants have toward the Dutch state to 'integrate', my respondents were in continuous contact with a variety of service providers who were leading them through the 'integration' process. Consequently, they did not have to engage in any kind of intensive networking within or outside their ethnic group in order to settle in the city.

The contacts with service providers started during the refugees' stay in reception centres (from several months to over a year). Although most people appreciated the fact that they were 'not left to their own devices', as a 51-year-old Bosnian man put it, the contacts with service providers were overwhelmingly perceived as lacking the knowledge about their individual needs and situations as well as about their culture(s) and backgrounds. Consequently, refugees complained about being taught how to use the lavatory while at the reception centres, as a 35-year-old Bosnian doctor recalled. A 48-year-old Bosnian nurse remembered being shown 'how to use the fridge and how to switch on the television', when

---

3 The information cited was provided by representatives of the NGO sector in the Netherlands during my exploratory visits in September 1999 and September 2000.

they moved to their own accommodation in Amsterdam. Such experiences were perceived as humiliating and unrelated to their needs. They were clearly embedded in the structural framework of a minority situation and a concept of cultural differences, in which the culture of the receiving society is ranked as superior (Knudsen 1991, p. 30-34). More importantly, these service providers were the key mediators and guides to Dutch society. Based on these contacts and experiences, and without closer, informal communication with other Dutch residents, many of the refugees gradually formed a perception of a profound cultural distance between Dutch society and their societies of origin. Consequently, their main micro-level social communication was limited and based on networks developed along ethnic lines or focused on family ties.[4]

The group of 20 refugees interviewed in Amsterdam was comprised of a large number of younger individuals (between 20 and 40 years of age) as well as a considerable number of older people (over 41 years of age) (See Table 1). Over half of the group were from urban areas, married with children. Approximately half of the interviewed were from semi-urban settlements. Interviewees in Amsterdam were well-educated, with approximately one third having a university degree, and an equally high number with a technical or other vocational qualification on a secondary level.[5] The group consisted almost exclusively of refugees from Bosnia-Herzegovina, who were overwhelmingly Bosniaks or of ethnically mixed families.[6]

The people I met during my fieldwork in Amsterdam all appeared to be relatively 'well-settled'. As shown in Table 1, almost all were Dutch citizens, around half of them were employed, and another quarter was studying or in the process of getting their formal skills recognised. The level of labour market participation of the group was similar to the general level of employment of refugees in the Netherlands. In 2000, the unemployment rate among Dutch population of working age was three percent, whilst the unemployment rate among refugees was 35 per cent.[7] Both those employed and unemployed enjoyed relatively good living conditions and had short and longer-term plans for their future. None had plans to return to Bosnia-Herzegovina, though some of those older and unemployed did not entirely give up the dream of going 'back home'. Although a tiny minority articulated their need to return 'for good' as soon as their children are 'up on their feet and independent', as a 51-year-old Bosnian man did, the majority saw their future in the Netherlands. Younger respondents who were studying or working did not think about returning. A majority of them shared the 'migration plans' and the attitude of a 42-year old woman, who explained:

> Since I arrived here [in 1993], I suppressed any thoughts about going back. I think that I've changed a lot, as well as the people I knew in Bosnia. It's a big gap between us now, and there's no way of bridging it. So, I am focused on my life here and I want to stay.

Despite their willingness to reconstruct their lives in Amsterdam, and their relatively good standard of living, enjoyment of fine public amenities and social tolerance, the refugees felt that they were not 'of Amsterdam', to paraphrase Mollenkopf's (2000, p. 127) view on

4 For more information and discussion on the character of the co-community ties among the refugees in Amsterdam see my article *Integration and How We Facilitate It: A Comparative Study of the Settlement Experiences of Refugees in Italy and the Netherlands* (Korac, 2003a).

5 Vocational high schools (the total of 12 years of schooling, with last four years in vocational education) were widespread in the education system of the former Yugoslavia.

6 The constitution of Bosnia-Herzegovina uses the term *Bosniak* to refer to Bosnian-Muslim.

7 Data provided by *Emplooi*, an organisation assisting refugees in finding employment in the Netherlands.

boundaries between immigrants and the Dutch in the city. The refugees continued to perceive themselves as the 'Other' and generally not accepted by the Dutch. The following is an account of a 35-year-old Bosnian man, in the Netherlands since 1994, on the type of 'otherness' he felt since in exile. This highly educated man who was among very few who were employed in their profession said:

> Foreigners are extremely marginalised here, although that is officially denied. Foreigners, except the Americans who work here, are usually portrayed in the media in a very bad way [...] I feel here pretty much the same as I felt in my hometown in Bosnia under the Muslim government during the war. They kept us [non-Muslims] there to show the world that they are a democratic state. It's the same thing here; they keep us here to show the world that some foreigners may be successful and 'well-integrated'.

Although the sense of marginalisation was often articulated as a feeling of 'otherness', the problem was experienced and strongly felt on another, micro-level of communication which was emphasised by all. A 'successfully integrated' Bosnian man explained the roots of his feeling of 'otherness':

> I am employed in a Dutch medical firm, I speak Dutch language well, my child goes to a Dutch school and soon he'll speak Dutch better than his mother tongue, but we live here a parallel existence, because we don't have real contact with Dutch society. We are neither accepted nor rejected. The biggest problem is that we don't have any friends among the Dutch here. We are here left to ourselves. I have a flat in Amsterdam, I live here, but I don't have any ties with Dutch people.

The experience of marginalisation did not originate in any form of open racism or discrimination; almost all of the refugees emphasised their appreciation of social tolerance of the Dutch. They did not have any 'bad experiences' in their (limited) informal communication with them, but they felt 'invisible'. The following account of a 27-year-old Bosnian student and an intern in a Dutch firm clarifies this point:

> I have a great desire to integrate, to the extent that is possible for someone who isn't Dutch. I want my life to be normal. I want to be accepted by the Dutch, but no matter how much I try, I feel invisible among my colleagues at work, for example. They are perfectly correct work wise, but when it comes to some kind of socialising at work or after working hours, they behave as if I am not there. Then I feel excluded.

During my fieldwork in Amsterdam, I realised that almost all of these 'well-settled' people felt socially isolated because they lacked any closer ties with the Dutch. This problem did not seem self-imposed, as the refugees emphasised the importance of establishing such informal contacts at and beyond working place. The absence of such contacts, I realised, was a 'missing piece' from their feeling of being included in Dutch society. It affected the formation of a boundary between 'us', refugees, and 'them', the Dutch.

In my search for more in-depth insights into the mechanisms leading to such social isolation and the consequent feelings of non-belonging, I explored more closely the process through which the refugees were reconstructing their lives in the Netherlands. Their accounts on the situation and choices they faced during this process pointed to the problems within highly centralised, state-sponsored settlement programmes.

Most refugees I interviewed experienced this phased, state-led settlement as a pressure to 'adjust in the way the Dutch see fit', as a 37-year-old Bosnian man put it. This man who was still in the process of getting his professional skills recognised, perceived his integration experience, as did many of my other respondents, as a form of social control which hardly left any space for the process of mutual adjustment and individual agency. The 'successfully integrated', 35-year-old Bosnian man summarised the views of my respondents:

> I do what I am told to do, and everything is going according to 'integration' rules that we 'refugees' have to follow. We didn't have to integrate really, you see, we just had to do what we were told.

Those employed or studying felt particularly exposed to this 'all-embracing pressure to adjust, both at professional and personal level', as one of them put it. Many were in fact underemployed because of the many structural and social barriers in the Dutch labour market and society. It took on average up to seven years for those few who were resourceful, patient and lucky enough to undergo the process of skills recognition, to be back in their professions.

Many of older or less educated people responded to the perceived control and pressures of integration by reducing their life aspirations and by effectively excluding themselves from wider society; they had opted for the unemployment/social benefit strategy of 'integration'. This choice, articulated by many as an 'early retirement', was overwhelmingly, although not exclusively, gender specific. Women in their late 40s or older who could not find employment in their professions, were more likely than men to take jobs that pay the same or slightly better than social benefits. In most cases, their spouses would spend most of their days in their local community organisations, either working as volunteers or socialising.

The difference in attitude between men and women concerning underemployment revealed in my Amsterdam study is linked to the issue of how men and women develop survival strategies in exile (Eastmond, 1993; Friere, 1995; Matsuoka and Sorenson, 1999; McSpadden, 1999). Friere's (1995) psychodynamic assessment of exile experiences of Latin Americans in Canada demonstrates that, given comparable time in a new country and similar settlement experiences, gender identity associated with women's traditional roles and responsibilities seems to be linked with the development of successful survival strategies in women. In most societies and cultures, Friere points out, 'work only adds an additional, secondary role to their [women's] core identity as mothers and wives' (1995, p. 21). Men's core identity is by contrast, work-related and supported by a number of traditional socioculturally established roles of 'authoritative figure', 'provider' and 'protector' within the family and community (Friere, 1995; McSpadden, 1999). In exile, as Friere further points out, men become painfully aware that their occupational status, sources of power, and political agendas are non-existent or meaningless in the receiving society. She argues that although both women and men in exile experience psycho-emotional disorganisation and individual identity crisis, women tend to reconstruct their core sense of identity more successfully than men; they are more likely to achieve a sense of a continuity of meaningful vital roles in exile than men (Friere, 1995). Consequently, I would add, women tend to be more open to whatever opportunities arise in exile.

Dutch policies of integration render refugees 'passive recipients of aid' (Harrell-Bond, 1986): refugees are seen as policy objects, rather than agents in the settlement process. Consequently, many refugees in the Netherlands remain unemployed and dependent on social funds because they are not motivated to enter the labour market to earn an income that hardly exceeds the social benefit they are entitled to. Many are not able to practice their professions, not because their skills are not needed in the Dutch labour market, but because of the many structural and social barriers that prevent them to do so.

The Dutch 'top-down' approach to integration and the consequent feelings of detachment from the society seems to have increased the refugees' fear of the officialdom and the state, despite being naturalised in the Netherlands. A few respondents who were Dutch citizens expressed a degree of uneasiness or fear of a possibility of their citizenship being revoked if the political situation in the Netherlands was to change and somehow turn all non-native Dutch into undesired aliens. Wallman's (1979) argument that a social boundary has two kinds of meaning — structural or organisational, and subjective — helps explain this seemingly paradoxical situation. Wallman suggests that "[b]ecause a social boundary is about the organisation of society no more and no less than it is about the organisation of experience, neither element has more or less reality than the other. Both the difference and the *sense* of difference count" (Wallman, 1979, p. 7). Among my respondents, the social distance from the Dutch was translated into doubts concerning equality of citizenship rights between the two groups. In the context of the Dutch 'integration model', citizenship was perceived as yet another way of state control rather than a guarantee of equality and full participation.

Surviving the 'Chaos' in Italy

Italy lacks legislative framework that could be a basis for social policy pertaining to reception and integration of refugees. This situation is caused by two factors. First, Italy was until relatively recently a country of emigration and a transit country, through which refugees and other migrants only passed on their way to other European and overseas destinations. Although the situation changed in the 1990s, the experience of the previous decades still shapes the institutional memory of many governmental bodies, which still find it difficult to acknowledge that many of the refugees and other migrants actually come to stay. Second, Italy's welfare system is relatively underdeveloped, which has led to a corresponding approach to assistance available to those seeking and/or granted protection. The assistance is minimal and it is assumed that those in need will resort to self-help within refugee and migrant networks, and that this will encourage them to become self-sufficient in a short period.

The absence of both a national integration strategy and a corresponding welfare structure have contributed to the situation in which both government organisations and the NGO sector in Italy continually deal with emergencies. The Italian NGO sector, with a mandate to assist asylum seekers and refugees, is also a relatively recent phenomenon. Most of the organisations were founded at the beginning of the 1990s. They are unevenly spread across the country and less numerous than church organisations, which offer assistance to the destitute in general, including refugees. Church organisations and NGOs provide various types of assistance, ranging from emergency accommodation and free meals to language courses. However, the assistance they are able to offer cannot meet the needs of a growing number of asylum seekers and refugees.

The group of 40 refugees interviewed in Rome consisted overwhelmingly of relatively young (between 20 and 40 years of age, see Table 2), urban, and well-educated people, predominantly single or cohabiting, without children, overwhelmingly from Bosnia-Herzegovina, most of whom were either Bosniaks or of ethnically mixed families. Even after seven or more years in Rome, single people, but sometimes also couples, often lived in shared accommodation with other refugees from the former Yugoslavia, immigrants from other countries or Italians who were also newcomers in the city. Only those married to Italians had Italian citizenship, very few had time-limited work-permits to stay, and the rest (a majority) had a temporary permit to stay, issued for humanitarian reasons and renewable on a yearly basis, which included the right to work and study. This temporary status was usually granted without any lengthy determination procedure. It was based on a special government decree introduced in 1992 to regulate the status of refugees from the former Yugoslavia who were fleeing generalised violence and persecution and therefore could have not been judicially recognised in Italy, because its legislation refers solely to the Geneva Convention.

Although they were granted the right to stay without any special difficulties or delays, only a couple of respondents in my Rome study received some form of minimal assistance to settle. Consequently, refugees in Rome encountered profound problems in achieving financial security and their first years of settlement were characterised by a struggle for physical survival, ranging from finding shelter to learning the language and finding any kind of work.[8] Their settlement involved a degree of self-selection, because younger people and those without children were more likely to find ways into the 'system' and society, and of surviving in the city without any assistance. Others moved on to smaller towns in the north of Italy, where it was easier to find accommodation and work, or they tried to resettle to a third country. In a few families that stayed on, teenage children often had to work during their first year in Rome to contribute to inadequate family budgets.

For those who stayed in Rome, the experiences of hardship in finding shelter, learning the language, finding work and becoming independent without assistance were interwoven with feelings of self-respect for being active in finding a solution and for being self-sufficient. Immediately upon their arrival, they engaged in an intensive process of networking among the group(s) of compatriots, and formed a spontaneous self-reception system. Although the Italian 'system' rests upon the assumption that refugees and other immigrants will be assisted through self-help groups they form, the policy framework in the country does not specifically encourage the formation of immigrant and refugee organisations. Unlike in some other EU countries, where the state institutions create opportunities for the recognition of groups (Joly, 1996), in Italy, the formation of associations is not the main avenue to obtain support from the state. In such a context, intra-group ties and networks are primarily informal and formed spontaneously to facilitate the needs of individual members. The spontaneous networking among my respondents involved contacts across ethnic lines, as this type of contacts and communication was critical for their physical survival in Rome.[9] A 33-year-old single woman from Bosnia, in Italy since 1992, explained the character of these networks:

> Each of us had our own opinions about politics [...] We'd have disputes over that [...]But despite the political discussions, we'd help each other whenever we could, regardless of where

---

8 For information and discussion on the kind of difficulties these refugees encountered in Rome and the survival strategies they developed, see my article *The Lack of Integration Policy and Experiences of Settlement: A Case Study of Refugees in Rome* (Korac, 2003b)

9 For more on these networks in Rome see Korac (2003b).

> we were from and what our political views were. That attitude was essential, because we needed these contacts and each other's help.

I argue that the situation in Rome and the character of the policies pertaining to the reception of refugees in Italy had an unintended effect on (re)creating inter-ethnic links among the refugees, the links that were destroyed by war and conflict in the former Yugoslavia. These networks were characterised by 'weak' ties among their members, as they were not based on family, kinship or ethnic ties (Granovetter, 1974). Rather, their networks were geared toward fast mobilisation of resources, ranging from finding vital information to securing accommodation and jobs.

Most of the refugees in Rome, regardless of their education and skills, had low-paying jobs primarily in the service sector; they usually worked long and antisocial hours. They also often worked in the informal economy, despite their legal right to work. This was not because of any specific discriminatory practices toward refugees/foreigners, but because that is also the situation for many Italians. A 33-year-old woman from Croatia explained the situation in an IT firm where she works: 'everyone in the firm works like that [informally]; our boss decided not to have many legal [formally employed] workers.' Many were combining work and studying, because the war and subsequent flight had interrupted their education. They were experiencing many difficulties, which are briefly summarised in the account of a 25-year-old Bosnian man, in Rome since 1993:

> Since I started my studies here [in the autumn of 1997], I've learned a lot. By now I should have almost graduated but with my job that's impossible. I only managed to pass five exams to date, with high grades though, because I lack the time and concentration for studying. When you work until three in the morning [at a bar], you wake up at 10-11, you need time to pull yourself together, to sit and study, make lunch. So I have very little time for studying.

Many more had to abandon the idea of continuing their education because of their unfavourable circumstances in exile. Consequently, and unlike in my Amsterdam study, almost none felt that they had succeeded in settling in Italy so as to give them a sense of security in planning their future. Almost all of them wanted to stay in Rome and Italy, but did not feel that they were in position to make any long-term plans. Their experience of exile in Rome made them realise that the 'only thing that's important' to them is 'what will happen tomorrow', as a 33-year-old Bosnian woman emphasised. She was in Rome since 1991, and like many of my respondents was highly educated but underemployed, with a job in a bar-discotheque, and with temporary, humanitarian permit to stay in Italy. The absence of almost any plans for the future is understandable given their uncertain legal status and their profound difficulties in securing financial stability.

Although the importance of work in developing successful survival strategies was emphasised by all the refugees in my Rome study, it was not perceived as a straightforward way to achieving financial security or indeed to finding work compatible with their skills and education. They emphasised that the lack of an initial reception system forced them to become self-sufficient at a high cost: they were forced to enter a niche in the labour market from which it is very hard to move up the economic and social ladder. For those very few who were resourceful and lucky enough to succeed in finding better jobs, it took approximately the same number of years as for those in Amsterdam.

This grim picture of settlement in Rome is the outcome of the Italian 'system' of receptionand integration. In fact, it seems to mirror the government's intentions of minimising their assistance and fostering the development of spontaneous self-help systems among newcomers. Although the initial stage of settlement in Rome was characterised almost exclusively by the social networks of compatriots, the process of intensive networking between the refugees and Italians/residents of Rome emerged early in settlement. Instrumental to this type of networking were women who were initially almost exclusively employed as live-in maids and nannies. Their contacts with Italian families and networks of their friends were central to facilitating their further 'functional' integration (e.g. language training, skills recognition, etc.). The contacts and networks that women established were also invaluable for refugee men in finding their jobs and accommodation.

These and other spontaneous contacts with Italians they had to establish in various social settings, ranging from their neighbourhoods to the markets and cafés, while in search for vital information or some other kind of help, were not mediated through professional or voluntary service providers. Amin (2002, cited in Mumford and Power, 2003, p. 90) argued that these semi-invisible micro-links of undeclared sociability, such as casual contacts between diverse groups of people in public spaces, help people 'rub along together' and develop a positive web of support. Indeed, many of these social encounters were often characterised by both confrontation and misunderstanding, but because they were spontaneous and personalised, those involved in such social interaction were usually perceived as individuals, rather than representatives of a 'culture' or 'society'. This helped avoid a perception that differences between Italian and non-Italian identity and culture are set in opposition, and enhanced the openness of the refugees toward Italians and vice-versa. They also enabled refugees to distinguish between the mechanisms of exclusion and inclusion at the state institutional level and during their day-to-day social contacts with Italians.

The experience of inclusion at the everyday level was central to their general satisfaction with their situation in Italy. They felt 'good and safe', as a 50-year-old Croatian woman put it, because most Italians they knew were 'good and emotional', despite existing xenophobia in Italy, which is an issue that 'politicians keep up their sleeve when they need someone to blame'. These day-to-day informal interactions and bridging social networks with Italians helped the refugees adjust to the new culture and the 'rules' of the new society. Some of these contacts developed into closer ties described as good friendships, regular outings, joint holidays and also marriages. By the time of my research, which was undertaken after the respondents had been in Rome for between 7 and 8 years, over a half of the group had more contacts with Italians than with people from their countries of origin.

The openness of the refugees toward their new environment in Rome did not mean, however, their willingness or need to abandon ties with their own culture, roots and identity. The following account of a well-educated but underemployed 38-year-old man from Serbia, in Italy since 1992, echoes the attitude of many of the refugees in my research:

> The only way to become integrated somewhere is to be in contact with local people. That means stepping out of a kind of 'national scheme'. Limiting yourself to what you see as your own identity prevents you from accepting whatever may be outside it. Some, for example, speak perfect Italian, even the *Romanacio* dialect, so there's no way you can recognise us as foreigners, they are well adapted. However, there's still a difference [between the well adapted refugees and Italians], which isn't bad at all. From what I've seen it's not a disadvantage and I'd like to keep that distinctive quality.

Spontaneous and individualised contacts with Italians were perceived as 'two-way' encounters and catalysts to the process of change. The sense that 'many Italians managed to learn something from us, too', as a 25-year-old Bosnian man put it, was very important to all. The intensity and quality of micro-level contacts with Italians contributed to the feeling of the Roman respondents that they were 'of Rome', that they are part of the social fabric of city life. They defined loses involved in their flight and exile as losses of economic welfare or uncertain prospects for their future, not as loss of personal agency or social contacts leading to social isolation.

CONCLUDING REMARKS

This chapter revealed how different policy approaches to integration in the Netherlands and Italy contribute to the shaping of refugee strategies of adjustment and their settlement outcomes. In both contexts, though in a different way, micro-level social interaction along, across and outside ethnic boundaries, was to a certain extent shaped by the settlement policy or the lack of it, and played a critical role in how refugees adjust and perceive their new social environment. Moreover, bridging social networks or ties with the established community at a micro-level were in both contexts identified by the refugees themselves as an important determinant of integration. My research revealed that the refugees in Amsterdam and Rome experienced different levels of success in achieving this important goal. It is important to add here that the relative success or failure of the refugees to establish bridging social networks cannot be attributed solely to the character of the policy and reception system. Indeed, the compatibility of cultures and lifestyles in the receiving and sending societies play a role in establishing closer social ties between the refugees and the native population. Unlike in my Amsterdam study, refugees in Rome perceived the 'Italian life-style' as similar to that in their countries of origin. Some aspects of interpersonal communication, 'café culture', some values and traditions among Italians in Rome were found to be familiar if not identical; and were helpful in forming a positive attitude toward the receiving society. However, despite the role that different levels of compatibility of cultures may have, this study strongly suggests that the assessment of integration success, as defined by refugees themselves, goes beyond simple, measurable indicators, such as individual occupational mobility or economic status. It importantly includes the existence, quality and strength of bridging social networks.

In the Dutch context, social contacts outside the group of compatriots were almost entirely reduced to the communication with numerous service providers. Such formal social encounters were overwhelmingly embedded in a minority situation framework and therefore they could not lead to establishing bridging social networks. In conjunction with the experience of a prolonged stay at reception centres, the character of refugees' contacts with service providers contributed to the perceptions of a cultural distance between the Dutch society and the sending society. This led to the experience of social isolation and feelings of detachment from the Dutch and the society at large.

In the Italian context, the absence of an organised assistance programme, and of experience of reception centres and contacts with professional or voluntary aid workers, meant considerable hardship in settlement. By the same token, the lack of integration policy saved the refugees in Rome from systematic bureaucratic labelling, which usually implies a dependent role and the lack of agency (Zetter, 1991). In their effort to reconstruct their lives, the refugees had to engage in intensive social networking outside their ethnic groups in order to survive and settle in the new society. As these social contacts were spontaneous and personalised, they shaped the attitudes of refugees toward their new social environment in a positive way. The experience of the bridging social networks also tended to compensate for their dissatisfaction with their socio-economic status.

The discussion in this chapter should by no means be understood as an argument for the absence of any assistance and strategy for integration. Moreover, the core of the argument is not that welfare programmes, such as Dutch, necessarily create lasting reliance on government support and undermine refugees' chances to integrate. Rather, the discussion aimed to emphasise the connection between specific policy contexts, structural constraints they embody, and the type of human agency they engender in the process of structuring and re-structuring social relations in societies undergoing social change due to migration and diversification. Further exploration of these connections, of the specific outcomes and meaning that they have for the actors involved in the process of adjustment and integration could lead to the development of policies that would provide initial conditions for a long-term formation of bridging social capital in the receiving societies.

References

Bauböck, R. (1996). Introduction. In R. Bauböck, A. Heller, & A.R. Zolberg (Eds.), *The challenge of Diversity – Integration and pluralism in Societies of Immigration.* Aldershot: Avebury.

Bloch, A. (2002). *The Migration and Settlement of Refugees in Britain.* Houndmills and London: Palgrave Macmillan.

Bourdieu, P. (1984). *Distinctions: A Social Critique of the Judgement of Taste.* Cambridge, Mass.: Harvard University Press.

Castles, S., Korac, M., Vasta, E. & Vertovec, S. (2003). *Integration: Mapping the Field.* London: Home Office. On-line Report. Retrieved August 15, 2003 from http://www.homeoffice.gov.uk/rds/pdfs2/rdsolr2803.doc

Dekker, P. & Uslaner, E. (2001). Introduction. In P. Dekker, & E. Uslaner (Eds.), *Social Capital and Participation in Everyday Life.* London: Routledge.

Duke, K., Sales, R. & Gregory, J. (1999). Refugee resettlement in Europe. In A. Bloch, & C. Levy (Eds.), *Refugees, Citizenship and Social Policy in Europe.* Basingstoke: Macmillan.

Eastmond, M. (1998). 'Bosnian Muslim Refugees in Sweden', *Journal of Refugee Studies, 11*(2), 161-181.

_____ . (1993). Reconstructing Life: Chilean Refugee Women and the Dilemmas of Exile. In G. Bujis (Ed.), *Migrant Women: Crossing Boundaries and Changing Identities.* Oxford: Berg.

European Commission. (2001). *Study on the legal framework and administrative practices in the Member States of the European Communities regarding reception conditions for persons seeking international protection.* Final Report, DG for Justice and Home Affairs.

Fernandez-Kelly M. P. (1995). Social and Cultural Capital in the Urban Ghetto: Implications for the Economic Sociology and Immigration. In A. Portes (Ed.), *The Economic Sociology of Immigration: Essays on Networks, Ethnicity and Enterpreneurship.* New York: Russell Sage Foundation.

Freire, M. (1995). The Latin American Exile Experience from a Gender Perspective: A Psychodynamic Assessment. *Refuge 14*(8), 20-25.

Gold, S. (1992). *Refugee Communities: A comparative field study.* London: Sage Publications, Series on Ethnic Relations, Vol. 4.

Granovetter, M. (1974). *Getting a Job: A Study of Contacts and Careers.* Cambridge: Harvard University Press.

Harrell-Bond, B. (1986). *Imposing Aid: Emergency Assistance to Refugees.* Oxford: Oxford University Press.

Indra, D. (1993). Some feminist contributions to refugee studies. *Gender Issues and Refugees: Development Implications.* Conference papers, Vol. II, pp. 757-66. Toronto: Centre for Refugee Studies, York University.

Joly, D. (1996). *Haven or Hell? Asylum Policies and refugees in Europe.* Basingstoke: Macmillan.

Knudsen, J.C. (1991). Therapeutic Strategies and Strategies for Refugee Coping. *Journal of Refugee Studies 4*(1), 21-38.

Korac, M. (2003a). Integration and how we facilitate it: A comparative study of settlement experiences of refugees in Italy and the Netherlands. *Sociology* (BSA), *37(*1), 51-68.

_____ .. (2003b). The lack of integration policy and experiences of integration: a case study of refugees in Rome. *Journal of Refugee Studies*, *16*(4), 398-421.

Lechner, F. J. (2000). *Managing others: Minorities policy and National identity in the Netherlands.* Claus M. Halle Institute for Global Learning, Emory University, Atlanta, Georgia. Occasional Paper.

Matsuoka, A. & Sorenson, J. (1999). Eritrean Canadian Refugees Households As Sites of Gender Renegotiation. In D. Indra (Ed.), *Engendering Forced Migration - Theory and Practice.* New York, Oxford: Berghahn Books.

McSpadden, L. A. (1999). Negotiating Masculinity in the Reconstruction of Social Place: Eritrean and Ethiopian Refugees in the United States and Sweden. In D. Indra (Ed.), *Engendering Forced Migration - Theory and Practice.* New York, Oxford: Berghahn Books.

Mollenkopf, J. (2000). Assimilating immigrants in Amsterdam: A perspective from New York. *The Netherlands' Journal of Social Sciences*, *36*(2), 126-145.

Mumford, K. & Power, A. (2003). *East Enders: Family and community in East London.* Bristol: The Policy Press.

Putnam, R. D. (2000). *Bowling Alone: The Collapse and Revival of American Community.* New York: Simon & Schuster.

Robinson, V. (1986). *Transients Settlers and Refugees: Asians in Britain.* Oxford: Clarendon Press.

_____ . (1998). Defining and measuring successful refugee integration. Report of conference on *Integration of Refugees in Europe.* Antwerp, November 12-14. Brussels: European Council on Refugees and Exiles.

Van Hear, N. (1998). *New disporas: the mass exodus, dispersal and regrouping of migrant communities.* London: UCL Press.

Wallman, S. (1979). Introduction: The Scope for Ethnicity. In S. Wallman (Ed.), *Ethnicity at Work.* London: Macmillan Press.

Weiner, M. (1996). Determinants of Immigrant Integration: An International Comparative Analysis. In N. Carmon (Ed.), *Immigration and Integration in Post-Industrial Societies: Theoretical Analysis and Policy-Related Research*. London: Macmillan Press.

Zetter, R. (1991). Labelling Refugees: Forming and Transforming a Bureaucratic Identity. *Journal of Refugee Studies*, *4*(1), 39-62.

In: Homeland Wanted ISBN 1-5945
Editors: P. Waxman and V. Colic-Peisker, pp. 109-125

Newyork.

Chapter 6

BOSNIAN REFUGEE RESETTLEMENT IN ST. LOUIS, MISSOURI

Hisako Matsuo

ABSTRACT

This chapter explores Bosnian refugee resettlement in St. Louis, Missouri, USA, using qualitative data collected through face-to-face interviews with 38 Bosnian refugees, eight service providers at local resettlement agencies, several representatives of federal and state offices, and participant observations of six Bosnian families and attendance at meetings of volunteer organizations. There are about 35,000 Bosnians refugees in St. Louis (about 12 percent of the population of the city), creating a critical mass for this group. Bosnians are described as resilient and hard working people by many service providers, making them a model group among refugees. Although many Bosnians experienced occupational downward mobility, an economic boom in St. Louis coupled with Bosnians' strong family ties have created an opportunity to capitalize on family human resources. A large ethnic enclave also provides an information network, through which Bosnians seek educational and financial upward mobility for their children. Although many Bosnian refugees in St. Louis are Muslims, they have never experienced prejudice and discrimination, unlike Middle Eastern Muslims. Being Europeans and also secular Muslims have reinforced each other, rendering Bosnians racially 'invisible' in American society, which continues to appreciate whiteness.

Key words: Bosnian refugees, group size, family human resources, secular Muslims, European refugees

INTRODUCTION

American sociology has produced an array of literature on refugees in the past few decades (Back, 1980; Cohen, 1981; Garcia, 1996; Gold, 1992; Liu, Lamanna, and Mirita, 1979; Nguyen, 1997; Portes and Bach, 1985). These refugees primarily came from Latin America (mainly from Cuba) and Southeast Asia (US Department of Commerce, 1999). The demographics of refugees have dramatically changed since the breakdown of the former Soviet Union in the late 1980s and the war in the former Yugoslavia in the early 1990s. More than 50 per cent of the refugees who came to the US since that time are Eastern Europeans (US Department of Justice, 1999).

Since the end of the Bosnian war 1992-1995, the number of immigrants from Bosnia-Herzegovina (hereafter the term Bosnians will be used) admitted as refugees and as a part of family reunification process has been increasing. For example, Bosnians were the largest group (27,840 people) among refugees admitted in fiscal year 1997 (77,600 people, US Department of Justice, 1999). According to the International Institute of Greater St. Louis (2002), the US government specified St. Louis, Missouri, as one of the preferred resettlement areas for Bosnian refugees in order to avoid ethnic competition among different immigrant groups for low-wage jobs, such as has been observed in New York and Los Angeles (St. Louis Post-Dispatch, 1998). Furthermore an increasing number of Bosnians who have resettled in other areas are currently migrating to St. Louis because of the lower cost of housing here compared to other large cities, bringing the estimated number of Bosnians in this area to 35,000, or about 12% of the population of the city (International Institute of Greater St. Louis, 2002a).

St. Louis is located in the geographical center of the United States, about 300 miles (480 kilometers) southwest of Chicago, Illinois, which is know as one of the traditional gateways for immigrants (The Brookings Institution, 2004). The city's population is a little over 300,000, and the metropolitan St. Louis area about two million. Although there were only 13 Bosnian families who resettled in St. Louis in 1993, the number increased rapidly during the following years. It is worthy to note that there are refugees with other ethnic backgrounds, who resettled in the St. Louis area, such as Russian and Ukrainian (about 3,900), Middle Eastern (about 2,300), Asian (about 8,500), African (about 1,200), and others (about 500), bringing the estimated number of refugees over 50,000 (International Institute of Greater St. Louis, 2002a). However, these numbers include neither the refugees who came to St. Louis as a secondary migration from other parts of the US nor their American-born children. Therefore, the number of refugees and their children in the area may be close to 100,000.

To date, literature on Bosnian refugees in the US is limited and mostly focuses on mental health and psychosocial and personal issues (Geltman et al., 2000; Kopinak, 1999; Stein et al., 1999; Wein et al., 1998). Although these studies explore important aspects of Bosnian refugees' lives, they ignore the effort that these refugees make in order to find a niche in American society. Being a refugee does not necessarily imply low psychological well-being (Mayadas and Segal, 2000; Van Selm et al., 1997). Unlike Bosnian refugees in European countries, Bosnians in the US do not have a fear of possible expulsion because they become eligible for status adjustment to permanent resident after one year. Heavy emphasis on the mental health of refugees stigmatizes the group and overlooks other important aspects of the group's dynamics to reestablish their lives in a new environment.

Although since the 1960s many studies on immigrants have made a clear distinction between voluntary immigrants and refugee immigrants, these studies placed too much emphasis on the disadvantaged situation and coercive assimilation of refugees, seeing them as powerless groups dependent upon public support. They also ignored refugees' cultural orientation, autonomy, and ethnic diversity (De Voe, 1981; Rynearson 1999). During the past decade, however, studies have started to view resettlement as a phenomenon on a continuum between "proactive" and "reactive", exploring the issues of group solidarity and ethnic identity of refugee immigrants (De Voe and Gold, 1993; Gold, 1992; Juan and Jason, 1998;

Somach, 1995). Instead of focusing solely on mental health issues, the latter approach integrated the aspects of employment and identity in the process of resettlement

Table 1. Refugee Presence in the St. Louis Area in 2002

Nationality	Refugee Population
Near / Middle Eastern	
Afghan	800
Iraqi	1,000
Kurd	500
Other	30
Eastern European / Russian	
Bosnian	35,000
Russian	2,675
Ukrainian	680
Other	600
Asian	
Lao	675
Vietnamese	7,800
Other	50
African	
Ethiopian / Eritrean	600
Somali	300
Other	340
Cuban / Haitian	480
Total	**51,530**

Source: International Institute, December 2002

Refugees in the US have several advantages compared to voluntary immigrants, such as eligibility for status adjustment to permanent resident after one year upon resettlement, welfare support for families with dependent children ('Temporary Assistance for Needy Family'), Refugee Cash Assistance for seven months, Refugee Medical Assistance for eight months, and language and job training provided by the refugee resettlement agencies. Yet, a major disadvantage of refugees is the impossibility to plan for their migration and to prepare for living in a new culture, including acquiring language skills. The example of previous refugee groups illustrates this disadvantage: more than 80 per cent of the first wave of Vietnamese refugees who arrived in the mid-1970s had less than seven days to prepare for their exit (Liu, Lamanna, and Mirata, 1979), which has affected the group's economic adjustment and upward mobility. The first wave of Cuban immigrants between 1960 and 1973 experienced downward mobility in America in spite of their English competency and high socioeconomic status in the country of origin (Garcia, 1996).

For both voluntary immigrants and refugee, one of the strategies used to find an economic niche has been the development of an ethnic enclave where they reside and open small businesses (Bonacich, 1973). While ethnic enclaves provide shelter for immigrants, they hinder upward mobility if these immigrants stay self-employed over generations, which has been the case with Cubans (Portes and Bach, 1985). Some immigrant groups, and especially those from less developed countries, may become a new underclass which lacks the potential for acculturation and upward mobility (Nguyen, 1997).

Unlike the earlier refugee cohorts from Southeast Asia and Latin America, Bosnians are Europeans. In spite of their potentially disadvantageous refugee status, their whiteness coupled with their religious background makes this group unique for exploring how refugees find their economic, social and cultural niches in the US. Although there are some Croats (mainly Catholic) and Serbs (mainly Orthodox) among Bosnian refugees in St. Louis, the majority are Bosnian Muslims (Bosniaks). However, they are predominately secular Muslims who do not practice their faith. Further, their racial background makes them 'invisible' in the predominantly white US, while refugees in the past, such as Cubans, Vietnamese, and Laotians have often been discriminated against (Lutheran Immigration and Refugee Services, 2003). Over the decade of their resettlement in St. Louis, Bosnian refugees became visible in the city because of its group size, but remain 'invisible' as individuals. The remainder of this chapter explores some aspects of Bosnian refugee resettlement process and community integration in St. Louis.

METHODOLOGY

My research interest in Bosnian refugees was sparked in the late 1990s by increased media coverage about Bosnian resettlement in the St. Louis area. This study started as a pilot study in order to explore three questions:

1. What are the major problems that Bosnians face in the process of resettlement?
2. How do Bosnians find their economic niches in American society?
3. Howe do Bosnians reconstruct their identity as a result of forced migration to the US?

The qualitative data were mainly collected through face-to-face interviews and informal observations. The interviews were conducted with 38 Bosnian refugees, eight service providers at resettlement agencies, four Americans who have assisted refugees in their resettlement and several representatives from the International Institute of Greater St. Louis, Catholic Charities, Missouri Department of Social Service, and the Lutheran Immigration and Refugee Services. The participant observations of six Bosnian families through informal interactions and attendance at meetings of voluntary organizations also provided useful data. Clips of local newspaper articles related to Bosnians provided anecdotal stories during the process of data collection. Data were collected from January 2001 to May 2002.

One of the major difficulties in researching ethnic groups is gaining trust from members of the community. Finding informants in the Bosnian community and establishing rapport were the first barriers during the formative period of the project. As an additional difficulty, the Bosnian community became suspicious of Americans after a Bosnian girl was murdered by an American man who disguised himself as a public health care provider. This happened in 1998 in a Bosnian neighborhood of St. Louis, just as Bosnians started to establish themselves there. For many Bosnians, it was difficult to accept strangers into their community and share their refugee experiences with them. Another difficulty was the language barrier, because many Bosnians, especially people in their 40s and older, spoke little English and there were very few professional Bosnian interpreters available. I was fortunate to meet a Bosnian college student, who arrived in St. Louis in 1996 as a 15-year-old refugee with his parents. He was invaluable for the project in the role of bilingual research assistant: he translated documents, introduced Bosnian families, arranged interviews, interpreted during the interviews and translated and transcribed audiotapes into English. Introducing myself to the community as an immigrant often helped to break the ice. Once I was accepted by several families, a rumor about my project traveled forth and facilitated further contacts. Although the formal data collection ended in May 2002, I remained engaged in ethnographic observations by participating in the network of refugee service providers.

Another difficulty encountered in this study was obtaining aggregate demographic data on Bosnian refugees. Although Bosnian refugee resettlement in St. Louis started in 1993, the International Institute of Greater St. Louis only started to computerize refugees' demographic data in 2000. Therefore, demographic information including sex, age, education, previous occupation, family structure, and previous resettlement sites between 1993 and 2000, were not available. After contacting about 40 local resettlement agencies in major US cities, I found that this was also the case elsewhere. Furthermore, the US 2000 Census surveyed only 7,000 Bosnians in St. Louis because many Bosnians were unable to fill out the form in English and because some Bosnians did not receive surveys due to change of residence.

The present study used a grounded theory method for sampling, data analysis, and theorization. Although the project started as an exploratory study for conceptualization and scale development for further quantitative data collection, it also used the adaptation model developed by Baker (1989) for initial conceptualization, focusing on such variables as the size of the group, employment, presence or absence of ethnic enclaves, language skills and discrimination. Baker's adaptation model combined previous adaptation literature on refugees from Southeast Asia (Back, 1980; Cohen, 1981) and studies of Slavic peoples in North America (Weinfield, 1981). It also integrated Feagin's (1984) concept of modernity which argued that European immigrants to North American no longer come from rural folk cultures.

Interviews were conducted both in English and Bosnian; 15 Bosnians were interviewed by the author in English, and 23 by the author through a Bosnian interpreter. Each interview lasted between two and five hours and some participants were interviewed twice. The study used both snowball sampling (asking participants to recommend further respondents) and theoretical sampling (Schatzman and Strauss, 1973). Several informants from the International Institute of Greater St. Louis, Catholic Charities, Saint Pius Church, Immigrant and Refugee Consortium, and other voluntary service programs also provided names of potential subjects. A semi-structured interview schedule was used, and it was revised as incoming data provided new themes. Data were transcribed and prepared for manual and computer-aided (QSR NUD*IST) data coding and analyses.

Of the 38 Bosnians interviewees, 25 were women and 13 men. Respondents were between 21 and 76 years old and originally came from Sarajevo, Srebrenica and Banja Luka. Most of them came to the US after staying in countries of first asylum such as Hungary, Germany, Croatia, and Austria. Their occupations in Bosnia varied from factory worker, waitress, electric and mechanic to schoolteacher, accountant, lawyer, and doctor. Their occupations at the time of interviews included housekeeper, janitor, factory worker, truck driver, interpreter, etc. The length of stay in the US varied between two and nine years with five of the respondents having become US citizens. Most of the subjects achieved junior high school to high school education, while two people had university education and three graduate degrees. At the time of data collection three of the respondents were students attending college in St. Louis.

GROUP CHARACTERISTICS OF BOSNIAN REFUGEES IN ST. LOUIS

Bosnians in St. Louis are a diverse population in terms of their socio-economic background, rural or urban origin, war experience and history of exodus from Bosnia. The caseworkers whom I interviewed assumed, from their own experiences with Bosnians, that many of them were blue collar workers in Bosnia. According to the data obtained form the International Institute of Greater St. Louis (2002b), the educational attainment of a majority of the Bosnian refugees was high school/trade school or lower, and less than five per cent held a university degree or higher. Many Bosnians came to St. Louis in family units, and a majority of Bosnians were between 30 and 50 years of age. Unlike other refugee groups from Africa and Middle East, both men and women were equally present in this group (International Institute of Greater St. Louis, 2002b).

Although Bosnian refugees faced many problems, such as language barriers, different educational and health systems, transportation problems, and lack of sufficient financial support (Somach, 1995), they were working hard on establish themselves in the foreign environment. There were some negative comments made about Bosnians by Americans living in the neighborhood where a large number of Bosnians were concentrated. American service providers interviewed in this study mentioned that neighbors of Bosnians were irritated by smokehouses Bosnians used to smoke meat; others were concerned about a potential outbreak of conflicts between Bosniaks and Serbs in St. Louis; some expressed concerns about a large number of Bosnians living in one household. Yet, many caseworkers argued that Bosnian refugees, as a group, have created a positive image to St. Louisans.

Caseworkers interviewed in this study mentioned their perception of common group characteristics. One of them was assertiveness. When I interviewed a Catholic nun who had been teaching English to refugee women from various countries, she compared Bosnians with Vietnamese: "Bosnians are very assertive. When we have some activities at our church, Vietnamese are sitting at the back quietly, but Bosnians usually sit in the front. They try to communicate with us even though they don't speak good English." A superintendent of one school district commented: "We tell people, 'don't mess with Bosnians. You'll never win the argument with them." Resilience seemed to be another Bosnian characteristic. When the Historical Society of Missouri held an exhibition on Bosnian refugees in 2000, its main theme was "We will survive." Many Bosnian refugees had been suffering from post-traumatic stress symptoms as victims of the war and humiliations of being forced to leave their homeland (Dugan et al., 2004), but they presented the strong will to survive. They usually say "What doesn't kill me makes me stronger." American social workers made similar observations on Bosnian refugees' resilience. A similar concept which seemed to characterize Bosnians is "sense of coherence" (Antonovsky, 1984), a term which was originally used to explain some of the Jewish Holocaust survivors' ability to find meaning about their fate under adverse circumstances. Bosnians seem to find meaning in a strong will to overcome the difficulties and they tend to see their circumstances as warranting the investment of energy. Bosnian refugee children in St. Louis showed better adjustment skills than American children on the standardized test of anxiety (Legett et al., 2001).

Despite a lack of English proficiency, many Bosnian refugees stared working at two or three casual jobs within weeks of arrival in the US. There was no option but to seek employment because financial support was inadequate for families' basic needs. Many Bosnians stopped receiving Refugee Cash Assistance soon after arrival and some even purchased a small house within a few years, trying to recreate a normal life in St. Louis, similar to the one that they had in Bosnia. Many Bosnian homes that I visited for interviews were nicely furnished, with comfortable sofas laid in the living room, and art and crafts brought from Bosnia or other countries arranged on the shelves and the walls. A Bosnian woman in her early 40s, who had stayed in Germany with her family for seven years, replied to my question, "how did you feel when you first came to the US?" in the following way:

> That's a tough question. How did I feel? Just imagine the hardest feeling of depression being on your chest constantly throughout the whole time. That's how I felt. The reason was my father. He stayed in Germany, and I left him in a very bad medical condition. Everything that I felt at that time was only family in Germany. That is all. .... How did I feel? There was a feeling of freedom, sadness, and closure. Period of three months after I left Germany were really hard on me. My dad died two months after I left. I couldn't see him for the last time (sigh), a fact that bothers me from time to time quite a lot. But everything goes away. Heart is tougher than stone. My children are here... I live for them. And while there is hope for them I will be fine. My first impressions, hmm, good, I would say. I can't say anything bad really... And now, I live a normal life. Life in the US is something completely different. My husband said, the moment he arrived in St. Louis, he said that he felt as if he was born again. He says that Germany or Bosnia has nothing to do with us anymore, and that this is a place for us (translated from Bosnian).

This woman's strong will to survive echoed in other interviewees' responses. Although some Bosnians, who were temporarily protected in Germany before coming to the US might have brought some savings because they were allowed to work there, they had to start their lives in the US 'from zero'. Yet, homeownership among Bosnian refugees was very high (about 75 percent), at the time of data collection, and they expressed relatively high satisfaction with their lives in the US (Matsuo, 2004). Besides resilience and hard work, what made it possible for them to achieve relative success within a few years after coming to the US as refugees? The next section explores some factors which contributed to the process of recreating a normal life.

Capitalizing on Family Human Resources

The process of refugee resettlement is supported by local voluntary agencies and state and federal governments, with economic self-sufficiency being the main objective of the US refugee resettlement program. When Bosnian refugees become economically self-sustaining, they often sponsor their relatives to migrate to the US and provide assistance to newly arriving refugees (Holman, 1996). Further, Bosnians are a strongly family-oriented group, and the notion of family extends to kin. Many Bosnian households consist of husband, wife, children and sometimes grandparents and/or other relatives. Although official statistics on the proportion of single-headed households among Bosnians in St. Louis were not available, representatives at the International Institute of Greater St. Louis assumed that there were not many such cases among Bosnians. As mentioned, within a few months of arrival in the US, a majority of adult members of Bosnians families no longer accessed Refugee Cash Assistance. Instead, they were employed in low-wage jobs which did not require English language competency, and saved money to send to their relatives abroad or to sponsor them to come to the US. Annual family remittances that Bosnians in my sample were sending to their relatives in Bosnia and other countries ranged between $2,000 and $5,000.

The fact that Bosnians lived in family units and had relatives in their neighborhood provided them with the opportunity to capitalize on family human resources. For example, a wife and a husband took different work shifts so that either one could be at home to take care of their children. Because their relatives lived close, they were providing childcare when needed. This was not only because of the high cost of hiring baby-sitters but also because of their culture which extends mutual support to kin.

For many Bosnians who had children, one of the reasons why they stayed in the US is to enable their children to access good education, which has not been available in Bosnia since the beginning of the war. The respondents in this study were also very conscious of the quality of education that their children were receiving. Although resettlement agencies had originally prepared housing for newly arrived refugees in the inner city where rent was inexpensive, many Bosnian families soon moved out of the inner city of St. Louis because of the low quality of education and safety issues in the area. While many racial minority families have been on welfare for generations and trying to get a grip on education in the inner cities of the US, Bosnians have wasted no time in seeking better educational opportunities for their children.

Families 'invested' not only in their children's education but also in those adult members who had the potential for upward mobility. Almost all Bosnian refugees who had held professional jobs in Bosnia experienced downward mobility because of a lack of English competency and a lack of recertification programs in the US. For these professionals, to reestablish a normal life in the US meant to obtain the same professional status they had in Bosnia. A Bosnian man in his early fifties who was a medical doctor in Bosnia said; "I am fortunate to be able to work in a hospital even as a janitor, but I want to die as a doctor." He knew, however, that his desire to go back to medical school in the US in order to become a doctor was unrealistic when he considered his English competency, his age, financial and other investments on his recertification process, and return on these investments. By the time he completed his internship, he would be in his early 60s and would be able to work only a few years. However, some families tried to capitalize on family human resources by considering not only one's needs but also one's abilities, especially the ability to be certified in their professional areas. One woman in her mid-30s, who was a doctor in Bosnia and was certified in the US by taking intensive courses, provided a success story in the Bosnian community:

> Yes. It was tough, but you know what, at that time I could talk in English, but all those medical terminology wasn't familiar to me and I had a lot of problems with behavioral science because there was a lot of words that I didn't even understand. Then I had to take a dictionary looking for that and all my books were actually [scribbled] with words. But when you're listening to tapes and you're reading constantly you just get it. And the test is in English and the test is really tough, I mean really tough even for an American student. Because I was taking exam with American students from Medical School so it's the same, and there is no difference between me and them on the test and we have to pass it. (Interview was conducted in English.)

Capitalizing on family human resources is possible when there are concerted efforts among family members, and when these members understand the meaning of postponing immediate fulfillment in order to achieve a better outcome in the future. Bosnian refugees in St. Louis have demonstrated an outstanding work ethic. Regardless of their region of origin, and urban or rural origin, Bosnians showed thriftiness and incentive in goal-oriented financial investment. One Bosnian woman whose family purchased a house two years after arrival in the US said:

> "When we studied English at a resettlement agency, they taught us how to use money. We knew that. We were living in a civilized country. We don't eat out so frequently like many Americans. … Buying a house is very important for us, and if you are thrifty, it is not that difficult to buy a house."

Bosnian work ethic and their strong desire for homeownership coincided with American values and created a positive public image of this refugee community in the St. Louis area.

Community Networks

Although some Bosnians moved to the surrounding St. Louis County, in some areas of the city of St. Louis they reached critical mass creating ethnic enclaves. As various immigrant groups in the US experienced in the past century, the ethnic enclave provides information networks and mutual support for new arrivals to the community. Bosnians exchange information about affordable housing, used cars, less expensive grocery stores, after-school activities for children and cheaper English classes. They also help each other by providing their own skills in car repair, plumbing, electronics and other areas which would be costly if they had to use paid services.

There is also a visible presence of Bosnian-owned small businesses, such as restaurants, grocery stores, bakeries, video stores, travel and real estate agencies. Although the exact number of Bosnian-owned businesses is not known, there must be more than 50 such stores. One American caseworker observed that "We don't know exactly how many such Bosnian stores are there, but if you walk in the area where Gravois and Chippewa meet, you will find many Bosnian restaurants, cafés, and bakeries." A Bosnian woman in her late 20's said:

> I like to walk along Gravois because it makes me feel [as if] I am in Bosnia. People walking on the street are Bosnians, talking [in] Bosnian … I like to go to a café with my Bosnian friends and talk. That's what we used to do in Bosnia. We just sat at a café, and talked many things. I also take my grandma to a café occasionally. She likes to see her friends there because there is nothing to do for her, you know. Talking to her friends in Bosnian [is] very good for her… It brings back all the memories about Bosnia. (Interview conducted in English)

Bosnians organized a Bosnian Chamber of Commerce (originally called the Balkan Chamber of Commerce) for the area with the assistance of the St. Louis Development Corporation. Those who opened their own businesses arrived from other countries with some savings, and also saved money in the US. Despite a number of Bosnians having an entrepreneurial background, without the presence of a critical mass of Bosnians in St. Louis, there would not have been many Bosnian businesses, as they primarily cater for Bosnian customers. These businesses became central to the Bosnian community life in St. Louis.

There are also Bosnian media. *South Side Journal*, a regional weekly newspaper in the area, has a one-page Bosnian section "St. Louis Novosti" which publishes news and information in Bosnian. In addition, there are a few Bosnian radio and TV stations with an estimated audience of 10,000 or more. These stations broadcast Bosnian programs within limited time slots and are very popular among Bosnians. One Bosnian man in his mid-sixties commented:

> "These shows are very interesting. When I listen to them, I think of my people in St. Louis. Since I don't have a car, I cannot go to the Bevo area [where Bosnian cafés are]. ... It [listening to Bosnian radio] is like many Bosnians going through a time tunnel together."

The ethnic enclave situation made Bosnians visible as a group. A large presence of an ethnic group is often perceived as a threat among mainstream Americans and may raise hostility toward the ethnic group (Bonacich, 1976). This has been observed in major cities with large intakes of immigrants, such as Los Angeles and Chicago. The US government's decision to specify St. Louis as one of the Bosnian resettlement cities, coupled with an economic boom in the area in the 1990's, increased the group's visibility. Although there are about 20,000 Asian Indians and almost an equal number of Koreans living in the metropolitan St. Louis, Bosnian refugees became synonymous with immigrants in the area.

Formal organizations are vital for the community to come together, enabling it to assemble resources and exchange information (Colic-Peisker, 2003; Neuhaus and Berger, 1977, Shelly, 2001). These organizations serve as a mediating structure among service providers, political representatives, and refugees. The network of service providers in St. Louis is well developed. A Yellow Page of refugee service providers in St. Louis lists several dozen voluntary service agencies and refugee programs. Some programs are targeted at specific ethnic populations, such as African, Bosnian and Vietnamese refugees. Other programs are based upon objectives of services, such as health, education, employment or housing. A Listserv (a list of e-mail addresses to send bulk e-mail messages) consisting of refugee service providers, also provides information and news relevant to refugees in other parts of the US and occasionally in other countries. Although the International Institute of Greater St. Louis and the Catholic Charities are key players in this service provider network, many individuals and small service programs are also linked into the information network.

Under the leadership of a Bosnian Imam (an Islamic spiritual leader), members of Bosnian community sought funding and contributions from various Bosnian and American organizations and purchased a building which they then transformed into a mosque in 2001. The mosque is not only a place of religious observance and spiritual support but also a place where the community gathers and where educational and cultural services, such as preschool education, summer school and Sunday school for children, and English classes and marriage counseling for adults, are provided. As mentioned, many Bosniaks in St. Louis are secular Muslims, and do not practice their religion as much as Middle Eastern Muslims do. However, the process of building a mosque has provided them an opportunity to reaffirm their ethnic identity, and the mosque has become a symbol of ethnic solidarity to some Bosnian refugees. This is comparable to the process of community building and reaffirmation of ethnic identity among Bosnian refugees in Western Australia through the construction of a Bosnian Community Center (Colic-Peisker, 2002).

A Catholic religious leader also organized an association called the Southside Bosnian Collaborative (SBC) in 2000, housed in one of the Catholic churches in St. Louis. The membership of the Southside Bosnian Collaborative is fluid, and consists of service providers, political representatives, business owners, and members of the Bosnian community. A major task of the organization is to disseminate information on health, education, and political issues by providing translated materials to the Bosnian community. For example, the SBC has translated the Missouri State Driver's Test into Bosnian, which has reduced the number of Bosnian refugees driving without a driver's license. They have also translated health related information, and distributed translated flyers at Bosnian grocery stores and restaurants. Health related information is also disseminated through a Bosnian TV show in order to make Bosnian refugees aware of the threats and risks of HIV and drug abuse. These activities were undertaken in conjunction with the Health Departments of St. Louis County and St. Louis City. In 2004, the SBC developed a proposal to recognize and acknowledge the large presence of Bosnians in St. Louis by designating the Bevo Mill area in which many Bosnians live as 'Little Sarajevo.'

Several mainstream organizations and educational institutions, including the St. Louis public school system and some universities, were also a part of this mediating structure. Needs assessments for adult refugees, refugee children and voluntary service providers were conducted with the assistance of university researchers and a national refugee organization, and recommendations given to the local, state, and federal governments. Some university researchers were involved with community projects targeted at solving problems, such as "prevention of drug use among Bosnian children," "providing health education to Bosnian women," and "AIDS prevention education for refugee youth".

Since many of these programs have been developed only in recent years, many Bosnians did not have the opportunity to access them. Also, Bosnians tend to use their own community resources more often than services provided by local resettlement agencies. There may also be a lack of awareness of the existence of some of these programs among refugees. There is no systematic assessment which evaluates the impact of these service programs on refugee communities. However, networks of formal organizations of service providers, which already existed in St. Louis, have been strengthened by the presence of a large number of Bosnians, connecting members of the refugee communities, service providers and researchers at various levels. Critical mass seems to be very important for ethnic groups to create solidarity and mutual support in a new environment (Baker, 1989; Colic-Peisker, 2002; Matsuo et al., 2002).

THE PRIVILEGE OF BEING EUROPEAN

The fact that most Bosniaks are secular Muslims as well as Europeans presents an interesting ethno-religious intersection, which has some bearing on their resettlement in the US. Muslims in America have experienced discrimination and have been denied full and equitable access to opportunities (Leonard, 2003). Immediately after the terrorist attack of September 11, 2001, some Middle Eastern Muslims in St. Louis experienced harassing incidents (Lutheran Immigration and Refugee Services, 2003). These incidents were targeted not only at immigrant Middle Eastern Muslims but also at American-born Muslims of Middle Eastern descent. The September 11 attack happened during my data collection and I explored its impact on the Bosnian community in St. Louis. No one in this study reported experiencing harassment. A woman in her late 50s said:

> I was watching TV, two buildings were falling apart. I cried and cried all day. It brought back the memories… Harassment? Never. I take a bus to work, and at the bus stop, nobody looks at me. We were persecuted because of our Muslim names, but here nobody knows that we are Muslims.(interview was conducted in Bosnian)

Bosnian women do not usually wear traditional Muslim veils, and many Middle Eastern Muslim women of the third and fourth generations do not either. Yet the latter group has experienced harassing incidents. This fact sheds light upon the importance of Bosnians' racial background as Europeans.

Discrimination based on minority's skin color and racial status still exists in the US. Although Vietnamese refugees have spent almost three decades in the US, they continue to face discrimination in many areas of social life (Fong, 1998; Lutheran Immigration and Refugee Services, 2003). Some African refugees for the first time experienced discrimination based upon skin color upon their arrival in the US. Bosnians, however, did not report the experience of prejudice and discrimination. They seem to be aware of their 'privilege' in being European refugees in American society, which continues to appreciate whiteness. A Bosnian man in his late twenties said:

> I am so grateful for what was given to me. I came here [as a] refugee, but they accept me. I speak English with accent, but they listen to me. In Germany, we were treated badly. You live in Germany 50 years, no citizenship. I am a permanent resident here, and can apply for a citizenship next year. No discrimination against Muslim names... People say America is a land of opportunity. It is true. All different people, they are all treated equally. Umm... I never experienced discrimination. We are Europeans. We are not black. (Interview was conducted in English.)

Although many Bosnians have experienced downward mobility and are in a lower income bracket (Matsuo, 2004) than the national median income of $42,000, they seem to prefer to identify themselves along racial lines, as 'whites' rather than along the lines of socio-economic position, which would place them to the lower rungs of society. Many caseworkers and university researchers whom I interviewed agree that the pride of being European is a feature unique to Bosnian refugees. Bosnian refugees seem to learn the fact that St. Louis is one of the most segregated cities in the US and that social class parallels racial lines. They also tend to think that those on welfare resent their past fate without striving to achieve better lives. A woman in her early 40s, working as a translator, mentioned:

> We came here without money… If you need money, you should take any job. My first job was housekeeping. … They are lazy. They think, 'we did not choose [to come] here, we were slaves.' We [Bosnians] did not choose America, either, but we have to work to survive.

A few Bosnians mentioned that they had some uncomfortable experiences initiated by American co-workers, but discrimination came in the form of jealousy about Bosnians' work ethic, rather than stemming from the prejudice against them.

One of the major problems that refugees face when they first arrive in the US is the language barrier. This especially pertains to Bosnians in their 40s and older. Although resettlement agencies provide English courses free of charge, it is difficult for older people to learn English as quickly as their children do. Another problem associated with English competency is the timing of refugees' entry into the labor market. A caseworker at one of the resettlement agencies observed: "The first two years are very important for refugees to spend some time to learn English. However, because of a lack of financial support in the beginning, many of them need to start working. Many of them do not have time to go to English classes."

However, it seemed that Bosnians tend to have a relatively better command of English than refugees from other ethnic backgrounds, such as Vietnamese and Africans who have lived in the US for the same length of time. A similar observation echoed among caseworkers and ESL instructors: "We have refugees from various ethnic backgrounds in the same class. Progress in learning, of course, depends on students' educational background and age. But in general, Bosnians seem to learn English faster than refugees from other countries." One of the reasons for this may be that many Bosnians already had the experience of learning a foreign language, because they migrated to the US after spending some time, and sometimes years, in Germany and Austria. Another reason may be that the Bosnian language is linguistically closer to English than many Asian and African languages are; some Bosnian words are spelt exactly the same way as in English.

Many caseworkers and researchers anticipate a faster integration of Bosnian refugees into American society than has been the case for other refugees groups. In the concluding section I analyze how these factors, such as group characteristics, family human capital investment, community networks and racial and religious backgrounds impact on Bosnian refugees' social integration and generational upward mobility.

Conclusion: The Prospects of Social Integration of Bosnian Refugees in the US

Some minority groups remain trapped at the bottom of the American social structure; Bosnians, however, seem to be achieving slow but steady success in their resettlement process. Most Bosnians in St. Louis are from working-class backgrounds. However, their resilience and a strong work ethic enabled many of them to lead fulfilling lives despite having gone through the ordeals of war, refugee camps and temporary protection. Once admitted as permanent residents, Bosnians set their goals: to recreate a normal life similar to the one they had in Bosnia and to provide good education to their children.

Figure 1 shows how major themes which emerged from the data, are related to each other. Besides group characteristics, accumulation of human capital was a driving force for Bosnians in setting their goals and striving to achieve them. The fact that most Bosnians came in family units provided them with a mechanism to retain many of their cultural values. One of these is an emphasis on family solidarity, which extends to kin. Another aspect of cultural values that they have retained is their work ethic, which parallels the 'protestant work ethic', that is self-discipline in postponing instant gratification for the sake of future goals and rational investment to realize these goals (Weber, 1958).[1] Although it was out of necessity,

[1] Japanese Americans' economic success in the past century, in spite of their racial minority status, is often explained by their work ethic (Biernat et al., 1996; Matsuo, 1992; Woodrum, 1981).

concerted efforts of family members during the early stage of resettlement have led to a relatively fast economic adaptation in the American setting. The speed of adaptation among the first generation is crucial in providing opportunities for upward mobility of the second generation (Portes and Zhou, 1993). Furthermore, although the educational level of many adult Bosnians was not high, they have placed a high value on their children's education. Although local resettlement agencies usually provide apartment housing in the inner city of St. Louis, where racial minority groups are concentrated because of low rents, many Bosnians have moved out of the inner city, seeking better educational opportunities for their children. Social workers and researchers in the St. Louis area anticipate greater economic success among Bosnian refugees and their children than among racial minorities who are relatively segregated from the rest of the society.

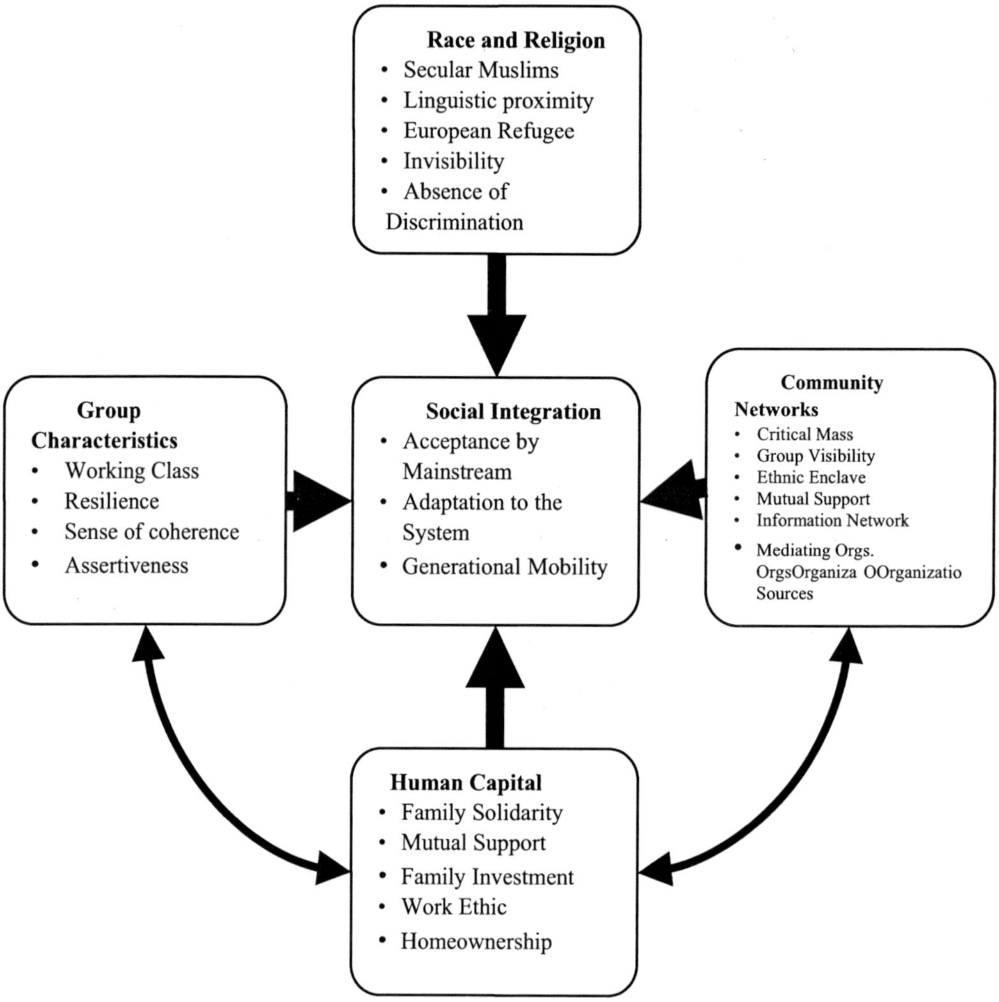

Figure 1. Bosnian Refugee Resettlement.

The resettlement of Bosnians in St. Louis would have had different dynamics if it was not such a large community. Baker (1989) argued the importance of the presence of critical mass for refugee groups to become self-sustaining in the new environment. The numerical strength of Bosnians has led to internal and external community networks and dynamics which are vital to accruing social capital of the group. Internally, the Bosnian community has provided necessary support to its members, ranging from Bosnian grocery stores and cafes, to ethnic organizations and Bosnian media. Externally, voluntary organizations, social workers and researchers have provided continuing support by arranging programs, events, and projects. In addition, local media have conveyed a mainly positive image of Bosnians which, in turn, facilitated their interaction with the mainstream society. The media coverage and a large number of Bosnians in St. Louis made the group visible and lead to its acceptance by mainstream Americans, which has not been the case with refugees from some other ethnic backgrounds. Bosnians' religious background as secular Muslims and their racial background as Europeans seem to have contributed to their acceptance by the mainstream society, rendering Bosnians racially 'invisible' in the American society which continues to appreciate whiteness.

ACKNOWLEDGEMENTS

I thank the Beaumont Faculty Fund at Saint Louis University for their support for the data collection of this study. I am also grateful to my research assistants Sara Garrow and Sara Beck and to Ademir Koric who was a translator for the data collection. Finally, I thank the respondents in this study for their valuable time and their feedback on my writing, and the reviewers of this chapter for their valuable comments.

REFERENCES

Antonovsky, A. (1984). The sense of coherence as a determinant of health. In J. Matarazzo (Ed.), *Behavioral Health: A Handbook of Health Enhancement and Disease Prevention.* New York: Wiley.

Back, R. (1980). Employment characteristics of Indochinese refugees. *Migration Today, 8*(3), 10- 12.

Baker, R. P. (1989). Eastern European Refugees: Implications for Social Work. *Journal of Sociology and Social Welfare, 16*(3), 81-94.

Biernat, M., Vescio, T. K., Theno, S. A. & Crandall, C. A. (1996). Values and Prejudice: Toward understanding the impact of American values on outgroup attitudes. In C. Seligman & M. James (Eds.), *The psychology of values: The Ontario symposium on personality and social psychology.*

Bonacich, E. (1973). A Theory of Middleman Minorities. *American Sociological Review, 3,* 583-594.

_____ . (1976) Advanced Capitalism and Black/White Relations in the United States: A Split Labor Market Interpretation. *American Sociological Review, 4,* 34-51.

Brookings Institution .(February 2004). The Rise of New Immigrants Gate Ways. *Living Cities Census Series.* Washington D.C.: Center on Urban and Metropolitan Policy.

Cohen, J. D. (1981). Psychological adaptation and dysfunction among refugee. *International Migration Review, 15*(1), 263-266.

Colic-Peisker, V. (2002). The process of community and identity building among recently arrived Bosnian Muslim refugees in Western Australia. *Mots Pluriels* No. 21. Retrieved from *www.arts.uwa.edu.au/MotsPluriels/MP2102vcp.html*

_____ . (2003). *European Refugees in (White) Australia: Identity, Community and Labour Market Integration.* National Europe Centre Paper No. 111, Retrieved from *http://www.anu.edu.au/NEC/vpeiskerNECpaper.pdf*

De Voe, D. (1981). Framing Refugees as Clients. *International Migration Review, 15*(1), 88-94.

De Voe, P. & Gold, S. J. (1993). Refugee Communities; A Comparative Field Study. *American Anthropologist, 95*(2), 467-468.

Dugan, M, Cook, C. & Kryah, R. (2004). *War related trauma and acculturation of Bosnia-Herzegovina refugees in St. Louis.* Paper presented at the Creating Livable Communities Symposium: Lining Research, Policy, and Practice, St. Louis, MO.

Feagin, J. R. (1984). *Racial and ethnic relations.* Englewood Cliffs: Prentice-Hall, Inc.

Fong, T. P. (1998). *The Contemporary Asian American Experience.* New Jersey: Prentice Hall.

Garcia, M. C. (1996). *Havana: Cuban Exiles and Cuban American in South Florida, 1959-1994.* Los Angeles, CA: University of California Press.

Geltman, P., Augustyn, M, Harnett, E. D., Klass, P. & Grove, B. M. (2000). War trauma experience and behavioral screening of Bosnian refugee children resettled in Massachusetts. *Journal of Developmental & Behavioral Pediatrics, 21*(4), 255-261.

Gold, S. J. (1992). *Refugee Communities.* Newbury Park, CA: Sage Publications.

Holman, P. A. (1996). Refugee Resettlement in the United States. In D. Haines (Ed.), *Refugees in America in the 1990's.* Westport, Connecticut: Greenwood Press.

International Institute of Greater St. Louis. (2002a). Refugee estimates for population with more than 500 individuals.

_____ . (2002b). Demographic Data on Bosnian Refugees Resettled. [Unpublished data].

Juan, R. & Leonard A. J. (1998). Job Interview Social Skills Training for Asian-American Immigrants. *Journal of Human Behavior in the Social Environment, 1*(4), 11-25.

Kopinak, J. K. (1999). The health of Bosnian refugees in Canada. *Ethnicity and Health, 4*(1-2), 65-82.

Liu, W. T., Lamanna, M. & Mirita, A. (1979). *Transition to Nowhere: Vietnamese Refugees in America.* Nashvill, TN: Charter House.

Legett, S, Karahodzic, E., Hemley, K, Klie, M., Kleeper, N., Klutho, R., Homan, S. & Noguchi, A. (2001). Health status of Bosnian children in St. Louis, Missouri. *Society for Pediatric Research* 40-154A (abstract).

Leonard, K. I. (2003). *Muslims in the United States: The State of Research.* New York: Russell Sage Foundation.

Lutheran Immigration and Refugee Services. (2003). *Direction in Service Provision: Findings From Needs Assessments of Refugee Youth, Children, and Parents.* Baltimore, MD. *www.lirs.org.*

Matsuo, H. (1992). Identificational Assimilation of Japanese Americans: A Reassessment of Primordialism and Circustantialism. *Sociological Perspectives, 35*(3), 503-523.

_____ . (2004). [Research on Bosnian Refugees]. Unpublished raw data.

Matsuo, H., Garrow, S. & Koric, A. (2002). 'Resettlement Process of Refugee Immigrants from Bosnia and Herzegovina in St. Louis: Finding Material and Emotional Niches'. Paper presented at the *XV World Congress of Sociology*, Brisbane, Australia.

Mayadas, N. S. & Segal, U. A. (2000). Refugees in the 1990s" A US perspective. In P.R. Balgopal (Ed.), *Social work practice with immigrants and refugees*. New York: Columbia University Press.

Neuhasu, J. R. & Berger, P. (1977). *To Empower People: The Role of Mediating Structures in Public Policy*. Washington, DC: American Enterprise Institute for Public Policy Research.

Nguyen, M. N. (1997). Vietnam Amerasians: Assimilation and Adjustment Problems in the United States. *Journal of Multicultural Social Work*, 6(1-2), 77-91.

Portes, A. & Bach, R. (1985). *Latin Journey: Cuban and Mexican Immigrants in the United States*. Berkeley, CA: University of California Press.

Portes, A. & Zhou, M. (1993, November). The New Second Generation: Segmented Assimilation and Its variants. *Annals of the American Academy of Political and Social Sciences*, *530* ,74-96.

Rynearson, A. (1999). Gatekeepers and Culture Brokers: Refugee Access to American Institutions. In J. Lipson & L. McSpadden (Eds.), *Negotiating Power and Place at the Margins*. Vol. VII. Arlington, VA: American Anthropological Association.

Schatzman, L. & Strauss, A. (1973). *Field Research*. Englewood Cliffs, NJ: Prentice-Hall.

Shelly, N. M. (2001). Building Community from "Scratch": Forces at Work among Urban Vietnamese Refugees in Milwaukee. *Sociological Inquiry*, *71*(4), 473-492.

Somach, D. S. (1995). *Proceeding of Meeting the Needs of Bosnian Refugees*. Washington, D.C.: Center for Applied Linguistics, Refugee Service Center.

Stein, B., Comer, D., Gardner, W., & Kelleher, K. (1999). Prospective study of displaced children's symptoms in wartime Bosnia. *Social Psychiatry & Psychiatric Epidemiology*, *34*(9), 464-469.

St. Louis Post-Dispatch. (1998, October 25). Bosnians Put Down Roots in St. Louis, They are Buying Homes and Opening Businesses. Record Number: 9810250191.

US Department of Justice. (1999, July). Refugees, Fiscal Year 1997. *Annual Report of Office of Policy and Planning*. No. 4, 1-10.

US Department of Commerce. (1999, October). *Statistical Abstract of the United States: The National Data Book.*

Van S., Karin, D., Lackland S. & Van Oudenhoven, J. P. (1997). Life satisfaction and competence of Bosnian Refugees in Norway. *Scandinavian Journal of Psychology*, *38*, 13-149.

Weber, M. (1958). *The Protestant Ethic and the Spirit of Capitalism*. New York: Scribner's.

Weine, S., Kulenovic, A. D., Pavkovic, I. & Gibbons, R. (1998). Testimony psychotherapy in Bosnian refugees: a pilot study. *American Journal of Psychiatry*,*15*(12),1720-1726.

Weinfield, M. (1981). Myth and reality in the Canadian mosaic: Affective ethnicity. *Canadian Ethnic Studies*, *13*(3), 80-100.

Woodrum, E. (1981). An Assessment of Japanese American Assimilation, Pluralism, and Subordination. *American Journal of Sociology*, *87*, 157-169.

In: Homeland Wanted ISBN 1-59454-266-X
Editors: P. Waxman and V. Colic-Peisker, pp. 127-145

Chapter 7

SURVIVING WAR, STARTING OVER: ADAPTATION OF BOSNIAN REFUGEES IN UPSTATE NEW YORK

Reed Coughlan and Judith Owens-Manley

ABSTRACT

This chapter explores the resettlement experience of a sample of 20 Bosnian families who recently arrived in a small city in upstate New York. We used open-ended questions to elicit narratives that would help us to understand the experiences of these Bosnians before the war in their homeland, during the conflict and in the period of resettlement following transit. We wanted to learn as much as possible about Bosnian society and culture before the war in order to more fully appreciate the adaptation these refugees were required to make in resettlement. The families in this sample appear to have successfully resettled as a result of the services provided by the local refugee center, a labor market that provides employment to those with limited English proficiency and a housing market that supplies affordable homes. This combination of variables has contributed to a sense of independence, autonomy and self-efficacy, even though many of them are unable to fully integrate and acculturate because of limited English language skills.

Key words: Bosnian refugees, resettlement, acculturation, adaptation, displacement, integration.

INTRODUCTION

Before the war in the 1990s, Bosnia-Herzegovina, more commonly known as Bosnia, was one of six republics comprising the Federation of Yugoslavia. In the wars that followed the dissolution of Yugoslavia, hundreds of thousands of Bosnian civilians were displaced and sought refuge internally and abroad. Between 1993 and 2002 more than 100,000 Bosnians were relocated to the United States and about 12,000 of them came to New York State (Bureau of Refugee and Immigration Affairs [BRIA], 2004). Of these, 4,500 Bosnians moved to the City of Utica in upstate New York (Mohawk Valley Resource Center for Refugees

[MVRCR], 2004). This chapter focuses on Bosnian families who were resettled in Utica, N.Y.

Over the past two decades, the MVRCR, an affiliate of the Lutheran Immigration Refugee Services (LIRS), has helped to resettle more than 10,000 refugees from more than 20 countries in Utica, New York. The three major refugee groups in Utica are Bosnians, Russians, and Vietnamese. Refugees are estimated, conservatively, to comprise about twelve percent of Utica's population of 60,651 — the fourth highest per capita refugee population in the country (Coughlan & Owens-Manley, 2002a). Only Phoenix, Chicago and St. Louis have a higher refugee density (Hassett, 1999).

The 1980 Federal Refugee Act fashioned a national Refugee Resettlement Program for the United States from a network of private resettlement agencies and public agencies (BRIA, 2004). Resettlement programs are operated by nonprofit groups affiliated with ten agencies nationwide, including the Lutheran Immigration and Refugee Services. The Department of State contracts with the ten agencies to place refugees in host communities, and each state participating in the national program is represented by a State Refugee Coordinator. In New York State, the BRIA supports the work of the Coordinator, primarily through contracts with local service providers. The main programs that BRIA administers are the Refugee Social Services Program (RSSP), which provides job training and placement services and the Targeted Assistance Grant (TAG) for refugees who need continued employment assistance as a result of layoffs, job upgrades, or for individuals with multiple barriers to employment (BRIA, 2004). There is no specific requirement that they be employed within six months, but the federal funding to cover basic living expenses, administered through the national voluntary agencies and state offices, rarely extends beyond six months. The actual legislative language does not give a specific time frame, but says repeatedly that refugees should be "self-sufficient as quickly as possible" (IRSA, email communication with Shannon Dennet, 29 July 2004). A refugee may change his or her legal status to a legal permanent resident after one year, and after five years, refugees may apply for citizenship (Mamgain & Collins, 2003).

Bosnians who may have relocated since their initial resettlement in Utica have been replaced with individuals and families who are attracted to the available employment and inexpensive housing, along with a strong center for refugee support. Thus, Bosnians in Utica are estimated to number at least 5,000, about half of the refugee population that has resettled there (MVRCR, 2004). Bosnian refugees began arriving in Utica in 1993, with arrivals peaking in 1997 when more than 1,100 individuals were resettled (MVRCR, 2004). After September 11, 2001, the influx of refugees slowed down as immigration restrictions tightened for family reunification. The family re-unification program for Bosnians has now closed.

Prior to our study, little was known locally of the Bosnian refugees. In keeping with policies and funding streams for refugee resettlement, MVRCR, their initial source of help in Utica, is most active in the lives of refugees in the first six months, promoting English language skill acquisition and employment. There is often little further contact with the agency once refugees find employment.

We sought to explore how Bosnian families adapted to life in this community. As researchers we come from different theoretical and empirical backgrounds. This influenced both the direction of the research and the lenses we used to view the findings. Coughlan is a sociologist with expertise in ethnic conflict, drawing us to focus on the origins of the war and the Bosnians' understandings of what the war was about. Owens-Manley is a social worker and psychotherapist with expertise in psychological trauma and a board member with

MVRCR. The latter perspective drew our attention to the long-term impact of war and displacement on people's lives.

Difficulties in adaptation have been documented for refugee groups that resettled in the last two decades, especially for the Southeast Asians (Mollica et al., 1987b; Beiser et al., 1989; Matsuoka & Ryujin, 1989-90; Montgomery, 1991; Mollica et al., 1992; Pernice & Brook, 1996; Nicholson & Walters, 1997). Studies of Bosnian refugees were relatively sparse until the late 1990s when a number of researchers began to separate pre-migration and transit effects from post-migration stressors and to document their impact on the well being of refugees. In addition, most of the literature has focused on clinical populations or on refugees early in their adjustment period. Researchers have increasingly focused on how refugees, especially after experiencing the atrocities and deprivations of war, adjust in the communities that received them (Van Selm et al., 1997; Waxman, 1998; George & Tsang, 2000; Waxman, 2001; Miller et al., 2002; Colic-Peisker & Walker, 2003; Kelly, 2003; Korac, 2003).

Miller et al. (2002, p.342) describe "…the profound crises of meaning, faith and identity that may result from forced migration and exposure to extreme violence", and many Bosnian refugees had such experiences. Their personal crises are difficult to understand without a rudimentary grasp of the Bosnian war and its consequences, which we acquired during our research. This chapter cannot cover the complexities of the Bosnian war, but over the past decade plentiful literature has dealt with it (Malcolm, 1994; Burg & Stroup, 1999). It should be mentioned that in the context of the community of Bosnians that we studied in upstate New York, more than half of the families came from the Northwest corner of Bosnia that engaged in a Muslim-against-Muslim civil war. This little known conflict continues to generate tension in the Bosnian community in Utica.

This chapter reports on the tales of struggle and survival told by 20 Bosnian families, a subset of a larger study of 100 families whom we had interviewed earlier in the year 2000. We wanted to interview families in a non-clinical population who had been relatively successful in their adaptation and who had been in the country for several years prior to our fieldwork. These interviews helped us to learn about three important periods of time in the lives of Bosnian families adapting to life in upstate New York: their lives before the war, their experiences during the war and its immediate aftermath, and their experiences adapting to life in the United States. We describe the resettlement experience of these families in three domains of adaptation — economic, socio-cultural, and psychological (Berry, 1992) and we suggest that there are three principle explanations for the relative success of Bosnians in upstate New York: the availability of a central resource center for refugees, the opportunity for employment and the opportunity to own a home.

METHODOLOGY

The design of our study was informed by our research questions. We wanted to learn about how individuals and families adapted to life in their new communities and how their adaptation was influenced by the contexts of their lives before and during the war. We also learned about their wartime experiences. Our interest in learning about these experiences derived from our awareness of the potential impact of trauma and loss upon resettlement and acculturation efforts (Weine, 1999; Fullilove, 1996).

The qualitative study of 20 families presented here (a subset of the larger study of 100 families referred to earlier) combined use of qualitative and quantitative methods. The larger study focused on a population of Bosnian refugees in Utica, New York, who had either purchased a home or had passed their citizenship tests. The larger study employed a semi-structured interview questionnaire that included variables such as employment, wages earned, language skill, and life satisfaction, as well as open-ended questions. The 20 families in the subset were chosen for a second, more in-depth, open-ended interview because of concerns about the elevated emotional distress levels that they had demonstrated in responses to the Hopkins 25 Symptoms Checklist (Mollica et al., 1987a) which they had completed in the first round of interviews. Following a participatory model of community-based research (Williams, 1999), we felt obligated to contact this group of families again in order to offer referrals to community mental health agencies.

In the sub-sample of 20 families, similarly to the larger sample, 65 per cent of the heads of household were under forty years of age; all but one family had children; all but two were homeowners; and, about 60 percent came from the northwest corner of Bosnia. The average age of these heads of household, usually male, was 38, while 50 per cent were younger than 36, and only four in the sample were over 60 years old. Most families had young children.

The instrument for the second round of interviews reported here consisted of general categories of prompts for discovery which elicited narratives of experience. For instance, we asked open-ended questions about material culture and the rhythms of work and leisure before the war. We also inquired about events that stood out during the war, stories during transit, including countries of first asylum, as well as current challenges. All completed the Hopkins 25 Symptoms Checklist (Mollica et al., 1987a), and most heads of household and, sometimes the partners, completed the Trauma Events Questionnaire (Mollica et al., 1992).[1] The 20 families were interviewed in their own homes. Our interpreter scheduled the interviews. Both authors conducted all interviews with the assistance of a primary interpreter, who was male, and a female interpreter, who assisted when it seemed important to speak separately to the woman of the household. The interviews took approximately one and a half hours. We did not audiotape interviews due to concerns about language barriers and about the integrity of transcription with the use of interpreters and multiple speakers, but we took copious notes.

Summaries were prepared from the twenty interviews in Word documents and loaded into QSR NUD*IST (Richards & Richards, 2000). Coding processes followed procedures recommended by Miles and Huberman (1994). From there, we chose to let the data inductively emerge into categories. This method is consistent with the grounded approach favored by Strauss (1987).

RESEARCH ON REFUGEE RESETTLEMENT

The process of refugee flight and recovery has been conceived of three stages, namely, pre-migration and departure, transit, and resettlement (Drachman, 1992). However for our purposes, we have defined the stages as: life before the war, experiences during war and

---

[1] Both instruments are included in the Harvard Trauma Questionnaire, Harvard Trauma Manual, Harvard Program in Refugee Trauma, Harvard Medical School. The manual provides Bosnian translations.

transit, and experiences in resettlement. The literature on refugee resettlement, in our view, pays too little attention to the first two stages, with the exception of the work by Weine and colleagues (Weine et al., 1995; 1998; Weine, 1999; Weine & Kuc 2001) who primarily focus on experiences in war. Miller et al. also draw attention to pre-war life as an important context for refugees to define their current lives, noting that "life prior to exile becomes a central reference point among refugees for the evaluation of their present life circumstances" (2002, p. 342). We, too, believe that it is important to consider refugees' lives before the war because it is a frame of reference for evaluating and comparing their current experience in the host society (Owens-Manley & Coughlan, 2002).

A few researchers have begun to develop theoretical models with implications for long-term adjustment and adaptation (Searle & Ward, 1990; Berry, 1992; Aycan & Berry, 1996; Montgomery, 1996). Aycan & Berry, (1996) emphasize economic adaptation, socio-cultural adaptation and psychological adaptation as three distinct and equally important measures of successful adjustment in a new host country. Studies designed to evaluate refugee adjustment along these dimensions have tended to emphasize objective measures (Lamba, 2003; Mamgain & Collins, 2003) whereas Montgomery (1996) makes the observation that subjective perceptions on the part of refugees can be as important as objective measures of adaptation and adjustment.

Miller et al. (2002, p. 341) take a broad view of the "stressors of exile" and argue that the effects of war trauma are significantly compounded by sources of post-migration distress such as lack of adequate income, language barriers and social isolation. Their inductive methodology employs semi-structured interviews that allows them to describe, in more depth, variables that have been overlooked in the empirical literature such as "social isolation, and the loss of community, separation from family members, the loss of important life projects, the lack of environmental mastery, poverty and related stressors" (Miller et al., 2002, p. 341).

Resettlement, Adaptation and Acculturation

Displacement for refugees is generally associated with significant underemployment and downward mobility. Consequently, variables that affect economic adaptation are an important concern (Aycan & Berry, 1996). Many studies report on the unemployment rate among refugees being considerably higher relative to the rate in the host society (Eastmond, 1998; Waxman, 2001; Colic-Peisker, 2003; Korac, 2003). This is an important consideration, since unemployment is associated with dependency and this, in turn, is a major obstacle to shedding the negatively stereotyped role of refugee (Harrell-Bond, 1999). Colic-Peisker identifies "labour market integration [as] the single most important aspect of successful resettlement and social inclusion in general" (2003, p. 17, see also Colic-Peisker & Waxman, this volume).

Three recent studies of the economic adjustment of refugees included Bosnians in their samples and concluded that English language proficiency is the best predictor of success in the labor market. Mamgain and Collins (2003) evaluated the experience of a mixed sample in the town of Portland, Maine in the United States. Besides this anticipated finding, there was the suggestion that education was helpful for women, but less so for men (Mamgain & Collins, 2003). Lamba (2003) examined the effect of human and social capital on employment of 525 refugees in Canada, more than half of whom were from the former

Yugoslavia. Lamba (2003, p. 1) observed downward occupational mobility in his sample and noted that human capital among those refugees has "little or no value in the Canadian labour market."

Waxman (2001), who studied the economic adjustment of refugees from Bosnia, Afganistan and Iraq in Sydney, Australia, found, like Lamba, that education had no impact on employment outcomes. His recommendations include the provision of more English language instruction for refugees, more training in job skills and providing employment counseling (Waxman, 2001). In another study, completed in the city of Utica, New York, Hagstrom concluded that "...while the returns are slow and modest in magnitude ... refugees [are] net contributors ... their participation in labor markets leads to growing benefits for the community" (2000, p. 44).

The Relevance of Resettlement Policy and Services

The experience of resettlement for refugees will vary depending on the policies that govern the process and the nature and extent of services offered in the host society. Colic–Peisker and Walker (2003) suggest that the choice of acculturation strategy adopted by refugees is influenced by the human capital they bring with them and whether they come from an urban or rural background. Those from rural areas will be more likely to adopt a collectivist resettlement style and reside close to their co-ethnics, while urban dwellers will be apt to engage in individualistic strategies and will blend more readily into the host society (ibid., 2003, pp. 351-352). However, refugees' choices are also constrained by structural realities such as resettlement policies, the receptivity of the host society and by policies that govern the recognition of foreign qualifications (ibid).

An early and extensive analysis of Bosnian refugee resettlement in the US was developed by Somach (1995), who reached the conclusion that, "the services available to refugees varies widely by state, city [and] agency" (1995, p. 2). A study of resettlement experiences in Canada concluded that Bosnians experience three types of resettlement difficulties: immediate problems with language, employment and housing, problems with access to services, and problems of isolation (George and Tsang, 2000, p. 391). The authors believe that some of these problems could be mitigated by a further development of Canadian settlement policy, a recommendation not unlike the one implied in Somach's (1995) analysis of American resettlement policies. A more recent evaluation of service provision in Australia called for greater consultation and coordination of services (Waxman, 1998).

A comparative study by Korac (2003) contrasted the highly centralized Dutch resettlement program with the Italian model under which refugees are provided minimal assistance. Korac found that the Dutch resettlement program tends to create dependency among refugees and to undercut their sense of self-esteem and empowerment. While recognizing the initial adverse effects of the lack of refugee assistance in Italy, she believes that, in the long run, this may help forge diverse "spontaneous and individualized" social networks, and achieve social inclusion that eluded the Bosnians in the Netherlands (Korac, 2003, p. 61; see also Korac, this volume).

BOSNIAN FAMILIES IN UTICA, NY: EMERGENT THEMES OF REFUGEE ADAPTATION

Families who we interviewed differed in the emphasis that each gave to particular parts of their stories. Some families provided greater detail about their pre-war and post-war lives, while other respondents focused on stories of the war. In the larger sample of families these discussions were emotionally difficult and for the 20 families selected for the second interviews, this was especially true. Our respondents spontaneously supplemented accounts of their lives prior to or during the war in Bosnia with photographs or videotapes. These visual materials showed their villages and landmarks, or funerals at which relatives were buried, or signs of destruction following ethnic cleansing, or the exodus from hometowns brought about by the approach of an enemy army. Their recollection of those experiences through the telling of their stories brought a myriad of feelings into play, but also demonstrated their commitment to survival and to the future — an altered future from the one they had anticipated prior to the war.

War and displacement brought an abrupt end to what many described as the "beautiful life." For many Bosnian refugees, life in America pales in comparison to recollections of life in Bosnia before the war. In resettlement, the experience of having lost everything was paramount – even loss of a personal sense of self. The finding that, in spite of everything, many or most refugees rated their current life as good to excellent was surprising, and we address that in our discussion and conclusions.

All but two of the heads of household whom we interviewed were employed and about half were still in the original jobs they had first taken. These were usually unskilled positions, making less than $7.00 per hour. Those who had changed jobs had moved to a higher wage of between $7.00 and $10.00 per hour, and a few men were making more than $10.00 per hour. Two men had completed a university degree in Bosnia, eleven had completed secondary school, and four had only finished primary school.[2] For about half of the men, their current jobs represented a change in employment from their occupation in Bosnia and resulted in lower income and status. This is consistent with the finding that downward economic mobility is common among refugees whose previous skills are either not acknowledged or are not transferable in the host society (Lamba, 2003; Mamgain and Collins, 2003; Colic-Peisker 2003).

Most of the families arrived in the United States between 1995 and 1998, but some had left Bosnia as early as 1992. Some families from eastern and central Bosnia spent two or more years in Germany or Pakistan before arriving to the US. Families from the northwest corner of Bosnia were usually in refugee camps in Croatia for some time before coming to the US. All but three families had purchased homes in Utica; and more than half of the homeowners had been here only two to three years. Seven of the homeowners had homes that included at least one rental unit; several others had that capability, but they used the whole house for extended family members without collecting rent. All but three families had also owned homes in Bosnia; two others had been living with their parents in Bosnia, who also owned their homes. In earlier papers we had reported that home ownership was a strong value

---

2 Educational levels were unavailable for three interviewees.

for the Bosnians we had interviewed (Coughlan & Owens-Manley, 2002a; 2002b; see also Colic-Peisker, 2003).

Sixteen of the twenty respondents suffered from depression or distress. The 12 men who completed the Trauma Events Questionnaire reported experiencing a range of traumatic events. These events could be reported and taken into account as an important determinant of resettlement only in a qualitative study, as numbers in the Trauma Events Questionnaire cannot express the range of horrific experiences that traumatized many people. The following discussion identifies themes that emerged from interviews with the twenty families and sketches stories about their lives before the war, their experiences during war and their adjustments to life in a new country.

Pre-War Bosnia: 'A Beautiful Life'

As mentioned, life in Bosnia before the war is remembered as "*the beautiful life*" or "*the perfect life*"; filled with family, close friends, with travel, and having a more relaxed lifestyle than they would find in America. The following quotes[3] evoke nostalgic memories for two young adults:

> We had such a nice life, a little farm. My father built a big house. He said, 'do something.' I liked to go out with friends after school, play handball, play billiards, play soccer, go on river. (66)
>
> I had a beautiful childhood, playing outside and going to the sea sometimes. In high school and after, I played in a band and had a wonderful youth, vacationing without parents from the age of 16 or so with friends. We were able to travel cheaply, stay in homes on the Adriatic Sea. (6)

Respondents described rich social networks and close family ties in contrast to the family separation they have experienced since the war. Rural life was described through idyllic images:

> We had enough money for ourselves, had good friends, good neighborhood, houses far but not too far, in village. Farmers were up at 5:00 a.m. I baked bread and had sheep. In May, we had shearing, and wool was dyed for me to weave rugs, very attractive. We also had a cow, horse, and grew all our own vegetables and canned for winter. Food was mostly meat, potatoes, beans, and I made different pitas. (65)
>
> I had animals, orchards, vegetable garden. In summertime, I woke at 5:00 a.m., milked cow, take care of kids, go to garden. Raised mostly enough for us. Sometimes I take break from sun mid- day and go back and work in evening. (54)

Young parents described their life in urban settings as one in which you could rely on neighbors and friends.

> Children played everywhere in safety without parents, with a key around their neck to get into home. Everyone watched all of the children. Here it is very hard to be a parent. No one helps you, and you are responsible alone for everything. (6)

---

3 Each number found within the parentheses represents a different respondent, thus allowing anonymity to be maintained.

We were told that in rural Bosnia the man of the household typically worked outside of the home while his wife tended the subsistence farm. Under this arrangement, "there was a better life in Bosnia before the war than here. We worked less than here and could do more with money." (54) Similarly, several men whom we interviewed commented that they "felt rich" in Bosnia, because they owned two or more homes, with one in the mountains or by the sea. In contrast, their perception was that they had to work harder in the US and will have less to show for their efforts.

Bosnia is also described as a multicultural society in which no one knew or cared if you were Croat, Serb, or Muslim: "Before war, we had that 'brotherhood and unity' and everything was good." A typical pre-war description of the country was, "Yugoslavia was its own country with no ethnic tensions." Responses are often nostalgic.

> Before everyone was the same – everything is different now. It was a good, nice life. I don't know why. Everyone was like brother, sister, you go to work you like, building house and everyone comes. Not now, attitudes have changed, not friends. Now about money, changed because of war. (75) Nearly everyone reported that ethnic tensions did not exist in the multicultural Bosnia.

> No one asked about religion or ethnicity. It didn't happen and would have appeared as something wrong with questioner.
> Differences were there, but it was like in the United States, everyone celebrated all the holidays together. Before the war, no one really cared about the ethnic background of anyone else.

The contrast with the ethnic hatred that had been generated by war is striking. The outbreak of war suddenly engendered distrust between groups that had previously existed side-by-side.

These depictions of an idyllic life in pre-war Bosnia obviously gloss over the actual political and economic conditions that led up to war. The crumbling economy and massive inflation of the late 1980's and the ascendance of nationalism are detailed in the literature on the antecedents of the war (Woodward, 1995; Silber and Little, 1996). The trauma of war and displacement and the stressors of resettlement can engender nostalgia for a romanticized past that may bear little resemblance to reality. Nonetheless, our respondents recollect that they were surprised by the outbreak of war; most of them did not see it coming.

'War Is Hell: We Had no Control, the World didn't Help, Families Suffered'

War is described as happening almost overnight. Escape was dangerous, especially for men, who were conscripted into as many as three or four different armies during the war.

> It was unbelievably sudden. We knew there was fighting in Croatia, but we never thought it would come to us. April was a funny month in Sarajevo in 1992. The war had started, but you could still travel around the city. Just needed papers and you would be checked. (6)
> Nobody believed war would come. Now my father has been missing for seven years, and I don't know what happened to him. (81)

The war experience for those caught up in the Muslim versus Muslim civil war in the northwest corner was difficult for all to describe and difficult for us to understand. The boundaries of identity and of constructed "enemy" were blurred and easily crossed. There has been some open dissension within the Bosnian community in Utica. Many of those whom we interview speak of bad feelings between the two groups of Muslims in the city. Those feelings appear to be fading as time passes, but quarrels and brawls at work, at clubs, and at athletic events are known to have occurred.

This little known conflict toward the end of the war in Bosnia did not involve ethnicity. There was little to differentiate soldiers on one side— the army of the local Muslim warlord — from the other — the official Bosnian (predominately Muslim) army. It was difficult to tell whose side an individual had taken. We were told that it was an individual choice. People told us stories of being forcibly conscripted, imprisoned, tortured and humiliated by one (or both) of the two armies, and described circumstances which forced them to change sides in the war, sometimes more than once. In addition, men often had no choice about fighting, or indeed, about what they were sometimes forced to do if they were captured.

Many respondents shared a belief that other countries should have provided more assistance, both during the war and afterwards. Although not all respondents discussed this, the ones who did, expressed both bitterness and ambivalence. Some gave credit to the United States for providing opportunities to start over. This was especially true when compared with Germany, which did not give Bosnians access to permanent residency or citizenship (see Halilovich, this volume). However, several men were pointed in their criticism of the US and other countries for not intervening in the war earlier. This middle-aged respondent's words are both typical and fervent:

> We were all just victims, nothing else. The world didn't intervene when we died. 100,000 people were taken to concentration camps in the first two months. When we started winning, the US and Europe intervened. They didn't want a Muslim country. (81)

During the war, families suffered from deprivation, separations, and losses of family members and friends. Men described to us, often with their wives interjecting, the struggle to survive during war.

> I had to do everything while my husband was a soldier – son helped. We would see each other once in a while. Grenades and bombarding were common. The garden was a little far, and I made a home in the tool shed. I stayed there off and on. It was dangerous, but we were lucky. No one was hurt. His cousin was killed in the war. (54)
>
> I came to US May 7, 1996. Wife and children came November 20, 1996. Separated from wife and children August 1995 until November 1996. Wife was pregnant first time I was captured. She and children went to Cazin [a town in northwestern Bosnia] in August 1995. I saw my daughter for first time when they arrived in the US in November 1996. (91)

Deprivation was often severe, even for those not in the direct line of fire.

> Food was getting scarce, roads were closed, stores closed down. We were stuck there – nobody could get in or out. We had flour – couldn't get sugar, salt, oil, detergent for two years. Kids started getting sick, two children died of starvation. People who didn't store ahead and didn't have farms were very bad off. No money – nothing could be sent. (75)

Our respondents from Sarajevo described the precarious life in the capital divided along ethnic lines. A respondent told of the circumstances surrounding her mother's experience with ethnic violence:

> My mother was a telecommunications planner, so there were maps in the house. Muslim neighbors came and beat her and robbed her because they said she was spying for the Serbs. They said she left laundry on balcony as signal to Serbs. My uncle was shot in the head by snipers and Muslims were happy for that. 'You will be dead too' they told my mother. (6)

Resettlement: 'We've Lost Everything, Life has Changed, Look to the Future'

The initial resettlement experience, difficult for nearly everyone, was usually expressed as fear, confusion, and even anger.

> Everything was difficult when we first came. The language, the airport, not knowing what any of the signs mean or where to go. I was crying all of the time when I first got here – it was so hard to understand.
> At first, I was lost. I had never left my parents or family before. Everything was confusing – day- by-day. I'm sorry now that I didn't learn English [in Bosnia]. (91)

One man tells us about his unsettling experience on arriving at JFK airport and then, shortly afterwards, in Utica.

> JFK Airport was a big shock to us after glossy airport in Frankfurt, Germany. Everything was so old and dirty. People walked, actually they ran, in funny clothes. Everything looked like a big joke. This was America?!? Through the mass of people I went outside the building to light up my cigarette. An old van was parked in front of the entrance. Its body was rusted, dirty with lots of holes on it. Bumper was made of wood?!? What is this? Where are the big buildings? Where are people in suits and ties? Where are limousines? This cannot be America! My wife was crying. We were all sweaty. It was June 26, 1996. The heat was incredible. What are we doing here? That day they sent us to Utica. Our apartment was its own story. If it weren't sad we would have laughed about it. But it was sad. Sad and scary. Out on the street was loud. Some people were screaming. Glass was breaking somewhere. Three houses across the street were burned almost to the ground. Is there maybe a civil war in America that we didn't know about?(6)

Families experienced tremendous losses of all kinds. Two older men describe the pervasiveness and the permanence of the sense of loss:

> I lost things, family, friends, house. I cannot go back to those. Some of those friends are not alive. (84)
> We've lost everything we had. Our soul is empty. I have feelings of emptiness inside. All of my life I tied to make something, I lost it all, and now hands are tied, I'm stuck. (45)

Some sense that their identity is lost when their culture of origin is not recognized or known, an experience that causes some indignation:

> Many Americans are unaware of our cultural identity. Some people ask where Bosnia is – in Middle East? Asked did we have TV in Bosnia?(84)

As reported, the experience of loss goes much further — the loss of youth, of profession, of status.

> When the war started, it just cut off my youth. My youth was stolen. I had to assume the life of an adult when I was 19 or 20. (6)
>
> You lose everything you've had, start from scratch, do very simple work here and have a very low income. You lose your ranking in society. Used to work in office, in profession, required very specialized skills. (84)
>
> It was difficult for us because we had everything in Bosnia and here we have nothing. Many of us have college degrees and many work in simple jobs – low-paying and not in areas for which we prepared. (84)
>
> In Bosnia I owned two houses which I built myself. We lost everything. Came with empty hands. Here nobody helps. (65)

But for others, especially rural Bosnians who had been engaged in subsistence farming, life now seems easier and more comfortable. The husband spoke first:

> We like to work and we like to have everything. We're in a hurry. (85)

His wife describes her duties on the subsistence farm and says,

> Work here is much easier than work I had to do in Bosnia. I miss the beauty and countryside, but I would never go back to that. (85)

When talking about their satisfaction with life, most men and women had mixed feelings. War brought significant life changes, and many expressed those as a change in their emotional state, or a sense that something within them had been altered. Again, the contrast is evident with life as it was before.

> War changed me, makes me easily upset. I'm changed – I cry very easily. I didn't sleep for two years after the war, at my mother's. My heart is heavy. Kids forget fast, but older people can't. (69)
>
> Life is hard, not really good friends like I had in Sarajevo. Life is just okay, needs more lightness and fun like before. (6)
>
> We're scared from the problem in our country, still scared in the head. The kids are always with me or husband or his brothers and sisters. (57)
>
> Now, life is nothing very special. Everybody has to work and not a lot of time to be together. All those payments... money... I can't have everything I'm supposed to have after working so hard. (54)
>
> Small things make me really mad. I'm supposed to be satisfied because I'm still alive, but who knows how much good I will be. Before the war, I had an excellent memory. .. now I can't remember my own phone number. (91)
>
> I get nervous really easily. I don't know how people who've been through worse things can be calm at all. (45)

The Bosnians we interviewed exhibited various attitudes toward life. Some seemed optimistic in spite of their experiences of war and disruption. Others seemed to have been broken by them. The following two quotes represent these contrasting viewpoints. A woman in her early thirties expressed a sense of optimism and determination,

> The good change is I like staying here. I can see better things for me, for husband, for kids. Every new life is hard. If you tell yourself you can do it, you can. (69)

A man in his late forties told us that he has lost enthusiasm for life,

> All those good things you have in your life I had. War is over, I'm a little older. I'm just living to survive. I lost pleasure and interest in things. I'm not healthy, and I don't have a need for anything. (37)

In several families, parents anticipated the future for their children, not for themselves.

> It's better for my children to be here. Bosnians are always thinking about children. My daughter is in National Honor Society... . I wish to live because of the children. (45)
> I was glad I came here and still today, I'm glad to be here. Didn't see any sense to live in Bosnia and any future for children. We lived life for children always, before the war too. (65)
> I don't care what happens to me, only for him [young son]. (66)

to be read

DISCUSSION AND CONCLUSIONS

Our data shed light on three periods of time in the lives of Bosnian families; their lives before the war, their experiences both during the war and its immediate aftermath, and the initial period of their adaptation to life in the US. While the small size of our sample limits our ability to generalize, the 20 families are similar to the sample in our larger study (Coughlan & Owens-Manley, forthcoming) in that they reside in a relatively circumscribed neighborhood, in close proximity to their co-ethnics. Most of the heads of household are from rural areas and most arrived with a secondary school education and virtually no knowledge of the English language.

Their refugee narratives highlight the importance of understanding the impact of the first two periods of refugee experience on efforts to resettle and acculturate. Our subjects demonstrated varying degrees of successful accommodation in the three domains of adjustment – economic, socio-cultural, and psychological.

Economic adaptation seemed difficult for those who had completed university education and who had held professional positions in Bosnia. These individuals expressed dismay at having to work in a factory for low wages and at having no prospects of regaining the status they had enjoyed in their country of origin. Some respondents thought that they had been better off in Bosnia where they "felt rich." For others, and especially people from rural areas, economic adaptation was less problematic because their material lives in upstate New York were superior to the living standards they had achieved in Bosnia.

Socio-cultural adaptation is facilitated by good language skills, a necessary precursor for integration to the new society. Many respondents mentioned difficulty with the acquisition of adequate English skills. Most respondents spent only three to four months in an English language class and few believed their English was adequate for the demands of daily living. Because many Bosnians work in settings with others who speak their language, the tendency to be grouped together can work against the English language acquisition and inhibit creation of broader social networks. Family separations, in a culture where strong family bonds are crucially important, have taken their toll, and networks of friends have changed for most people. Even though families in Utica send money to relatives left behind in Bosnia and are in frequent contact with them by phone, they exhibit much distress and fear for their relatives' well-being because of the poor economic conditions and continued political tensions in Bosnia.

Several family members who were experiencing distress were seeing general practitioners for symptoms including headaches, stomach-aches, nervousness and sleeplessness; the large majority of those had been prescribed some form of medication. Most of our subjects continued to mourn the loss of their way of life before the war and consistently compared their current experiences with their pre-war lives. The authors feel a profound sense of sadness for what many of these families were continuing to experience and have a deep concern for their struggles to cope with the past and adjust to their new lives.

Yet, in spite of our respondents continued sadness and distress, the large majority have indicated that life in Utica is "fair to good," and some said "very good" or "excellent." This finding stands in contrast to other studies that are not sanguine about the adaptation of Bosnian refugees. For example, Waxman (2001) and Lamba (2003) document the difficulties Bosnians have encountered in their efforts to find employment in Australia and Canada. George & Tsang (2000) and Plante and colleagues (2002) identify broader challenges in the resettlement efforts of Bosnians in Canada, the United States and internally in Bosnia. Weine (1999) has exhaustively recounted the emotional and psychological obstacles which Bosnian refugees continue to encounter. The sample of Bosnian refugees that Miller et al. (2002) studied in Chicago included many who were unemployed and who complained of poverty and associated stressors.

Three principle explanations for the successful resettlement of Bosnians in upstate New York are a coordinated source of assistance, a labor market that afforded entry level opportunities for those with limited English proficiency, and a plentiful supply of affordable housing. One center in Utica organizes a myriad of services under one roof. Although there were a few complaints about services, especially in 1997 when there was a large increase in the number of Bosnians moving to Utica (service demand exceeded capacity until the center caught up), more than three-quarters of the Bosnians in our larger study were employed within four months of resettlement here. That brings us to the second factor accounting for the finding of successful resettlement, namely, jobs.

Bosnians tend have strong work ethic (see Matsuo, this volume). The ready availability of jobs in Utica fosters a sense of independence and feelings of self-efficacy. Two respondents were not satisfied with their jobs and three were unemployed, but fifteen said that they were satisfied with their work. The importance of work as a source of meaning, as an anchor in the lives of Bosnian refugees, is well documented (Miller et al., 2002; Colic-Peisker & Walker, 2003). Although jobs typically involve low wage employment, hard work has enabled these Bosnians, in their views, to achieve material well-being in a relatively short period of time. For most of the Bosnians in our sample, this has included the purchase of a home. This brings us to the third reason for the relative contentment of this sample of Bosnian refugees.

Home ownership is a strongly articulated value for many Bosnians, especially those who had lived in rural areas in Bosnia (Bringa, 1995; Coughlan & Owens-Manley, 2002a, 2002b,

Colic-Peisker & Waxman, this volume). Bosnians tend to rent or own homes in East Utica where housing costs are low and socials networks and mutual support are close-by. Home ownership has been possible for the Bosnians within just a few years of arrival. We believe that this has helped with feelings of self-sufficiency and successful adjustment.

This group of Bosnian families demonstrated an acculturation strategy that Berry (1992) conceptualized as 'separation', and their resettlement style may be characterized as collectivist and oriented toward the establishment and maintenance of ties within their ethnic community (Colic-Peisker & Walker, 2003). However, if we recall that separation involves a commitment to the old culture with little or no interactions with the host society, it may be more accurate to portray this as a transitional strategy. Bosnians are increasingly visible and active in workplaces, in supermarkets and other retail outlets, on soccer fields in parks throughout the city, even though they remain residentially clustered in East Utica. It is our impression that Bosnians would integrate more if they could, but that the language barrier makes this difficult. Separation is not so much a choice, as a strategy of temporary necessity that is adopted until their acquisition of better language skills allows further integration.

Recommendations for Community Work with Refugees and Future Research

Below are some recommendations for intervention and further research in the area of refugee adaptation.

Both researchers and service providers need to pay more attention to the unfolding of the life story of each individual and family in order to discover the discrepancies between the *old* life and the *new* life. It is important to help refugees re-establish social networks, to mourn the losses they have experienced, including the intangible losses, and to rebuild their human and social capital in ways that will be meaningful to them. Greater efforts could be made to acknowledge the skills and prior social status of incoming refugees to ease their transition. At the very least, we can assist refugees by acknowledging these as important losses.

If we promote the connection of recent refugees to networks both within and beyond the refugee groups, we will facilitate employment opportunities through these new social networks. Opportunities for greater contact between refugees and groups in the host community can be maximized through the design of resettlement programs with this purpose in mind. Communities that encourage, tolerate, and facilitate multiple perspectives, values, and traditions are healthier for ethnic minorities, particularly minorities which have already experienced persecution. The MVRCR has begun to design more aggressive programs to educate the general community regarding the culture and history of newcomers and to encourage a welcoming response. Outreach by community volunteers can help isolated groups, such as the elderly, who need assistance with English language acquisition to pass the citizenship test.[4]

Primary care physicians have had the most direct contact with those refugees who continue to experience distresses that interfere with their ability to adapt psychologically and to recreate a satisfactory life. Physicians and other medical providers need training to

[4] Hamilton College and Utica College received a SHINE (Students Helping in the Naturalization of Elders) grant in 2003 to assist elder immigrants and refugees to acquire English language and citizenship skills that will help them achieve American citizenship. SHINE has assisted thousands of refugees nationally since the program was begun in the 1980s at Temple University (Philadelphia, Pennsylvania).

understand the refugee experience, and they need to acquire cross-cultural competence in providing medical services. They need access to and support in using screening tools for assessment and treatment. Immigration and Refugee Services of America (IRSA) formed the National Alliance of Multicultural Mental Health to serve as a resource for mental health needs of refugees in 1997 and created a Medical Case Management Program in 1999 to provide technical assistance for organizations that resettle refugees with special health needs (Immigration and Refugee Services of America [IRSA], 2004). Yet, our impression in Utica is that both health and mental health providers have a limited understanding of their patients' refugee experiences and that few have had access to or have availed themselves of refugee-specific training. It is possible that in smaller communities such as Utica there are advantages such as a tighter community network, but also liabilities, such as the absence of a medical teaching center and other multicultural resources.

We need to continue to increase our understanding of what will help refugees upon resettlement. This enhanced understanding should inform our delivery of frontline services, as well as program design and policy development. Attention is currently too often reactive and given only when people are already symptomatic and in great distress. Research designed to explore family and community support that provides safety nets for individuals and families before they encounter difficulties would be a valuable addition to the literature. We believe than an inductive methodology that employs semi-structured interviews and narrative accounts of refugee experiences may be well-suited to elucidate the needs of the refugee community and hence can lead to the development of improved support services to refugee populations.

References

Aycan, Z., & Berry, J. W. (1996). Impact of employment related experiences on Immigrants' psychological well being and adaptation to Canada. *Canadian Journal of Behavioural Science*, *28*(3), 240-251.

Beiser, M., Turner, R.J., & Ganesan, S. (1989). Catastrophic stress and factors affecting its consequences among Southeast Asian refugees. *Social Science and Medicine*, *28*, 183-195.

Berry, J. (1992). Acculturation and adaptation in a new society. *International Migration*, *30*, 69-85.

Bringa, T. (1995). *Being Muslim the Bosnian way; identity and community in a central Bosnian village*. Princeton, New Jersey: Princeton University Press.

Bureau of Refugee and Immigration Affairs, New York State Office of Temporary & Disability Assistance, (2004). Albany, New York. Retrieved from *www.otda.state.ny.us/otda/bria/default.htm*

Burg, S.L. & Stroup, P.S. (1999). *The war in Bosnia-Herzegovina*. Armonk, New York: M.E. Sharpe, Inc.

Colic-Peisker, V. (2003). Bosnian refugees in Australia: identity, community and labour market integration. *New Issues in Refugee Research*, Working Paper No. 97. UNHCR, Evaluation and Policy Analysis Unit.

Colic-Peisker, V., & Walker, I. (2003). Human capital, acculturation and social identity: Bosnian refugees in Australia. *Journal of Community & Applied Social Psychology, 13*, 337-360.

Coughlan, R., Owens-Manley, J. (forthcoming) Bosnian refugees in America: New communities, new cultures. Sociological Practice series, Kluwer-Plenum Publishing.

_____ . (2002a). The new face of immigration: Bosnian refugees in transition. In J. Pula, (Ed.) *Ethnic Utica,* Utica, New York: Oneida County Historical Society.

_____ . (2002b). Adaptation during cross-cultural transitions: Bosnians in upstate New York. In J. Fure and L. Ytrehus (Eds.), *Crossing borders, changing minds?* Bergen, Norway: *Kulturstudier,* The Norwegian Research Council, Programme for Cultural studies and The Norwegian Academic Press.

Drachman, D. (1992). A stage-of-migration framework for service to immigrant populations. *Social Work*, *37*, 68-72.

Eastmond, M. (1998). Nationalist discourses and the construction of difference: Bosnian Muslim refugees in Sweden. *Journal of Refugee Studies*, *11*(2), 161-181.

Fullilove, M.T. (1996). Psychiatric Implications of Displacement: Contributions from a Psychology of Place. *American Journal of Psychiatry, 153*(12), 1516-1523.

George, U., & Tsang, A. K. T. (2000). Newcomers to Canada from former Yugoslavia. *International Social Work, 43*(3), 381-393.

Hagstrom, P. (2000). *The fiscal impact of refugee resettlement in the Mohawk Valley.* Clinton, NY: Hamilton College, Arthur Levitt Public Affairs Center.

Harrell-Bond, B. (1999). 'The experience of refugees as recipients of aid. In A. Ager (Ed.), *Refugees: perspectives on the experience of forced migration.* London and New York: Pinter.

Hassett, K. (1999, November 21). 'Refugees blend rich past, hopeful future in Utica'. *Observer Dispatch,* pp. 1A & 9A.

Immigration and Refugee Services of America (IRSA): IRSA mission and programs. (2004). Retrieved from *www.irsa-uscr.org.*

Kelly, L. (2003). Bosnian refugees in Britain: questioning community. *Sociology*, *37*(1), 35-49.

Korac, M. (2003). Integration and how we facilitate it: A comparative study of the settlement experiences of refugees in Italy and the Netherlands. *Sociology, 37*(1), 51-68.

Lamba, N.K. (2003). The employment experiences of Canadian refugees: Measuring the impact of human social capital on quality of employment. *Canadian Review of Sociology & Anthropology, 40*(1), 45-64.

Malcolm, N. (1994). *Bosnia: a short history.* Washington Square, New York: New York University Press.

Mamgain, V., & Collins, K. (2003). Off the boat, now off to work: Refugees in the labour market in Portland, Maine'. *Journal of Refugee Studies*, *16*(2), 113-146.

Matsuoka, J.K., & Ryujin, D.H. (Fall/Winter 1989-90). Vietnamese refugees: An analysis of contemporary adjustment issues. *The Journal of Applied Social Sciences*, *14*, 23-45.

Miles, M.B., & Huberman, A.M. (1994). *Qualitative data analysis* (2nd Ed.).Thousand Oaks: Sage Publications.

Miller, K., Muzurovic, J., Worthington G., Tipping, S., & Goldman, A. (2002). Bosnian refugees and the stressors of exile: a narrative study. *American Journal of Orthopsychiatry, 72*(3), 341-354.

Mohawk Valley Resource Center for Refugees (2004). Utica, New York. Retrieved from *www.mvrcr.org*

Mollica, R., Wyshak, G., de Marneffe, D., Khuon, F., & Lavelle, J. (1987a). Indochinese versions of the Hopkins Symptom Checklist-25: a screening instrument for the psychiatric care of refugees. *American Journal of Psychiatry, 144*, 497-500.

Mollica, R.., Wyshak, G., & Lavelle, J. (1987b). The psychosocial impact of war trauma and torture of Southeast Asian refugees. *American Journal of Psychiatry, 144*, 1567-1572.

Mollica, R., Caspi-Yavin, Y., Bollini, P., Truong, T., Tor, S., & Lavelle, J. (1992). The Harvard Trauma Questionnaire: validating a cross-cultural instrument for measuring torture, trauma, and posttraumatic stress disorder in Indochinese refugees. *Journal of Nervous Mental Disorders, 180*, 111-116.

Montgomery, J. (1991). Predicting Vietnamese refugee adjustment to Western Canada. *International Migration, 29*(1), 89-118.

Montgomery, J. (1996). 'Components of refugee adaptation. *International Migration Review, 30*(3), 679-702.

Nicholson, B.L., & Walters, T.K. (1997). The effects of trauma on acculturative stress: A study of Cambodian refugees. *Journal of Multicultural Social Work, 6*, 27-46.

Owens-Manley, J., & Coughlan, R. (2002, June). *Psychosocial wellness in refugee resettlement: Attending to family well-being*. Paper presented at the National Alliance of Multicultural Mental Health annual conference, Atlanta, Georgia.

Pernice, R., & Brook, J. (1996). Refugees and immigrants' mental health: association of demographic and post-immigration factors. *The Journal of Social Psychology, 136*, 511-519.

Plante, T.G., Simicic, A., Andersen, E.N., & Manuel, G. (2002). Stress and coping among displaced Bosnian refugees: An exploratory study. *International Journal of Stress Management, 9*(1), 31-41.

Richards, T., & Richards, L. (2000). QSR NUD*IST (N5) [Computer Software]. Thousand Oaks, CA: Scolari: Sage Publications Software.

Searle, W., & Ward, C. (1990). The prediction of psychological and sociocultural adjustment during cross-cultural transitions. *International Journal of Intercultural Relations, 14*, 449-464.

Silber, L., & Little, A. (1996). *The death of Yugoslavia*. New York: Penguin.

Somach, S.D. (1995). *Bosnian refugee resettlement in the U.S.* Washington, D.C.: Center for Applied Linguistics.

Strauss, A. (1987). *Qualitative analysis for social scientists*. Cambridge, UK: University of Cambridge Press.

Van Selm, K., Sam, D. L., & Oudenhoven, J.P. (1997). Life satisfaction and competence of Bosnian refugees in Norway. *Scandanavian Journal of Psychology, 38*, 143-149.

Waxman, P. (1998). Service provision and the needs of newly arrived refugees in Sydney, Australia: A descriptive analysis. *International Migration Review, 32*(3), 761-777.

_____ . (2001). The economic adjustment of recently arrived Bosnian, Afghan and Iraqi refugees in Sydney, Australia. *International Migration Review, 35*(2), 472-505.

Weine, S. B., Daniel F, & McGlashan, Thomas H. (1995). Psychiatric consequences of "ethnic cleansing": clinical assessments and trauma testimonies of newly resettled Bosnian refugees. *The American Journal of Psychiatry, 152*, 536-542.

Weine, S. M., Vojvoda, D., Becker, D. F., McGlashan, T. H., Hodzic, E., Laub, D., Hyman, L., Sawyer, M., & Lazrove, S., (1998). PTSD symptoms in Bosnian refugees 1 year after resettlement. *American Journal of Psychiatry, 155*(4), 562-564.

Weine, S. (1999). *When history is a nightmare*. New Brunswick: Rutger University Press.

Weine, S., & Kuc, G. (2001). PTSD among Bosnian refugees: A survey of providers' knowledge, attitudes and service patterns. *Community Mental Health Journal 37*(3), 261-271.

Williams, L. (1999) Participatory research, knowledge, and community-based change. *Research in Community Sociology, 9*, 3-40

Woodward, S. (1995). *Balkan tragedy: chaos and dissolution after the Cold War*. Princeton, N.J.: Princeton University Press.

In: Homeland Wanted ISBN 1-59454-266-X
Editors: P. Waxman and V. Colic-Peisker, pp. 147-164

Chapter 8

THREE GENERATIONS OF UGANDAN ASIAN DIASPORA IN SWEDEN

Charles Westin and Catarina Nyberg

ABSTRACT

In 1972, 70,000 Asians who were expelled from Uganda by Idi Amin, were dispersed to a number of receiving countries in the West, among them Sweden. This article reports on the subsequent process of integration in Sweden over a thirty years period, starting in a refugee camp in southern Sweden. The study is based on four different data collections over the years, the most recent one still ongoing. The article gives an historical background to the Asian settlement in East Africa during the colonial era. The expulsion and initial resettlement is outlined. A following section looks at community development, social mobility and adjustments that people had to make of their traditional ways with regard to the structures of opportunity in Swedish society. The final section surveys identities and identifications among the young Sweden-born generation of Asians. The community in Sweden is small and highly dependent for its continued existence on the transnational connections it has with the broader Ugandan Asian diaspora in the West.

Key words: forced migration, resettlement, Ugandan Asians, diaspora, transnationalism, identities

INTRODUCTION

The concept of diaspora originates from antiquity. It referred to the Greek settlements outside Hellas itself, in southern Italy, northern Africa and other places around the Mediterranean. In more recent usage it has come to denote a people in exile due to a specific chain of events that led to their exodus from a historic "homeland".[1] The concept of diaspora

---

1 The classic example is the Jewish diaspora that started with the imprisonment of the Jews in Babylon and centuries later with the definite dispersal after the destruction of the second temple in Jerusalem in the year 70 A.D. The Armenian diaspora following the Armenian Genocide in 1915-20; and the Circassian diaspora when Russia annexed the Circassian homeland in the Caucasus to the Czarist Empire in 1864, are other well-known

was reintroduced in to the discourse on forced and voluntary migration in the early 1990s. An important contribution was made by Clifford (1994, pp.302-308) who referred to specific qualities in the life situation of people in exile that are not captured by terms such as exile, forced migration or flight, terms that bring out administrative rather than theoretical conceptualisations. According to Clifford, a particular series of events in the past has led to the exodus of a diasporic group from a former homeland and in time, the group develops a mythology about the homeland. This serves, among other things, to reinforce a distinctive group identity and to counteract cultural assimilation in to host society. Political movements may arise that aim for a return or "repatriation" to the lost homeland.[2]

Theorists in the field of international migration, interethnic relations and transnational studies soon adopted the concept of diaspora. Cohen (1997, pp. 177-187) proposed to extend the concept to also include categories of migrants arising through trade and commerce, labour migration and colonial settlement. Important contributions to the discourse on diasporas have been made among many others by Giles, Moussa and van Esterik (1996), van Hear 1998) and Vertovec and Cohen (1999).

This chapter is about the Ugandan Asian diaspora, a global victim diaspora resulting from the expulsion of the Asian communities of Uganda in 1972.[3] The Ugandan Asian diasporic communities are found in Africa, Asia, Europe and North America. A small number of Ugandan Asians resides in Sweden. The original members of this community (approximately 1,000) were the first non-European refugees to be accepted by Sweden. In this chapter we look into the 30 years of their settlement in mainstream Swedish society.

METHODOLOGY

We draw upon data collected by Charles Westin in fieldwork carried out in 1973, 1974 and 1979, which included participant observation and interviews. Members of 33 families were interviewed. The first interviews were carried out in a refugee camp in southern Sweden and later fieldwork in eight towns of settlement. All interviews were taped, transcribed and analysed with the aim to outline the process of integration in to mainstream society and the effects this had within the community in terms of strategies of action, organisational structures and internal relations (Westin, 1986).

In 1997, a questionnaire was distributed to 343 "Ugandan" Asian households in Sweden, the aim of which was to survey geographical and social mobility in Sweden over the (then) twenty-five years of settlement. Defining the population was not as straightforward as it had been in 1973 due to the fact that many of the elderly settlers had died, their Sweden-born children were now grown-ups, marriages had brought in new family and community members (in a few cases through marriage with ethnic Swedes) with no relationship at all to Uganda.

examples. Even the African American population, descendants of the slaves that were brought to the Americas up until the 19th century, are referred to as a 'victim diaspora' (Harris, 1993).

2 Zionism is the classic example of such a movement.

3 A note on terminology: While the early Gujarati and Punjabi settlers in East Africa, both Hindus and Muslims, came from British India, and thus were "Indian", the separation of India and Pakistan in 1947 and the establishment of the two independent states, created a problem with the term "Indian" as it was interpreted as not including Punjabi Muslims whose region of origin by then was situated within the state of Pakistan. It is reasonable to conjecture that the term "Asian" was introduced in the East African context at this point in time so as to refer to both Hindus and Muslims.

Identifying members of the community is discussed further on. We looked for "structural" information in the sense that we sought to unravel the whereabouts of the family and household in the social and geographical landscape and timescape. Questions were asked about family origins, religious and sectarian affiliation, caste and sub-caste, places of residence, education, profession, experiences of working life and experiences of discrimination. We did not seek to uncover individual attitudes or values (Westin, 2002, p. 125).

In this chapter we also report from a study in progress carried out by Catarina Nyberg. Her study focuses on the experiences of the second generation, children of the original Ugandan Asian settlers. These children were born in Sweden or came to Sweden as infants. They were in their twenties and early thirties when Nyberg met them in interviews or at various social functions. Nyberg set out by following the social networks of a daughter of one of Westin's key informants. Several, though not all, of Nyberg's 20 principal informants had parents participating in Westin's studies in the 1970s. All interviews were taped, transcribed and analysed in accordance with a grounded theory approach. Key questions that Nyberg addresses are those of conflicting identities as members of Swedish society of (South) Asian cultural origin, sense of belonging, experiences of discrimination, academic and professional achievements, friendships and marriage.

In order to grasp the process of integration in Sweden, we need to understand the social and cultural mindsets that the refugees brought from Uganda, as notions of community relations were developed through collective experiences of the earlier emigration from India and settlement in East Africa. We base our overview on the anthropological work of Morris (1968) and the historical work of Gregory (1971; 1993). The history of the Asian communities in East Africa is also written by Mangat (1969) and Ghai and Ghai (1970).

We seek to outline the cultural and social background in East Africa, relating back to the origins in western India. Thereafter, three sections deal with the process of adjustment to conditions in Sweden. Finally, based on material from the ongoing study we comment on the situation of young members of the Ugandan Asian community in Sweden. This paper therefore reflects experiences of three generations, the first born and socialised in India, the second born and raised in Uganda, and the third born and acculturated in Sweden.

The Origins of a Transnational Minority

The British colonised Zanzibar, Kenya and Uganda in the late nineteenth century (Gregory, 1971, p.30). Indentured labour was brought from the Punjab to construct a railway from Mombasa to Lake Victoria. Traders from Gujarat followed, establishing trading posts along the line. These Gujarati-speaking tradesmen remained in East Africa and encouraged relatives to join them. Basically, the Asian minority in East Africa descends from these traders. Lohanas and Ismaelis were the most populous of the Asian groups in Uganda. A third large group, the Patels did not arrive on the East African scene until later. Emigration was selective: most migrants to East Africa were located within the lower ranks of the caste hierarchies, and were not necessarily traders by caste.

Asian settlement in East Africa brought about changes to traditional ways of life, and new organisational and social structures emerged. The caste hierarchies were never reproduced (Morris, 1968, p. 45), and caste and sectarian divisions were instead endowed with new meaning. Three larger communities (Ismaelis, Lohanas and Patels) and a number of smaller distinctive communities evolved. The essential East African experience was the development over time of new organisational structures and cultural models, founded on social categorizations inherited from India.

The emergence and consolidation of distinct caste and sectarian-based communities within the Asian population was occasioned by continuous migration to East Africa from the 1890s up until 1960. Settlement and community building required far-reaching adjustments of organisational structure (Morris, 1968, pp. 40-43). The communities were engaged in stiff commercial competition with each other. This produced organisational innovation and political re-orientation among people who otherwise were tradition-bound in many respects. The Asians combined traditional Indian ways and attitudes in family life with progressive Western ideas of business, economy, organisation and education in the public sphere. The communities provided for cultural and religious needs, temples and mosques, graveyards, community-run schools, medical and health-care facilities, banks and insurance companies and so on

Upon Uganda gaining independence in 1961, the Asian population in the country was 80,000 (Kuepper, et al., 1975, p. 3). At this point in time, East African Asians started to emigrate to Britain because many leaders were in doubt whether their communities would enjoy a secure future under African rule. It was not uncommon that the Asians were blamed for being loyal servants of British colonialism. In Britain, the large influx of Asian migrants from former African colonies in the 1950s and early 1960s brought about the Commonwealth Immigration Act of 1962, the aim of which was to stop continued post-colonial immigration of British-protected persons.

Milton Obote, the first president of Uganda (1966-1971), strove to develop an African brand of socialism, which met with widespread distrust among Asian communities. Many were therefore reluctant to naturalise to Ugandan citizenship. Quite a few chose to maintain their status as British protected persons despite the fact that the Commonwealth Immigration Act no longer entitled them to settle in the UK. Leaders of the Asian communities actually welcomed the coup, staged by Idi Amin in 1971, that overthrew Obote. However, the interim was only too brief. A year later, in August 1972, General Amin announced that British citizens – British protected persons – were to leave the country within three months (Mamdani, 1973, p. 23; Kuepper et al., 1975, pp. 3-6). In the chaotic situation that arose, even those who had opted for Ugandan citizenship were deprived of their passports and turned stateless. Bands of soldiers robbed people of jewellery, money and even family photos. Men were beaten up and women were raped. Family members were often separated from one another in the rush out from chaos. Kenya and Tanzania, but also India and Pakistan soon closed their borders. Approximately 70,000 persons were forced to leave Uganda, abandoning their properties and personal belongings.

In this mass flight emergency, international relief operations were quick to act. An airlift between Uganda and Europe was put in operation. Refugees were placed in temporary camps in Italy and Austria. In these exceptional circumstances, the UK accepted those who could prove that they were British-protected persons (Kuepper et al., 1975, p. 18). Canada and the USA opened their borders to young, well-educated academics and professionals, but not to large penniless families.

INITIAL SETTLEMENT IN SWEDEN

Sweden was one of several European countries to accept stateless Ugandan Asians. Approximately 800 persons arrived in Sweden in December 1972. Family reunifications took place in the following months. Thus the initial Ugandan Asian community numbered approximately 1,000 persons. They represented different sects and castes, within the main cleavage between Hindus and Muslims.

The refugees were placed in a reception camp in southern Sweden for health checks, language training, and were informed about family reunification procedures, schools, job opportunities, vocational training, language courses, rights and obligations, housing, social security and many other basic facts. People from all parts of Uganda assembled in the camp. Most were strangers to each other. They were of all ages, professions, castes and sectarian faiths. Some were single and others belonged to large families. There were marginalised individuals, some perhaps with a shady past, as well as people of high repute, who less than six months earlier had been well off. The camp represented, as it were, a cross section of the Asian society in Uganda. Most people felt lost and insecure about what the future might bring. People were traumatised by having been forced to abandon their homes, strains of the flight, uncertainty about the future, and involuntary separation from family and kin. To each and everyone, the life one had led in Uganda was very much present by being so obviously absent (Westin, 1986, p. 10).

In this situation people were trying to make sensible decisions about the future. Should they stay in Sweden, or try to get to some other country? What sort of future could they hope for in Sweden? Could they join family in other countries? Or vice versa? How could they get into business? People in the camp were soon involved in a process of defining positions in relation to one another, negotiating identities and seeking leaders. New bonds of friendship developed while at the same time ethnic and religious boundaries between various Asian groups were emphasised, usually in a friendly manner, but sometimes in confrontation.

The flight from Uganda was in the hands of the international refugee organisations and being placed in a Swedish camp meant that these people were subject to what might be called a process of collective "patience" (as opposed to agency). They received loads of information and they could accept or reject various proposals presented to them. Essentially, however, planning, initiatives and the course of events were determined by the Swedish authorities for quite some time. This loss of agency, however, did not apply to interrelations within the camp. From the very first day, younger people were seeking the advice of elderly men of high reputation about where to settle, what jobs to accept, and so on.

The time that was spent in the reception camp may be seen as a focal point of their resettlement. During the first few months in the refugee camp, in what might be called a period of post-traumatic unawareness, group boundaries were relieved on the interpersonal level. The refugees were forced to associate with each other in these exceptional circumstances. At times traditional differences would flash up in the pervasive feeling of powerlessness. In moments of frustration and grievance, some might resort to the old ways from East Africa by expressing solidarity to one's own particular group and manifesting opposition to others. People from different parts of Uganda — geographically, socially, religiously and culturally — were brought together and subjected to the same treatment and working arrangements. Their only possessions were the clothes they wore: they had no personal belongings, no money in the bank and no certificates of education. No one, however, could rob them of their previous experiences and skills, their family links and transnational networks, or their ideas of what they wanted to do. Subsequently they dispersed from the camp according to the resettlement program devised by the Swedish authorities.

A first test was to settle for a job among various offers that were presented by the labour market office. This would have consequences for where one was to settle. The flow of information coming from the National Board of Labour, prospective employers, trade unions, municipal councils, schools, day nurseries, etc. was truly overwhelming, and the Asians lacked an overall understanding of Swedish society. Thus, important decisions were based on limited understanding. A majority believed that the town they decided to settle in was where they would spend the rest of their life. Decisions of settlement were determined less by information disseminated by the Swedish authorities and more by considerations within the group. When, for instance, a man of high esteem decided that the town of Mariestad and work at the Electrolux factory was the best choice, other more indecisive families followed. Other considerations concerned whom of one's new friends one wanted to be close to, and in a few cases, whom one wanted to avoid.

In the various towns of Asian settlement Swedish neighbours treated them politely. Individuals volunteered to welcome the refugees, but lasting bonds of friendship with Swedish families rarely developed. Local NGOs took part in programs that were intended to facilitate the settlement of the Asian families. For the majority of the Asians it took many years to fully understand the workings of Swedish society and the opportunities that were available to those who had ideas and knew what they wanted to achieve.

Some co-operation between different Muslim sects as well as between different Hindu castes was initiated at an early stage. It could not be said that the Asians integrated into Swedish society, but they were not totally dissociated from it either. In certain respects the general situation resembled that in East Africa some eighty years earlier. Most people had a realistic understanding of their situation in exile. When the Amin regime collapsed in 1979, people appreciated that return to Uganda was out of the question: the society they had been forced to leave no longer existed. This painful insight meant, however, that they could look realistically upon their future in Sweden. Whether one liked it or not, there was no other alternative.

The vast majority of people were under heavy pressure to reorganise their lives during the first years in Sweden. The elderly were acquainted with Swedish institutions and social conditions only in a superficial sense. After about four months stay in the reception camp, all men and many women belonging to the middle-aged generation were given unqualified factory work. This was a central element of the integration procedure organised by the National Board of Labour. In some towns of settlement, jobs could not be found for women who wanted to work. No one found a job commensurate with qualifications or previous work experience. Most people found factory work unrewarding and physically exhausting but still coped reasonably well and regarded factory work as a temporary solution. When asked in 1979, no adults admitted experiencing discrimination or racism. Negative encounters were explained as individual incidents, misunderstandings or ignorance. Teenagers and young children were more open about hostility directed at them and prejudicial attitudes among their Swedish peers. Frustrating experiences of various kinds during those early years created a strained atmosphere within the Asian community. This did not primarily manifest itself in discontent aimed at Swedish society or Swedish authorities, but was manifested in internal discord through group-distinguishing processes along the traditional lines of division in East Africa. Conflicts among young Hindu and Muslim boys led to rows between families and the traditional support networks did not function as well as in Uganda. In some towns, the Asian communities lacked clear leadership to provide moral support and guidance during those early and for many difficult years.

However, as time passed, people began to settle down. Some managed to set up their own small-scale businesses. A few with academic training found jobs as language teachers. Tensions between people of different backgrounds eased. People were marrying, children were born and life continued. Many individuals and families eventually found their niches. By 1979 an overall union, the "Asian Cultural Society", had been founded in the towns of Jönköping and Mariestad, the aim of which was to promote joint interests of the Asians (both Hindus and Muslims) in cultural and social matters and to serve as partners in discussion with the local Swedish authorities in questions concerning the welfare of the group. Elsewhere, Hindus and Muslims founded separate organisations. Initially, the Mariestad union was not particularly strong but yet its existence was an indication of social integration and the transcending of the ethnoreligious and social differences between families.

A Generation Later

In several countries where the Ugandan Asians resettled, the qualification *Ugandan* (and even *East African*) is gradually losing in importance. A generation has been born and raised in the West without any personal attachment to East Africa. It is an open question whether the Ugandan Asian groups in Sweden are gradually merging with other migrants from India and Pakistan in terms of organisational infrastructure. In 2002, there were approximately 25,000 migrants from countries of the Indian subcontinent residing permanently in Sweden, 12,000 of whom were from India (Statistics Sweden, 2003). If we include their children born in Sweden, the community consists of about 40,000 persons. However, only about 1,500 persons are affiliated with the Asian Cultural Societies tracing their origins back to the Ugandan expulsion.

The names and addresses of most Ugandan Asians in Sweden are listed in a telephone directory compiled by the Asian Cultural Society in Mariestad, one of the centres of Ugandan Asian settlement since 1973. In a short preface, the expulsion from Uganda is mentioned as the event that triggered the diaspora, and hence was relevant to the creation of the Asian Cultural Society. The preface, however, also addresses the young generation as well as members who have come later from India and Pakistan.

Not everyone listed in the directory has personal roots in the Asian communities in Uganda. Indeed, many on the roll, and family members of those listed in the directory, have come from India or Pakistan. Some have even come from the UK, Kenya, Tanzania and Norway. Most importantly, a large number of family members are born and raised in Sweden. The Ugandan Asian label, then, refers to the *origin of the community* in Sweden. The Asian Cultural Society only includes among its members those who experienced the expulsion themselves, their descendants, and later arrivals who through family ties identify themselves with the aims of the Asian Cultural Societies.

In our 1997 survey, questionnaires were sent to 343 first names listed in the directory. In the analysis of the data, education, housing and occupation were used as indicators of social position. Dealing with a process of change over three generations, and migration between three continents was a complicating factor. This meant that only rather crude indicators would work as least common denominators. The respondents' parents were referred to as generation 1. Consequently, the respondent and his/her spouse were referred to as generation 2, and their children as generation 3. Each generation in this sense covered a wide range of years. Those classified as belonging to the same generation did not necessarily belong to the same age cohort. There was, however, a centre of gravity. Typically, generation 1 was born in India, generation 2 grew up in Uganda, and generation 3 had spent most of their life in Sweden.

Practically all those referred to here as generation 1 had had their schooling in India. It was more surprising that almost half of those belonging to generation 2, that is, the respondents themselves and their spouses, also had their primary schooling in India (and in what is now Pakistan), the other half in Uganda. Most of those belonging to generation 3 have had their schooling in Sweden, in some individual cases in Uganda. Broadly speaking, the educational opportunities have differed considerably for the three generations. What they appear to have in common, however, is the belief that education promotes the chances of social mobility: all generations appear to value education highly.

A large majority of the respondents' parents (generation 1) had had about six years of schooling, though for women generally less than three years. Surprisingly many men belonging to this first generation, however, had had some university-level training. The relatively high degree of university attendance has only increased marginally for men but substantially for women of the following generations. The marked gender difference in access to higher education for the first generation has more or less levelled out for the Sweden-born third generation. When the Ugandan Asians families came to Sweden, they maintained rather traditional gender values stressing the husband's bread-winning role and his wife's domestic responsibilities. These customary roles have not prevented women of the second and third generation from pursuing secondary, and not infrequently, also university education. Gender roles still differ in many respects from the Swedish ideal of gender equality, but as far as higher education is concerned, young Asian women have not been discouraged from study.

Many immigrants to Sweden live in low-status housing estates situated on the outskirts of cities where cheaper accommodation is available. These estates were built in a nation-wide effort to ease the serious housing shortage. When they arrived in the 1970s, the Ugandan Asians were provided with apartments in these estates. The material standard of these apartments is generally good but the neighbourhoods have poor social infrastructure – run-down schools, lack of jobs, unsatisfactory public transport, high unemployment rates, high crime rates and widespread social welfare dependency (Westin, 1998, pp. 15-25; Westin, 2000, pp. 32-36, 41-49). Increasingly these housing estates have become identified as immigrant ghettos. Obviously, the structure of the Swedish housing market differs considerably from the situation in Uganda before the expulsion and in India before that. Initially in Sweden, rented accommodation was the only option. The respondents reported a drastic change of living conditions experienced as a result of the expulsion. They abandoned privately-owned homes in Uganda, to be resettled in rented flats in low-status neighbourhoods in Sweden. Most people have moved once or twice during the years in Sweden. One motive has been to distance oneself from the immigrant-dominated neighbourhoods. The aggregated outcome of these moves is an increasing proportion of privately-owned homes. Moving to middle-class neighbourhoods and privately-owned housing may be seen as an indicator of social mobility.

Having looked at education and housing, a third indicator of change in social status pertains to one's occupational career. Regardless of people's qualifications and experiences from Uganda, the Swedish labour market authorities initially treated the Asians as though they were unskilled labourers. As mentioned earlier, unskilled factory work were the only jobs available from the start. Academic qualifications, previous work experience, personal merits and skills were given no consideration when people were allocated to jobs: the labour market determined the outcomes. The Ugandan Asians arrived at a time when immigration to Sweden was regarded as a matter of labour recruitment. Resettlement policies were about getting people into the labour force as soon as possible. As the demand for low-skilled labour declined in the 1980s, the Swedish integration policies changed radically, laying greater stress on vocational training and Swedish language courses. Over the years, a gradual mobility to occupations of higher status has taken place among Asian immigrants: about half of them improved their occupational status. This means, however, that the other half have remained in unqualified positions at the lowest rung of the occupational hierarchy. These persons were predominantly middle-aged or even elderly when they came to Sweden.

The results of the 1997 survey point to social mobility in terms of education for the young (third) generation, geographical mobility to middle-class neighbourhoods (often only within the town of residence), and an improvement of one's occupational status for about half of the population. Jointly these indicators support the hypothesis that the Ugandan Asians as a distinct community in Sweden are "migrating" from an initial position of unskilled labourers living in working-class and immigrant-dominated housing estates, to occupations of higher social prestige and middle-class neighbourhoods. This supports the view that, as a community, the Ugandan Asians in Sweden seem to have done better than most other migrants and refugees from non-European countries. These results are consistent with findings of various British and American studies (Bose, 1982, pp. 456-458; Robinson, 1993, pp. 237-241; Strizhak, 1993, pp. 263-264).

Mastering Swedish was an obstacle to many of the middle-aged and elderly. Lack of proficiency in Swedish meant that after some years, elderly men of high prestige in Uganda gradually lost their positions as leaders to younger men who were able to negotiate with the local authorities in Swedish, and who had been successful in establishing businesses. Those who came to Sweden as infants did not have to face the problem of mastering a foreign language or having to learn to deal with subtle cultural codes, alien practices and unknown rules.

Timing was to the advantage of the Ugandan Asians: in the early 1970s, there was a demand for labour. The Asians did not have to face a period of long-term unemployment as was the case with many later refugees. Although they were dissatisfied with factory work, it nevertheless provided them with an entry into the labour market. Spatial location was another important factor. The Ugandan Asians preferred to settle in small towns. In the early 1970s, the choice to settle in small or medium-sized industrial towns was opportune as it was easier to acquire an understanding of the workings of Swedish society, to establish useful contacts, and to exploit the structure of opportunities there.

A cornerstone of Swedish integration policy has been to encourage migrants permanently residing in the country to naturalise. The requirement for Swedish citizenship is five years of residence. Stateless persons are entitled to apply after four years of residence. Citizenship is seen as one of the essential means of integration because it brings people into the polity. Practically everyone affiliated with the (Ugandan) Asian community is now a Swedish citizen. Most naturalisations were concentrated in the years from 1976 to 1980 (Westin, 2002, p.133). Practically everyone who was made stateless applied for Swedish citizenship at the earliest opportunity.

THE RECONSTRUCTION OF COMMUNITY

For most people, the essential part of the settlement process is to try to reconstruct what had been lost through the expulsion. Those accepted by the UK could link up with the East African Asian communities already existing in Britain. Such communities were well established in places like Leicester (Pardesh, 1994; Robinson, 1992). In Sweden, on the other hand, the reconstruction of an Asian community was a lot more complex because the numbers were small, they were divided and there was virtually nothing to build on. People were conscious about their identities and the status associated with caste and sectarian membership, as these categories had applied in East Africa. A very first step in the community reconstruction process was to define oneself in relation to others. However, this had to be undertaken in a situation in which the customary markers of identity that had been significant in the East African context lacked roots in Swedish society, as there was no social structure to support the old hierarchies. This could lead to unexpected and problematic outcomes in definitions of self and others and in the attribution of status.

It soon became clear that social divisions based on sect and caste membership were not functional in Sweden: these distinctive identities could not continue to be asserted against one another. Hindus of different caste backgrounds found ways to co-operate to achieve joint aims as did Muslims of different sectarian denominations. The local Swedish authorities generally took a benevolent view to requests for graveyards, temples and mosques voiced by Hindus and Muslims. Cultural support was another domain that the authorities understood: local libraries received extra grants to purchase Indian books, journals and films. In the educational field, the organisation of mother-tongue instruction (in Gujarati) provided jobs for a few qualified teachers.

Over time, sense of common destiny evolved within the community. Friendships developed across boundaries that normally would have been difficult to bridge in Uganda. An important explanation for the relatively smooth integration of the Ugandan Asians in Sweden in the 30-years perspective — despite the adjustment problems of the early years — pertains to social cohesion within the group. Consolidating the Asian community meant exploiting the opportunities that the Swedish integration and immigrant policy provided for the benefit of all, and hence forming organisations to promote common interests once these were identified. This meant downplaying differentiating factors – caste, sect and religion – and promoting or emphasising factors that were common to all. However, this reorientation did not come about overnight.

The Ugandan Asian community in Sweden is approximately one-third Muslim and two-thirds Hindu, as it was in Uganda before the expulsion. Sectarian distinctions are mainly typical of the Shia Muslim community. In our questionnaire, most respondents were reluctant to reveal their sectarian identity, which contrasts with both the situation in Uganda before the expulsion and at the time of arrival in Sweden. Surprisingly few mention affiliation with the Ismaeli community, which was the sect with the strongest sense of group distinctiveness in Uganda. In the 1997 questionnaire, a majority of the Hindus also refrained from referring to caste categorisations: for them as well it appeared to be important to downplay divisions within the community. Emphasising sectarian or caste distinctiveness in the Swedish context was rightly seen as an obstacle to achieving common goals. People have generally accepted that co-operation rather than competition is necessary for a small community to survive.

Yet, caste and sectarian associations do exist, and members meet on various occasions. In other circumstances that might materialise in the future, organisations founded on these identities could come to play a more active role. A decisive condition for history to repeat itself in this respect is numerical growth of the community. However, at present no indications point to such a development.

A gradual reorientation and adjustment to life in a modern welfare state is taking place among the Ugandan Asians. In general, it appears that religious duties are not practised as actively as before. Visiting the mosque or temple is done on a weekly rather than on a daily basis that used to be the norm in Uganda (Westin, 1986, p. 149). Working hours, dispersal of residence, and the secular nature of Swedish society are factors that affected the religious practices. However, these changes do not mean that people's faith is necessarily in decline, but rather that it has assumed new forms of practice that are functional in the Swedish context with regard to the general conditions of working life and family economy.

Another obvious change is that family size is conforming to the Swedish norm, which is partly a result of marriages taking place later in young people's lives. Husbands participate in household chores and are more directly involved in the care of young children, which was not the case before. These are experiences that all the Asians have in common, regardless of one's former position in Uganda. The changes are largely determined by the economic and structural realities in Swedish society – wage levels, income taxes, social security, working hours, housing conditions, educational opportunities, the labour market, and so on.

Common language is an obvious factor uniting a majority of the Asians. All but one respondent mention that the language spoken mutually by parents (generation 1) was an Indian language, predominantly Gujarati. In the family (generation 2), spouses communicate with one another in Gujarati (or one of the other Indian languages) in 87 per cent of the cases. Swedish is used as the family language by about eight percent of respondents. Finally, 25 per cent mentioned that Swedish is the language spoken by their children (generation 3) in mutual conversation. Therefore, Indian languages still predominate by 70 per cent. In a long-term perspective, Swedish will inevitably increase its hold over the young generation. Proficiency in Gujarati – for many, also in Hindi and Urdu – enables people to share Indian/Pakistani cultural works – media, films, videos, books and, above all, music.

The survey also showed that many elderly and middle-aged regularly wear traditional clothing at home, but young people only on festive occasions. Practically all families predominantly cook Indian/Pakistani food.

The total population of the "Ugandan" Asian community in Sweden is increasing at a very slow rate, in contrast to the trend for other refugee communities in Sweden. Young families have adapted to the western norm of only having one or two children. For persons with moderate incomes, there are compelling economic reasons to limit the size of the family. A second reason for the slow population increase is a constant drain of young people to the UK, the USA and Canada for purposes of marriage and studies. In the long run, the slow growth of the community is a threat to its survival. The drain of young people needs to be balanced by immigration. This can only be done through marriage because Sweden does not have a labour migration programme, and the refugee gate is no longer open to prospective Asian migrants from East Africa, or from India and Pakistan (Hammar, 1999, pp. 173-179).

In East Africa, the Asians as a rule observed strict principles of endogamy. Ideally marriages were arranged. For most Hindus, a marriage partner would have to conform to a set of criteria with regard to family, villages of origin and caste. Differences of status between families would be given due consideration in negotiations about dowries. Similar rules applied to the Muslims, though for them sectarian membership was the most important criterion.

In the 1960s, the marriage institution was gradually modernised. Love marriages were accepted as long as the liaison conformed to the rules. During the early years in Sweden, arranging appropriate marriages was of great concern to parents. They became more active than before in finding suitable marriage partners for their sons and daughters. This return to traditional ways was a response to one's position as newcomers to a society of which one had little knowledge. Families needed to be strong and consolidated. Moreover, adhering to the traditional rules represented an opportunity to expand the community by bringing in new members. Practically all marriages within the Asian community have taken place with persons accepted as members. Quite a few of the respondents were married before they came to Sweden but 75 per cent of the marriages in generation 2 have taken place in Sweden after the expulsion from Uganda. In most of these cases, spouses were brought from India and Pakistan. It has proved more difficult to find a partner from the UK willing to marry in Sweden than vice versa. Only a very few marriages with Swedes have taken place and these out-married persons often become marginalised to the Ugandan Asian community.

Respecting the rules of endogamy means reasserting the importance of caste and sect, so bringing in marriage partners from Gujarat goes against the adaptive strategy of downplaying traditional categorisations. As mentioned, the Asians seem to live in two different worlds: traditional divisions of rural Gujarat and an emerging ecumenical community in Sweden. The ecumenical community is a practical and functional solution to constraints that the international system of states has placed on the movement across international boundaries and that affects this group of people who happened to end up in Sweden.

The community in Sweden, however, has family connections to the larger communities in the UK. The Ugandan Asian diaspora is a typical transnational community if ever there was one (Hannerz, 1996, p. 6). French anthropologist Levi-Strauss stated that there were three principal types of exchange that characterise relations between communities in interaction with one another (Levi-Strauss, 1967). The Asian community in Sweden is highly dependent upon contacts with other Asian communities abroad for these same reasons:

- Business is the first domain in which the personal international links play an important role. Spices, food and items of clothing are imported via connections and business partners in countries with larger South Asian communities than Sweden.
- The second domain concerns information and knowledge. Films, magazines, records and books are distributed to consumers in Sweden from shops in the UK for entertainment and leisure but also, and perhaps more importantly, to keep people updated about cultural, political and social developments in the wider transnational community of which one is part.

– The international community plays an important role as a pool of potential marital partners. Most members have visited the UK many times to see family and friends and to be introduced to possible marriage partners, with many (about 70 per cent) having also visited India or Pakistan for the same reasons. The contacts with East Africa are less frequent.

Thus the Ugandan Asian community in Sweden is part of the broader South Asian diaspora (Westin, 2002, p. 139). This is epitomised through the international e-mail network *Namascar-Africana* to which we were invited to join. Some members of the Asian Cultural Societies in Sweden are active in this network. Over a period of four years we received more than 20,000 e-mails (an average of 14-15 e-mails per day), touching upon all possible subjects relating to the diaspora. Many comment on current events, world politics and sports (for instance, test matches), usually with some Indian angle to it. Others discuss issues of identity, nostalgia and memories more directly. Some thirty persons were active over the entire period, participating in discussions more or less on a daily basis. A considerably larger number (several hundred persons) take part less frequently, participating only for a brief period or discussing a particular topic. *Namascar-Africana* is an illuminating example of how modern information technology is used to revitalise a sense of community by people sharing a similar background but now dispersed all over the world.

Identities in Transition

In our ongoing study, we are looking at how young people who, according to our classification belong to the "third" generation, manage their lives in Sweden. We have established contacts with key informants who came as infants, or were born in Sweden during the 1970s. We conducted a series of interviews with these informants and participated in various social events, sports tournament, the annual Diwali celebration among the Hindus and other functions. At these social gatherings we have been able to extend our network of informants, participate in informal conversations and acquire a deeper understanding of identity transactions.

A first general observation is that the young generation is well educated, with many having studied at universities and holding academic degrees. Those who have completed their studies and entered the labour market have good, well-paid jobs with excellent career prospects. Some, who work in the public sector, may not have high salaries but, nevertheless, hold important, influential positions. Several respondents were working within the field of information technology as computer consultants. Some were in business, banking and the stock market while others had jobs in engineering companies; a few were teachers and some worked in medical professions. Although unemployment rates in Sweden have risen to much higher levels than before, and people of migrant origin have been harder hit than those with a Swedish background, the young generation of Ugandan Asians in Sweden has not encountered serious problems in finding jobs.

Most informants were in their twenties and early thirties at the time of the recent interviews. They had grown up in the small and middle-sized towns of initial Ugandan Asian settlement. Unlike their parents, however, once they entered the labour market, many moved to major cities, predominantly to Stockholm and Gothenburg. One obvious reason is that these cities offered skilled jobs in fields such as information technology and engineering, economics and business. Furthermore, most of those who continued into tertiary education had to live away from home during their years of study. Thus, they had already taken a first step away from their childhood homes in Mariestad, Jönköping, Trollhättan and other towns of Ugandan Asian settlement.

Children who started school in Sweden grew up to be bilingual, but the Swedish language was dominant. It was the language that the young generation mastered, both in its oral and written form, while Gujarati was understood in terms of a restricted code. For example, respect towards one's elders was expressed in Gujarati, and this could not be easily translated into Swedish. However, Gujarati was not the language through which the young Sweden-born generation developed intellectual skills: it was the family language and the language of religion, used at social functions where all generations were present, just as it had been to the generation born in East Africa. According to several informants, the Gujarati spoken at home is more archaic than modern Gujarati spoken in India.

Among this generation, many respondents reported that as children, before they reached their teens, they thought of themselves as being no different from native Swedish children and felt like a part of Swedish society. However, in teenage, this sense of belonging was challenged and even abandoned by some: their awareness of phenotypal characteristics grew and impacted on their sense of belonging. As almost all of our young respondents reported, one just felt that one did not conform to the stereotype of the blond, blue-eyed Scandinavian. Although practically everyone denies that they were victims of overt discrimination, there seems to be indirect evidence that in junior high school in particular they quite often had to put up with racialised insults and subtle forms of exclusion. When pressed for information and details, respondents usually related many such incidents but still denied that they experienced the instances of discrimination. Instead, they describe the incidents as unfair treatment and some even reported that the "insults", within a general non-aggressive atmosphere, were returned. It seems that these youngsters were unwilling to assume the role of victims and that they would not let confrontations of this kind depress them.

Parents worried that their children would be affected negatively by western youth culture and premarital sexuality. They thought Swedish life-styles differed considerably from their own traditional ways of handling attraction to the opposite sex. Thus young people grew up with conflicting sets of values. Swedish standards of achievement applied in the education and career domains and parents did not try to prevent their children from taking active part in sports, as long as family values and traditional social life were not jeopardised. Many of the young people interviewed explained that they felt it was their own family, and in a wider setting, community expectations that held them back from moving on into Swedish society, not racism or discrimination emanating from individual Swedes or Swedish institutions.

Feeling that a Swedish identity was largely denied them, many young people sought to explore what an Indian identity would imply and developed a strong sense of Indian identity. However, several informants reported that the first visit to India really was an eye-opener. It was all too obvious that one had very little in common with the makings of Indian identity as expressed in India and that one's outlook on many vital existential, social and political issues (such as gender roles, for example) was coloured by values underpinning Swedish society. Those who spent time in Britain did not feel at home within Indian communities in the UK, as these were either too Anglicised or too orthodox. One felt that this was a great contrast to the situation for the community in Sweden, which had achieved a balance between Indian ways and Swedish context. These visits to India and the UK made them aware that they had a Swedish outlook on many important issues concerned with cultural identities, gender roles, social welfare, justice and equality.

An interesting observation is that the term "Asian" is no longer used by the young generation. The generation of adults who came to Sweden in 1972 and 1973 had lived with the term "Asian" during most of their lifetime, so it was natural for them to name their joint organisation "The Asian Cultural Society". However, to the young generation that had grown up in Sweden the term "Asian" lacked the reverberations that it had to their parents. After all, a majority of the immigrants in Sweden from Asia are not from, or do not have origins in, the Indian subcontinent, but come from Iran, Iraq and Turkey. Reverting back to the term "Indian" is, then, about an identity definition in cultural terms rather than with reference to geographical origin. But what does the term "Indian" mean to the young generation? Does it include the Muslims? As our informants use the term "Indian" it seems to be open to interpretation. In some contexts, it refers to all people with origins in the Indian subcontinent. On other occasions, it obviously applies to Hindus only by Hindus, or more narrowly to Gujaratis. Sometimes it is used even more restrictively to refer only to those with origins in the Ugandan expulsion. An even narrower usage is about caste categorisation. Thus, the term "Indian" is used with a variable degree of inclusion and exclusion, depending, it appears, on the social context. It seems to have several layers of meaning. In modern society, the identity concept is important for a variety of reasons. One reason emanates from the quest for identity as an aim of minority groups to assert distinctiveness and to gain recognition. Castells (1997) points to another reason. Social stability and cohesion in contemporary (Western) societies are, to a lesser extent than just a few decades ago, consequences of the inertia of social structure. Globalisation of the economy and information flows and intercultural encounters on a hitherto unprecedented scale, bring the question of identity to the fore. In this age of the network society with its rapid 'information revolution', individual identity stands for a kind of psychosocial inertia. All this contrasts, of course, to conditions in societies not very far back in time when people were tied to one more or less fixed location and one specific collective. Categorisations have always existed but assignment to some particular category was previously not an identity project as it has become today.

This brings us to the issue of whether or not the time-old categorisations defined by caste and sect are meaningful to the young generation in Sweden in terms of identity projects. Our interview data indicate that these demarcations are still an important part of people's identities, although in a diluted form. Recognising the significance of these classifications is closely linked to parental authority and respect of one's elders. It is an integral part of one's Gujarati background and thus it will inevitably be part of one's identity. The traditional caste in terms of the *varna* system, with its roots in Vedic mythology, is no longer politically accepted in India, and East African Asians adhered to the *jati* (or sub-caste) classification based on membership of traditional guilds and passed it on to the next generation. Among the Hindus, marriage rules were intrinsically bound to *jati* classifications. Young people attend functions organised by the caste associations (for instance, the Lohana organisation and the Patel organisation) to meet friends and relations. Unlike the situation in East Africa where caste communities served as corporate interest organisations, the associations that have emerged in Sweden seem to serve social purposes. Although most are critical of the caste organisations, by the very fact of attending the functions, young people acknowledge and at least indirectly, support the existence of caste classifications. Sectarian denominations within

Islam are not equally problematic because they do not invoke status classification in the same way, nor are they prohibited. Moreover, the freedom of religious belief is stated in the Swedish constitution.

The real challenge is to combine life and work in Sweden with the traditional Gujarati values. Obviously, there is no problem in consuming cultural commodities: eating Indian food, listening to Indian music and watching Indian films. Wearing traditional Indian clothes may be more problematic as it represents a public statement of identity. Generally, young generation only does this on festive occasions. Several informants stressed the point that one should not mix the Swedish and Indian sides of one's identity in practice. In other words, one should not act in accordance with Swedish norms in an Indian context, and vice versa, because this will be experienced by others as conflicting and confusing. It appeared from the interviews that most young informants were believers and took active part in religious celebrations, visited the temple or mosque on a regular basis, and prayed regularly, some of them every day. This is one way through which Indian identity may be expressed in private without complications in relation to the mainstream society.

The young generation expresses a pan-Indian identity. At the same time, however, people are involved in identity negotiations that, in effect, are about differentiation between various groups in terms of religion, caste, (Swedish) towns of origin (actually to the Ugandan Asian communities in these towns), generation, gender, and so on. These identity transactions are also about relations to the Swedish majority population and to other people of migrant origin. Generational differences are very obvious in all migrant groups. The young generation is born and raised in Sweden, Swedish is their first language and they have no experience of life in other countries, apart from visits, mainly to the UK and India. Informants generally regarded their parents as liberal and understanding. Conflicts with parents may arise but the impression conveyed is they are resolved through discussion.

The true test of this complex identity situation is marriage. This is something everyone in the young generation is very concerned about. Within the Ugandan Asian community in Sweden, there is not a sufficient number of marital partners matching the traditional criteria of eligibility. This often means abandoning the traditional rules, which conflicts with the wishes of parents and expectations of the community. Marrying a Swedish partner does not necessarily mean that one is ostracised from the community, but it will involve redefinitions of position and identities. Some informants report that mixed marriages have caused tension in families. However, it is not easy to comply with parental wishes. Several informants mentioned that they had been introduced to a number of potential partners in marriage on various occasions, quite often on visits to the UK. Sometimes it worked but it usually involved moving to England. The problem is that qualifications and exams from Swedish schools and universities are not accepted in the UK. This creates another type of problem.

A temporary solution seems to be to postpone marriage. This means marrying at a considerably older age than previous generations. The problems of finding a partner who is acceptable according to the traditional criteria and meets with the approval of the parents, and at the same time defend career positions that have been achieved in Sweden, affects young women much more than young men because of conflicting views on gender equality. With increasing age, the strict adherence to the rules may be relaxed, and issues of eligibility may be dealt with by redefining people's positions and qualifications, or possibly by reinterpretation of the criteria of eligibility.

CONCLUSION

Returning to the telephone directory of the Mariestad Asian Cultural Society, we note that it only lists those who *identify* themselves as members of the (Ugandan) Asian communities in Sweden and who are *accepted* as members by these communities. Individuals who don't identify themselves with these communities even though they may have been victims of the expulsion, and those who are for some reason excluded from the community, are not listed in the directory. Some who have married Swedes are not listed as members. The roll of names in the directory, reflecting the body of people behind it, indicates that the vast majority of migrants from India and Pakistan are not associated with the Asian Cultural Societies referred to in this directory.

The roll may be seen, then, as a statement of self-defined collective identity. Although the *Ugandan* label is rarely used nowadays in public self-references, the collective memory of the expulsion is emotionally highly significant and a source of distinctiveness. Using Cohen's terminology (1997, p. 178), the expulsion turned the earlier Gujarati trade diaspora into a victim diaspora. It was a traumatic event binding those who experienced it, and their descendants and relatives by marriage together into a distinct group. Cohesiveness within the Ugandan Asian community is rooted in the common experience of the expulsion trauma. Memories of the trauma have been reinforced in recent years by virulent racism in Sweden of which the Ugandan Asians have had their share as victims.

The history of the Asian communities in East Africa shows how the Asians, with their roots in rural Gujarat, exhibited a strong sense of continuity in family life, social life and language, while at the same time these communities adapted well to the colonial society in business, politics and education. The small Ugandan Asian community in Sweden is an appendix to the wider South Asian diaspora in the UK and North America. There is reason to assume that a similar development to that experienced in Sweden is taking place elsewhere within the diaspora. The Asian communities in the West are well integrated into modern society and all aspects of its economy. Still, there is a strong sense of unique identity and cultural continuity that may be traced back to the Gujarati origins.

REFERENCES

Bose, M. (1982, 16 September). The Ugandan Asian Success Magic. *New Society,* 456-458.

Castells, M. (1997). *The Power of Identity*. Oxford: Blackwells.

Census Commissioner for India (1961). *Census of India 1961*, vol. 1 – 26. 1962-1966. New Delhi: Census Commissioner for India.

Clifford, J. (1994). Diasporas. *Cultural Anthropology*, *9*, 302-38.

Cohen, R. (1997). *Global Diasporas*. London: UCL Press.

Ghai, D.P. & Ghai, Y.P. (1970). *Portrait of a Minority. Asians in East Africa*. Oxford: Oxford University Press.

Giles, W., Moussa, H. & van Esterik, P. (1996). *Development and Diaspora.* Dundas, Ontario: Artemis.

Gregory, R.G. (1971). *India and East Africa. A History of Race Relations within the British Empire*. Oxford: Clarendon Press.

______ . (1993). *South Asians in East Africa. An Economic and Social History 1880-1980.* Oxford: Clarendon Press.

Hammar, T. (1999). Closing the doors to the Swedish welfare state. In Brochmann, G. and Hammar, T. (Eds.), *Mechanisms of Immigration Control. A Comparative Analysis of European Regulation Policies*. Oxford: Berg.

Hannerz, U. (1996). *Transnational Connections*. London: Routledge.

Harris, J. E. (Ed.). (1993). *Global Dimensions of the African Diaspora.* Washington, DC: Howard University Press.

Kuepper, W.G., Lackey, G.L. and Swinerton, E.N. (1975). *Ugandan Asians in Great Britain.* London: Croom Helm.

Lévi-Strauss, Claude, (1967). *Structural anthropology.* Garden City, N.Y.: Doubleday.

Mamdani, M. (1973). *From Citizen to Refugee. Uganda Asians come to Britain.* London: Francis Pinter.

Mangat, J.S. (1969). *A History of Asians in East Africa 1945-1996.* Oxford: Clarendon Press.

Morris, H.S. (1968). *The Indians of Uganda.* London: Weidenfeld & Nicholson.

Pardesh, Desh, (1994). *South Asian Presence in Britain.* London: Hurst & Co.

Robinson, V. (Ed.), (1992). *The International Refugee Crisis.* London: Macmillan.

_____ . (1993). Marching into the Middle Classes? The long-term resettlement of East African Asians in the UK. *Journal of Refugee Studies*, *6*, 230-247.

Statistics Sweden, (2003). *Population Statistics 2002.* Örebro: SCB.

Strizhak, E. (1993). The Ugandan Asian expulsion. Resettlement in the USA. *Journal of Refugee Studies*, *6*, 260-264.

Twaddle, M. (1975). *Expulsion of a Minority.* London: The Athlone Press.

Van Hear, N. (1998). *New Diasporas. The Mass Exodus, Dispersal and Regrouping of Migrant Communities*. Basingstoke: UCL Press.

Van Veer, P. (Ed.). (1995). *Nations and Migration. The Politics of Space in the South Asian Diaspora.* Philadelphia, PN: University of Pennsylvania Press.

Vertovec, S. and Cohen, R. (Eds.). (1999). *Migration, Diasporas and Transnationalism.* Cheltenham, UK: Edward Elgar.

_____ . (1986). *Encounters. The Ugandan Asians in Sweden.* Stockholm: Ceifo.

_____ . (1998). On migration and criminal offence. Report on a study from Sweden. *IMIS-Beiträge*, 7-29. Osnabrück: Institut für Migrationsforschung und Interkulturelle Studien, Universität Osnabrück.

Westin, C. (2000). *Settlement and Integration Policies towards Immigrants and their Descendents in Sweden.* International Migration Papers 34. Geneva: ILO.

_____ . (2002). The Ugandan Asians in Sweden – Twenty-five years after the expulsion. In S. Fenton and H. Bradley (Eds.). *Ethnicity and Economy. 'Race and Class' Revisited.* Basingstoke: Palgrave Publishers.

In: Homeland Wanted ISBN 1-59454-266-X
Editors: P. Waxman and V. Colic-Peisker, pp. 165-189 © 2005 Nova Science Publishers, Inc.

Chapter 9

RESETTLEMENT AFTER DETENTION: HAZARA REFUGEES FROM AFGHANISTAN IN AUSTRALIA[1]

Diana Glazebrook

ABSTRACT

Ineligible for resettlement services offered by the Federal government to refugees on permanent visas, Hazara refugees on temporary protection visas are required to manage their own 'resettlement' in Australia. Ethnographic research undertaken among Hazara refugees from Afghanistan living in Dandenong, Victoria, offers insight into their everyday activities of association, work, and study. These activities are facilitated by the mobile phone which provides a point of contact, and mediates the circulation of critical news and information. The author argues that Hazara mobile phone use can be conceived as an activity of resettlement, particularly in the first 12 months after release from detention.

Key words: refugee, resettlement, temporary protection, mobile phone, Hazara, Afghanistan.

INTRODUCTION

Conditions of the temporary protection visa (TPV) have required Hazara refugees from Afghanistan to be resourceful in managing their own 'resettlement' in Australia. This chapter examines how Hazara refugees evolved activities of resettlement in response to an asylum regime that denied TPV holders' entitlement to the full range of resettlement services available to permanently protected refugees.[2] Central to the discussion is an ethnographic

1 Aspects of this chapter were first published in the 2004 journal article 'Becoming mobile after detention' in *Social Analysis: The International Journal of Cultural & Social Practice* 48 (3). Many thanks to those Hazara people in Dandenong whose comments on this written chapter improved the final draft enormously, to Val Colic-Peisker, Nicholas Hall and Toni Wills for their close reading and recommendations, and to the Feith and Lim families in Melbourne for hosting me during the period of fieldwork.

2 Asylum seekers who have arrived by sea and subsequently claim asylum are considered unauthorised and unlawful, contrasting the lawful application of asylum seekers 'offshore' i.e., in the nearest Australian mission overseas or UNHCR office (DIMIA 2004).

account of the uses Hazara have made of their mobile phones. The axis of discussion revolves around what mobile phone practice says about experiences of temporary protection and resettlement. The fieldwork-based research focuses on a particular TPV population in a defined place, three years after release from detention. It was undertaken between December 2003 and March 2004 in the industrial region of Dandenong (south-east of Melbourne, Victoria) where about 700 Hazara refugees lived and worked.

During a three-year period between 1999 and 2001, approximately 9, 524 asylum seekers, mainly from Afghanistan and Iraq, arrived in Australia by boat. Of these, 3,597 asylum seekers from Afghanistan (including 2,500 Hazara) were subsequently recognised to be refugees and issued with TPVs. Conditions of this visa include the limitations of three years of temporary residency after which the applicant must re-apply for continued protection; no right of family reunion in Australia with spouses or children remaining in either the country of origin or the transit country of first asylum, and no right of re-entry for travel outside Australia; restricted access to the Federal government-funded Integrated Humanitarian Settlement Strategy;[3] no access to longer term resettlement services provided by the Community Settlement Services Scheme; no access to the 510 hour free English language training provided by the Adult Migrant Education Program, and no access to job training or placement services under the Job Network Intensive Assistance scheme. In terms of entitlements, TPV holders are eligible for income assistance under the Special Benefit scheme, free public health care under Medicare, and counselling from the Program of Assistance for the Survivors of Torture and Trauma. TPV holders are permitted to work.

An extensive published literature based on primary source material has assessed the social impact of temporary protection in Australia to be profoundly negative. Three studies: *Temporary protection visa holders in Queensland* (Mann, 2001), *Politics of social exclusion: refugees on temporary protection visas in Victoria* (Mansouri & Bagdas, 2002) and *Lives in limbo: voices of refugees under temporary protection* (Leach & Mansouri, 2004) find that neither state or local government services, nor community organisations, were able to meet the settlement needs of TPV holders, especially in the areas of housing and education. The evocative study *A life devoid of meaning: living on a temporary protection visa in Western Sydney* (Barnes, 2002) reveals that TPV holders made secondary movement to locations where members of their own ethnic community had settled. However, ethnic communities were similarly unable to meet their resettlement needs. Barnes' report analyses the dilemma of resettlement service provision and TPV policy. Community organisations funded by the Federal Department of Immigration, Multicultural and Indigenous Affairs (DIMIA) have been precluded from providing services to TPV holders. This exclusion has threatened these organisations' relationship with their constituent communities, and pushed service provision onto organisations that receive no DIMIA funding and have limited resources. Pickering et al.'s 2003 study *We're working with people here: the impact of the TPV regime on refugee settlement service provision in NSW* focuses on the way settlement service providers have "accommodated, negotiated and subverted" the temporary protection regime. Marston's (2003) study *Temporary protection permanent uncertainty* proposes direct and indirect discrimination in TPV holders' attempts to access housing, income support, the labour market

---

3 The Department of Immigration, Multicultural and Indigenous Affairs' (DIMIA) Integrated Humanitarian Settlement Strategy identifies initial settlement needs and provides matching services (e.g., initial information and orientation assistance, accommodation support, household formation, early health assessment and intervention services) with the goal of achieving "self-sufficiency in the settlement process" (DIMIA 2003d).

and health services in Victoria. In his monograph *Labour rights and border protection: attempts at a viable life on the temporary protection visa,* Hoffman claims that the temporary protection regime has created a new class of workers with minimal refugee rights, and has also reduced human, civil, and labour rights.

The chapter begins by exploring some methodological issues that arise from doing qualitative research among refugees whose protection is temporary. From this entry point, TPV holders are located historically by tracing the formation of a temporary asylum regime in Australia. For Hazara who have a documented history of persecution, the possibility of forced return to Afghanistan implied in the conditions of temporary protection, has profoundly affected their experience of temporary protection. I use news-gathering and news-telling practices as a lens to view Hazara anxieties about the past and the future. The focus moves to Dandenong in the present where Hazara live in group households that function communally; shop and socialise in an Afghani trading precinct; work alongside other Hazara in local factories and abattoirs; study English together in classes led by local university students; and gather en masse to celebrate religious events, and commemorate Shia and Hazara martyrs. These activities of community formation forge and intersect social networks of local Hazara. Public meetings 'about the visa' — on which Hazara futures are contingent — are occasionally convened in Dandenong. But most information about the visa is passed on via the phone. I examine the way Hazara have made use of the mobile phone for orientation and navigation, for making sense of and circulating news, and for 'maintaining' long-distance relations with family in Afghanistan. My analysis demonstrates that in a situation where they are only entitled to a level of support to "tide them over" for a period envisaged by the federal government as temporary (Barnes, 2002, p.10), the mobile phone has become fundamental to Hazara management of their own resettlement in Australia.

METHODOLOGY

To initiate contact with Hazara in Dandenong, I chose a large social gathering attended by over one hundred Hazara men and families. This end-of-year social event hosted by the Monash University Student Association's 'English tutors for TPV holders' program, provided opportunity to speak informally with Hazara about the research project, and exchange mobile phone numbers with men and family groups interested in participating. Of these original contacts, four became regular respondents, and subsequently introduced me to other Hazara. Over a period of ten weeks, I carried out 42 two-hour semi-structured interviews with a core group of fourteen men and four family groups. I also made social contact with about fifty other Hazara people in Dandenong. Except for two families, all of these people were TPV holders. Interviews with men were conducted primarily in English and with women primarily in Persian. Interviews took place in people's houses, or in a café located in the air-conditioned Dandenong Plaza, depending on the preference of the respondent and the heat of the summer day.

Undoubtedly, speaking rough Persian and demonstrating knowledge of Hazara populations in Iran paved my entry. Twelve months prior to undertaking the research, I had enrolled in an intensive course of Persian. Dari is a lingua franca of Afghanistan described by Hazara as an older version of Persian, but not a dialect, whereas Hazaragi is a dialect of Persian spoken by Hazara (Mousavi, 1997, pp. xv, 24). In mid-2003, a two-month trip to Iran

— a country of first asylum for some two million Afghani refugees — allowed valuable practise of colloquial Persian. It also provided insight into the different experiences and aspirations of Tajik and Hazara refugee families with whom I lived in Tehran and Mashhad (Glazebrook & Abbasi-Shavazi, forthcoming).

In Dandenong, I gathered data through in-depth, semi-structured interviews, as well as some spontaneous group discussions. Hazara friends and other Hazara household members were sometimes present when I arrived for an interview, or arrived during the course of an interview, and stayed around to participate in the conversation. In another setting, Omidian (2000, pp. 51-52) has described in cultural terms, participation by entire Afghani households (kin-based family groups) in interviews. Interviews become inclusive because Afghani conceive themselves as family members rather than individuals, and it would be unusual for a family member to invite someone into their home, and then exclude others from participating in the discussion. Participation in social gatherings in public places and people's homes further extended my understanding of people's everyday lives. McMichael describes this as one method informing another "to create an iterative process that could produce an ethnographic understanding" of everyday life (2002, pp.175-176).

I did not tape interviews. Most of the people that I interviewed were waiting on the verdict of a claim for permanent protection to DIMIA, or an appeal to the Refugee Review Tribunal (RRT).[4] Early in the research I was advised by Payendah, a straight-talking young man, that several Hazara were unclear about my motivations for doing research in Dandenong. They feared that any recorded comment critical of DIMIA could compromise their current application for permanent residency, in the event of it 'getting back' to DIMIA. Likewise, any comment deemed to be critical of the former Taliban or Northern Alliance regimes could endanger that person's future in the event of their forced return to Afghanistan. I resolved not to ask questions that would solicit comment about DIMIA or various regimes in Afghanistan. If this information was offered, I composed follow-up questions carefully. Omidian (2000, p.56) has described such fears as 'reality-based paranoia'; Afghani refugees have learned to survive repressive forms of government and their fear is based on their actual experience.

Payendah's warning affected my research method. Like other researchers of political refugees, "in order to know, I had to become expert in demonstrating that there were things, places, and people I did not want to know" (Feldman in Malkki, 1995, p.51). I did not ask people their name, place of origin, political allegiance, or details of events surrounding flight. This information was already contained in DIMIA's dossiers. Given DIMIA's approach to refugee narrative as forensic evidence, I did not want to appear to be developing a second dossier that could contradict the first in a court of law. I was also vigilant about not using people's conversations as the subject of discussion with others. Disclosing something said by another, suggested that I could likewise disclose what that person said to others.

Omidian learned that note taking was an issue among Afghani due to their "distrust of those who may record what they say and do" (1994, pp.156-158). I wrote notes by hand in interviews, and occasionally respondents requested that notes not be taken on a particular subject of conversation. I explained to respondents that identities would be coded in the raw data, and in published material, pseudonyms would be adopted, and place names and

4 The Refugee Review Tribunal reviews decisions made by DIMIA to refuse or cancel protection visas to non-citizens in Australia.

occupations changed. I offered to circulate a draft of any published material for Hazara respondents' comment prior to submission for publication, and did so with this chapter. During interviews I tried to transcribe phrases and longer 'monologues', and these are represented in italics in the text. I chose to retain the original expression as the intent is plain enough and compelling.

The fieldwork focus on mobile phone use emerged in the course of the research. I had initially set out to look at resilience in terms of religious ritual providing refuge, configuration of household space offering familiarity, and new modes of social attachment affecting sociality. It was in the course of fieldwork that I abandoned the first two presuppositions regarding resilience, as the men I interviewed were mainly secular, and their houses were apparently functional spaces where they rested between fatiguing shifts in nearby factories. The question of sociality was more promising. Doing research in Dandenong revealed a plethora of activities in which Hazara participated, and gave me insight into a process of community formation. But it was in interviews frequently interrupted by respondents' mobile phone conversations in Dari, that my curiosity was particularly aroused: how had mobile phones come to be integrated into their everyday lives, and what difference did the mobile phone make? Before moving forward to the interview data, it is necessary to outline the conditions and formation of temporary protection.

A History of Temporary Protection

A genealogy of temporary protection introduced in 1999 reveals selective immigration policies dating back to the first Immigration Act in 1901. For example, Pashtun Afghans migrated from the 1860s until the Immigration Restriction Act controlled immigration, naturalisation and movement in 1901.[5] In force until 1948, Australia's first immigration policy was characterised by exclusion based on race. Since the 1970s, Australia has maintained an annual humanitarian quota of 12,000 places across four categories: refugee (off-shore applicants); special humanitarian (applicants with sponsors); special assistance (applicants with close family sponsors) and onshore protection visas (those in Australia eligible for refugee status) (Jupp 2002, p.34). Hazara people from Afghanistan were not the first asylum seekers to arrive by boat to Australia, experience mandatory detention, or receive temporary protection. Vietnamese people arrived by boat in 1975, Cambodian asylum seekers were detained at Port Hedland and Curtin in 1991, and temporary safe haven visas were offered to groups of East Timorese, Sri Lankans and Kosovar asylum seekers. The contribution of these events to the formation of a temporary protection asylum regime in Australia has been traced (e.g., MacCallum 2002; Mares 2002; Jupp 2002; Manne & Corlett 2004). Prior to October 1999, asylum seekers arriving by plane or boat who were recognised to be refugees according to the UN Convention, were automatically offered permanent protection visas (PPV) which provided permanent residency.[6] The safe haven policy has been

5 Rajkowski (1987) and Stevens (1989) have documented the contribution of camel transporters from Afghanistan in the development of the interior of Australia.

6 Fitzpatrick (2000) has examined the trend towards temporary protection and demonstrates plans to codify temporary protection to be based on retrogressive and progressive impulses. Codifying temporary protection could allow protection for 'non-Convention' refugees; allow group-based protection when individual status is indeterminable, and allow for policy makers of conservative domestic constituencies to offer 'discreetly humane' protection. However, where temporary protection is offered as substitute protection to Convention

described as a precedent, preparing public acceptance for the idea of temporary protection (Mares 2002, p.191). During the 1998 Australian federal election, the conservative political party 'One Nation' campaigned on the issue of immigration, proposed temporary protection to refugees, and won almost a million votes (Maley 2001, p.5).

In 1998-99, 42 boats arrived in Australian territory carrying 921 asylum seekers mainly from Afghanistan and Iraq (DIMIA 2003b). Under the mandatory detention regulation, they were indefinitely detained in one of six onshore immigration detention centres. From 1998, the metaphor 'queue jumper' entered Australian public discourse as a pseudonym for asylum seeker. It originates from DIMIA's collapsing of the number of onshore arrivals (by boat) with offshore visa applicants into one category. According to this view, every asylum seeker arriving by boat and recognised as a refugee within the UN Convention guidelines could be seen to be unfairly denying a visa to an offshore applicant who has gone through proper legal process (Mares, 2002, p.24). Researchers emphasised that increased secondary movements from the country of first asylum to Australia was directly related to deterioration of refugee protection in the countries of first asylum (e.g., Pakistan and Iran) in the same period (Maley, 2001, p.10).[7] They drew attention to two aspects of secondary movement. First, asylum seekers may flee a country of first asylum due to discrimination amounting to persecution on the grounds of their nationality (Human Rights Watch, 2002, p.24). Second, in transit countries such as Indonesia, asylum seekers face notorious difficulties gaining access to the UNHCR determination and resettlement system (Human Rights Watch, 2002, p.38).

It was not until October 1999 that migration regulations were changed to introduce temporary protection. A temporary protection visa also known as visa subclass 785, was to be issued to onshore arrivals found to be refugees. At the expiry of this visa, individuals could apply for a PPV which granted Australian residency status. Subsequent legislation added further visa restrictions. The 2001 federal election campaign fell almost two years after the introduction of TPVs. During this period, 9,233 asylum seekers were transported in 171 boats (DIMIA, 2003b). In a six-day period during the election campaign, three boats arrived carrying almost 1000 asylum seekers. The arrival of a fourth boat which was rescued by the Norwegian freighter *MV Tampa* resulted in the Federal government introducing new legislation in the form of seven bills (Mathew 2002, p.1). It was the political exploitation of the *Tampa*'s arrival by the Howard federal government in a post-September 11 election campaign that saw the *Tampa* become an icon of border-protective nationalism. The seven bills were passed fifteen days after the destruction of the World Trade Center in New York on September 11, 2001, and after a link had been manufactured in public discourse between terrorism and boat people from Muslim countries.

The bills limited the Refugee Convention definition of 'refugee'[8] and enacted new powers of interception at sea with six of the seven bills validating the actions related to the *Tampa*. Glossed as 'the Pacific Solution', one of the bills excised Christmas Island, Ashmore and Cartier Island, and Cocos (Keeling) Islands from the Australian migration zone so that

---

refugees (e.g., Australia), it effectively undermines the Convention because it does not guarantee non-refoulement to a Convention refugee.

7 The Government of Iran ratified the UN Refugee Convention with reservations regarding articles 17 (wage earning employment), 23 (public relief), 24 (labour legislation and social security), and 26 (freedom of movement) (http://www.refugees.org/world/countryrpt/mideast/2003/iran.cfm). The Government of Pakistan is not a signatory to the UN Refugee Convention.

8 For example, by redefining 'social group' as a basis for persecution, and disallowing consideration of persons who fear persecution based on the past persecution of a family member (Crock & Saul 2002, p.66).

boats landing there were deemed not to have entered Australia.[9] This rendered their passengers ineligible for asylum. All intercepted asylum seekers were to be removed offshore (transferred to Nauru, and Manus Island, Papua New Guinea) or forcibly returned to Indonesia from where they could apply to enter Australia (DIMIA 2003c). The new legislative regime which included the 'Pacific Solution' added two further temporary visa classes, and changed the terms of the original temporary Visa 785 for those arriving after September 2001.[10] These changes revealed the government's intention to discipline boat arrivals, and reward those who 'queued' off-shore. Refugees who had been granted a TPV and had not applied for permanent protection before September 2001, were now precluded from doing so. Refugees who had spent seven days in a country where they could have sought 'effective protection' en-route to Australia also became ineligible for permanent protection. In short, refugees granted TPVs since 2001 would not have the right to apply for permanent protection (Marston, 2003, p.15).

By the beginning of 2004, many temporary protection visas had expired. The period of fieldwork research for this chapter coincided with the expiry of TPVs held by Hazara. Most Hazara people that I interviewed had their subsequent claim for permanent protection rejected by DIMIA, and were actively preparing their case for appeal to the RRT. Because they applied to maintain their TPV status before its expiry, these people were allowed to maintain their TPV status (work rights, access to Special Benefit payments and Medicare) until their case has been finally determined. However, the expiry of TPV visas created extreme confusion and only the very literate viewed this change as pragmatically as Musa who: "read on the DIMIA website that we had the right of appeal to RRT and then the High Court. I knew this rule and so I didn't have any confusion." The perceived threat of forced return to Afghanistan was profoundly unsettling for Hazara refugees in Australia.

Temporary Protection and the Issue of Return to Afghanistan

Persecution of Hazara in Afghanistan

Hazara people are distinctive in their homeland Afghanistan. They typically have a Central Asian rather than southern European phenotype (Maley, 2001), are considered to be of mixed Moghol, Turkic and Persian ancestry (Mousavi, 1997, p.43) and are a Shia Muslim minority in Sunni-dominant Afghanistan. Although Hazara live scattered throughout Afghanistan, particularly in the urban areas of Kabul, Herat and Mazar-e Sharif, their cultural homeland is considered to be the Hazarajat, covering three provinces of Afganistan (Bamiyan, Orozgan and Ghur) and parts of Herat, Farah, Qandahar, Ghazni, Parwan, Baghlan, Balkh and Badghis (Mousavi, 1997, p. xiii). In Afghanistan, discrimination against Hazara has been grounded in "sectarian antagonism and social closure" (Maley, 2001, p.8),

9 These islands and reefs lie to the north of the Australian mainland, in close proximity to Indonesia from where most boats carrying asylum seekers have been launched.

10 Visa 447 is a three-year visa issued to asylum seekers found to be refugees and apprehended on boats bound for Australia. 447 holders are precluded from applying for a permanent visa whereas visa 451 is a five-year visa issued to asylum seekers found to be refugees in transit countries. 451 holders are permitted to apply for a permanent protection visa at the expiry of their temporary visa (Human Rights Watch, 2002, p.83).

resulting in severe displacement and massive exodus in the 1890s, and again from the late 1970s. It is these "sufferings and humiliations of previous generations" that have been internalised by younger Hazara, and are a component of an emerging Hazara ethno-nationalist consciousness (Canfield, 2004). Since 1979 following Soviet occupation, civil war and Taliban rule, more than one million Hazara have joined other Afghani refugees seeking refuge in Iran and Pakistan. Maley (2001, p.6) has explained the reason for refugees from Afghanistan seeking asylum to be complex and based on an interaction of such factors as: "state disintegration, political mobilisation based on ethnic and sectarian social cleavages and a criminalised economy, and gross human rights violations".

From 1996, Shia Hazara were particularly targeted as heretics by powerful Taliban leaders (Maley, 2001, p.8). Hazara land was seized, assets looted, and mass killings carried out. Among many of the Hazara with whom I conducted research, one event stood out as a catalyst. In August 1998, the Taliban slaughtered two thousand Hazara in Mazar-e Sharif incited by anti-Hazara broadcasts by the Taliban Governor of that province (Human Rights Watch, 1998). Seventy to eighty per cent of Hazara asylum seekers who arrived to Australia since 1999 were aged between 18 and 30.[11] Hazara people explain this narrow demographic to be due to the fact that it was young men in this age bracket that the Taliban were forcibly conscripting into their front line against the Mujihadeen opposition. Hazara have also suffered persecution under those who formed the Northern Alliance, and who now constitute the interim administration in Kabul (Human Rights Watch 2002:9).[12] An example of this is the massacre of Hazara residents of the Afshahr district of West Kabul in February 1993 (Mousavi, 1997, p.198).

During the period of this research, both the Federal Government and the Embassy of Afghanistan in Australia made public statements about the negligible risk of return for asylum seekers and refugees. The Embassy of Afghanistan published a news release to its web site, and published a letter in national daily newspapers claiming that "assertions that members of the Hazara community or other ethnic minorities are still subject to persecution does not hold ground on closer scrutiny".[13] The statement made by the Second Secretary of the Embassy of Afghanistan, A.S Qassem, was responded to vehemently in several letters including one by M.A. Fayazi of the Association of Hazaras in Victoria[14] who detailed incidences of abuse of Hazara reported by the BBC. Every Hazara person that I spoke to about the Second Secretary's claim responded similarly with a detailed inventory of recent incidents of disappearance and murder of Hazaras, sourced from the internet and reported by Reuters, BBC and Amnesty International.

11 Without recourse to published or at least official statistics, unless otherwise cited, figures in this chapter relating to Hazara refugees in Australia are estimates that have been corroborated by Hazara community leaders.

12 The Northern Alliance is an alliance of non-Pashtun parties and forces that formed in 1992 after the withdrawal of the Soviet Union, and re-aligned to oppose the Taliban after Kabul was captured in 1996.

13 Qassem 2004.

14 Fayazi 2004.

Figure 1. Kabul is listed as a premier travel destination in the window of a flight agency in Dandenong.

The Risks of Hazara Return

The story of TPV holder Fatih Ali's voluntary return to Afghanistan and his subsequent flight to Pakistan was circulated among some Hazara in Australia and acted as a warning of the risks of Hazara return. I have reconstructed this story about Fatih Ali from rough notes taken during a conversation with Qasim — for whom Fatih Ali was like a father. Together they travelled in the same boat from Indonesia, were detained in Woomera detention centre together, and shared a house on release from Woomera.

> Qasim: Fatih Ali was about 52. He paced the house most of the night, and on the street, and spoke out loud to himself. Both Fatih Ali and I feared that he was becoming crazy. He decided to leave Australia and return to Afghanistan. He said to me that if he did not go back then maybe he would become completely crazy. He sent a letter to me from Pakistan about his experience. He said that on his arrival to Kabul, he exited the airport and immediately someone pointed to him on the street and said he was Hazara. After than he felt everyone to be looking at him and watching him, especially militia. People said that returnees had abandoned Afghanistan during the Taliban and were only returning for a share of the spoils in a time of peace. He noticed that everyone in Kabul carried a gun, and that all returnees were vulnerable because people assumed they had prospered in exile. Fatih Ali advised me: better to go back into detention in Australia and remain indefinitely than return to Afghanistan and risk death.

A second story about the suicide of Hazara TPV holder Dr Habib relates to the unbearable decision-making of return to Afghanistan. It is also a warning of the risks of thinking too much about the future, causing *andesh* (sick with worry). According to the storyteller Choli, a person can die from *andesh*, but Dr Habib killed himself out of *andesh*. From the outside, Habib's dilemma appears to be: he would kill himself if he had to return to unsafe Afghanistan yet his family was there, and he would kill himself if he had to remain in 'safe' Australia without his family. Dr Habib's suicide coincided with the release of DIMIA's Reintegration Package for TPV holders from Afghanistan.[15] In the narrative below, a Hazara community leader in Dandenong told the story of Dr Habib as a lesson of the risks associated with searching for news, reading 'bad' news, and worrying about news.

> We (the Hazara Community Association of Dandenong) told the message to the community that Dr Habib's problem is the same problem for us. Too many times we talk with the people and tell them if they are feeling depressed or anxious, do something about it. Talk with someone, leave your work, change city and relocate to be closer to your close friends or family from your area [Afghanistan]. Don't stay in the same house if you are depressed. Dr Habib was all the time searching the internet – his English was good enough for this. All the time searching for news about Afghanistan, about Australia, about the visa. Everytime he would arrive home from work he would immediately begin searching on the internet. At that time too many bad news for refugees. His friends always were telling him to stop searching. He thought the Immigration was everywhere, was coming to find him, knew what he was reading.

15 In May 2002, a memorandum of understanding signed between the Australian Immigration Minister and Afghanistan's Interim Administration introduced a 'reintegration assistance package' which offered an amount of money ($AUD200 per adult, $AUD10,000 per family) to Afghani asylum seekers in detention, and to Afghani TPV holders if they volunteered to return to Afghanistan (DIMIA 2003a).

Telling and Receiving Bad News

People's attitudes towards telling news about Afghanistan and the visa situation were apparently contradictory: news was both the subject of proscription, and an inevitable subject for speech. On the one hand, respondents believed that telling bad news diminished people's '*ruh*' (spirit). On the other hand, telling news about the visa was inevitable because it shaped their everyday lives so radically. Choli explained:

> Sometimes I say to my friends when we are together or we are at a party: don't talk too many about the news. Talk instead about what has happened to you, about your job, what is good for you. In the beginning at a party we make an agreement: don't talk about news and visas. But then the conversation always turns back to the news. For example, if one of our friends is absent I will ask why and it will happen that he has an interview the following day with his lawyer about his visa and then the conversation turns back to news.

Many Hazara trawled internet sites daily for news of Afghanistan and visa policy. The month of January 2004 carried much news categorised by Hazaras to be 'bad'. First, Hazara asylum seekers on Nauru, after facing forced return to Afghanistan following DIMIA's rejection of their application for refugee status, carried out a prolonged hunger strike with sewn lips that threatened their lives and long-term health.[16] Second, consultations by the interim government of Afghanistan resulted in a Constitution judged by many secular Hazara in Australia to be embedded in Islamic law which discriminates against secular citizens. Third, public statements were made by the Embassy of Afghanistan denying any risk of return to Hazara based on their ethnicity. There was another tension about news. News was sought for reasons that were simultaneously contradictory: to verify Afghanistan as both safe and unsafe. On the one hand, Hazara sought to learn of the situation improving in Afghanistan because of the possibility of their forced return and out of concern for their family's well being. On the other hand, they were required to gain evidence of Afghanistan's 'unsafeness' in order to substantiate their claim for extended visa protection. According to Choli, Hazara perceive much news as 'bad' and subsequently become *andesh* because they interpret news literally. It was explained to me that Hazara who are neither formally educated nor functionally literate in Dari or English, tend to hear all reported news as fact, rather than as part of a discourse which includes opinion, rhetoric and propaganda.

Fieldwork research for this chapter was conducted between December 2003 and March 2004 during a period when a confluence of factors invoked a low nadir in Hazara people. I have outlined these factors to be: domestic and international political news considered to be bad for Hazara; the expiry of their visas which required another drawn-out cycle of complex legal review, contest, and verdict; and prolonged and indefinite separation from their families. Against these events, the place of Dandenong provided a relatively stable and hopeful place to live and work.

---

16 These asylum seekers on Nauru had no review rights in the Refugee Review Tribunal as they were deemed to have not entered Australian territory, and therefore did not have the same appeal rights as TPV holders.

FORMATION OF A HAZARA COMMUNITY IN DANDENONG

At the time of the research, about 600-700 Hazara men and a few family groups lived in the region of Greater Dandenong, considered to be one of the most disadvantaged in metropolitan Melbourne. According to the 2001 Australian Bureau of Statistics Census figures (ABS, 2002), Dandenong residents collectively have low individual incomes (median weekly income $AUD200-$299), low home ownership (30 per cent of all occupied dwellings are rented) and large household size (median household size is 2.8). A high concentration of residents are non-English-speaking-background migrants, and forty-nine per cent of residents were born overseas including the UK (4 per cent), Sri Lanka (3.9 per cent) and Viet Nam (2.6 per cent). Almost 11 per cent of the labour force are unemployed, and 29 per cent are employed in the manufacturing industry. Hazara learned about Dandenong's classification as 'disadvantaged' when they were required to pay an annual risk premium for motor vehicle insurance amounting to $AUD100.

Figure 2.Dinner for twenty-three around the desterkhan (tablecloth), suburban Dandenong.

Figure 3. Banner of the Hazara Australian Community Association.

Hazara began arriving in Dandenong following their release from detention in mid-2000. Also residing in Dandenong were several hundred family groups from Afghanistan who arrived in the 1980s and had been granted permanent residency.[17] The first group of 29 TPV holders, including 27 Hazara, came to Dandenong because of the presence of Dari-speaking Pashtun and Tajik people, and the offer by a Pashtun community association to provide limited support. Subsequent groups of Hazara then followed this first group to Dandenong. Others made secondary movement to Dandenong from other states and regions. Mohib explained to me that there was no grand plan: "[I]t just happened like that. All Hazara people are coming here. When Hazara were gradually released from the detention centres they would contact each other and ask: who's living here [in Dandenong]?" Choli explained that a history of Pashtun persecution had produced in Hazara, a natural ability to commune. He used a Hazara proverb and shepherding analogy to illustrate the tactic of Hazara when threatened: a single sheep separated from the mob is vulnerable prey. Hazara have not always been perceived by outsiders as united however. The representation of Hazara as fractious has been glossed as the "amity of wolves" by Canfield (2004), who proposes that it is in the past two decades that Hazara have practiced brotherhood due to a rise in their political consciousness.

At the time of their release from detention, many Hazara people lived for two or three weeks with previously released friends, who then helped them find somewhere to live locally. After several Hazara households established their reputation as reliable tenants, local real estate agents ceased to discriminate against Hazara applicants for not holding tenancy records and references.[18] Biki explained that Hazara encouraged their friends to relocate: "If others contacted us, we would say, live close to us – here, you get a job, you get a house close to us." Some of these relations were long-lasting and could become reciprocal for purposes like loaning money. In Dandenong, Hazaras live together in groups of three or four in shared houses and flats.

Households tend to be based on shared region of origin in Afghanistan or shared place of detention in Australia. Sometimes people from the same workplace live together and share a car for commuting to work. Many Hazara have moved two or three times between houses which have become 'Hazara households' with revolving membership. Households act to some extent as family groups: party invitations are extended at the level of the household, and parties are hosted by entire households. In Shokur's words: "If I invite a guest, everyone in the house must look after you, like a family." Household members prefer to eat together at mealtimes around a *desterkhan* (tablecloth of any size spread on the floor). Symbolising an Afghani custom of hospitality, the ample *desterkhan* can host many guests, unlike a table with chairs.

Thomas Street, Dandenong boasts about eleven Afghani shops including four Hazara-run grocery shops and three restaurants. Shops like the Bamyan grocery shop recall the Buddhist statues in the Hazarajat, whereas the Balkh restaurant/bakery is named after the Balkh area which is imagined nostalgically as a sort of heartland of the Afghanistan nation. Grocery

---

17 The 2001 Australian Census listed 11,264 people born in Afghanistan, an increase of 93 per cent from 1996. Since the early 1980s — coinciding with the Soviet occupation of Afghanistan and the Mujihadeen resistance — Afghani (including Pashtun, Tajik, Uzbek and Qizilbash) have immigrated to Australia with approximately 4,000 settling in Melbourne and elsewhere in the state of Victoria (Immigration Museum of Melbourne 2003). A history of Afghani in Australia was the subject of an exhibition in 2003 titled *Safar-e Ma* (Our Journey) at the Melbourne Immigration Museum.

18 The dire housing situation of other TPV holders in Melbourne (extremely limited access to public housing and difficulties in obtaining housing on the open rental market) is documented (Marston 2003, pp. 34-38).

stores stock food imported mainly from Iran and India, and CDs, videos and DVDs from Afghanistan and Iran. All of these shops use their street-side window space as public billboards notifying customers in Persian and English about music concerts, legal forums, migration agents, etc. Local Afghani tradesmen also pin their business cards here.

Figure 4. The Bamyan Shop, Thomas Street Dandenong with Balkh Kebabery opposite reflected in the window.

The availability of factory employment close to the residential area of Dandenong is attractive to new residents. The rate of employment among Hazara in Dandenong is estimated by community leaders to be near to 90 per cent, including a small percentage of men who have casual or seasonal work and experience periods of unemployment between jobs. Those who are not working at all include some older men who are frail and men who have sustained workplace injuries. According to community leaders, most Hazara own second-hand cars as employees are required to have their own transport. The rate of Hazara employment in the Dandenong region is in stark contrast to the aggregated TPV population unemployment figure of 50 per cent in 2003. Unemployed TPV holders receive income assistance from the Federal Government in the form of Special Benefits (Marston, 2003, p.39).

Hazara people in Dandenong come from a variety of backgrounds. In Afghanistan they worked as small-scale farmers of sheep and goats; labourers; shopkeepers; machinists; teachers, and nurses. Some were students in secondary school and university (law, engineering, literature, literacy and education, and medicine). The entry of recent Hazara arrivals into the local labour market was eased by the reputable work practice of other Hazara. For example, at different times Hazara have comprised over 25 per cent of the local abattoir workforce of 450. Most Hazara are employed in factories where they process food and manufacture products such as car parts, tyres, flags and tents, shower screens, couches, plastic bottles, chemicals, galvanised iron. Other Hazara work as taxi drivers, forklift operators, bricklayers, painters and tilers, bakers and pizza makers, farmhands, Persian carpet sales, recycling company rubbish sorters, machinists and railway station sweepers.

Many Hazara are enrolled in English language courses at local Technical and Further Education (TAFE) colleges in Dandenong. News about courses travels by word of mouth among Hazara. In 2004, TPV holders became eligible to study full-time and at the time of writing, many Hazara were enrolled part-time and full-time in courses including English language, IT studies, and accounting. About a dozen Hazara work full-time and study full-time. The shift in TAFE policy in 2002 to allow TPV holders enrolment at domestic tuition fee rates was considered by some Hazara to be a significant turning point in their circumstances. Until that time, TPV holders in Dandenong had been restricted to volunteer-staffed English classes provided by the local library and Adult Migrant English Scheme. Students from the local Monash University also offer English language tutoring several evenings per week in Dandenong. All TPV holders remain ineligible for the 510 hour English language training under the Adult Migrant Education Program offered to refugees with permanent protection.

There are two Hazara community associations with elected leadership based in the Dandenong region: the Hazara Australian Community Association of Victoria, and the Association of Hazaras of Victoria. The Hazara Australian Community Association of Victoria hosts annual cultural and religious events in Dandenong attended by up to 450 Hazara. Annual events celebrated locally include *Eid* (close of the fasting month of Ramazan); *Moharam* (commemoration of the Shia martyr Imam Hossein at Karbala, Iraq); *Mazari* (commemoration of Abdul Ali Mazari, martyr and leader of the Hazara Party of Unity *Hesb-e Wahdat* killed by the Taliban in March 1995), and *Nawrooz* (the celebration of New Year according to the Persian Solar Calendar). The Hazara Australian Community Association also arranges information sessions for TPV holders, and office bearers are in constant mobile phone contact, advocating and advising community members, as well as reading government correspondence received by members who cannot read English. The Association of Hazaras of Victoria focuses on public affairs matters and publishes a 12-page monthly newsletter in Persian named *Aarmaan* (Desire), which is distributed among Hazara throughout Australia. *Aarmaan* contains visa information, aspects of immigration law, RRT decisions on TPV holder appeals, as well as news about the interim government of Afghanistan. Office bearers of this organisation advocate on behalf of members, and provide a free translation service for documents relating to applications for permanent protection. They also publish information relating to Hazara diaspora on their own website www.bamyan.org.au.

Mobile Phone Use and 'Resettlement'

Establishing a Point of Contact

Much of Hazara communal life detailed in the section above has been facilitated by the mobile phone. Analysis of Hazara mobile phone use begins with their release from detention and the imperative of establishing a point of contact. From mid-2000, Hazara asylum seekers recognised to be refugees were released in stages from six detention institutions. Newly-released Hazara made contact with members of their social network who had been released previously. The bases of a Hazara social network might be traced to shared village of origin; shared school or university in Afghanistan; shared boat journey; shared detention centre; or shared region of resettlement or workplace in Australia. Newly released TPV holders relied on members of their personal social network to provide them with the 'know how' to self-administer their everyday lives. Some of this knowledge originated from orientations session provided by the Ecumenical Migration Centre (EMC).[19] For example, information was provided about how to apply for employment and government income assistance, and a tax file number; applying for a government health card; finding and leasing a house; understanding changes in visa policy and obligations; applying for and keeping a drivers licence; financing and insuring a car; opening a bank account and using an automatic teller machine, and selecting and servicing a mobile phone.

In 2000, pre-paid mobile phones were not cheap. Contract or plan mobile phones that offered free handsets required proof of identity such as a driver's license. In Australia, financial contracts require proof of identity based on a points system. Identity documents are accorded a value and an applicant must produce documents to the value of 100 points. A mobile phone contract is worth 15 points. For TPV holders, a mobile phone contract became part of their identity documentation. Ironically, however, a visa does not constitute proof of identity outside of the government sector. Coming into contact with this bureaucratic irony, Shokur observed: "the visa I have, but *they* don't have it on their system".

A single home-line in a shared house accommodating three or four adults was impractical. Where the shift-work hours of household members coincided, people inevitably wanted to use the phone at the same time. Some households elected not to connect the single home-line, and instead, all of the occupants purchased their own mobiles. Sometimes a mobile owner shared his phone with other members of a household until they could afford to buy their own. For example, Qasim bought his first mobile after four months. He lived with two close friends, with whom he had previously studied at the University of Mazar-e-Sharif in Afghanistan and had also lived with in detention. Released together, Qasim bought a phone and the others used this number to give to prospective employers until they found jobs and could afford to buy their own phones.

Government forms inevitably require telephone contact details. Employers also routinely request telephone details in order to contact an applicant in the event of a vacancy. If a home-line is engaged or if a person is away from the house and misses the call, an offer of work may be missed. For example, Mohib applied for up to fifty jobs: "When they call for us we have to have a mobile. The first question they ask is your contact number. During the day we were not at home. After two or three weeks there is no way, we have to get a mobile." Considered most dire was the risk of missing a call from one's lawyer. During the period of research, most Hazara were either in the act of lodging a claim, or appealing DIMIA's rejection of their application for permanent protection. Either way, they were in various states of expectancy: anticipating news to come at any time about their claim. Qasim explained to me that whereas in the first twelve months he kept his phone switched on 24 hours per day in case a friend called, three years later, he keeps his mobile phone switched on in case his

[19] EMC is a non-government organisation funded by the Victorian state government to develop basic co-ordinating structures for reception, emergency accommodation and information/referral of refugees released from detention.

lawyer calls: "I feel if something happens with my case, I will know very quickly, or if something [else] happens I will know very quickly."

On release from detention, the majority of Hazara TPV holders were not functionally literate in the Arabic script of Persian,[20] or English. It is the immediacy that the mobile phone allows that lends security to the lives of people who speak negligible English, especially when they are alone and outside of the household that they share with fellow Hazara. Payendah reflected on this experience: "When I first arrived I had many, many problems. I could not ask for help in English. One way was with a mobile phone. I could just ask for help, just call one of my friends. All the time I would call a [Dari-speaking] friend who could speak English." Free calling[21] offered by most mobile phone providers in Australia has extended conversations between Hazara people across Australia allowing for easy circulation of news.

Making Sense of News

At least in the first 12 months after release from detention, most Hazara could neither understand English language news on the television, radio or newspapers, nor could they read news in Persian on the internet. In the period following 11 September, Hazara anxiously sought out news about the US occupation of Afghanistan and the interim administration in Kabul, as well as changes to visa policy in Australia. Television footage relaying images of Afghanistan and detention centres in Australia prompted Hazara to seek out the commentary from others who comprehended English. Many people listen to the weekly, sixty-minute news broadcasts in Persian on local Melbourne radio stations. But most Hazara relied on their social networks for news which was circulated via the mobile phone.

Free calling allowed Hazara to contact their friends dispersed across Australia, and provided Hazara working in rural locations with access to news. The practice of circulating news via mobile phone networks was understood by some to carry risks. Choli's experience as a professional teacher had taught him: "If people are not educated they cannot relay the news exactly, maybe similar but essentially incorrect." Choli's comment is part of a wider Hazara discourse about the dangers of illiteracy, underwritten by a belief that illiteracy produced war in Afghanistan. News may also be distorted when people misinterpret visual footage on television news and pass this on.

Since release from detention, Hazara have routinely spent hours in daily discussion about news. In the twelve month period leading up to the expiry of their visas, this practice is still linked to the conditions of temporary protection. News is soughtabout: what to do when one's visa expires; how to appeal against the Department of Immigration's determination; the outcome of other Hazara TPV holders' appeals; mooted and actual legislative changes vis a vis. TPVs; the status of Hazara in other western countries; the situation in their immediate region in Afghanistan in the event of their forced return, and conditions of DIMIA's reintegration package (see DIMIA 2003a). Much of this news has originated from the twelve-

---

20 According to Choli, a university-qualified teacher, over 80 per cent of the population of Afghanistan including Hazara, are functionally illiterate i.e., they may be able to read parts of the Qaran in Arabic, but may not be able to read, write and comprehend Persian which also uses Arabic script.

21 For example, one provider offered free calls from 8pm until midnight (Mondays thru Fridays); another offered free calls from 9pm until 7am, and another offered weekend calls at $AUD 0.20c for ten minutes to any mobile network.

page monthly newsletter *Aarman* distributed among Hazara throughout Australia, by the Association of Hazaras of Victoria, based in Dandenong. While some of this discussion about the visa happens face-to-face, much of it happens by mobile phone facilitated by free calling.

Some Hazara have tried reducing their mobile phone use, conceding that free calling has produced health problems. For example, Choli worried that: "Sometimes my head is confusing, I think the room is moving, sometimes my ear is aching. Sometimes I have a headache, [if] I open my mobile I feel more headache." Some have taken to switching off the ring, others switch off completely. But Qasim acknowledged: "most Hazara can't control themselves talking because it is free call." It is a free call that produces unmeasurable social capital. Knowledge about their political and legal circumstances, and exposure to other people's experiences and perceptions, aids Hazara in their decision making. Knowing about Afghanistan and the visa, has instilled in Hazara a small measure of confidence that there is some 'order' both in the way things have happened, and in the way things may proceed. News about people's village and region could also be gleaned by phoning family in Afghanistan, but this contact was inevitably unsettling.

Phoning Family in Afghanistan

Hazara men imagined their families to be waiting anxiously for reunion and this increased the men's discomfort. Shokur explained:

> When we were released from detention we were very happy. We don't want to stay at home, always on picnic. Since the first group got the refused letter from the DIMIA there is a change. We are no longer going too much for sightseeing. Before, every weekend we had four or five visitors in the house for dancing and eating and drinking tea. Now everyone is sleeping. All come back from work but just want to sleep. Everyone is very sad. When we were released from detention our families [in Afghanistan] were happy. When our visas expired they asked: what is happening to you, what is the future? Many, many pressures. Families are waiting. Last night in my house until 2 am a group of us sat around. There was no television on, no drinking tea. Just speaking about the situation and what we should be doing.

Hazara community leaders estimated that 45 per cent out of a population of 2100 Hazara men on TPVs in Australia are married with wives and family in Afghanistan. All Hazara men in Australia are integral members of extended families that include elderly parents and younger and older siblings. By 2003, Hazara had been separated from their families for up to four and a half years. If permanent residency is granted, family reunification rules will prolong separation further by a minimum of two years (Marston 2003, p.25). In the long and uncertain separation of families, telephone contact has offered the only possibility of connection.

Contact with one's family in Afghanistan is entirely dependent on their location. In Afghanistan, there are very few mobile phones and even fewer home-lines.[22] Ghazni Province

22 The Afghan Wireless Communication Company publication *A Nation on the line* (2002) reported that in November 2001, Afghanistan had approximately 20,000 working telephone lines for a population of 27 million. Outside of Kabul, only expensive satellite phones and a few private systems could make international or inter-city telephone calls. By 2002, Afghan Wireless had installed base stations in Kabul, Herat, Mazar-e Sharif, and Kandahar, and hosted 30,000 mobile phone subscribers.

- from where most Hazara in Dandenong originate – has neither land-line nor postal service. Connection is extremely fraught for Hazaras in Australia and Afghanistan: it is costly, dangerous and unsettling. Several mobile phone owners make it their business to put international callers in touch with their relatives. A mobile phone operator may summon a family member to come to his shop at a time prearranged with the caller in Australia. The family member pays a summons fee, and a tariff per minute for use of the operator's phone (seven Afghani or $US 15 cents per minute). Some operators may take their mobile to the home of the family where they can take the call. The system is time consuming and costly. It frequently happens that the operator has been unable to summon the family, or the family does not turn up on the appointed day or precise time. In this case, the caller from Australia must go through the rigmarole of trying to establish contact again. Some families in urban centres use the service of the *mokhabarat* (payphone shop) where they are charged per minute for international calls.

Using the mobile phone service in this way is not without risk. A family summoned to the public area of a crowded shop to receive the call of their son or husband in Australia becomes vulnerable to people pressuring them for money. Choli knows this too well:

> All the people know if I'm calling by mobile phone in the shop, the people know Choli is calling and talking to his family. Too many people are staying, hearing. They are thinking where is Choli now? If someone has a mobile it is also not safe. If someone finds I am in Australia, they push my family to pay money because they think Choli has too many dollars now. These mobiles are not safe. Now we have examples of people have a problem.

Like Choli, Jarghiw contacts his family intermittently as they live in an isolated area. He is contemplating purchasing a mobile phone for his wife at a cost of $US800, but worries that this would make her vulnerable to suspicion. After all, in Afghanistan "mobiles tend to belong to people engaged in business, politics, or war" (Plant n.d., p.27). In July 2003 when Jarghiw last spoke with his wife, she begged him not to hoard money to send to the family, but rather, spend this money on regular phone contact. From Australia, it costs $AUD 2.50 per minute for calls to Kabul and $AUD 5.00 per minute for calls outside of Kabul. (Unfortunately unlike Iran and Pakistan, cheap international phone cards do not yet extend to Afghanistan.) Jarghiw is faced with a dilemma when his wife and family ask him when they will be reunited: "I tell them six months, two months, four months. When that time expires I must set another time. I feel like I am lying."

Sadali avoids phoning his family because it takes him a week after phoning them to 'recover' from his sense of helplessness and shame in their separation.[23] After a month he is feeling better again having placed those feelings to one side. A new call invokes the same feelings again: "For one week after I call I feel worse. After not calling for a month, I feel better; I try to forget them. Sometimes they ask me why you didn't call? I reply that it is very expensive. I talk for one hour every month. For one hour I ask for everything and speak to everyone." Sadali recalled a time when he asked the question "who has died?" in his small village. The reply disturbed him profoundly because he had known all of those people who had died.

---

[23] The mental and emotional impact of indeterminate separation on TPV holders is documented (e.g., Fernandes, 2002; Steel, 2001).

Some families in Afghanistan are able to make contact with their Hazara menfolk in Australia. But they do so to check on a man's welfare in a strange land, rather than to divulge any detail of tragedy in their own lives. They perceive their son or husband to be more vulnerable than they are, because he is alone and they do not want to burden him further with sad news. Further, if the tragedy has happened unexpectedly there is nothing that can be done to help. According to Ali: "It is more likely if someone has been killed in Afghanistan that the news will be concealed as the family will fear that I will return home upon hearing the news and will also be at risk of being killed." It is their physical distance that makes Hazara men in Australia unable to receive tragic news, and so they are kept out of the loop, often until they find out indirectly.[24]

If the mention of a particular person is avoided in conversation or s/he is repeatedly absent at the time of a telephone call, people suspect bad news. Choli implored his family not to leave him to worry about tragic news: "Maybe before the news is revealed I feel I already suspect the truth. I know in fact what has happened because they avoid that news." By way of example, Tizak recounted the story of his brother. Tizak requested his brother to travel from Ghazni Province to Kabul to fax some documentation that Tizak required for the preparation of his appeal to the RRT. During his journey home from Kabul, Tizak's brother was mugged and sustained a head injury which left him unable to talk or walk, and he spent one month in hospital. Tizak phoned twice to check the whereabouts of the documents. Both times his family claimed that his brother was unable to come to the phone. On the third call he pressed his family to tell him what had happened, but in the meantime he had worried himself sick about the actual fate of his brother.

Undoubtedly, mobile phone contact between Afghanistan and Australia can connect family. But the possibility of contact does not mean that families will share bad news, and knowledge of this cultural proscription of telling tragic news increases anxiety in Hazara. Further, the indefiniteness of a person's visa situation may discourage contact: they have no good news to bear and the long distance connection may be disorienting. In the first twelve months after detention, communication facilitated by the mobile phone enabled Hazara to get their 'bearings' in order to negotiate a complex urban setting of regulation, procedure, and responsibility. It is this use which I have framed as an enabling and positive activity of resettlement, whereas mobile phone connection to families in Afghanistan can intensify feelings of separation.

Conclusion

Conditions of temporary protection created specific patterns of mobile phone use among Hazara. Ineligible for Federal government-funded resettlement services offered to refugees on permanent visas, Hazara made use of their mobile phones to establish a point of contact on release from detention. Then, drawing on their social networks facilitated by the mobile phone, they identified other Hazara households and houses in which to settle, and jobs. Ineligible for AMEP's 510 hour English language training, and further disadvantaged by high rates of functional illiteracy in Persian and English, they have drawn on these social networks

24 Omidian (1996, pp.161-164) has also written at length about protection from tragic news in the context of Afghani in California.

for translation and interpreting, as well as making sense of, and circulating important news. Hazara have used their mobile phones to reposition themselves at the center of their own social network in Australia, producing a new social space which has partially alleviated their separation and distance from family.

Hazara men remain profoundly affected by their temporary status. For married men particularly, anxiety associated with separation has not diminished with the passing of time and their lives in Australia remain precariously contingent. This chapter confirms what the earlier literature on temporary protection of refugees found (Mann 2001; Mansouri & Bagdas, 2002; Barnes, 2002; Marston, 2003; Pickering *et al.*, 2003; Hoffman 2004): that refugees granted temporary protection are released from detention into the community without the support structures deemed essential for other refugees. This research moves beyond this fact to examine the convergence of Hazara in the place of Dandenong some three years after release from detention. It finds that the combination of work, study and association has affected Hazara stamina to endure the vagaries of their temporary protection. Particularly in the first 12 months after release from detention, these activities were facilitated by the mobile phone which provided a point of contact and mediated news and information required by Hazara to manage their own resettlement. It is these uses made of the mobile phone -- common among Hazara in Dandenong -- that can be conceived as an activity of resettlement.

EPILOGUE

In May 2004, five Hazara men with whom I worked closely during the course of this research, were granted permanent protection visas after appealing DIMIA's judgement at the RRT. Three others were granted a permanent protection visa by DIMIA at the expiry of their TPV. In the period between 1 July 2003 and 31 May 2004, 290 appeals were made by applicants from Afghanistan (mainly Hazara) in the RRT. In 30 cases the original DIMIA decision was upheld, and in 258 cases (i.e., 89 percent) the DIMIA decision was overturned and permanent protection granted (RRT 2004), allowing residency and family reunion in Australia. The dissonance in determination can be explained in terms of interpretation (D. Manne 2004). Drawing on the 1951 Refugee Convention's Article 1(c) known as the Cessation Clause, the RRT requires the authorities to: "show why that refugee status has ceased." Whereas, DIMIA requires the applicant to: "demonstrate a well-founded fear of persecution" based on Article 1(a) of the Convention. From my reading of RRT decisions in relation to Hazara appeals (published on the RRT website http://www.rrt.gov.au), it is apparent that whereas it is no longer accepted by the RRT that Hazara Shia have a well-founded fear of being persecuted by the Taliban because it is claimed that the Taliban no longer 'exist' as a political movement, it is increasingly accepted by the RRT that Hazara ethnicity remains a well-founded basis of persecution. Additionally, Hazara religious (including atheist) and political (including Communist) affiliations are accepted as grounds for persecution from religious and political leaders. It is also accepted by many RRT members that there is currently no recourse to protection from the Afghanistan state.

REFERENCES

Australian Bureau of Statistics. (2002). 2001 Census Basic Community Profile and Snapshot, Greater Dandenong City. Retrieved 10 August 2004, from *http://www.abs.gov.au/Ausstats/abs@census.nsf/Lookup2001Census/B2BCA07B39EB088BCA256BBF0000A161*

Afghan Wireless Communication Company (AWCC). (2002). A nation on the line: the story of the Afghan Wireless Communication Company. Retrieved 30 May 2004, from *http://www.telsysint.com/AWCC%20Brochure%20012703.pdf*

Barnes, D. (2002). Life devoid of meaning: living on a temporary protection visa in Western Sydney. Sydney: Centre for Refugee Research, University of New South Wales, Retrieved 30 May 2004, from *http://www.refugeecouncil.org.au/docs/current_issues/life_devoid_of_meaning.pdf*

Canfield, R, L. (2004). New trends among the Hazaras: from the 'amity of wolves' to 'the practice of brotherhood. *Iranian Studies*, 37:2.

Crock, M. & Saul, B. (2002). *Future seekers, refugees and the law in Australia*. Sydney, NSW: Federation Press.

Department of Immigration and Multicultural and Indigenous Affairs (DIMIA). (2003a). Fact Sheet 80a: Reintegration Package for Afghan TPV holders. Retrieved 30 May 2004, from *http://www.immi.gov.au/facts/pdf/80a_tpv_reintegration.pdf*

DIMIA. (2003b). Fact Sheet 74a: Boat arrival details. Retrieved 3 May 2004, from *http://www.immi.gov.au/facts/pdf/74a_boatarrivals.pdf*

_____ . (2003c). Fact Sheet 70: Border Control. Retrieved 31 May 2004, from *http://www.immi.gov.au/facts/pdf/70border.pdf*

_____ . (2003d). Fact Sheet 66: Integrated Humanitarian Settlement Strategy. Retrieved 31 May 2004, from *http://www.immi.gov.au/facts/pdf/66ihss.pdf*

_____ . (2004). Fact Sheet 60: Australia's Refugee and Humanitarian Program. Retrieved 6 August 2004 from *http://www.immi.gov.au/facts/pdf/60refugee.pdf*

Fayazi, M. A. (2004, January 15). Hazara Returnees Targets of Violence in Afghanistan. The Age. Retrieved 10 August 2004 from *http://www.theage.com.au/articles/2004/01/14/1073877895956.html?from=storyrhs*

Fernandes, P. (2002). Trauma strikes the soul: an attempt to explore and understand the impact of the temporary protection visa on clients in New South Wales. Mots Pluriels 21, May, 2004 . Retrieved 20 May 2004 from *http://www.arts.uwa.edu.au/MotsPluriels/MP2102pf.html*

Fitzpatrick, J. (2000). Temporary protection of refugees: elements of a formalised regime. *American Journal of International Law, 94* (2), 1-32.

Glazebrook, D. & M. J. Abbasi-Shavazi. (2005). Pilgrimage aspirations and practice of Hazara mohajer in Iran and the question of repatriation to Afghanistan. *Journal of the Anthropological Association of Iran*.

Glazebrook, D. (2005). Becoming mobile after detention. *Social Analysis: the international journal of social and cultural practice, 48* (3), 40-58.

Hoffman, N. (2004). *Labour rights and border protection: attempts at a viable life on the temporary protection visa*, Monograph Number 4. Sydney: University of New South Wales Studies in Human Resource Management and Industrial Relations in Asia.

Human Rights Watch. (1998). *Afghanistan: the massacre in Mazar-e Sharif.* New York: Human Rights Watch.

_____ . (2002). *'By invitation only': Australian asylum policy.* New York: Human Rights Watch.

Immigration Museum of Victoria. (2003). *Safar-e-ma, our journey: Afghan immigration to Australia.* Melbourne: Immigration Museum of Victoria.

Jupp, J. (2002). *From White Australia to Woomera: the story of Australian immigration.* UK: Cambridge University Press.

Leach, M. & Mansouri., F. (2004). *Lives in limbo: voices of Refugees under Temporary Protection.* Sydney: UNSW Press.

McMichael, C. (2002). Everywhere is Allah's place: Islam and the everyday life of Somali women in Melbourne, Australia. *Journal of Refugee Studies, (15)* 2, 171- 188.

MacCallum, M. (2002). Girt by sea: Australia, the refugees and the politics of fear. *Quarterly Essay, 5*, 1-73.

Maley, W. (2001). *Security, people-smuggling and Australia's new Afghan refugees*, Working paper No. 63. Canberra: Australian Defence Studies Centre.

Malkki, L. (1995). *Purity and exile: violence, memory and national cosmology among Hutu refugees in Tanzania.* Chicago: University of Chicago Press.

Mann, R. (2001). Temporary protection visa holders in Queensland. Brisbane: Queensland Government . Retrieved 31 May 2004, from *http://www.premiers.qld.gov.au/library/pdf/temp_visa.pdf*

Manne, D. (2004). Temporary Protection Visas. *The Law Report.* ABC Radio National, 8 June. Retrieved 16 June 2004 from: *http://www.abc.net.au/rn/talks/8.30/lawrpt/stories/s1125918.htm*

Manne, R., & Corlett, D. (2004). Sending them home: refugees and the new politics of indifference. *Quarterly Essay, 13*, 1-95.

Mansouri, F. & Bagdas, M. (2002). *Politics of Social Exclusion: refugees on temporary protection visa in Victoria.* Geelong, Victoria: Deakin University.

Mares, P. (2002). *Borderline*, Sydney, NSW: UNSW Press.

Marston, G. (2003). Temporary protection, permanent uncertainty. Melbourne: Royal Melbourne Institute of Technology (RMIT). Retrieved 30 May 2004, from *http://mams.rmit.edu.au/k2vavbh0g5ik.pdf*

Mathew, P. (2002). Australian refugee protection in the wake of Tampa. *The American Journal of International Law*, July, 661-676.

Mousavi, S. A. 1997. *The Hazaras of Afghanistan: an historical, cultural, economic and political study.* New York: St Martin's Press.

Omidian, P. A. (1994). Life out of context: recording Afghan refugees' stories. In L. A. Camino & R. M. Krulfeld (Eds.), *Reconstructing Lives, Recapturing meaning: refugee identity, gender and cultural change.* USA: Gordon and Breach Publishers.

_____ . (1996). *Aging and family in an Afghan refugee community: transitions and transformations.* New York, London: Garland Publishing, Inc.

_____ . (2000). Qualitative measures and refugee research: the case of Afghan refugees. In F.L Ahearn (Ed.), *Psychosocial wellness of refugees: issues in qualitative and quantitative research.* Oxford, New York: Berghahn Books.

Pickering, S., Gard, M., & Richardson, R. (2003). We're working with people here: the impact of the TPV regime on refugee settlement service provision in NSW. Retrieved 31

May 2004, from *http://www.refugeecouncil.org.au/docs/current_issues/tpvr_report_3_11_3.pdf*

Plant, S. n.d. On the mobile: the effects of mobile telephones on social and individual life Retrieved 30 May 2004, from *www.motorola.com/mot/doc/0/234_MotDoc.pdf*

Qassem, A. S. (2004, January 8). Afghans Find Imposters Among the Asylum Seekers. The Age, 8 January. Retrieved 10 August 2004 from *http://www.theage.com.au/articles/2004/01/07/1073437342653.html*

Rajkowski, P. (1987). *In the tracks of the camelmen.* North Ryde, NSW: Angus and Robertson Publisher.

Refugee Review Tribunal (RRT). (2004). RRT Statistics database, Cases finalised by country in 2003/04. Retrieved 30 May 2004 from *http://www.rrt.gov.au/stats/finalised%20by%20country%20this%20year.pdf.*

Steel, Z. & Silove, Z. (2001). The mental health implications of detaining asylum seekers. *Medical Journal of Australia, 175,* 596-599.

Stevens, C. (1989). *Tin mosques and ghantowns: a history of Afghan camel drivers in Australia.* Melbourne: Oxford University Press.

In: Homeland Wanted ISBN 1-59454-266-X
Editors: P. Waxman and V. Colic-Peisker, pp. 191-208

Chapter 10

TRANSNATIONAL IMAGINATION AND MORAL OBLIGATIONS: OROMO REFUGEES IN MELBOURNE, AUSTRALIA

Greg Gow

ABSTRACT

This chapter explores the challenges presented to settlement planners by the increasingly transnational dynamics of refugees settling in urban centres of the West. It provides an empirically grounded study of Oromos from Ethiopia who have begun settling in Melbourne, Australia. The discussion explores how Oromo refugees in Melbourne imagine themselves as members of a transnational collective (or diaspora), and how they position themselves in relation to it. It asserts that a transnational perspective on "settlement" will require moving beyond state-centered approaches and placing it in a multidisciplinary conceptual space.

Key words: Oromo, Australia, transnationalism, home, settlement

INTRODUCTION

The United Nations High Commissioner for Refugees typically deals with the "refugee problem" via the so-called "three durable solutions": integration in the country of first asylum, repatriation to the home country, or assimilation in a third country of resettlement (UNHCR, 1995). But such categorization implies too much: refugees may be more inclined to see themselves simultaneously moving in and across multiple countries and maintaining transnational connections (Van Hear, 2002). Many researchers of refugee resettlement, myself included, are confronted with the question of how to deal with the irreducible complexity of the issue.

To convey this complexity, Munzoul Assal (2004) speaks of the "rich ambiguities" produced by criss-crossing transnational connections among refugee groups. His emphasis upon ambiguity and "messiness" seems justified. Nowadays, there is a lack of clarity about the meaning of resettlement of refugees in the West. This chapter deals with this reality through an empirically grounded study of Oromos from Ethiopia who have begun settling in Melbourne. Like other refugee groups, their story is one of persecution, escape, flight, fraught existence in a country of first asylum, and eventual reassembly in a Western country (Gow, 2002).

This chapter is an attempt to challenge conventional settlement frameworks. In Australia, settlement discourses remain state-centred. The common assumption is that humanitarian arrivals will begin to live and think as national citizens within the container of the Australian state, and that what is needed for this to occur is the correct mix of resettlement services. Instead, as I show in relation to the Oromo, the reality is that most refugees live and think transnationally, that is, ambiguously combine multiple national loyalties and identities (cf. Beck, 2000). Therefore, I propose transnational imagination and moral obligations as analytic constructs from which to approach the complexities of refugee settlement in the West.

This chapter analyzes how Oromo refugees in Melbourne imagine themselves as members of a transnational collective (or diaspora), and how they position themselves in relation to it. As will become clear, the imagination informs the daily lives of Oromo refugees in myriad ways and allows them to deal with experiences of displacement and settlement, and to design new forms of belonging (cf. Appadurai, 2001, p. 6).

My analysis is informed by the recent literature on the interactions between transnationalism, diaspora, citizenship, and the nation-state, which are situated under the broad multidisciplinary umbrella of transnational studies (Hannerz, 1996; cf. Cohen, 1997; Van Hear, 1998). Here "transnationalism" typically refers to the processes by which immigrants forge social relations that link together their societies of origin and settlement; these processes build connections that cross geographic, cultural, and political borders (cf. Basch et al., 1994, p. 7). Throughout this chapter the emphasis is upon "transnationalism from below"— the non-institutional agency of individuals and collectives acting across borders (Smith & Guarnizo, 1998).

I am aware that the label "refugee" is not always desirable or appropriate. In the Australian context it remains loaded with negative associations. Nevertheless, I use the term in reference to Melbourne's Oromos because nearly all of them have settled under the humanitarian program, and even those who travelled under family reunion schemes often present themselves as "refugees" from Ethiopia. In addition, because of relations within the state of Ethiopia, even Oromos who are now Australian citizens remain inclined to see themselves as refugees. Oromo nationalist imaginaries reject Ethiopia and everything it stands for. In this sense, being labelled a "refugee" is not a negative, but more likely a positive source of affirmation.

The first part of the chapter outlines the research methodology and offers a sketch of the Oromo people, their conflict with the Ethiopian state, and patterns of displacement, refugee settlement and diaspora. Preliminary details are provided about Oromo refugees in Melbourne. The second part picks up the idea of resettlement complexities created by transnational imagination and moral obligations, combining theory with selected ethnographies. The chapter ends with consideration of how my study of Oromo refugee experiences may contribute to further understanding refugee resettlement in the West.

RESEARCH METHODOLOGY

From the outset, a study of Oromo refugees settling in Melbourne was full of exciting ethnographic possibilities. My concern as a researcher was to explore the cultural dimensions of displacement and settlement among the recent arrivals. I wanted to investigate how refugees with rural backgrounds renegotiate their lives upon settling in urban Melbourne. Tied to this were themes of identity, belonging, homeland, imagination, community and transnational ties.

My interest in the Oromo grew from an association with a number of recently arrived people in Australia. In 1996, the leaders of the Oromo Community Association in Victoria (OCAV) initially asked me to consider a research project with their members. By no means did this represent an invitation from the whole community but it did indicate that I would be warmly welcomed. Accordingly, my research has been supported in various ways by probably all the Oromos I know.

The project was designed as an ethnography of displacement (cf. Malkki, 1992). Ethnography appealed because of its capacity to draw out wider implications from very particular (and focused) case studies. Through the application of ethnographic methodologies — specifically, variations of participant observation and semi-structured interviews — theorizing from within the particularity of the everyday seemed possible (Geertz, 1973).

The six-year project (from 1996 to 2001) began in and around the suburb of Footscray in Melbourne's western region and quickly moved to a global scale. In many respects, it is a multi-sited ethnography: the "sites" for data collection were both face-to-face single-site locations and the spaces of networks and associations that reach across national borders (cf. Gupta & Ferguson, 1997). Via extended family and hometown/village networks, I mapped criss-crossing flows between people in Australia, Ethiopia, Kenya, Djibouti, Canada, the United States, Germany, and England.

Throughout the research and writing process I resided in the Footscray area. There remained a regular flow of new arrivals whom I would meet in the street, and visit and welcome as they moved into the area. Meeting people in the neighbourhood led to further introductions and the formation of a broad network of Oromo contacts, not only in Footscray but throughout Melbourne.

This way I began a cartography of daily life: by spending hours with Oromo people in varied settings, listening and later writing notes. Much of the research was conducted with small groups of participants in bi-lingual contexts which minimized the reliance on interpreters. My visit to Oromia was a defining point, as too were visits to other diaspora communities in Toronto, Washington DC, Minneapolis, Atlanta and London. Importantly, these exposures enabled me to gain a transnational picture of the movement of Oromo people.

To claim a representation of Oromo refugees was a complex and problematic endeavour, not least because those participating in the research expected my writings to promote their political struggle. At times this meant numerous pre-publication meetings with community members to discuss the contents of my writing. On one occasion I was called to meet with fifteen elders who admonished me for misrepresenting conflicts within the community and insisted that I omit an entire draft chapter. I reluctantly aligned my writing with their directives (cf. Kirsch, 1999).

Another problem related to the gendered dimensions of the research task. As a male researcher it was difficult to document the experiences of women in the community. In the company of their spouses and other male members of the community, the women usually remained quiet and frequently offered little towards the discussion. It was not until the final stages of the research process that I gained access to various women's oral histories. To obtain their input it was necessary for me to be accompanied by another Oromo woman close to those with whom I was seeking to talk. I attempted to meet with the women in a space that was free of the influence of their spouses and other adult male family members. Formal meetings seldom worked and most of the material was derived from impromptu discussions.

Notwithstanding these difficulties, the research became a dynamic process whereby significant data were collected through the status of the research method as a social relationship (cf. Moss, 2002). It could not be otherwise, simply because, above my research role, the Oromo apparently regarded me as a "person". Not only did they see me as a "person", but also as one of them or, at least, one with them.

Conflict, Displacement and Diaspora Formations

Since the early-1990s, thousands of people from the Horn of Africa have fled conflicts and settled in urban centres of North America, Europe, Australia, and New Zealand. Meanwhile, masses await resettlement in cities such as Nairobi, Khartoum, Djibouti, Jeddha, Cairo, and in camps like Kakuma in Northern Kenya. The Oromo are among the most recent, fastest growing and most disadvantaged of the refugees from the Horn of Africa. They are an ethno-national group who originate from the region which goes by the name of "Ethiopia". While demographically the largest ethnic group in Ethiopia, they have limited access to economic, political and social status within the nation-state. The describer "Ethiopian" is full of difficulties when related to them.

The Oromo are a religiously plural collective. Those from the Eastern and South Eastern regions (Hararghe and Arsi) are generally of Sunni Muslim background, whereas Oromos from the West, Central and Northern regions (Wallaga, Shoa, and Wollo) have Protestant, Orthodox Christian, and Sunni Muslim backgrounds. At the same time, more ancient indigenous religious beliefs and practices dominate among the southernmost Booran Oromo. Despite the religious differences, one can speak of an indigenous outlook shared by most Oromos, which stresses blessings, fertility and peace (*nagaa*). These dispositions are tied to discourses about the Oromo land and its sustenance of all living things (Baxter, 1990; cf. Bartels, 1994; Megerssa, 1996).

The Oromo-Ethiopian Conflict

The longstanding Oromo-Ethiopian conflict is about the resources of the vast Oromo land, known today as Oromia (or *Oromiyaa*) — an area of six-hundred thousand square kilometres located mainly within the south, east and west of Ethiopia. Control of Oromia, and by extension the Oromo, is an economic imperative for the Ethiopian government as the fecund area functions somewhat like a "bread bowl" for the arid northern regions (Keller, 1995; Hameso et al. 1997).

The Oromo have lived under Ethiopian rule since the late-nineteenth century. They were politically, linguistically, economically, and historically marginalized on their own land — starting with the Abyssinian forces of Emperor Menelik II, continuing with the reign of Emperor Haile Selassie, and later Mengistu Haile Mariam's junta. As documented elsewhere (Baxter, 1978; Holcomb & Ibssa, 1990; Jalata, 1993), the formation of what is today recognized as the Federal Democratic Republic of Ethiopia occurred through the expansion of the mostly Orthodox Christian kingdom of Abyssinia. The expansion entailed the Abyssinian conquest of numerous "nations" south of Abyssinia (the Oromo being the largest) through the physical appropriation of land and the pursuit of cultural hegemony.

In response to such longstanding cultural, economic and political oppression, the Oromo nationalist movement has gained massive support over the past two decades, within Oromia and among the burgeoning diaspora populations. Oromo nationalism is a political-cultural movement that centres around the assertion of a pan-Oromo identity (*Oromumma*, "Oromoness"). Like all identity politics, Oromo nationalism sanctions exclusion and, characteristically, leads to violence.

The vanguard Oromo Liberation Front (OLF) have engaged in a protracted twenty-nine year armed struggle against consecutive Ethiopian governments. Over the years, the organization's objectives have shifted between the idioms of secession and self determination. In 1991, conflict briefly ceased following the demise of Mengistu's junta. The OLF participated in the Transitional Government of Ethiopia (TGE) and the autonomous Oromia Regional State was established within Federal Ethiopia in 1992. It became lawful for the first time to teach or publish in the Oromo language (*Afaan Oromoo*) using the Latin alphabet. Such changes brought some hope for peace and democratic development as masses of Oromos went public in their support for the OLF's nationalist program. However, such hopes were soon frustrated.

The OLF were to participate in the 1992 Oromia Regional State elections. However, following an outbreak of violent clashes with the Tigray People's Liberation Front (TPLF), the OLF again went underground and the executive leadership fled the country. The TPLF client party Oromo People's Democratic Organization (OPDO) spuriously won the Oromia Regional State elections and remains, at least formally, the ruling party in Oromia Region (cf. Lata, 1998).[1]

Immediately following the OLF withdrawal in 1992, the TPLF dominated the TGE security forces and with the cooperation of the OPDO commenced a systematic round-up of suspected supporters of the OLF—which was virtually wiped out inside Ethiopia during the 1990s. Thousands of Oromos have been killed or imprisoned without trial, many of them with earlier experiences of Mengistu's gulag—the extent of arrests and of extrajudicial killings since 1992 is documented in consecutive Annual Reports from Amnesty International (cf. Keller, 1998).

Masses of Oromos have fled Ethiopia and many have resettled in Western countries. Mekuria Bulcha, the leading authority on Oromo refugee populations, estimates that two-hundred thousand Oromos are scattered around the world, with one-hundred thousand now living in North America, Europe and Australia (2002, pp. 174-175). At least another hundred

1 The TPLF represent the Tigray people of Northern Ethiopia. They were the major rebel fighting force against Mengistu's junta and over the past decade have maintained political dominance within the ruling Ethiopian People's Revolutionary Democratic Front (EPRDF), of which the OPDO is a member.

thousand have made their way to Kenya, Djibouti, Sudan, Saudi Arabia, Egypt and Somalia—most remaining unregistered with the UNHCR (cf. Fossati et al., 1997).

An Emerging Diaspora

The Oromo outside of Ethiopia are an incipient transnational social collective which may be called a "diaspora". I use the term cautiously. As Ang (2001, p. 89) contends, the diaspora metaphor is quite limiting because it reduces disparate masses to a "sameness-in-dispersal." The displaced populations are a multifarious collective, as Kumsa (2002) emphasizes in relation to Toronto's Oromo.

At the most basic level, the Oromo disapora are a series of relatively autonomous extended family and hometown/village networks criss-crossing over multiple locations. Paraphrasing Werbner (2002, p. 123), chaotic order (or chaorder) is the principle of organization: the displaced populations are characterized by multiple discourses, internal dissent, and competition between various sectarian, regional, gendered or party political groups, all identifying themselves with the same diaspora.

Diaspora is a metaphoric label for imagined collective. Its power is ideological and emotional rather than institutional (Ang, 2001, p.84). Diaspora imaginaries are typically fuelled and authorized by the cultural works and discourses of artists and intellectuals who, among others, purvey themes of ancestry, roots, homeland, tragedy and obligation. Among diasporic refugee groups, such imaginaries create new possibilities beyond the boundaries of the nation-state. But diaspora is also dystopic. Loss, anguish, divided loyalties and the longing for cohesion and community feature in the lives of displaced people. In Western settlement contexts, experiences of discrimination and exclusion negatively constitute diaspora consciousness. For instance, Kumsa (2002, p. 480) speaks of Oromos in Toronto fending off the larger world of change and flux by retreating to the intimate "little worlds" or "cocoons of *Oromummaa*" (Oromoness).

Of course, settlement experiences differ from one context to another. A useful comparison can be made between the Oromo populations in Germany and Australia. The Oromos in Germany number little more than four hundred, with a high proportion of educated men from Central and Western Oromia. In Australia, the Oromos number over three thousand, with the majority originating from Eastern and South-Eastern Oromia (Gow 2002). There are more or less equal numbers of men and women and very few have any formal education. They are Australian citizens, whereas the German population are mostly students and professionals seeking asylum.

Having emphasized different positions, I also want to signal a commonality which extends my earlier point about shared outlooks. As I discuss elsewhere (Gow, 2001; 2002), in diaspora contexts, indigenous outlooks are performatively articulated via a myriad of ritual activities around childbirth and naming, engagement and marriage, death, the changing of seasons, and the need for protection and blessing. Even basic greetings entail lengthy references to peace and blessings for the land. Megerssa (1996) statically labels this outlook *Oromumma* and Baxter (1990) describes Oromo culture as floating on a "river of prayers and blessings". It is inappropriate to simply dismiss this as nativist rhetoric. Homeland attachments seemingly are critical to Oromo wellbeing and the identities refugees gain from their association with Oromia are vital to their resettlement (cf. Kibreab, 1999, p. 407), but not for all people at all times, as I will show later.

Among the displaced populations, connections with homeland localities are perpetuated (and transformed) in a variety of ways (cf. Bisharat, 1997). Translocal links are typically constructed and reinforced through remittances, migration networks and practices directed at improving the lives of kin in the homeland. The intersection of these activities with rural outlooks enables diasporic Oromos to imaginatively relocate themselves from marginalized city-bound people to city-based Oromos with rural identities.

Oromo Refugees in Australia

Since the mid-1980s, Melbourne has been the settlement centre for Oromo refugees arriving in Australia. In July 1997, the Australian Oromo Community Association (AOCA) conducted a headcount. The total number of adults and children living in the Melbourne metropolitan area was 465—241 male and 224 female. By the year 2003 there were more than three thousand. The overwhelming majority have travelled to Australia under UNHCR resettlement programs.

Stateless Minority

The Oromos represent a distinct pattern of immigration to Australia and collectively contrast with other African refugee groups (e.g. Ethiopians and Somalis) because they are difficult to classify in the Australian system of multiculturalism, with its focus on "birthplace", which is seen as synonymous with a nation-state. Research participants frequently put it to me that Oromos resent their classification as "Ethiopians" by Australian authorities. In this regard, the Oromos may be thought of as a "stateless minority": a group who sees itself as having a "homeland" which is currently not a nation-state, but which, to varying degrees, they would like to establish through struggles for independence. For example, Kurds born in Iraq speak of Kurdistan, and Oromos born in Ethiopia speak of Oromia, as their homelands.

More broadly, "minorities" may be defined as groups who are marginalized within Australian society on the basis of socially constructed markers such as race, nationality or culture. They are also groups with some degree of collective consciousness based on a belief in shared language, traditions, history and experiences. Stateless refugee groups are relatively "invisible minorities within minorities" (Castles & Davidson 2000, p.63).

The idea of "invisibility" relates to the incapability of government authorities, service providers, the mass media, and the general public to recognize particular communities. The "invisibility" of stateless refugee groups leads to settlement problems exceeding those experienced by other refugee groups. Stateless minorities are often deprived of culturally appropriate services and funding for their own community development because the Australian Bureau of Statistics (ABS) Census does not accurately count them.[2]

---

2 Until 2001, the only Census figure available was the "language spoken at home" category, which is of little assistance because it grossly reduces the size of the community. The accuracy of a recently introduced ancestry question remains to be seen.

Settlement in Melbourne

Although Oromo people have been in Australia for twenty years, they are still categorized as an emerging community. The earliest Oromo refugees arrived in 1984. As Zeyneba[3] recollected:

> There were about ten Oromos in Melbourne when I arrived in 1985. The first group arrived in 1984, then one year later we came from Cairo. By the end of 1985 more refugees were coming via Egypt ... When five of us arrived together we stayed at the Midway Migrant Hostel in Maribyrnong. I think we were the first black people that had been there and everybody stared at us ... I remember after the first day we went outside to look around the Footscray shops and everybody stared at us. It felt strange in the city and I wanted to tell people to stop looking—they were not used to seeing black people.

Like these early arrivals, many Oromos are unaccustomed to the dynamics of city living and feel disheartened by urban surroundings.

There are numerous familial and social networks within the broader Oromo community in Melbourne and, in general, people tend to relate foremost to those with the same tribal affiliation — usually from their own village/town and rural area of Oromia. As my study evolved, a large network of over three hundred people, mostly from Eastern Oromia, who lived in and around Footscray, were the most accessible and with them I most closely bonded.

The research participants were mostly semi-skilled or unskilled workers with little or no formal education. Illiteracy or semi-illiteracy remains high, especially among the women. With low levels of proficiency in English and few marketable skills, many of them were unemployed, and those with jobs commonly work as cheap labour in difficult conditions: often as factory hands, process workers, taxi drivers and cleaners. While a few have accumulated a small amount of capital and mortgaged houses, the majority live in privately rented flats or in government-subsidized rental properties located on public housing estates in the western suburbs of Melbourne.

The public housing estates, with their nearby shops, community services and cafés are a microcosm of the Horn of Africa: residents form a cross-section of national/ethnic groups and clan affiliations including Somalis, Oromo, Amhara, Tigray, Gurage, Harari, Afar, Eritreans, and Southern Sudanese peoples including Dinka, Nuer, and Nuba live there. In Australian society, these recently arrived "black Africans" are socially and economically compelled to live close to each other.[4]

Settlement Ironies

"Settlement" is a problematic construct. As mentioned earlier, among service agencies, church groups and immigration officials working with refugees, "settlement" remains tied to state-centred assumptions about what it means to be a "good" refugee and would-be citizen. This is what Malkki (1995) coined "the national order of things", which, put simply, assumes that refugees will never settle until they find a nation-state to which they can belong. But do

---

[3] The names of Oromo individuals featured throughout this chapter are pseudonyms.

[4] I use the term "black Africans" to denote the representation of these diverse peoples as an homogenous group by service providers, the mass media and various research publications (cf. Cox et al., 1999; Udo-Ekpo, 1999).

refugees ever "settle" in a globalized world? The refugee regime and its settlement policy are geared around the idea that they do.

In new urban places of settlement, Oromo refugees can reconstruct identities, and learn to be Australian — if this means making a new home, putting down some roots, and becoming individually responsible subjects of a neoliberal market society (Ong 2003). Yet, to differing degrees they are faced with an unprecedented silence and deficit of meaning. They are compelled to look not only within the domain of Australian citizenship but also across borders for their collective and individual sense of place in the world. The following episode is illustrative:

Fatuma Mume is 27 years old and was born and raised in Haramaya — a small highland town in Eastern Oromia, about 25 kilometres south of the large town Dire Dawa. Since 1997, when she arrived in Australia, Fatuma has lived in the same Footscray neighbourhood as I. Her cousin Mohammed, who lives on a nearby public housing estate, sent her money while she was in Nairobi and helped her migrate to Australia.

One Friday evening I waited for her in Footscray at the 402 bus stop on Leeds Street. We agreed to meet and travel together to her cousin Ahmed's Flemington house. The streets were frantic with last minute shopping before the close of business, and about twenty people waited for the 402 bus to arrive. Fatuma rushed from home after a day's work in the Broadmeadows factory where she assembles electrical goods.

The brown 402 bus — running to East Melbourne via Kensington, North Melbourne, and Carlton — is among the most popular bus routes departing from Footscray. Locals refer to it as the "African Express" because of the many women from the Horn of Africa, loaded with shopping, who populate the bus stops with their children and talk loudly while travelling. The bus finally arrived and we boarded, purchased our tickets and sat at the rear.

At the first stop, a frail elderly woman boarded the bus and one passenger assisted by lifting her heavy shopping trolley up the steps. Affectionately looking at the woman, Fatuma recalled to me a frightening experience: "I will never forget what happened after I had been in Australia for just two months. Every day I used to see an old lady, just like her, who lived by herself in our street ... without any family. I think she was Australian [white Australian-born]. You might remember her, she used to walk down the street at the same time every morning with her shopping trolley ... always wearing the same clothes and a green hat." I vaguely remembered the woman. Fatuma continued, "Well, she used to walk past my house and I could see her from the lounge room window. We never spoke to each other and I didn't know her name, but sometimes I would wave to her. She was a nice lady, with a kind face."

All of a sudden Fatuma looked sad. "About three days went by and I didn't see her ... I started to worry where she was. Anyway, the next day an ambulance came and took someone away. I decided to go to her flat and see if she was all right. I knocked on the door and a young woman opened it ... I asked about the old lady ... She told me that she had died." Fatuma looked frightened, shaking her head in bewilderment and speaking in a muffled tone so the other passengers could not hear. "Her grandmother fell asleep on the couch and never woke up. I couldn't believe it ... that she could die without anyone knowing."

The story was finished. I was startled, not as much by the circumstances of the woman's death as by Fatuma's anguished response to it. As she put it, "In Oromia and in Kenya I had seen people die, but I never heard of anyone dying alone like this. I was frightened after that. It scared me that she had been lying dead in that flat for three days before they found her body. For the next few weeks I felt depressed — I thought maybe this could happen to me —

and from that day on I hated the loneliness and silence in this country." There was an irony manifest in her complaint: "I have money now and nice clothes, but I would rather be poor in Oromia than die alone like that in Australia."

If this is part of the experience of being an Australian, then evidently Fatuma does not want it. Her experience highlights how now, although "free" in Australia, Oromos variously encounter new forms of "silence". Certainly the conditions of liberty, compared with conditions in the Horn of Africa, make their personal advancement possible. But they also create anguish and divided loyalties as the values of self-reliance, privacy, and self-advancement in mainstream Australian society conflict with their longing for cohesion and community.

The idea of "silence" (and "silencing") relates to the condition of dislocation from family and homeland, and migration to an isolating Australian society — a condition located in a problematic transnational space. Borrowing from Bourdieu's (1991) economics of symbolic power, it is a space where, possessing little of anything that white Australians value (i.e. financial prosperity and sporting prowess), Oromos must struggle to acquire status.

Struggles for the acquisition of social, cultural and economic status have featured in the fracturing of Melbourne's Oromo community. The common complaint is that, despite the apparent personal freedom offered in Australia, many Oromos, like Fatuma, felt their lives more meaningful while living under conditions of immense deprivation and collective threat in places like Djibouti and Kenya. They prefer to reflect nostalgically upon the days before coming to Australia and talk about the times when they experienced a unity and cohesion necessary for common survival. Many cannot understand why things changed and speak of imagining a divisive "disease" the community "caught" after arriving in Melbourne.

Transnational Imagination and Moral Obligations

The "imagination" remains an important theme in cultural research. Charles Taylor (2002, p.91) recently undertook something of an archaeology of modern social imagination. In his words, the imaginary is "not a set of ideas; rather it is what enables, through making sense of, the practices of society." Put another way, imaginaries are a necessary navigational means. The key here is that by forming specific images of the social world, we also construct its meaning.

This is crucial when attempting to describe how refugees make their place in the world and, more specifically, in Western settlement contexts. For example, Fatuma's story signals a range of imaginings or images of the social world. She deflects and rejects Australian values and implicates herself in the "homeland", and in a quintessentially African perspective on death and dying. In the mind's eye, she puts herself in rural Oromia, never dying alone, while at the same time travelling on a bus in urban Australia.

For Oromo refugees settling in Melbourne, all everyday activities are understood and lived through what I call "transnational imaginaries". In terms of settlement experiences, this has potentially positive as well as negative effects. On the one hand, refugee imaginaries involve attachment of feelings toward their own homeland, histories and capabilities, and on the other hand, their detachment from disempowering conditions of life in the here-and-now (Battaglia, 1995, p. 77).

The imagination informs the everyday lives of Oromo refugees in a myriad of ways. It allows them to respond to experiences of displacement, exile and migration, and design new forms of associations and belongings (Appadurai, 1996; 2001, p. 6). Moreover, imaginaries function in relation not only to the homeland but to dynamics within the settlement country and among the wider diaspora.

The idea of transnational imaginaries provides a useful analytic construct from which to approach various practices among refugee groups. Returning to Taylor (2002, p. 107): "If the understanding makes the practice possible, it is also true that the practice largely carries the understanding." This expresses something of the dynamic relationship between practices and imaginaries. What I am calling "transnational imaginaries" occupy a middle ground between embodied practices and implicit self understandings (Gaonkar 2002, p. 11). They operate through a range of transnational social, cultural, economic and political practices which may be investigated using various empirical indicators. These include: private and public networks, decision making structures, marriages and kinship ties, literatures and media productions, routes of communications, travel and mobility, and activities in transnational initiatives and organizations (cf. Al-Ali et al., 2001; Beck, 2000).

There is always a bodily and sensory dimension to transnational imaginaries. They are experienced *physically* as embodied practices (Noble 2002, p.54). This implies that refugees may come to realize a productive capacity in their transnational imaginings, which become an important means of dealing with experiences of displacement and trauma (Battaglia, 1995, p. 78).

Tied to transnational imagination is the idea of moral obligations. Indeed, entwining the two provides a means of describing complex settlement dynamics. Werbner (2002, p. 129) takes up this theme by analysing the moral dimensions of diaspora in order to understand their internal complexity and affective power. She characterizes diasporas as "dispersed [imagined] communities of co-responsibility"; with the diasporic imagination being fed by a "compelling sense of moral co-responsibility" embodied in transnational practices.

Certainly Oromos in Melbourne feel varying degrees of moral co-responsibility. Their life-world criss-crosses multiple regions, with obligations extending to relatives and compatriots in Ethiopia, Kenya, Djibouti, Europe, the Middle East, North America, and Australia. In diaspora contexts, moral obligations require renewed national devotion to settle guilt for abandoning the homeland. It is against this backdrop that transnational connections are given priority over ties to the Australian state.

Like other stateless refugee groups (e.g. Kurds, Southern Sudanese, Palestinians), Oromo imaginaries are underwritten by a nationalist project which not only ties people to the homeland but intersects with symptoms of trauma and displacement. Paraphrasing Wise (2002, p. 116), the convergence of transnational imaginaries with trauma and displacement creates strong affective moral pulls toward the "national" community. They also serve as an affective means through which city bound Oromo refugees can share in and have a relationship to their rural homeland and also, as Werbner (2002) emphasizes, tie disparate diaspora communities together.

The idea of affective moral obligations closely relates to Hage's (2002) concept of "affective intensification" and Wise's (2002) "embodying exile". Exploring news reading practices among Lebanese migrants, Hage speaks of intense bodily dialogues and migrant strategies to implicate themselves in the homeland. Adapting Hage's concept, Wise (2002) highlights the affective dimension of protest and performance among East Timorese refugees as a means of dealing with trauma and repaying the debt owed to the homeland. However, it must be emphasized that, as with the imagining of "settlement", the "homeland" is also subject to a plethora of imaginings which are both complex and ambiguous.

Connecting Flights

Over the following pages I aim to illustrate the complex entwining of transnational imagination and moral obligations by way of two abbreviated case studies. The first recounts the homecoming to countryside Oromia of a young Oromo woman, Hawee, and her ties to family and nation. It is a story of anticipation, promise and shattered illusion. The second case study features a young Oromo man, Tofik, whose life journey spans from Oromia to Nairobi, through Europe, back to Nairobi, and then on to Australia. Like Tofik, probably every Oromo in Melbourne has relatives in Nairobi — the major Horn of African refugee hub — and the links between Oromia, Nairobi, and Melbourne remain at the forefront of people's minds.

Hawee's Connecting Flights

Hawee Sheko is twenty-nine years old and originates from Calanqqo—a small town in Eastern Oromia. She fled Ethiopia in 1995. Travelling alone, she undertook a long and arduous journey: "I went from Calanqqo to Dire Dawa, and then to Addis Ababa. Then I took the bus south to the Moyale border. I paid someone to get me into Kenya ... after that I paid Kenyan shillings to travel in the back of a truck for three days down to Nairobi. I registered as a refugee with the UNHCR and stayed there with my brother Ibsaa."

In October 1998, Hawee settled in Melbourne and within nine months found work, cleaning motel rooms. She is proud to be Oromo and takes an active role in the community. Hawee has two sisters in Toronto, an uncle and brother in Minneapolis, and her father and youngest brother in Nairobi. Her brother Ibsaa remains her only relative in Australia.

In the problematic settlement space of Melbourne, Hawee doggedly fulfils heartfelt, although burdensome, obligations to her family and nation. She supports the Oromo Liberation Front's armed struggle in Ethiopia via financial contributions and attending Melbourne branch meetings. As she put it: "I feel it ... the burden is on me ... now I have to give all the support I can to our struggle for freedom ... and to my family in Oromia and Kenya. Every month I am sending money and phoning."

In 2002, after four years of working and saving, she purchased an around-the-world ticket and flew to Toronto, then Minneapolis, on to Ethiopia, then to Nairobi, and back to Melbourne. In Minneapolis she married an older man called Ali (who also originates from Calanqqo). In the presence of her uncle, their marriage was consecrated in a combination of Islamic and Oromo ritual practices. Hawee explained to me that she chose to travel to the U.S. to marry Ali because she had little hope of finding a partner in Melbourne. Accordingly, she expressed uncertainty about their impending life together. As she described, "Sometimes you have to take a risk. I don't know him that well and I don't know how it will turn out. I will see when he comes to live in Australia."

Four weeks after the wedding, eager to visit her place of origin and following much deliberation, she embarked upon a return journey back "home" to Calanqqo. While aware of the security risks, Hawee anticipated a time of reunion and cultural renewal, of "being home". As she later reflected: "After my wedding I wanted to go to Calanqqo to see my mother and homeland. But I was scared. I didn't know whether I should go or not. It is risky because you never know what the government people will do... they are always watching Oromos. But I had to go."

She flew from the capital Addis Ababa to Dire Dawa and travelled overland to Calanqqo. As the aeroplane approached Dire Dawa, Hawee was overcome by sadness and secretly wept with her head between her knees. Contrary to her expectations, it did not feel like she was going "home"; rather, it felt she was going to a place where she could not fit in any more. In a strange way, she felt "homeless" in her own land.

Feeling terribly sad, defeated and insecure, she stayed in Calanqqo for only three weeks. She hurriedly arranged for her mother to travel to Nairobi with her — to facilitate her passage out of Ethiopia, reunion with her father, and hopefully on to a new life in the U.S. or Australia. Her imaginings of "home" as an unproblematic geographic location, the growing up place of coherence and familiarity, were undercut by the reality of oppression and struggle. Perhaps her journey meant confronting the unreality of her imagined constructions of "homeland" and "return"— the anticipation, promise and shattering of illusion.

Hawee returned to Australia feeling unsettled, but nevertheless satisfied with her efforts. Her feelings were mixed as the aeroplane landed at Melbourne Airport: she was happy to be back, but felt out of place. Hawee later reflected: "Right then I felt that Australia is good, and I am grateful to Australia... but I knew then that I will never really think of myself as Australian. I will always be thinking about Oromos... and being Oromo... Oromia is where I belong, I can't get away from it." Indeed, now she would have to find money to fund her relatives' living costs in Nairobi and Calanqqo, and to sponsor her husband's migration from the U.S. to Australia.

Tofik's Nomadic Urges

Tofik Obsii's story begins in 1975 with his birth in Dire Dawa, in a family with seven children. Tofik's memories of Oromia are obscure and the line between his own experience and what he was later told is blurred. His father was exiled from Ethiopia in 1981. Two years later Tofik, aged eight years, travelled with his family to join him in Nairobi. For the next seven years they lived together in a poor Nairobi neighbourhood.

In contrast to his blurred recollections of his early childhood in Oromia, Tofik clearly registered and fondly remembered Nairobi as the place of his childhood. It was there that early friendships were formed, and the childhood places of familiarity located. Alongside his inability to return, his departure at a young age has limited his identification with the place Oromia to the extent that Tofik speaks of his "roots" residing not in Oromia but Nairobi.

Given the precarious status of refugees in Nairobi and the danger of going back to Ethiopia, by the late 1980s many Somali, Ethiopian and Oromo refugees sought residency visas for North America, Europe, and Australia. Eventually, most of Tofik's childhood friends left the country to resettle in the U.S. or Canada. The departing Oromos insisted that Nairobi could never be "home" for them because "home" would always be Oromia, but they could never go back there.

In 1990, at the age of fifteen, Tofik decided to leave Nairobi. Unable to get a Swedish entry visa, he settled for Germany. Although various people told him Germany was not a good place for him to go, he decided, with a tourist visa in hand, to go and see for himself. Tofik spent three years there. Because he was under eighteen years of age and an asylum seeker, the German government sent him to an institution for homeless boys. Despite some friendships, Tofik never felt welcome because there was always some reminder that he was a stranger in a foreign country. He decided to leave and in 1993 boarded an aeroplane back to Nairobi. When the plane took off from Frankfurt, Tofik felt unsure about what lay ahead: lonely and sad with no future. Perhaps he was making a mistake returning to be stuck in Nairobi.

The point of tension in Tofik's narrative is the apparent juxtaposition of nomadic urges with his strong desire to feel "at home". Surveying the past, Tofik volunteered that the tension originated from his childhood experiences in Oromia. Being raised by relatives in Dire Dawa and growing up with the knowledge that Oromia was insecure for Oromo people, he never thought of it in familial terms. Additionally, losing significant people as an adolescent in Nairobi traumatized Tofik and eroded his sense of "rootedness" in that place. With neither physical attachment nor access to Oromia, the erosion of ties in Nairobi, and the experience of racism in Germany, Tofik could not feel very much "at home" in any of those places.

However, it was not long before Tofik moved to another place. Before he returned to Nairobi from Germany in 1993, one of his sisters had gone to Australia and settled in Melbourne, where she began the process of sponsoring her siblings. Tofik breathed a sigh of relief; he knew he was travelling again. Five siblings travelled together and arrived in Australia in 1995. After they arrived, they lived with their sister for one month. Meanwhile, his parents planned to leave Nairobi and join his oldest sister in Minneapolis.

Tofik's experience in Melbourne was different from his previous "homes". In terms of the present and the future, he felt more secure. Certainly life was not without its difficulties, but he was now able to have some control over it. With new citizenship he was at last free to stay somewhere and travel anywhere, including Ethiopia if he wanted. To this extent he felt that he was making a new start, free from the invisible chains that had previously limited his life.

If "home" is considered in nativist terms as the place of one's origin (i.e. birth), then Oromia could be Tofik's "original" home. But his experience problematizes any essentialist definition of "home". Perhaps for Tofik, Oromia is imagined as a de-territorialized nation, a national family of co-responsibility spread around the globe. Alongside his inability to return, his departure at a young age has limited his identification with the place Oromia to the extent that Tofik speaks of his "roots" residing not in Oromia but Nairobi. His parents' presence in Nairobi is the primary source of continuous identification with that place, to the extent that when they leave Tofik expects he will feel like "a tree that has lost its roots". Their departure will further displace his childhood and disjunctively erode a sense of continuity in his life.

Both Hawee and Tofik are inclined to see their futures moving in and across multiple countries and maintaining global connections. It is their Australian passports which provide the key to mobility. Their experiences return us to the key question of this chapter: how can we describe the irreducible complexity of refugee settlement in the West? Hawee and Tofik highlight the fundamentally ambivalent contingencies, and uncertainties which, at least conceptually, seem yet to be fully appreciated in the domain of refugee settlement discourse (cf. Beck 2000, p. 81; Assal, 2004).

CONCLUSION

What follows from my study of Oromo refugees in Melbourne? Apparently, refugee settlement experiences in the West would be improved if complex transnational realities were more comprehensively considered by government and non-government service providers, the media, and the general public. At present, however, settlement planners as well as refugee researchers are playing catch-up to globalized economic, social and cultural processes that speed ahead. Meanwhile, the extent of contemporary global transformations is challenging ideas which have guided the refugee settlement regime over the last five decades. The presumption that settlement in the West correlates with a passage of integration into a new (imagined) national community seems contentious.

Developing a transnational perspective on "settlement" will require moving beyond state-centered approaches and placing it in a multidisciplinary conceptual space that encompasses some of the most vexing contemporary issues: globalization, diaspora, hybridity, and post-national citizenship to name just a few (cf. Lee & LiPuma 2002, p. 191). This will entail displacing the nation-state as the a priori transcendent point of settlement discourse.

As I have stressed, refugees creatively engage with the complexities of displacement by looking further afield than the nation-state in which they have physically settled. And this suggests they are not primarily looking "above" to existing institutional (and narrowly bureaucratic) channels to establish transnational ties. Rather, paraphrasing Stuart Hall (in Ings 2003, p.10), they are moving laterally back and forth across borders and establishing networks of movement, literal and symbolic. There is very little that nation-states can do to regulate this "transnationalism from below".

This reality has major implications for settlement policy. A practical starting point will be recognizing the undocumented contributions refugees in the West are making toward development in their countries of origin, and among displaced relatives and compatriots abroad. In the Oromo case, contributions are also directed toward funding armed struggles against the Ethiopian state. As Shandy (2003, p.7) highlights in relation to Southern Sudanese refugees in the U.S., "third country resettlement" has significant "material and cultural impacts on refugees in Africa beyond the small numbers that actually board the plane and set off to Western countries." Perhaps in years to come transnational considerations will become the new order of the day.

Finally, Oromo experiences in Melbourne highlight the particularities of urban settlement among rural people with whom indigenous outlooks and perspectives remain intact. By and large, settlement policy assumes their capacity to assimilate into a Western urban-centered mode of being. This variously creates unsettling localized disjunctions, difficulties and existential dilemmas. To this extent, there is real ambiguity about settlement in the West and, at least, at the existential level, the describer "settlement" might be a misnomer.

REFERENCES

Al-Ali, N., Black, R. & Koser, K. (2001). The Limits to "Transnationalism": Bosnian and Eritrean Refugees in Europe as Emerging Transnational Communities. *Ethnic and Racial Studies, 24*(4), 578-600.

Ang, I. (2001). *On Not Speaking Chinese: Living Between Asia and the West.* London & New York: Routledge.

Appadurai, A. (1996). *Modernity at Large: Cultural Dimensions of Globalization.* Minneapolis: University of Minnesota Press.

_____ . (2001). Grassroots Globalization and the Research Imagination. In A. Appadurai (Ed.), *Globalization.* Duke University Press, Durham & London.

Assal, M. A. M. (2004). *Sticky Labels or Rich Ambiguities? Diaspora and Challenges of Homemaking for Somalis and Sudanese in Norway.* Bergen: BRIC University of Bergen.

Bartels, L. (1994). On Pilgrimage to a Holy Tree. In D. Brokensha, (Ed.), *A River of Blessings: Essays in Honor of Paul Baxter.* Syracuse: Maxwell School of Citizenship and Public Affairs, Syracuse University.

Basch, L., Glick Schiller, N. & Szanton Blanc, C. (1994). *Nations Unbound: Transnational Projects, Postcolonial Predicaments and Deterritorialized Nation-States.* Basel: Gordon & Breach.

Battaglia, D. (1995). On Practical Nostalgia: Self-Prospecting among Urban Trobrianders. In D. Battaglia, (Ed.), *Rhetorics of Self-Making.* Berkeley: University of California Press.

Baxter, P.T.W. (1978).Ethiopia's unacknowledged problem: the Oromo. *African Affairs, 77*(308), 283-296.

Baxter, P. T. W. (1990). Oromo Blessings and Greetings. In A. Jacobson-Widding & W. van Beek (Eds.), *The Creative Communion: African Folk Models of Fertility and the Regeneration of Life.* Uppsala: Acta Universitatis Upsaliensis.

Beck, U. (2000). The cosmopolitan perspective: sociology of the second age of modernity. *British Journal of Sociology, 51*(1), 79-105.

Bisharat, G. E. (1997). Exile to Compatriot: Transformations in the Social Identity of Palestinian Refugees in the West Bank. In A. Gupta & J. Ferguson (Eds.), *Culture, Power, Place: Explorations in Critical Anthropology.* Durham & London: Duke University Press.

Bourdieu, P. (1991). *Language and Symbolic Power* (Translated by G. Raymond & M. Adamson) Cambridge: Polity Press.

Bulcha, M. (2002). *The Making of the Oromo Diaspora: A Historical Sociology of Forced Migration.* Minneapolis: Kirk House Publishers.

Castles, S. & Davidson, A. (2000). *Citizenship and Migration: Globalization and the Politics of Belonging.* Basingstoke: Macmillan.

Cohen, R. (1997). *Global Diasporas: An Introduction.* London: UCL.

Cox, D., Cooper, B. & Adepoju, M. (1999). *The Settlement of Black Africans in Australia.* Bundoora: Department of Social Work and Social Policy, La Trobe University.

Fossati, B., Namarra, L. & Niggli, P. (1997). *The New Rulers of Ethiopia and the Persecution of the Oromo. Reports from the Oromo Refugees in Djibouti.* (M. Forsyth, Trans.). London & Zurich: epd-Dokumentation.

Gaonkar, D. P. (2002). Toward New Imaginaries: An Introduction. *Public Culture, 14*(1), 1-19.

Geertz, C. (1973). *The Interpretation of Cultures.* New York: Basic Books.

Gow, G. (2001). Viewing Mother Oromia. *Communal/Plural: Journal of Transnational and Cross-cultural Studies, 9*(2), 203-22.

_____ . (2002). *The Oromo in Exile: From the Horn of Africa to the Suburbs of Australia.* Carlton South: Melbourne University Press.

Gupta, A. & Ferguson, J. (Eds.). (1997). *Culture, Power, Place: Explorations in Critical Anthropology*. Durham & London: Duke University Press.

Hage, G. (2002). The Differential Intensities of Social Reality: Migration, Participation and Guilt. In G. Hage (Ed.), *Arab Australians Today: Citizenship and Belonging*. Carlton South: Melbourne University Press.

Hameso, S., Trueman, T. & Temesgen, E. (Eds.). (1997). *Ethiopia: Conquest and the Quest for Freedom and Democracy*. London: TSC Publications.

Hannerz, U. (1996). *Transnational Connections: Culture, People, Places*, London & New York: Routledge.

Holcomb, B. K. & Ibssa, S. (1990). *The Invention of Ethiopia: The Making of a Dependent Colonial State in North East Africa*. New Jersey: The Red Sea Press Inc.

Ings, R. (Ed.). (2003). *Connecting Flights: New cultures of the Diaspora. Debating Globalization, Diaspora and the Arts*. London: British Council & Arts Council England.

Jalata, A. (1993). *Oromia and Ethiopia: State Formation and Ethnonational Conflict, 1868-1992*. Boulder: Lynne Rienner Publishers Inc.

Keller, E. J. (1995). The Ethnogenesis of the Oromo Nation and its Implications for Politics in Ethiopia. *The Journal of Modern African Studies*, *33* (4), 621-34.

_____ . (1998). Regime Change and Ethno-Regionalism in Ethiopia: The Case of the Oromo. In A. Jalata (Ed.), *Oromo Nationalism and the Ethiopian Discourse: The Search for Freedom and Democracy*. Lawrenceville & Asmara: The Red Sea Press Inc.

Kibreab, G. (1999). Revisiting the Debate on People, Place, Identity and Displacement. *Journal of Refugee Studies*, *12*(4), 384-410.

Kirsch, G. E. (1999). *Ethical Dilemmas in Feminist Research: The Politics of Location, Interpretation and Publication*. Albany: State University of New York Press.

Kumsa, M. K. (2002). Negotiating Intimacies in a Globalized Space: Identity and Cohesion in Young Oromo Refugee Women. *Affilia*, *17*(4), 471-96.

Lata, L. (1998). The Making and Unmaking of Ethiopia's Transitional Charter. In A. Jalata (Ed.), *Oromo Nationalism and the Ethiopian Discourse: The Search for Freedom and Democracy*. Lawrenceville and Asmara: The Red Sea Press Inc.

Lee, B. & LiPuma, E. (2002). Cultures of Circulation: The Imaginations of Modernity. *Public Culture*, *14*(1), 191-213.

Malkki, L. (1992). National Geographic: The Rooting of Peoples and the Territorialization of National Identity among Scholars and Refugees. *Cultural Anthropology*, *7*(1), 22-44.

Malkki, L. (1995). Refugees and Exile: From "Refugee Studies" to the National Order of Things. *Annual Review of Anthropology*, *24*, 495-523.

Megerssa, G. (1996). Oromumma: Tradition, Consciousness and Identity. In P.T. W. Baxter, J. Hultin, & A. Triulzi (Eds.), *Being and Becoming Oromo: Historical and Anthropological Inquiries*. Uppsala: Nordiska Afrikainstitutet.

Moss, P. (Ed.). (2002). *Feminist Geography in Practice: Research and Methods*. London: Blackwell.

Noble, G. (2002). Comfortable and Relaxed: furnishing the home and nation. *Continuum: Journal of Media & Cultural Studies*, *16*(1), 53-66.

Ong, A. (2003). *Buddha is Hiding: Refugees, Citizenship, The New America*. Berkeley: University of California Press.

Shandy, D. J. (2003). Transnational linkages between refugees in Africa and in the diaspora. *Forced Migration Review*, *16*, 7-19.

Smith, M. P. & Guarnizo, L. E. (Eds.). (1998). *Transnationalism From Below*. New York & London: Transaction Publishers.

Taylor, C. (2002). Modern Social Imaginaries. *Public Culture*, *14*(1), 91-124.

Udo-Ekpo, L. T. (1999). *The Africans in Australia: Expectations and Shattered Dreams*, Henley Beach: Seaview Press.

UNHCR. (1995). *The State of the World's Refugees: In Search for Solutions*, Oxford: Oxford University Press.

Van Hear, N. (1998). *New Diasporas: The Mass Exodus, Dispersal and Regrouping of Migrant Communities*. London: UCL Press.

_____ . (2002). From "durable solutions" to "transnational relations": home and exile among refugee diasporas. Occasional Paper 23. Roskilde: International Development Studies.

Werbner, P. (2002). The Place which is diaspora: citizenship, religion and gender in the making of chaordic transnationalism. *Journal of Ethnic and Migration Studies*, *28*(1), 119-34.

Wise, A. (2002). No Longer in Exile? Shifting experiences of home, homeland and identity for the East Timorese refugee diaspora in Australia in the light of East Timor's independence. PhD Thesis. Centre for Cultural Research, University of Western Sydney.

In: Homeland Wanted
Editors: P. Waxman and V. Colic-Peisker, pp. 209-237
ISBN 1-59454-266-X

Chapter 11

The Outsider

Hariz Halilovich

To all those who did not make it

Introduction

In 1990 and 1991, while communism was caving in and Yugoslavia was about to fall apart, Sarajevo was probably its most politically vibrant capital city. New parties with different political platforms popped up like mushrooms. When armed conflict first broke out in Slovenia in June 1991 and a month later sprawled over to Croatia, demonstrations, rallies and concerts for peace were held almost daily. The Sarajevo Opera gave free performances for peace. An undergraduate student at that time, I became a sort of full-time demonstrator and peace activist, moving from one rally to another, from one peace concert to another peace-promoting event. At these occasions, my friend Sejo and I would rise on our feet and sing ecstatically the most popular peace song of the season:

Ljubav je nebo,
Ljubav je more,
Ljubav je ti kad budiš se
I kad je teško ljudi se vole
Samo u ljubav vjerujem!

Love is the skies
Love is the sea
Love is you when waking up
And when it's hard
People still love
I only believe in love!

In many ways, we felt and behaved like Western youth some twenty years earlier. Some others, however, like Munja, my distant cousin and best primary-school mate, decided to do something more, something different, and with no close friends or family in Croatia, he went to Zagreb to join the newly established Croatian National Guard. His motivation was purely idealistic: he did not want to miss this great opportunity to become a hero fighting for the right cause, defending Croatia and its people. We were 21 years old then. On his way to Zagreb, Munja stayed over at my student apartment which I shared with two of my friends, Samir, a Bosniak, and Željko, a Bosnian Serb. I sincerely believed and hoped that Munja wouldn't have an opportunity to become a hero as there couldn't be a real war in this country. Unfortunately, my optimism was misplaced. The news from Croatia worsened daily. It was hard to know what exactly was going on there, but it surely wasn't anything good.

VISOKI KOMESARIJAT
UJEDINJENIH NARODA
ZA IZBJEGLICE

UNITED NATIONS
HIGH COMMISSIONER
FOR REFUGEES

UNHCR Zagreb
Telephone: 38-41 613-266
Telefax: 38-41 530-101
38-41 530-390

Kupska 2
41000 Zagreb
Croatia

NA ZNANJE

Zagreb, 02 kolovoz 1993

Ovime potvrdjujemo da je gospodin HALILOVIC HARIZ, rodjen 15.01.1970. u Klotijavac, Srebrenica, Republika Bosna i Hercegovina, registriran kod Visokog Povjerenistva Ujedinjenih naroda za izbjeglice.

Gospodin HALILOVIC HARIZ nalazi se pod zastitom UNHCR-a za vrijeme dok ovaj Ured razmatra njegov slucaj.

Ovaj dokument je valjan do 02.10.1993.

Marco Roggia
Associate Protection Officer
OCM - Croatia

UNITED NATIONS HIGH COMMISSIONER FOR REFUGEES 210

Propaganda coming from Serbia spread paranoia about ‘endangered Serbs everywhere’, while the Yugoslav People’s Army (JNA), which over several months was transformed into a Serbian army, destroyed Croatian towns. With a dose of euphoria, I voted for the independence of Bosnia and Herzegovina in March 1992. My roommate Željko, like many other Serbs I knew, voted the same way with similar enthusiasm. We believed this was the only way to stop Milošević’s military from using Bosnian territory for its war against Croatia.

I also believed that this would stop his intentions for the subjugation of Bosnia as Bosnians of all ethnic groups would create a neutral Switzerland of the Balkans. We did not have and did not need an army: Like the Swiss, we had three ethnic groups living in a mountainous country. We had three main and a number of minority religions. The Swiss analogy helped me believe that Bosnia was soon to become a prosperous, diverse and in many ways a unique nation. Bosnians did not have a choice, did they, as the complex ethnic pattern ran not only through Bosnian towns and villages, but also through their streets, through their houses, families and bedrooms.

The idea of dividing Bosnia, the central of the six Yugoslav republics, along ethnic lines was seen as an absurd joke. 'Nadrealists' (Surrealists), an extremely popular Bosnian equivalent of *Monty Python*, picked up the joke in their sketch about the 'Sarajevo Wall', ridiculed it on television and exposed it as absurd. My impression was that no-one in Bosnia believed in the partition of the country along ethnic lines.

Ethnic and religious identity was of little importance to most Bosnians of my generation. We felt patriotic and proud about our Bosnian ethnic diversity and cultural mix. While the loyalty of many Bosnians was primarily with their soccer clubs, neighbourhoods and favorite bands, my sense of belonging was very much focused on my student 'commune' at the student village where I lived. Our roommates, friends and lovers were chosen for their sense of humor, their looks, their style, and their academic results regardless of their 'ethnicity'. Student 'communes' included people from other parts of Yugoslavia and a significant number of international students, mainly from Middle Eastern and African countries. Zijo, a good friend of mine, was Palestinian.

Sarajevo was diverse, vibrant and open. It had retained some of the 1984 Olympic glory and had the best rock'n'roll in Yugoslavia. The Bosnian sense of humor was legendary throughout Yugoslavia. Other nations told jokes about others, while most Bosnian jokes were about Bosnians themselves. This cultural practice indicated that Bosnians were confident about who they were. My girlfriend Zerina and I were going out for quite some time before I could draw any conclusions about her ethnic or 'religious' background. This did not matter at all: what mattered was that she was the best-looking girl in the lecture theatre. My reputation as the best student and the fastest swimmer may have helped me to win her over. Zerina and I spent almost every moment together, except when she used to go to her hometown of Prijedor to visit her family about once a month. Upon her return, I would wait for her at the railway station; we would have a feast with our friends, eating all the goodies that her mother had packed in her bags. I visited my own parents who lived near Srebrenica in Eastern Bosnia less frequently. I left home for school at 14 and was quite used to 'being away'.

As the war in Croatia raged on in late 1991, I felt sorry that the country I was brought up to believe was my homeland, Yugoslavia 'from Vardar to Triglav',[1] was melting away. But I had never imagined that I could lose my immediate homeland, Bosnia. It was clear that there was a definite relationship between Bosnian independence and the imminent dissolution of Yugoslavia. The country Yugoslavia could not continue to exist without its westernmost republics, Slovenia and Croatia, who had declared independence in 1991. Bosnia followed in 1992.

April 1992, the beginning of the Bosnian war, shattered my neat little world and my plans. While attending one of the biggest demonstrations for peace at the time, when Bosnian provincial towns close to the Serbian border were already under attack, I was shot at for the first time in my life. The shooting came from the Military Hospital and from one of the windows in the Holiday Inn Hotel. Thousands of people demonstrating, many of them miners from central Bosnia carrying photos of Tito, dispersed in panic. After the initial confusion, we realised that the Bosnian police were shooting back at the attackers. Something unexpected happened then: hundreds of people, encouraged by the presence of our police, got up from the ground and ran to storm the Holiday Inn. In front of me, a miner got hit by a bullet in the thigh. My friends and I carried him into a building some fifty metres away where I gave him first aid. By then a crowd of protesters and the police reached the hotel and the glass windows started crashing. We joined the crowd and entered the hotel through one of the broken windows on the ground floor. Minutes later, the police captured the first Serb snipers in Sarajevo. The angry crowd demanded that they be lynched, but the perpetrators were taken away in a police van. This was my first war experience, and many more were to come.

This was the last day public transport functioned in Sarajevo. The first casualties were counted. My friends left Sarajevo one by one. Earlier that month, Zerina had gone to visit her family in Prijedor. My student commune felt quite deserted and all the usual services ceased. I did not know what to do or what to expect. People were leaving Sarajevo by all available means and in all directions. Most roads and telephone lines with Eastern Bosnia were already seriously disrupted. I felt uncomfortable without my friends, but I did not think of leaving Sarajevo yet. I needed a bit more time to process events.

During April 1992, normality was replaced by complete horror and madness. Moral values, human virtues and common sense seemed to forsake Sarajevo. Out of the blue, heavy artillery started shelling the city around the clock. When the Bistrik district was shelled, I saw houses disappearing in fire and smoke for the first time in my life. My plans and dreams

---

1 A line from a political folk song that pledged loyalty to Yugoslavia: Vardar (a Macedonian river) and Triglav (a Slovenian mountain peak) were picked to signify its full territorial stretch.

evaporated with that smoke. I was preparing for my final physiotherapy exams in June, and then I was going to have an exciting, study-free working holiday in Austria. As a trained physiotherapist speaking good German, my Austrian relatives assured me I would easily get a job. There was a shortage of health professionals in Austria, and once in Vienna, I would just have to make a phone call, go through a routine interview and start work. But it wasn't meant to happen.

At the time Zerina invited me to visit her in Prijedor 'until the situation in Sarajevo calmed down a bit' so we could then return to our studies together. As hardly anyone was left in the student village, I thought this was the best option. The university closed and no-one knew for how long. I packed a bag with a couple of books and a few pieces of clothing, locked my room and, without suspecting it, started my seven-year journey into exile.

I walked about three kilometres to the Sarajevo main railway station, hiding behind buildings to avoid exposure to snipers. Chetniks (Serb militants) shot at everything that moved. I was stopped by a small group of local residents, defenders of Sarajevo who shared a gun or two, and who suspected I might be a Serbian infiltrator. It wasn't easy to convince them otherwise. I was ordered to drop my bag, hold my hands up and face the wall, with my legs apart. The situation was reminiscent of American movies. They apologised once they realised I was a harmless, hungry student trying to get out of the mess.

At the station, I was told that it wasn't known whether the train service still operated, but after a two hour wait, my train arrived. I didn't have enough money, so I bought a ticket only half-way. I told the conductor I was from Prijedor and going home. We agreed that I would pay the full fare 'next time'. What was normally a five-hour trip took eight hours that day. It was a relief to arrive in Prijedor as this part of Bosnia was still at peace and people, although worried about the situation in Sarajevo and Eastern Bosnia, appeared to be going about their daily business as usual. After a couple of days in Prijedor, I noticed groups of armed reservists in regular Yugoslav military uniforms. They looked unruly and malevolent. I was told that they were 'volunteers' from Montenegro in transit to or from the frontline in Croatia. At night we could hear distant explosions in Croatia across the river Sava. I thought of Munja. That night I decided to return to Sarajevo.

However, the trip back became impossible as armed Serb militias occupied Doboj, one of the most important railway crossings in Bosnia. All traffic to Sarajevo had stopped; Sarajevo was cut off and under siege. So were many other Bosnian towns. Before I could make up my mind to cross into Croatia, all the bridges between Bosnia and Croatia were destroyed. I was a visitor trapped in Prijedor and I could only wait anxiously for whatever was to come. What did come was worse than anything I could imagine.

Under Occupation

On 22 May 1992, Radio Prijedor — which had become 'Serb Radio Prijedor' that morning — announced the 'historic news' that the town had become 'Serb Prijedor' in 'the Serb Republic' overnight. Prijedor was the second largest city, after Banja Luka, to be totally taken by Karadžić's[2] forces. The strong presence of Serb forces and 'JNA reservists' from

2 At the time of writing (mid-2004), Karadžić, the leader of Bosnian Serb forces during the war, is still on the loose and hunted by international forces wanting to deliver him to the war crimes tribunal in The Hague.

Serbia and Montenegro prevented any resistance from Prijedor's majority population — the Bosniaks and Croats.

The day Prijedor was renamed 'Serb' Prijedor, the lives of non-Serb residents of Prijedor and the surrounding villages became worthless. Any armed Serb had 'by default' a license to rob, humiliate, kill, rape or detain anyone who was not a Serb. The surrounded villages were the first to experience the might of the Yugoslav weaponry in the hands of Karadžić's drunken militants. They targeted people's homes and mosques that couldn't be defended. I saw burning houses and people running across the river Sana, seeking shelter in the city. These refugees told horrific stories of murder, rape and pillage.

Shortly after 'cleansing' the villages, the Serb occupiers started arresting any Bosniak and Croat men found in the city of Prijedor. There was no way out for the hunted non-Serbs. The arrested men were detained in one of the newly established concentration camps. I was a 'multiple target' of such cleansing actions as I was not from Prijedor at all, which meant that I did not have a document issued locally and could only be regarded as a 'refugee'. Both my original hometown, Srebrenica, and my place of residence, Sarajevo, were resisting the Chetniks and were regarded by Serbs as enemy areas. I was a young Bosniak man, therefore a potential Bosnian soldier. My name might have been the greatest danger of all as it could easily be associated with some of the high-ranking officials in the Bosnian Army and Government. This would have been a reason good enough for any Chetnik to shoot me on the spot. The next three months I spent in hiding.

One morning I woke up with an AK-47 gun barrel aimed at my chest by a young Chetnik who raided Zerina's house with one of his older 'colleagues'. He was a bit nervous and asked me to move the blanket from my body. I obeyed but tried to defuse the tense situation by initiating some kind of conversation. He was not interested in talking and left me once his older colleague had checked the rest of the house and called him to leave as 'this house was okay'. Zerina's mother only presented her ID card and lied that I was her son. My next close encounter happened one evening when I was stopped on the street by two drunken Chetniks and 'arrested'. Before they took me to a 'restaurant' where they used to kill captives like me, I was ordered to take them to the houses of rich Bosniaks. I pretended to know a very rich house with two shops and tried to buy some time by taking them there. After a while, they lost patience and one insisted on slashing my throat if I didn't find the house in five minutes. They had long army knives and Scorpion pistols attached to their belts. They were drunk and looked murderous. I knew they weren't joking. Some thirty metres away I saw a Serb soldier leaving a house and walking towards a car and I suggested that he must know the place we were after. This distracted their attention from me as they headed towards the soldier. They called him and he stopped, but by then I had bolted in the opposite direction. I must have run for an hour before I stopped in a small park next to a bridge. I did not hear if they shouted and shot after me, but I knew that they would not get me that night. I made many detours to avoid the Chetnik checkpoints on my way back to Zerina's place.

The Concentration Camp

As days passed, most Bosniak and Croat men of Prijedor were either murdered or detained in one of the three concentration camps nearby. I knew about the killings and the bad treatment of the detainees and feared that the same fate awaited me sooner or later. There were rumors that one of our Serb neighbors might have provided some protection for our street where some ten young men, including myself, were hiding. I heard there was going to be a final raid in which all the remaining men were to be collected, transported to the concentration camp Trnopolje and then sent on a 'prisoner exchange' to Central Bosnia. Central Bosnia would mean freedom for me, as it was controlled by Bosnian Government troops. I decided not to hide any more. One hot day in July 1992, wearing my black cowboy boots and blue jeans, I was on the way to Trnopolje with dozens of other men. Our guards tried to be 'friendly'; I hoped this was a good sign.

Trnopolje concentration camp had by then been officially converted into a 'refugee collection centre'. This was a result of international pressure on Karadžić, initiated by the actions of brave individuals like Roy Gutman[3] for example, the first foreign journalist to visit Serb-run concentration camps and publish stories about them. The International Committee of the Red Cross (ICRC) was to be allowed occasional visits to selected camps and even register the detained. In Trnopolje, the blood-stained walls of the local primary school where hundreds of local Bosniaks and Croats were tortured and killed, were freshly painted and a sign 'Sabirni centar za izbjeglice' (refugee collection centre) was erected one day in August. The worst looking detainees, 'unworthy of being seen', mostly transferred from the Omarska and Keraterm camps, were selected for the 'prisoner exchange' and taken away. These men were never seen again. Most of them were taken to an area in Central Bosnia near the demarcation line, on the mountain Vlašić, and killed in summary executions.

By late summer, the inmate population of Trnopolje comprised not only Bosniak and Croat men but also many underage boys. At the time, the Serb military carried out one last 'cleansing of the terrain' (čišćenje terena) in the burned villages around Prijedor, as well as in those parts of the city known to be populated by a large proportion of Bosniaks and Croats. The resulting new intake radically changed the detainee population. In August 1992 the camp held some 3500 people in the local primary school called, by some bitter irony of fate, 'Bratstvo-Jedinstvo' ('Brotherhood and Unity'): at least half of the detainees were now women and children.

In addition to the daily disappearances of selected inmates and the torture, starvation and overcrowding of the camp, the lack of sanitation resulted in the spread of dysentery and other infectious diseases. A number of the weakest inmates, the elderly and the children, died as a result of this.

Trnopolje was the most miserable place imaginable: crowded with many once fit and healthy men, now walking skeletons and ghosts. Their eyes, the most prominent features on their frozen faces, were either full of fear or empty and expressionless. Three of these people recognised Nero, Zerina's brother, as one of their relatives and offered to share their improvised tent with us. The first long and sleepless night I could hear screams of tortured men and knew it was just a matter of time before it was our turn. Nero's relatives snored in their sleep: after three months they were quite used to this horror. I did not want to get used to it: I decided to resist mentally and try to keep my sanity. I did not have a plan or strategy as to how to do this yet.

While in the early months of the camp's existence routine torture and killings took place within the camp, from late summer onwards, the inmates were mostly selected and taken

[3] For his brave work Roy Gutman won a Pulitzer Prize in 1993. For more information about the first reports on Serb-run concentration camps in Bosnia see Gutman, R. 1993, *Witness to Genocide*, Macmillan, New York.

away. On a number of occasions Serb farmers would come to pick up the fittest men for forced labor on their estates. Such visits were particularly feared by the detainees as many of those previously selected had never returned. The guards were reluctant to insist that detainees be returned as long as they knew that they were not freed but executed. When Serbs suffered casualties in distant parts of Bosnia, revenge was taken on the camp inmates. Mobs of local Serbs, including relatives of Serb soldiers killed on the battlefield, were allowed to enter the camp and torture, humiliate and kill the detained men. Dozens of men would then be put on trucks and taken into the unknown. The recently discovered mass graves in this area contain a number of men killed in such raids.

Another feature of the Trnopolje concentration camp, and routinely practiced in the Omarska camp, was the institutionalised rape of women and girls. For this, a house outside the camp, some 300 metres on the camp's western side, was used. Women were selected both directly from the camp population and while 'cleansing the terrain' of the villages around Prijedor. The three-storey house confiscated by its Bosniak owners was turned into a 'pleasure house' for Serb soldiers and camp guards. The young Bosniak and Croat girls were picked up for their beauty and innocence to be exposed to the worst kind of physical abuse. Some were returned to the camp after a period of time spent in the 'white house'.

Nights brought nasty surprises and more suffering for the inmates as the often drunk Serbs would enter the camp and start a competition to humiliate the 'Balije' (a pejorative term for Muslims). The overcrowded, makeshift tents on the school sports ground became targets for the guards on check points around the camp. Lightning ammunition was used to make shooting at night more impressive. The only way for inmates to escape was to burrow into the muddy ground and protect each other with their bodies. Often the safer spots were given to the youngest inmates or a father would use his body as a shield for his son. Casualties were a regular result of these random shootings 'for fun' and some people lost their lives. The guards collected the wounded and removed them from the camp, which meant only one thing: these people disappeared forever. Thus badly beaten and wounded men hid in all corners of the camp to avoid being selected for removal. It was the survival of the luckiest.

The only way I could mentally deal with the reality of a concentration camp was to see myself as an 'outsider' with a mission. I became an informal chronologist of the camp, even more so after the International Committee of Red Cross (ICRC), on one of their first visits, nominated me as the camp medic. This resulted from my contact with one of the ICRC workers, Pierette, a nurse from Geneva. I tried to explain to her in German that I just happened to be there due to a number of unfortunate coincidences. I didn't belong there and I had nothing to do with all of this mess. I presented my 'UN Association for Bosnia and Herzegovina' membership card and my student booklet, both issued in Sarajevo. I asked the ICRC if they could take me with them to Sarajevo or Zagreb. The answer was a clear 'No', justified by the ICRC's 'neutrality and non-interference' policy. However, they were glad that I contacted them as they needed someone with a medical background to provide basic medical assistance to inmates.

Thus I started working as a camp 'doctor'. I was moved from my improvised shelter shared by three other inmates into a small cottage which was used as a school infirmary before the war. The cottage was close to one of the 'machinegun nests' which were always manned by one or more heavily armed guards. The ICRC supplied me with two boxes of bandages, disinfectants, basic remedies for the treatment of dysentery, painkillers and some antibiotics. The food they delivered for the inmates was, upon their departure, confiscated by the guards. The same happened to most of the medical supplies. In the following months, I performed more than five thousand 'examinations' and 'interventions' in the role of the busiest 'doctor' anywhere. My patients were mostly wounded and tortured men, but also children, women and elderly people with acute and chronic illnesses. From time to time, the ICRC sent or delivered some basic medicine which I was forced to share with the camp guards.

I wrote a detailed diary which I named 'Patient Register', and explained to the guards that I needed this in order to justify the medicine sent by the ICRC and to get more. The guards warned me not to write anything else and not to submit any information to the ICRC before they approved it. They did not have to tell me twice, but I found I could avoid their suspicion by using Latin and my own code words to describe what was going on in the camp. This included my description of eight murders I witnessed. One of them was a six year-old girl shot by a guard with his automatic Scorpion pistol. He often 'played' with his gun, aiming it at people behind the barbed wire and shooting over their heads or at their legs. He killed Emira 'just for fun' because she was walking close to the barbed wire surrounding the camp. Her mother brought her to me and Emira died in my arms. The blood pouring from her head stained the letter I had in my pocket from Zerina that had been smuggled into the camp to me. I still have this blood-stained letter as a proof that Emira once lived and was killed by those who created 'Republika Srpska'. She was buried in a corner of the camp and I was asked to sign a declaration that on the day Emira died there was no shooting around the camp and that she died from an 'unknown cause'. The same was to be repeated for seven other deaths which I was asked to diagnose.

Torture and death were not my only experiences as a camp doctor: I also assisted three women in the delivery of healthy babies. As a medical student I had attended births and the last subject I completed at Sarajevo University was Gynecology and Obstetrics, for which I was given the highest mark. However, being completely in charge of a situation where the lives of two people, mother and baby, were my sole responsibility, was a complete novelty to me. My passion for other clinical subjects in which I invested a lot of interest and time proved very helpful during my camp experience. I selected two 'assistants' from among the detainees to provide them with some protection rather than to actually have their assistance. One of them was Zerina's brother, an electrician. We shared the same tent before I became the 'doctor', and both my assistants had been tortured by the prison guards.

Many of my patients only wanted to tell me their stories. These stories were full of suffering, grief, loss and fear. Many men and women were completely broken and had lost every hope of ever getting out of the current situation: they could envisage nothing ahead. I listened to their stories and wrote down some of the details in my coded register. I promised myself to go back to my notes one day and write all of their stories. One of the most horrific came from Ibrahim who miraculously survived a mass killing of sixty-four men in a paddock near his village, squeezed between the bodies of his brothers and one of his sons, and with six bullets in his legs, the lower part of his body and both sides of his chest.

A Refugee in Croatia

After nine months of horror, I reached Croatia in January 1993. I was issued a document with a 'Serb Republic' stamp stating that I left Trnopolje to go to Germany 'for permanent resettlement'. This was the bureaucratic face of the 'ethnic cleansing' of non-Serbs. Before issuing the document, authorities of the so-called 'Serb Republic' demanded that each individual pay tax, electricity bills and council rates for the last year even though in many cases their houses had been destroyed or taken over by Serbs, and the electricity cut off in the spring of 1992. People also had to sign a statement saying that they left all their assets — houses, land, animals, furniture, cars — to the 'Serb Republic'. I was afraid that getting the exit certificate would expose me to additional risk as I did not own anything in this area. What could I leave to the 'Serb Republic'? A couple of books? My cowboy boots? The bureaucrat who issued my one-way ticket out of his republic was not very diligent that day, which might have saved my life once again. I got my exit permit to freedom.

Zerina was not allowed to leave Prijedor, the town of horror. Each night, the remaining Bosniaks and Croats went through hell as armed Serbs did whatever they pleased. It was a bitter-tasting freedom for me. I did not know anything about my family in Srebrenica or any of my friends and did not know what to do with my newly-gained freedom. I expected a return to normality but I soon realised that my normality was left behind somewhere in my past life that ended in April 1992 in Sarajevo. War was raging in my homeland and I knew how much suffering it caused ordinary people. I only wanted one thing: to go back to Sarajevo to join the Bosnian Army and fight against bloodthirsty Chetniks. I felt bitter and sad and also guilty to have survived. The only way to restore my purpose and dignity was to go back.

I hated being called a 'refugee' or a 'camp survivor' and after spending three days in a centre for concentration camp survivors in the former army barracks in the Croatian town of Karlovac, I decided to go to Zagreb and explore ways to return to Sarajevo. At that time, I submitted both oral and written testimony to the Hague War Crimes Tribunal. I was angry that my fellow ex-inmates, many of whom had been tortured and who also witnessed the rape, torture and death of other people, often members of their own families, now only dreamed about some bright future in another country. They believed the physical distance would help them forget the part of their lives they did not want to remember.

Zagreb, only 150 kilometres from Trnopolje, was like another planet. People walked freely on the streets. Shops were full of goods. No gunfire, no destroyed buildings, no sandbags and, most importantly, no Chetniks. It was a weird feeling, all this normality. My inner tension kept me on guard though: I couldn't relax. Both my body and my mind needed time to readjust. Like most Bosnian refugees in Croatia, I went to Zagreb's only mosque. Bosnians gathered there to hear the news from Bosnia brought by recent arrivals or radio amateurs. Some found their relatives, friends and neighbors there, and some were able for the first time to send a radio message to relatives somewhere in Bosnia. Those with connections and money could sometimes even talk to relatives over the radio. Many Bosnians working in Western European countries used to visit Zagreb regularly with the hope of finding family members or to make a donation to numerous fund collectors, many of whom turned entrepreneurs and made their fortune during the war.

As I approached the mosque, I became even tenser. Seeing a mass of people gathered around a modern, magnificent-looking building made me uncomfortable. I did not expect to see anyone I knew except some of my fellow survivors from Prijedor, so I ignored the hundreds of unhappy faces looking for someone or something. I made my way to the mosque's main entrance and was stopped by a security guard who advised me to wait till the noon prayer was finished and the mosque was vacated. I noticed a number of refugees sheltering in some of the rooms. The atmosphere was one of misery and desperation. I was about to leave the place when hundreds of people started pouring out of the mosque. Suddenly I started seeing faces I knew in the crowd, but all of them proved nothing more than wishful illusions. I looked again at the face of a dark skinned young man — and this time I recognised Zijo, my Palestinian friend from university. He couldn't believe it was me.

Zijo invited me to stay at his rented flat in the centre of Zagreb. He told me he had been allowed to leave Sarajevo with other foreign passport holders and ended up in Belgrade. From Belgrade he flew back to Lebanon, only to come back to Zagreb and enroll at Zagreb University as a 'guest student'. I told him my story; we talked for a week. In the next few days, I met a couple of other Palestinians I knew from Sarajevo. One of them now worked for an Arab humanitarian organisation involved in helping Bosnians.

I wanted to go back to Bosnia, but this proved very difficult. There was no regular way to return. My inquiries proved fruitless as most people were trying to get out of Bosnia rather than in. I could go to Northern Bosnia and join the united forces of the Bosnian and Croatian armies, but I wanted to go back to Sarajevo and this seemed impossible.

Zijo's hospitality helped me regain some sanity and see the situation I was in more clearly. He advised me not to rush into any decisions while I was still traumatised and disoriented by my recent experiences. He was right. I had terrible nightmares almost every night and was both physically and emotionally tense. I felt as if I was still in prison and in constant danger.

I felt guilty that I could walk freely and eat good food while Zerina was deprived of everything behind a curtain of fear in her hometown of Prijedor. I managed to find a way to send her a parcel through Merhamet, the only humanitarian organisation which was sporadically allowed to organise a convoy of humanitarian aid from Zagreb to Prijedor. Behind this dangerous and risky venture was a clever, brave man, a local imam from Prijedor. He managed to strike a deal with some of the most dangerous warlords in the town. For a safe passage in and out of Bosnia, he gave them half of the humanitarian aid he would bring in a couple of trucks from Zagreb. Still, on many occasions he was attacked, robbed and beaten up by local Chetniks. Regardless of this, he continued his humanitarian mission which helped to save the lives of many Bosniaks and Croats who remained in Prijedor. He also managed to bring legal documents, all sorts of transit visas and visas for third countries, which helped the local people obtain exit permits from the Serb authority in Prijedor. This good man might have saved my life too.

I wanted to send some of my Zagreb normality to Zerina. The parcel was limited to 10kg, so I had to choose carefully: In the end, the box included soaps and shampoos, Nivea creams, and a supply of Coke, coffee, sugar, bananas (her favorite fruit!) and chocolates. This was the first parcel Zerina, her mother and brother received from the outside world. In May 1993, Zerina and her brother were finally allowed to buy a one-way ticket and join one of the refugee convoys to Croatia. Their mother remained in Prijedor.

Zerina and I spent a month together in Zagreb and Rijeka where her father lived. This was the third chapter in our lives together. We romanticised the first one when we met in Sarajevo and wanted to erase the second bleak one in Prijedor. However, Zerina was in Zagreb only in transit as she accepted her uncle's invitation to join his family in Hamburg where they had lived for over twenty years. In May 1993, at Zagreb's international bus terminal, I kissed her goodbye and promised that we would reunite some time in the not-too-distant future. I fought the sadness of our farewell thinking how lucky we were that she was going to a normal country and that we were both alive. Many relationships like ours were physically destroyed and many surviving broken hearts were contributing to the ever-expanding Bosnian sadness. I felt I didn't have a right to be sad as I knew many tragic stories.

While my world was split between my physical presence in Zagreb and my thoughts back in Bosnia, Zijo convinced me to enroll at Zagreb University and complete my studies. I only had one semester to go. Not having anything better to do, I enrolled. Another friend helped me get a scholarship of 150 Deutschemarks monthly from his sheikh-boss, which was enough for me to rent a room in Novi Zagreb. I shared a flat with my landlord, an elderly artist who spent his days dressed in his run-down underwear, painting and writing, and a Canadian journalist and alcoholic who never got over the fact that his Spanish wife left him for another man.

My friend Klara, whom I met on the bus while traveling to Rijeka to visit Zerina's father, helped me find this accommodation through her church connections. This kind young woman studied theology and music and was in love with Jesus. I often visited the Zagreb Cathedral where she practised on the organ, studied and prayed daily. Being a rare true believer, Klara was not poisoned by the new nationalist pseudo-religion. Her spirituality was closer to Buddhism than to a decadent Catholicism resurrected in Croatia during the war. Religion, on the other hand, was a place that I visited often, but never managed to make my home. Klara never tried to convert me. She still corresponded with a Serbian friend from Belgrade, who apologised to her for what was being done in the name of her people and her country. This was in 1992–93 when only the bravest maintained such friendships.

I was surprised to see hundreds of young, urban-looking people attending various church activities. At one of them, a very popular priest played guitar, sang Jesus songs and told jokes about stupid Bosnians. He explained that by 'stupid Bosnians' he actually referred to Bosnian Muslims. Klara blushed for me and I pretended I didn't hear.

In the religiously ecstatic crowd of young Catholics, I recognised another face I knew from Sarajevo. It was a young woman from our student commune, my friend's girlfriend. To say the least, she was confused when she recognised me there. 'Don't tell me you are a Catholic?' I explained to her there was no need to worry about my heretic soul, as my visits to church had nothing to do with me getting 'Croatised' and looking for my Catholic roots. She explained her relationship with my friend was over as she was a devoted Catholic now and wouldn't have anything to do with a Muslim. Less then a year ago in Sarajevo she seemed to be a cosmopolitan girl free from nationalist bigotry. Now she appeared to be a brainwashed puppet suffering from cultural and emotional amnesia. I wondered how people could change so quickly and radically.

Resuming my studies at Zagreb University was a turning point in getting normal again. People at the university were helpful and sympathetic. I was allowed to enroll as a 'guest student' without having to pay fees. I didn't need to attend lectures and was only expected to do the exams. It was a great feeling doing all the normal stuff again, studying and having exams. I received high marks and encouraging comments from my professors. I started feeling more relaxed, having my place, friends and purpose in this city that I started to like.

One day I decided to look for Munja. I didn't know where he might be and if he was still alive. The only vague information I remembered was that he had joined the Croatian National Guard or police some two years earlier. I started my search at the Ministry of Interior and eventually got the information that Munja was one of the bravest soldiers and a member of the President's guard, but it turned out that Munja had been transferred into the regular police.

I found out which police station he belonged to and the next morning I was there, waiting for him to come out of the morning staff meeting. When a number of policemen in dark-blue uniforms walked through the waiting room on their way out, I recognised Munja and called his name. He stopped and looked at me in disbelief.

From that day on, we spent many evenings and weekends together. He told me how he took part in the initial fighting with the Serbianised Yugoslav Army as a member of the special police. As one of the best fighters, he was selected for the President's guard. There he also did his best and was soon promoted. Then, the President's guard was purged of anyone who was not a Croatian pure-blood and a Catholic. Munja was demoted and transferred to the regular police force. His current work consisted of harassing motorists and extorting money from them on the freeway near Zagreb. He and his colleagues shared the bribes they collected in a day, some 200 to 500 Deutschemarks, which for most people was a monthly wage at that time. Munja spent most of the money on the expensive nightlife which Zagreb didn't lack during the war. We didn't have to pay entry at exclusive nightclubs as Munja was an old customer.

Munja was now a Croatian citizen and with his newly acquired Zagreb dialect he blended well into the Croatian metropolis. I felt he was sometimes a bit annoyed or ashamed of my Sarajevo dialect which was not so popular in Zagreb in those days. I consciously adjusted to the dominant Zagreb slang. Witnessing this 'cultural transformation', I guess, he encouraged me to apply for Croatian citizenship and one day, dressed in his shiniest police uniform, he accompanied me to the place then processing possibly millions of citizenship applications. The main criterion of eligibility seemed to be a proof that the applicant was a Catholic. I had no evidence of this kind and I didn't mention in my application that my grandfather served as a Croatian 'Home Guard' in the Second World War and survived its final massacres among people now declared to be martyrs and Croatian heroes by the Tudjman government. Unsurprisingly, my application was not approved. Atheists, agnostics, followers of 'wrong faiths' and heretics like me were excluded from this 'Christian' nation.

I was not upset because my claim to Croatian citizenship was rejected. I enjoyed my guest-student status and because of it I was not categorised as a refugee. At the time Bosnian refugees were relegated to one of the overcrowded slums on Zagreb's periphery. An annoying fact associated with the stigma of being a Bosnian refugee was that survivors from Bosnia were treated differently according to their religion. Being a Catholic automatically meant being considered a Croat and a Croatian citizen. Bosnian Catholics were thus segregated from Bosnian Muslims (Bosniaks) and other Bosnians, and accommodated in luxurious hotels along the Adriatic coast. Still, they were resented by the local population who much preferred the hotels being filled with German tourists bringing hard currency.

In July 1993 I graduated from Zagreb University. My temporary student visa was to expire in August and I knew I would have to register as a Bosnian refugee. The political climate for Bosnian refugees in Croatia worsened daily as the Tudjman government, dominated by ultra-nationalists, sponsored and controlled criminal gangs of Bosnian Croats in Herzegovina. Their goal was to join parts of Bosnia to Greater Croatia. The separatist agenda was carried out through robberies and blackmail, and finally resulted in an armed conflict between the Croatian and Bosnian armies in Herzegovina and Central Bosnia. This was the first time in history that Bosnian Catholics (Croats) and their compatriot Muslims (Bosniaks) fought each other. However, the conflict didn't spread to other parts of Bosnia, where Croats and Bosniaks continued to fight together against the common enemy, the Serb Chetniks.

As a concentration camp survivor, I was under UNHCR and ICRC protection. I had a letter with my photo where this was stated; the letter was stamped with a disproportionately large UN stamp and signed by a UN bureaucrat. I also had my UNHCR 'case worker' who encouraged me to resettle in the US. Initially, I was against permanent resettlement anywhere as I still had no news at all about the fate of my family back in Bosnia. Besides, migrating to the US was never my fantasy. I knew no one there and was aware that I would not be able to meet the cowboy and Indian heroes from my childhood comic books and movies. Bjorn, my case worker, tried to persuade me that there was a future for me in San Francisco. There was a sponsor willing to assist and possibly to help me continue my studies to become a doctor. I wasn't sure that I wanted to become a doctor either, but finally gave in and accepted the offer. Bjorn promised that Zerina could join me if she wanted. The flight to America was to be organised in a fortnight.

Off to Austria

I called my relatives in Austria to tell them my decision. They were very sad about it and wanted me to reconsider my decision. We were not close relatives, but they were my only 'blood relatives' in the West. We had become very close since I arrived in Croatia and they had visited me occasionally in Zagreb. I developed an especially close relationship with my relative Sabina who was a couple of years my junior. It was an affectionate brother-sister relationship and we enjoyed each other's company very much. Hearing the news about my plans to migrate to the US, she was very unhappy and invited me to join them in Austria instead. Hajro, Sabina's father, told me that I could easily get a job there and he offered to cover my illegal trip to Austria as there was no legal way to enter the country with a Bosnian passport. I rejected his offer to pay a smuggler to get me into Austria, but I accepted the invitation to join them in Wolfsberg near Klagenfurt. The next morning I met with my UNHCR caseworker for the last time and told him I had changed my mind about migrating to America and preferred to remain in Europe.

My old Yugoslav passport was nothing more than a souvenir while the new Bosnian passport I obtained in Zagreb had a symbolic value to me as it proved that there still was a country that I could refer to as my homeland. Neither of them, however, could serve the purpose they were issued for: namely, to travel to other countries. I had to find a way to make my trip across the two borders to Austria. People smugglers were very expensive and I didn't trust them anyway. I knew, however, that there was no safe illegal travel and I looked for the least risky option that was in accordance with my limited budget of a couple of hundred deutschemarks.

Most of my budget I had to spend to 'borrow' a Croatian passport from a guy who was eight years older than me and didn't look anything like me, but he did not have any distinctive facial features either. I practised his signature and learned his basic biography: lives in Zagreb, demobilised, works as an electrician, married, one child... Munja helped me get unchecked onto the train in Zagreb and, off we go, I started my journey of an illegal migrant. My possessions had grown from a half empty plastic bag eight months earlier to a large travel bag and an overnight bag. The books I acquired during my stay in Zagreb formed the bulk of my luggage.

Some twenty minutes later, at the Slovenian border, two Slovenian guards entered the compartment I shared with three other passengers. Three of us presented blue Croatian passports while a middle-aged man handed over his old wine-coloured Yugoslav passport with a valid Swiss work visa. He was a 'Gastarbeiter' ('Guest worker') from Bosnia and was returning to Switzerland where he had been working for years. He did not have the new Bosnian passport and he tried to explain the reasons to the Slovenian border guards, but they showed no sympathy. He had to leave the train to be escorted back to the Croatian border. My heart pounded wildly. I pretended to be relaxed, starting to chat with a fellow traveler in my best Zagreb slang. We got our Croatian passports checked, stamped and returned to us without any additional queries. The border guards wished us a good trip and the train slipped through the tiny Republic of Slovenia. I tried not to think about the next border crossing.

A couple of hours later the train stopped again in the dark. The mixed Slovenian and Austrian border police performed the same routine of checking travel documents. This time I was asked about my destination and I quickly replied I was visiting 'my sister in Salzburg'. This seemed to be a good answer: 'my' passport was stamped again and returned to me. The next couple of minutes passed very slowly, but finally I was on Austrian soil. I made it!

Some time before midnight, I got off the train in the small town of Villach. The station was not in the town centre and no trains for Klagenfurt were shown on the timetable. I approached two railway officers who spoke what was for me an incomprehensible German dialect. Somehow, I made some sense of their instructions. After a three kilometre hike with my luggage, I managed to find the right station, waited for three hours for the train, and arrived in Klagenfurt the next morning.

To a sleep-deprived early morning arrival, seeing homeless people dressed in filthy rags sleeping on the bare shiny floor of the Klagenfurt Main Railway was sort of surreal. I managed to figure out how to use the public phone and rang Sabina. An hour later, she and her father picked me up in their new Opel. I felt happy and welcomed.

Ausländer in Austria

Getting legal status in Austria was the first step in looking for a job. Instead of a 'work visa' I was given a 'protection visa' which meant that I finally had to accept my new identity as a Bosnian refugee. Once I got a job, I would be able to change my visa category and I didn't waste a day before exploring avenues to do so. I had seven years of study in nursing and physiotherapy with excellent marks, some relevant experience and good references from my Zagreb professors. My German was functional, but I needed some time to pick up the local dialect. I was after any job in the medical field and didn't foresee too many barriers.

The reality, however, was completely different. After staying with my relatives for two weeks I started feeling a bit uncomfortable, as I hadn't planned to stay with them indefinitely. I moved into a refugee centre which hosted some fifty people from the former Yugoslavia, most of them Bosnians. The support provided included free accommodation and meals served at a boarding school. There was no financial assistance and no help to find work. Occasionally, refugees would go to local farms to do hard physical labor for miserable pay.

Younger refugees attended school, while adults were completely excluded from the local community. The only 'communication' was regular verbal abuse by the locals which went unnoticed by local authorities. Neo-Nazis were visibly active. Most local pubs, cafés and disco clubs were a no-go zone for the *Ausländer* (foreigners). Fights between Neo-Nazi gangs and refugees broke out frequently, sometimes resulting in broken noses, broken ribs and stabbings. Jörg Haider, the far-right politician and leader of the Austrian Freedom Party was omnipresent in the town. His posters with nationalist and sometimes openly racist messages were displayed everywhere. He seemed to have no opposition in the town. He owned a driving school, a restaurant and countless properties. He often visited the town and was apparently popular with the local population.

I was deeply disturbed and unhappy about having to be 'the other' in such a volatile environment. My attempts to find employment in the local hospital failed as my qualifications were not recognised and I would have to enroll at a medical school and study for a year or two in order to get the lowest nursing qualification partly recognised. There was no financial assistance provided to do this. I would have to pay the school fees, accommodation, exam fees… No-one cared that I was a refugee without an income.

Institutional discrimination was perceived as completely normal and none of the Austrians I had contact with thought there was anything strange in their system. I was told that we should be thankful to the Austrian people who gave us shelter and food and should never expect to have the same rights as them. One of the local 'liberals', a certain Herr Ragger, a journalist for a local paper, published a story about my experience as a camp survivor under the dramatic title 'No words to describe what he survived'.[4] I lent him the film negatives I had risked my life to smuggle out of Prijedor, so that he could include a picture in the story. He never returned the negatives and his colleague's name appeared as the author of the photo. The story disclosed all my personal details: my name, age and address, together with my photo. At the time a number of war criminals from Bosnia spent time in Austria and European countries to 'relax' and to lavishly spend the money they had extorted from their victims. One such 'tourist', Dušan Tadić, was not far from Klagenfurt at that time. He was captured soon after in Germany, and became the first war criminal to be tried and sentenced by the Hague War Crimes Tribunal. Ethical journalism was not what Herr Ragger practised. I was not paid a single schilling for his 'great story' and he knowingly exposed me to real danger.

According to him and other local 'intellectuals' I had an opportunity to meet in Wolfsberg and Klagenfurt, the conflict in the former Yugoslavia was explained by our 'brutishness' and a lack of democratic traditions. This was something inherent in our Slavic origin and our 'lateness in catching up with the Enlightenment'. They were convinced something so barbaric could never happen in their miniature civilised Alpine heaven. They were not aware of their own parochial and racist mentality. I did not want to offend them by mentioning the Third Reich and their most famous countryman who, fifty years later, was still inspiring their favourite politician. Instead, I said I loved Mozart and that I was sorry that a Serb terrorist had killed 'our' Archduke Franz Ferdinand, in Sarajevo in June 1914. They agreed the Serbs were the worst of all Slavs.

I tried my luck in other parts of Austria and, on my way through this beautiful country, I visited the old town of Steyr. My father's cousin Meho lived there. The town looked frozen in history and I liked it. Meho took me to a pub frequented by locally settled Bosnians where he

---

4 Ragger, G. 'Kaum Worte für das, was er erlebte!: Hariz Halilović überlebte drei Monate das Konzentrationslager der Tschetniks bei Banja Luka. Jetzt is er in Wolfsberg in Sicherheit', *Kleine Zeitung*, 18. October 1993, pp. 8–9.

introduced me like a hero to two of his friends sharing the table with us. They all wanted to buy me a beer and hear my story. One of Meho's friends was from the Prijedor region. Most of his relatives had been missing from their village since the summer of 1992. I remembered the name of the village and the story I heard from my fellow inmate at Trnopolje, the survivor of the mass execution. I told the story as I heard it in Trnopolje and Meho's mate broke down in tears. After a long heavy silence, he revealed that Ibrahim was his uncle and the men killed were his missing relatives. He didn't know the full story and had hoped that his brothers were possibly alive somewhere. I felt awful and guilty to be a messenger with such horrible news.

Around Christmas 1993, I received the first ICRC messages from my relatives in Srebrenica. The messages had been censored and many crucial words describing the situation there were darkened and unreadable. My family was close to starvation and they desperately needed money to buy food on the black market. My uncle Nasko wrote that my nine-year-old cousin Alma was badly injured by a missile fired from Serbia. She lost her left leg and was transported in a critical condition to the town of Tuzla. From there, she was flown to a Western European country and for more than six months they had no news of her. They asked me if I could find her and keep her with me till the war was over. I immediately started my search for Alma at the local Red Cross. The only way to be of any help to my suffering family was to earn some money. I intensified my job search but my efforts were fruitless. After six months of trying to find a job in all the major towns and realising that there was only one city in Austria where I could imagine living — Vienna — I decided to move there. But the beauty and charm of the old Vienna didn't change my situation: I was still a jobless Bosnian refugee, and this was what I didn't want to be.

WILLKOMMEN NACH DEUTSCHLAND!

Zerina's accounts of her life in Hamburg contrasted completely with my Austrian experience. However, deciding to join her in Germany meant I had to attempt another illegal border crossing. By then I had mailed back the borrowed Croatian passport and only had my two useless passports. Meho was an international truck driver and offered to take me to Germany on his next trip. I accepted. When we approached the border, I hid under the bedding in his sleeping cabin. Meho risked much more than I, as he could be labeled and charged as a 'people smuggler' if caught, whereas I would only be sent back to Austria. By now I was well and truly a refugee.

The border guards were friendly with Meho, chatting about the weather on that cold January morning. They checked and stamped his papers and did not search the truck. Minutes later, I was an illegal immigrant in Germany. In Nuremberg, Meho bought me a ticket and soon I was on a train to Hamburg. It was a whole day's journey. I enjoyed the landscape but couldn't wait to get to my final destination. I didn't know what to expect, but I was optimistic. It was a great feeling that someone very important to me was waiting for me there.

Maho, Zerina's uncle, his wife and two teenage kids were very hospitable. The next day Zerina took me to the *Ausländerbehörde* (Department for Aliens) in Amsinckstrasse, a place I was bound to visit frequently throughout the years we spent in Hamburg. We queued up with some two hundred other refugees, asylum seekers and ordinary *Ausländer* (aliens) from many different countries. We were given a waiting number and after waiting for most of the day, I was seen by an unfriendly bureaucrat who typed my statement describing how and when I came into the country. My story included a fictional German tourist who gave me a lift from Opatija, a famous resort on the Croatian Adriatic coast, and left me in Nuremberg where he lived. I then traveled by train from Nuremberg to Hamburg. Of course, I couldn't remember his full name and his car registration number. My train ticket was the only evidence I had to support the story. The bureaucrat in charge must have heard many less convincing stories than that one, and he did not ask any additional questions. We both knew no German tourist had visited Opatija since the beginning of the war in Croatia in 1991. My Yugoslav passport, which proved my Bosnian identity, was the document I declared. I signed a statement and was issued with a temporary three-month visa, *Duldung — die Aussetzung der Abschiebung* (tolerated — deportation postponed).

My accommodation, an eight square metre room in a hostel on the busy Borgfelder Strasse, was provided by the Caritas. Zerina left her uncle's place and moved in with me. Our furniture included a single bed, a fridge, a cupboard and a table with two chairs. This meant that there was about one square metre of unoccupied space in the room, but after being separated for so long we didn't mind this closeness. We shared a kitchen and a bathroom with five other families. Most refugees in Hamburg were accommodated on ships in the harbour, so our bed-sitter seemed a five-star hotel on solid ground in comparison. We made friends with three couples living in our building, all in mixed marriages between Bosnians and Croats. There were many more people there who didn't want to be anyone's friends. Alcohol abuse, non-stop partying, domestic violence, disturbance and provocations of all sorts happened daily.

The next couple of days I spent exploring the city and my first impressions of Hamburg were great. The city was beautiful and I fell in love with it immediately. In contrast to my experience of Austria, Hamburg seemed dominated by an urban, cosmopolitan culture. I believed I had finally found the place where I could start a new and happier episode in my life, but I had to find a job first. Zerina had a part-time job in a supermarket and also worked as an office cleaner, while I received some pocket money from Caritas. We wanted to rent our own place and start a normal life as soon as possible. I did not have a work permit, so I had to get a job which could not be mine until I convinced the prospective employer to apply for a work permit on my behalf. The Ministry for Employment would then take up to six weeks to process the application. Their decision was not always in the applicant's favour. Not surprisingly, this was not an attractive option for employers who normally needed an employee to start work immediately. After about two weeks in Hamburg, I found my first part-time job providing home aged care. I prepared meals and administered medication three times a day for Frau Radtke, a lady in her late eighties, who occasionally disappeared into her fantasy world. She had lost her husband during the Second World War, somewhere on the Eastern front, and had lived as a widow since then. She never had visitors and I was her only contact with the outside world.

Meanwhile, I looked for a full-time job in many Hamburg hospitals. I also worked as a casual journalist for the 'Bosnia Press International', a Bosnian language newspaper, and continued searching for my cousin Alma. At the Goethe Institute, I started an advanced German language course. Writing many job applications was good language practice. After about six weeks of intense job search, I finally had a job interview, for the position of psychiatric nurse at the Hamburg University Clinic. A day after the interview, I received a call on the only public telephone in the refugee hostel: I got the job! I was overjoyed. I was also lucky to get a three-month work permit.

I worked in a locked women's ward in the clinic. After three months on probation, my boss filled in a form for the Ministry of Health and I was fully recognised as a registered nurse and paid alongside my German colleagues. Soon after, my contract was rewritten and I became a permanent staff member. Working with mentally ill and very often acutely psychotic people was a completely new experience to me. Most of them were involuntary patients considered to be 'in danger of harming themselves or someone else' if not treated. Many of them lived in their fantasy world and wouldn't harm anyone in any circumstance. Frau P., a granny in her eighties, loved trains and would crisscross Europe whenever free. In her parallel reality, established rules for crossing the borders of nation-states did not exist. I felt Frau P. and I had something in common.

I worked in the ward for two years and learned a lot about the job and about the human psyche. There was truly a fine line between what was perceived 'normal' and 'not normal'. My patients told me great stories and I decided to write the second volume of Foucault's *History of Madness* one day. I quite loved my work and developed a high degree of professional confidence. Many of my colleagues became my good friends. They also had their stories. As most of us wore ordinary clothes, it was hard for an outsider to distinguish patients from health workers. The main difference was that we had keys and could leave after eight hours while most of the patients had limited or no access to the outside world.

As I was the only nurse on the ward with a university degree, in addition to my nursing qualification, I was perceived as overqualified for what I was doing. I didn't feel that way, but I accepted the offer by the clinic management to do some further training within the university hospital and eventually move into a counseling and psychotherapy program. I found the course program to be thoroughly enjoyable and completed it successfully. By then I had also completed the top level of German at the Goethe Institute with the highest distinction. I even managed to get rid of a foreign accent. I spoke *Hochdeutsch* and confidently used *Plattdeutsch,* the dialect of northern Germany. This was important as my verbal skills became my main trading tool. My teachers suggested I continue studying German literature at university, but I needed to work because many people now depended on my earnings.

I moved to the elite section of the clinic, the psychotherapy program. The program included individual counseling and group therapy for voluntarily hospitalised people suffering from depression and alcohol and drug addiction. The program was highly structured and staffed by experienced health workers. Gradually, I learned how to master psychotherapy sessions. I also found my soulmate there: Marion, a health worker for more than twenty years, who had also moved from nursing into psychotherapy. We became best friends and enjoyed working together and socialising privately. Differences in age and cultural background didn't matter, as we shared the same sense of humor. I felt I had much more in common with Marion than with most of my fellow refugees. I made many other friends, mainly with people from the University of Hamburg working at the same clinic. Some of them encouraged me to apply for the management position at the ward when it was advertised. I accepted their suggestion and went through a comprehensive and very competitive selection process, at the end of which I was appointed to the managerial position at the ward and sent to do the management course on full pay. I was the youngest and the only foreigner — a refugee — on the ward, and was now managing a team of sixteen Germans: an unusual situation, to say the least.

In the meantime, Zerina and I left the refugee hostel and moved into an apartment provided by the hospital. We finally had our own bathroom and 'normal' neighbours. Zerina found a job as a doctor's assistant in a prominent private clinic, where Hamburg celebrities and VIPs were regular patients. Zerina loved her new job and made many friends. We both earned decent salaries and worked in professions we were qualified for, while the majority of our compatriots and other refugees were less fortunate and, if allowed to work at all, worked as cleaners and unskilled laborers. Most of the relationships they had with Germans were based on an unequal power share.

Three-and-half years after Zerina and I were reunited, our son Suad was born. We lived in our new apartment in an affluent middle-class area of Hamburg. Our neighbors were all 'German bred' and, unintentionally, so were most of our friends. Only our name suggested we might not be from Hamburg. An elderly couple next door often invited us for coffee and cake. The only remark regarding our 'otherness' they once made was that our surname did not sound north German. They had a daughter who died of cancer in her twenties and had no younger relatives. When Suad was born in August 1997, they 'adopted' him as their grandchild. Their affection was genuine and we didn't mind sharing our happiness with them. Suad was a happy baby and enjoyed their attention, grabbing their noses and pulling their white hair which they enjoyed enormously.

Relatives in Srebrenica

From mid-1994, I started receiving ICRC messages from my family in Srebrenica almost regularly. After the initial 'we are OK — don't worry about us', most messages included references to their misery in the besieged town of Srebrenica. They desperately needed money to buy essentials for survival on the black market and I was looking for ways to send them money. I discovered a 'Dutch connection': a middleman from the UN Dutch Battalion, serving as a peacekeeper in Srebrenica, was able to take money to Srebrenica. He or she charged a ten per cent fee. I also succeeded in finding Alma: she was near Essen, in a UN rehabilitation centre for children from all over the world who suffered physical injuries in wars. I visited her and this was a very emotional moment for both of us. I could not take her with me as she was 'under UN protection'. Soon after that, while the war was still raging in Bosnia, she was taken back to Tuzla with dozens of other Bosnian children. They got their prosthetic arms and legs in Essen, learned how to use them and moved out to free up space for other maimed children. My uncle could not understand why I was not able to keep Alma with me until the war was over. The limited space of an ICRC message was not sufficient to explain the details to him.

My two brothers and my parents were alive, while a number of relatives including my grandparents and an uncle had died or been killed. Then there came a message saying that my 18-year-old brother had disappeared. He had had enough of the misery in Srebrenica and with two of his friends tried to escape by crossing into Serbia, hoping to reach Macedonia. From there he planned to contact me and find a way to come to Germany. He had been missing for many months and we feared the worst. Then one night the phone rang and someone asked if I wanted to speak to my brother. This was the first time in years I heard the voice of someone from my family. My younger brother was imprisoned somewhere in Serbia but he said he was okay and registered by the ICRC as a prisoner of war. The other voice was that of a prison guard who asked me to send a thousand deutschemarks and he would buy clothes and shoes for my brother. I knew very well what was going on there and I said that I would send the money. I knew my brother was safe while he was a source of money for his torturers. During the following months, I sent money to 'my brother' and on a couple of occasions he was allowed to talk to me, basically to ask for more money. He never received any of it, but was spared from physical abuse. Then, one day in November 1995, he was 'freed' by Milošević's 'amnesty decree'. By then, Milošević had started washing his hands of Karadžić and wanted to show the suspicious West that there were no concentration camps in Serbia. My brother was put on an aeroplane in Belgrade airport and sent via London to Australia.

While my brother was still held in the secret prison in Serbia, Srebrenica was taken over by Serbs and the worst massacre in Europe since the Second World War took place: between eight and ten thousand men and boys were shot in cold blood by Chetniks, while Dutch peacekeepers passively stood by. I personally knew at least a thousand of those massacred while my brother knew many more. Seventeen of our nearest relatives, including uncles and cousins were killed that July around Srebrenica. The youngest was our fourteen-year-old cousin Dino. He was taken away from his mother in Potočari where they had hoped to seek protection by the UN soldiers. The UN 'Blue Helmets' did not move a finger when men and boys were separated from women and children and taken to the killing fields by Chetniks with obvious murderous intentions.

I tried to help survivors in my extended family by sending money, food and clothing to everyone I knew. My older brother was one of the surviving few who fought their way through the Chetnik front lines and ambushes between Srebrenica and Tuzla. On the seventh day he collapsed, completely exhausted, not far from territory controlled by the Bosnian Army. Many hours later, another survivor, a school friend, found him and carried him for the last few kilometres to the Bosnian Army lines. This friend saved my brother's life and he never made a big deal out of it. His only comment was: 'Well mate, what else could I do? Although, I didn't think you were that heavy!'

WHERE TO NEXT?

Suad's birth had made me more aware of the uncertainty of our situation. A letter in his name arrived a week after he was born. I thought it was quite cute that someone had sent him a letter, but the content was not amusing. The four pages signed by a German bureaucrat explained to Suad that even though he was born in Germany he did not have any of the legal rights of a German citizen or a permanent resident. His parents were refugees and this was his status as well. He would be requested, in the not too distant future, to leave the territory of the Federal Republic of Germany. I didn't want my child to be born a refugee and to be legally defined as 'the other' even before he knew he was alive. I hated the situation we were in. We lived ordinary lives while 'the unknown' part of our lives included regular visits to the Department of Aliens to have our refugee visas extended.

When the war officially ended in late 1995, the German authorities became more rigorous over Bosnian refugee visas. The first deportations started, officially called 'voluntary repatriation'. In practice, once the temporary refugee visa was cancelled, one was doomed to the status of illegal immigrant. Anyone who refused to 'voluntarily' leave the country could be arrested in the middle of the night, put in a police van and kicked out somewhere on the southern borders. Our friend Marina, who worked as a civil engineer in a Hamburg firm, was one of the first Bosnians to be 'repatriated' this way. She only had time to collect her personal belongings before she had to leave Germany and return to her completely demolished flat in Sarajevo. Marina was not a criminal. She worked and paid tax. She wasn't a burden to the German state.

By this time, thousands of Bosnian refugees in Germany applied for permanent resettlement in third countries like the US, Canada and Australia. Almost none of them were rejected and thousands were soon on their way, heading further from their original homeland. My first preference was to stay in Germany and the second was to eventually return to Sarajevo, if the war really was over.

A Visit to Bosnia

In 1997, I was allowed to visit Bosnia for the first time. This was a generosity extended to Bosnians by the German authorities before we were finally asked to leave the country for good. I was shocked by the magnitude of destruction I saw in Bosnia. Nothing was in its place any more, neither people nor the physical infrastructure. The war had changed everything and everyone. The survivors were not happy because they lost the lives they once had and there was nothing in sight to replace them. The faces of people on the streets of Sarajevo were unknown to me. I felt ashamed that I didn't feel the joy of peace and that I could not reconnect with the city I once loved so much. Burned houses, demolished buildings, bullet-ridden facades, thousands of new graves and many broken people — that was the reality of Bosnian peace. The country I still called my homeland had been torn apart and taken away from me. Along with legalising the so-called 'Serb Republic' through the Dayton Peace Accords, the atrocities and ethnic cleansing were also legalised. More than 200,000 people killed, tens of thousands tortured and raped, and almost two million displaced were some of the foundations on which the 'Serb Republic' was built. My completely burned-down home in Srebrenica was now in the 'Serb Republic' and if I decided to live in Bosnia, I was to obtain legal documents from the 'Serb Republic', adorned with the very same symbols under which my relatives and friends were murdered. This was a brutal slap in the face to all the displaced and dispossessed survivors of 'ethnic cleansing'. I realised this place wasn't home anymore and decided not to return to live there ever again.

Ethnically Cleansed Once Again

When returning home to Hamburg, I started thinking of possibly joining my brother in Australia or migrating to the US. Before enquiring about these options, I applied for two jobs in Europe, one in Norway and the other one in Austria, but due to the 'limited freedom of movement' attached to my refugee visa, I was prevented from seriously pursuing these jobs. My employers were very supportive in all matters regarding my visa. They changed my job description to fit the criteria for the renewal of my work permit. They paid one of the best lawyers to represent my case and to look for options that would enable me to stay in Germany. My lawyer was optimistic but there were no positive results. My bosses, two university professors, wrote long letters of support and contacted the University's ombudsman to look into the human rights case of an employee who was a permanently employed public servant with a managerial position but also a temporarily protected refugee. The ombudsman recommended I marry a German woman and in that way avoid this institutional discrimination. Similar suggestions, as well as concrete offers, were made by my good friends. I rejected the offers, as Zerina and I were not prepared to go that far for the sake of getting a visa.

From time to time, I felt very angry that this discrimination was again based on my ethnic and national origins. I felt I was once again ethnically cleansed, as the only thing that separated me from my German friends and permanent legal status was my 'ethnic background'. My German looks, which sometimes confused even my Bosnian compatriots, my fluency in German, my role as a 'productive member of society' and a taxpayer were not sufficient to ensure me the treatment of an 'ordinary Hamburger'. Hamburg was the only place on the planet where I had an address and my home. The situation was bizarre: the state that wanted me out of the country had me as its public servant with a permanent contract. I had a number of hot debates with my 'colleagues', the public servants in Amsinckstrasse: they always made clear to me that I was 'the other' and did not belong.

The last remaining option was a 'temporary humanitarian visa', in exceptional circumstances issued to refugees with mental health problems due to war trauma. This visa, however, did not include a work permit so it was out of the question. I finally lodged my application to migrate to Australia. My brother sent me some forms and a statutory declaration in which he stated he would support my resettlement. The fact that Zerina and I were young and already had a beautiful little attachment, one-year-old Suad, might have played a role in us being assessed favourably. The procedure was lengthy and I hoped that in the meantime the German bureaucracy would recognise our status as 'ordinary residents' of Hamburg so we wouldn't need to migrate to the other side of the world.

Unfortunately, this was a vain hope and after about eighteen months on hold, our application to migrate to Australia started moving ahead very swiftly. We were asked to have our medical tests done and submit some additional documents, and then we had to book our flight before being issued with the 'visa for the future'. We had to pay all the associated costs — around 7,000 Deutschemarks. Finally, some time in August, we received our Bosnian passports back from the Australian Embassy in Bonn, with our permanent residency visas, subclass 202. My feelings were definitely mixed. On the one hand, it was a good feeling that there was a future for us somewhere, but having to leave our life in Hamburg was not easy. We planned our flight for the last day in October in order to have enough time to say good bye to everybody. We managed to visit Bosnia and see our parents once again and so they met their grandson for the first time before our departure for Australia. Although I had not lived with my parents more or less since I was fourteen, this last farewell was much harder than any before. I was leaving my aging parents with my older brother to look after them in a house that did not belong to them, my brother only occasionally earning some money as a laborer. They were displaced and dispossessed in their own country, but compared to the majority of people they knew they were the rare lucky ones as everyone in the immediate family was alive and well: for people from the Srebrenica region this was very rare indeed. This was the last time I saw my mother and it was the last time Zerina saw her father. They both passed away two years later.

Back in Hamburg, after wining and dining with our friends and a big farewell party, we started selling and giving away the assets we had acquired during our Hamburg years. We were only allowed eighty kilograms of luggage which was far below our needs. On the last day of October 1998, dozens of our good friends came to say good-bye at the station. Some of them even travelled with us for one or two stops. The train took us to Frankfurt from where we had to catch a plane to the southern hemisphere. I wanted to make sure that this was the last time I fled anywhere and, especially, I did not want my fourteen-month-old son to ever remember being a refugee. Somewhere there, on the other side of this unhappy planet, there was a homeland waiting for him, and I would adjust somehow.

A Journey to Australia

Apart from Suad's baby-talk, most of the trip to Frankfurt passed in silence. From the Frankfurt train station, we took a taxi to the international airport. The taxi driver was a friendly, chatty, middle-aged man. We talked a bit about the weather, politics and the government's plans to abandon the Deutschemark for the Euro. He asked about our flight destination and when we answered, his interest grew considerably. He said Australia was a place worth visiting, but the airfare was quite expensive. I answered that we were flying one-way and planning to settle in the country. His comment was: 'Lucky you! How did you manage to get the visas? I heard it's very hard.' I explained that we had Bosnian passports and were migrating under the humanitarian program. He looked at me confused and asked how we got Bosnian passports. 'We are Bosnians and refugees and we've been ordered to leave the country or the German police will deport us!' I replied impatiently to this seemingly ignorant German. Once again, he looked at all three of us in disbelief and said he had never met *Ausländer* that seemed so German. He seemed quite upset for the rest of the trip and apologised for his government's wrongdoings. 'They are forcing such nice people to leave Germany while there are so many Turks, Russians and criminals from all over the world destroying this country from inside…' I didn't bother responding to his 'sympathetic' remarks as we reached the airport.

Before we took off and left Germany, we had to make one last sacrifice to our transitional homeland. Our luggage was thirty kilograms too heavy and we were asked to pay 50 marks per kilo or part with something. We knew we had a lot of sentimental junk, so we decided to take the second option. We would get new things in our new life. In the departure lounge of the Frankfurt international airport, I finally parted with my cowboy boots which dated back to my student days in Sarajevo...

After almost 24 hours high in the skies, we finally reached the red continent, our designated homeland that we had never seen before. The only person I knew there was my brother, whom I had not seen for seven years. He was waiting for us at the airport. Our reunion was a mixture of feelings: too much joy and too much sadness coming together. My brother tried his best to make us feel welcome in Australia. I was deeply disturbed at having to build a life in a country where nothing seemed to be quite as I knew it in continental Europe. I had never learned English before. I had to start building friendships and social networks all over again, but without good English this seemed impossible. I felt like a baby that needed to learn about every single thing in a big strange world. Expelled from urban Hamburg, the cultural centre of northern Europe, we ended up living in a poor — I later learned to call it 'disadvantaged' — suburb in Melbourne's West, mainly inhabited by new migrants, the unemployed and the 'socially deviant'. Becoming a Centrelink 'customer', after having earned a good regular income, was a blow to my self-esteem. Even driving was an issue: back in Germany, I was an experienced driver and had crossed half of Europe in my Volkswagen Golf without ever being involved in an accident, but here in Australia, driving on the 'wrong' side of the road proved to be a serious challenge and in my first three months in the country I had three car accidents. Fortunately, none of them involved casualties.

Soon after arrival, I enrolled in an English course for adults (meaning: 'migrants'). I was placed in the same class as people who had been attending for six months and were still not able to put together a proper sentence in English. I was frustrated as I did not have time to waste: I wanted a 'turbo' English course that would enable me to communicate with other people ASAP. I spent a lot of time in the school library endlessly writing e-mails to my German friends with whom most of my thoughts were. I hated being approached by friendly teachers and asked questions I could not understand. One of them was particularly annoying as she always tried to start a 'conversation' in which I felt handicapped. I started avoiding the library when she was around. She later became my teacher and thanks to her, my English indeed progressed at a 'turbo' speed. Elsie, the teacher, became one of my first Aussie friends.

Overcoming the culture shock included coming to grips with some elements of the 'Australian mentality'. The generally casual and relaxed attitude was the opposite of the highly structured and formal German way of thinking and acting. As I felt homesick for Hamburg, the casual Aussie-style was a frustrating rather than an enjoyable change. For example, two of the three people I encountered through car accidents did not have any car insurance. None of the cars would have passed a roadworthy test. One of the drivers did not even have a driver's licence. Such things were unimaginable in Germany. To get your car registered in Germany you needed valid car insurance and a rigorous yearly car inspection. Not many people in Germany would take the risk of driving without a licence. I preferred the German way. I also missed recycling and environmental protection. I could not believe people could wash their cars in front of their houses or anywhere they wanted. The uncontrolled use of plastic bags was another shocker. And all the consumerism: while the most dominant message on German streets seemed to be 'Sparen' (saving), in Australia the emphasis was on spending. The sales, discounts, bargaining and buying on credit were not part of my German experience.

On the other hand, I enjoyed the Australian egalitarianism: addressing and treating people equally, with no special formalities and little special consideration of their status and 'importance'. I easily got used to calling people by their first names. I had difficulties being constantly greeted with the question 'How-a-ya?': In no other culture I knew would this question be asked without a keen interest in someone's wellbeing. One afternoon, a salesman 'ambushed' me with a new question 'How's-your-day-been so far, mate?'. My brother laughed when I started describing in detail what I'd done in the last couple of hours. In a matter of months, I was using these phrases myself and I even made weatherman comments like 'Nice day, isn't it?'.

The best part was that I finally did not need to queue to get my visa extended. I was able to 'hide' my refugee background by being just another European immigrant. My Slavic-Germanic accent became my enemy with which I'd been fighting a losing battle; old dogs don't learn new tricks. I found migrant and ethno-specific agencies providing services exclusively to migrants or 'members of disadvantaged communities' much too patronising: a multicultural window-dressing rather than taking a genuine interest in 'ethnics', so I avoided them. I just wanted to be an ordinary mainstream guy.

In the following years, I completed my degree in Social Science/International Studies, initially hoping to get a job with the Department of Foreign Affairs. It would be nice to be sent back where I belonged, to an Australian embassy in Europe, preferably Vienna or Berlin. But instead, here I am, working in a number of other jobs: a census officer, a counselor, a research assistant, a teacher… Zerina studied tourism because she wanted to work exclusively with 'happy people'. That was at least what she believed tourists were before she started working in the complaints department of a large tourist agency.

Being formally invited to join the Australian nation should have been the last step in my evolution from a displaced refugee into a 'normal' person with citizen's rights and obligations. The most visible change, however, came in the form of the Australian blue passport with a golden kangaroo and emu on the cover. Finally, I could move freely with a travel document in my own name. What's more, as clearly stated in my passport, '…Her Majesty Queen Elizabeth the Second requests all those whom it may concern to allow the bearer to pass freely without let or hindrance and to afford him or her every assistance and protection of which he or she may stand in need'. I didn't feel I needed the 'assistance and protection' of such an important lady, but then, hey, where's the problem...? So, long live the Queen! Just in case…

Over the years my Australian friends have multiplied and I would not do them justice by only mentioning them briefly in this place. Zerina and I now live an 'ordinary' (sub)urban Aussie life; paying off our home loan and leading active social and professional lives. Two years ago we provided permanent residency to a refugee dog, Lily, and regardless of her suspicious genealogy we have legalised her status.

Australia has slowly grown on me and I have developed affection for my new homeland. This does not mean that I can forget all that happened to me and my original homeland. I don't constantly express my gratitude to 'my' Prime Minister who let me into 'his' country. As a citizen of this country, I am aware of my responsibilities, rights and privileges and I frequently use them to express my opinions about issues I feel strongly about. One of them was a speech I gave as a member of the Western Peace Alliance, while standing on a truck in front of a colorful crowd of a couple of thousand people, on a drizzly day last year (2003):

Good day peace-lovers!

I come from Bosnia and I survived a war that took the lives of a quarter of a million of my countrymen. I lost dozens of friends, relatives, school mates... Many of my dear friends and relatives — just ordinary folks like you and me —- were maimed, tortured and killed in summary executions in Srebrenica and across Bosnia. I witnessed killings of people regardless of age or gender. A five-year-old girl and a 77-year-old grandfather died in my hands after being shot by uniformed soldiers.

I know that war is the most destructive form of violence and I'm here to say something against the war hysteria which has been propagated by a couple of powerful leaders that have never and will never smell blood mixed with gunpowder, feel misery, hunger, and fear... and will not lose their friends and relatives. They don't know what this means and how ordinary people become refugees.

This day coincides with Bosnian Independence Day. On the same day, 11 years ago, when Bosnian citizens expressed their opinion in a referendum about the future of their country, Milošević was finalising his war plans to attack this multicultural and peaceful place — a country that did not have an army or any kind of armed forces.

The attack on Bosnia was a 'pre-emptive strike' which was psychologically prepared by the Milošević propaganda machine, the Serbian media, and executed by his military. It took many months, and even years, till a critical mass of Serbian people started to believe what the propaganda was promoting. The war was justified as an ultimate fight for the Serbian nation, culture, religion, history and territories. Milošević's propaganda made his people believe if they did not attack first they would be attacked. In April 1992, Milošević's forces attacked Bosnian towns and villages with all the military capabilities possible, including heavy guns, tanks, airplanes, missiles, snipers... People all around the world could see this genocide, known as 'ethnic cleansing', in their homes, on their TV screens. You could see it and I WAS THERE.

And every time I see scenes of war and preparations and justifications for a war I panic, because I know what it means for hundreds of thousands of unknown people who will lose their lives, their relatives, their homes and their place on this planet... It always takes more than one generation to recover after a war and our lives are too short and too precious to be wasted on wars and their aftermaths.

Even today, when the war in Bosnia is over and I'm standing here while Milošević is in jail in The Hague for the war crimes committed in my country, I don't feel the sweetness of victory and justice. There is no victory that will give me back my relatives, my friends, my schoolmates and the way of life I once had.

With this I want to say that regardless of the final outcomes of a war, the majority of the people on all sides come out as losers. Don't let us all become losers! Don't let us allow one single person to get killed or displaced due to a decision made in a cabinet representing us!

Thank you for your attention!

EPILOGUE

Some three years after I arrived in Australia my older brother and his family joined me here. When my mum passed away in Sarajevo, I brought my father here, but he also left this world forever two years later. His grave is in Melbourne and it has become a new family shrine we all often visit. The strongest, if not the only, sentimental connection with Bosnia remains the white marble monument on a hill near Sarajevo with my mother's name inscribed on it. I need to visit this place from time to time and to pay respect to my motherland. But when I visited my 'old world', I was disappointed in my inability to reconnect and could not wait to get back home to Australia to do all the normal stuff in my normal life.

My old world, with all the happy people and places, now only exists in my timeless memories. On my last return to Bosnia in autumn 2003, I visited Srebrenica and saw the burned-down ruins of my home for the first time. The place was covered in green weeds and one red rose looked like a defiant reminder that a family had lived there in some happier times. I saw ruins of many houses and I knew no-one will ever visit them, because there were no survivors among families who used to live in them. These people were my neighbors, my childhood friends and relatives. The remains of seven of them were recovered, identified, and put to rest at the Srebrenica memorial in Potočari: people born on different dates but who died together in July 1995.

I also visited Prijedor and had the same feeling of discomfort that I had had ten years earlier. The Trnopolje camp was deserted and the empty school building had been painted. There was no reminder whatsoever that ten years earlier innocent people had been tortured, starved and killed here. Then again, I reminded myself not to dream a naïve dream; would the Nazis ever have acknowledged Auschwitz if they had not been defeated? On the spot of the notorious 'machinegun nest' in the camp, a Serbian eagle was erected as a memorial 'to the fallen Serb heroes who gave their lives for the foundation of the Serb Republic'. What an irony, what a denial! No Serb had fallen here, not even by 'friendly fire': only Bosniak and Croat detainees were killed. But 'he who controls the present also controls the past' and the people who engineered and participated in ethnic cleansing are now bureaucrats and administrators in the 'Serb Republic'. I do not think the blame is solely on Milošević, Karadžić and a few psychopathic killers. Karadžić had his willing executioners in many places and some of them were 'ordinary people' like my former teacher who taught literature in the high school in Zvornik.

I visited the school where I think I spent the four happiest years of my life as a teenager in the mid-eighties. The walls of the once multiethnic and secular school were decorated by old and new Serb military heroes and Orthodox saints. My favourite teacher became Chetnik, a little Goebels in this town in 1992. She was spreading hatred through the local radio, giving a 'moral boost' to local Chetniks. She recognised me and pretended to be 'normal'. She wasn't ashamed of all the scary Chetnik iconography covering the school walls. She didn't seem to care if I knew about her war role. She proudly told me that both her children worked as doctors in the local hospital. I remembered her daughter Sanja who was a below-average student and compared her to my friend Sejo who was among the best students in our generation. Now, instead of being a doctor in his hometown, he was a nurse in Austria, his mother internally displaced, his father missing since 1992 and probably killed and his grandmother killed in her own house. Once upon a time, this was Sejo's and my city and our literature teacher was a respected citizen. Now Zvornik was a weird place where familiar faces had cold ghost-like expressions. I couldn't wait to leave the place and when I said to my former teacher that I migrated to Australia, she said it was better for me to live there. I agreed. We did not wish each other well at the end of that odd brief encounter in a death-ridden town.

The reality I encountered was the best remedy for nostalgia. A week later, I flew back to this side of the planet. It took me many days and nights to get rid of the images that threatened to overshadow my treasured memories of people and places. The fresh breeze off the southern Pacific helped me blow away the memories of the return to my dismembered homeland. Here at home, in a completely different sort of reality, I had an urgent domestic issue to deal with: to scare away a pesky pelican that was threatening, first thing in the morning, to eat the last fish in my little backyard fishpond.

NOTES ON CONTRIBUTORS

Morton Beiser is Professor of Psychiatry at the University of Toronto, founding Director of the Toronto Centre of Excellence for Research on Immigration and Settlement (CERIS), and National Scientific Coordinator of the Reducing Health Disparities Initiative of the Canadian Institutes of Health Research. He worked in the US, at Duke, Cornell and Harvard Universities, and since returning to Canada in 1975, he has focused his scholarship in the field of immigration and resettlement. Between 1981 and 1991 he was the Principal Investigator for the *Refugee Resettlement Project*, a ten-year study of the health and experiences of more than 1,300 'boat people' from Southeast Asia resettling in Canada. In 1986, Prof. Beiser chaired a national task force to address the mental health of immigrants and refugees in Canada, and wrote the final report *After the Door Has Been Opened.* In recent years, Prof. Beiser has been the Principal Investigator in a number of studies focusing on the heath of immigrants and refugees, as well as indigenous Canadians. Prof. Beiser has authored more than 150 scientific papers and is the author of *Strangers at the Gate*, University of Toronto Press 1999, and co-editor of *Immigration, Ethnicity and Health*, University of Toronto Press (in press). He recently created educational materials titled *Strangers Becoming Us*, which are in use in public elementary and high schools in Canada. Prof. Beiser is a recipient of numerous awards, the most recent being the Queen's Golden Jubilee medal (2002) and the Order of Canada (2004). Email mortonbeiser@rogers.com

Alice Bloch is a lecturer in the Department of Sociology at City University, London where she is currently working on a study of the transnational activities of Zimbabweans in the UK and South Africa. She has published widely in the area of refugee studies and is author of *The Migration and Settlement of Refugees in Britain*, published by Palgrave MacMillan in 2002. Email a.bloch@city.ac.uk

Stephen Castles is Professor of Migration and Refugee Studies, and Director of the Refugee Studies Centre at the University of Oxford. He has carried out research on migration, ethnic relations and citizenship in Europe, Australia and Asia, and is the author of many books on these topics. In 2003, his book *The Age of Migration: International Population Movements in the Modern World* (with Mark Miller, Basingstoke, Palgrave-Macmillan) appeared in a third revised edition. Other new publications include: *Migration in the Asia Pacific: Population, Settlement and Citizenship Issues*, (co-edited with Robyn Iredale and

Charles Hawksley, Cheltenham and Northampton MA: Edward Elgar, 2003); and *States of Conflict: Causes and Patterns of Forced Migration to the EU and Policy Response*, (with Heaven Crawley and Sean Loughna, London: Institute of Public Policy Research, 2003). Email stephen.castles@queen-elizabeth-house.oxford.ac.uk

Val Colic-Peisker is a Research Fellow at Murdoch University, Perth, Western Australia. She holds degrees from the University of Zagreb, Croatia, the University of Western Australia and Murdoch University, in political science, teaching, women's studies and sociology. Her doctoral and postdoctoral research was focused on the Australian settlement of migrants and refugees from the former Yugoslavia, notably Croatians and Bosnians. Her articles in the area of migration and refugee studies have been published in the *Journal of Sociology*, *International Migration*, *Journal of Community and Applied Social Psychology*, *Journal of Ethnic and Migration Studies* (forthcoming in 2005) and elsewhere, as well as online. Her most recent publication is *Split Lives: Croatian Australian Stories*, published by Fremantle Arts Centre Press. Email v.colic-peisker@murdoch.edu.au

Reed Coughlan is professor of sociology at Empire State College/SUNY. He writes about ethnic conflict and refugee studies. His main areas of interest include Northern Ireland, Cyprus and Bosnia. His recently published volume, *Enosis and the British: British Official Documents,* Greece and Cyprus Research Center, 2004, contains a compendium of documents drawn and selected from Colonial Office correspondence. His latest book, *New Communities, New Cultures: Bosnian Refugees in Transition*, co-authored with Dr. Owens-Manley, is to be published in 2005 by Kluwer-Plenum. Email Reed.Coughlan@esc.edu

Don DeVoretz is co-director of RIIM (Vancouver's Centre of Excellence – Research on Immigration and Integration in the Metropolis) and a Professor of Economics at Simon Fraser University, Canada. His current research focuses on the economic impact of citizenship ascension of immigrants. He was recently visiting the Malmö University, Sweden as the Willy Brandt Guest Professor. Email devoretz@sfu.ca

Diana Glazebrook's previous anthropological research at the Research School of Pacific and Asian Studies, Australian National University (ANU), examined decision-making by West Papuan refugees from Irian Jaya living in exile in Papua New Guinea, at a time of unprecedented political reform in Indonesia and asylum policy change in PNG. Her current postdoctoral work at the Centre for Cross-Cultural Research, ANU, is concerned with refugee experiences in the conditions of temporary protection in Australia and focuses on the ideas of resilience and resettlement in relation to Hazara refugees from Central Afghanistan. Email diana.glazebrook@anu.edu.au

Greg Gow is an ARC (Australian Research Council) Postdoctoral Research Fellow at the Centre for Cultural Research, University of Western Sydney, and is currently undertaking a major project investigating the transnational dynamics of emerging and stateless refugee groups. His book *The Oromo in Exile: From the Horn of Africa to the suburbs of Australia* is published by Melbourne University Press in 2002. He has also published papers in *Communal/Plural: Journal of Transnational & Crosscultural Studies*, *Social Analysis: The*

International Journal of Cultural & Social Practice, and the *International Journal of Cultural Studies*. Email: g.gow@uws.edu.au

Hariz Halilovich works as a Counsellor at the Victorian Foundation for Survivors of Torture and as a Researcher at the Globalism Institute, RMIT University, in Melbourne. His current research is primarily in the areas of cultural hybridity, identity, displacement, refugees, the politics of violence in former Yugoslavia, nationalism, ethnocentrism and globalization. He has published in Bosnian, German and English, and is a recipient of National (Australian) Writing Award in the short story category in 2001. Email hariz.halilovich@ems.rmit.edu.au

Janet Hannah is Senior Lecturer in Continuing Education and Deputy Director of the Centre for Comparative Education Research at the University of Nottingham, having worked previously at Newcastle Polytechnic and Ruskin College, Oxford. She has extensive teaching and research interests in the field of international workers' education and migrants and refugees' access to education, training and the labour market. She has worked with development agencies, trade unions and educational institutions in the UK, Brazil and Australia, and has conducted joint research with colleagues in these countries. She is currently Visiting Fellow at UNESCO's International Institute for Educational Planning in Paris, researching the experience of Technical and Vocational Education Institutions in areas with large migrant and refugee populations. Email Janet.Hannah@nottingham.ac.uk

Maja Korac is a Senior Lecturer in the School of Cultural and Innovation Studies at the University of East London. Her research interests are in the area of forced migration, conflict and post-conflict situations. Maja worked and did research in Britain, Canada, Italy, the Netherlands, and former Yugoslavia. She has published extensively in the field of refugee studies. Email m.korac@uel.ac.uk

Hisako Matsuo, Ph.D. is an Associate Professor in the Department of Research Methodology at Saint Louis University in St. Louis, Missouri, USA. Her research focuses on the migration of organizations and people across borders. For the former, she has studied subsidiaries of Japanese multinational corporations in the US, focusing on the transfer of human resource management. For the latter, she has studied Japanese Americans who migrated to the US around the turn of the 20th century. In the past few years, she has been conducting research on Bosnians refugees in St. Louis and on the American attitudes toward immigrants. Email matsuoh@slu.edu

Catarina Nyberg is a Ph.D. student at the Department of Education, Stockholm University. Her area of research is international migration and ethnic relations, with a specific interest in ethnicity and identity. Email Catarina.Nyberg@ceifo.su.sc

Judith Owens-Manley is the Director for Community Research in the Arthur Levitt Public Affairs Center at Hamilton College in upstate New York. She earned her Ph.D. from the State University of New York at Albany, in the School of Social Welfare and also works as a psychotherapist, providing individual and family therapy. At Hamilton College, Dr.

Owens-Manley teaches Program Evaluation and supervises independent studies in community-based research. She has published journal articles and contributed to books on human service issues in the community such as welfare, domestic violence and refugee resettlement. She is currently writing a book with Dr. Reed Coughlan, her co-author in this volume, about Bosnian refugees in upstate New York. Email jowens@hamilton.edu

Sergiy Pivnenko received his first degree at the University of Kiev-Mohyla Academy, Ukraine, and his Master's degree in economics at Simon Fraser University, Vancouver, Canada, in 2004. His Master's thesis investigated the economic integration experience of Ukrainian immigrants in North America. He is currently employed as a Senior Researcher at RIIM, (Vancouver's Centre of Excellence – Research on Immigration and Integration in the Metropolis), studying the economic implications of citizenship ascension of immigrants. His previous work on immigrant public finance behavior is published in the *Canadian Journal of Urban Research.* Email: spivnenk@sfu.ca

Peter Waxman is an urban economist in the Faculty of Design, Architecture and Building at the University of Technology, Sydney. Although Property Studies is the main focus of his teaching and research, due to his family history he developed a keen interest in refugee issues and wrote his PhD thesis on the early resettlement adjustment process of Iraqi, Afghani and Bosnian refugees in Sydney, Australia. Articles based on his refugee research can be found in journals including the *International Migration Review, Immigrants and Minorities* and *Urban Policy and Research*. The sixth revised edition of his book *Investing in Residential Property: Understanding the Australian Residential Market* was published in 2004 by John Wiley & Son. Email Peter.Waxman@uts.edu.au

Charles Westin, trained as a psychologist, is Professor of migration and ethnicity studies. He is director of the Centre for Research in International Migration and Ethnic Relations at Stockholm University. Email Charles.Westin@ceifo.su.sc

INDEX

A

B

C

S

T

U

V

W

X

Y

Z